PIMLICO

9 7

THE RISE AND FALL OF MAYA CIVILIZATION

Sir Eric Thompson was born in London and educated at Winchester College and Cambridge University, where he studied anthropology. On graduating, he was appointed Assistant Curator in Central and South American Archaeology and Ethnology at the Field Museum of Natural History, Chicago. He subsequently became Senior Archaeologist at the Carnegie Institute of Washington, where he worked for many years.

Eric Thompson made numerous archaeological field expeditions to the Mayan areas of Mexico and Central America. He was knighted in 1975 and was a Fellow of the British Academy. He was also awarded the Mexican Order of the Aztec Eagle and was a commander of the Spanish Order of Isabel la Católica. His publications include *Maya History and Religion, Maya Archaeologist, Maya Hieroglyphic Writing: An Introduction* and *Mexico Before Cortez*.

THE RISE AND
FALL OF MAYA
CIVILIZATION

———

J.ERIC S. THOMPSON

Revised Edition

PIMLICO

P I M L I C O

An imprint of Random House
20 Vauxhall Bridge Road, London SW1V 2SA

Random House Australia (Pty) Ltd
20 Alfred Street, Milsons Point, Sydney
New South Wales 2061, Australia

Random House New Zealand Ltd
18 Poland Road, Glenfield
Auckland 10, New Zealand

Random House South Africa (Pty) Ltd
PO Box 337, Bergvlei, South Africa

Random House UK Ltd Reg. No. 954009

First published in the U.S.A. by the University of
Oklahoma Press, 1954
Second edition 1966
First published in Great Britain by Pimlico, 1993

1 3 5 7 9 10 8 6 4 2

© the University of Oklahoma Press 1954, 1966

Printed and bound in Great Britain by
Mackays of Chatham PLC, Chatham, Kent

ISBN 0-7126-5654-5

To Florence
Almost thirty-nine years after our honeymoon at Coba

Preface to First Edition

For reasons explained in the text I have not given individual credit for the many discoveries in the field and at the desk which have made possible the writing of this book. Nevertheless, I wish to express my indebtedness to my colleagues and, particularly, to my fellow members, past and present, of the Department of Archaeology (formerly the Division of Historical Research), Carnegie Institution of Washington. I have drawn heavily on their ideas, and owe much to them for their constructive criticisms of the manuscript of this book. The drawings are the careful work of Miss Avis Tulloch, staff artist in the department.

It is a pleasure to acknowledge how much I owe to my Maya friends and workmen. In their homes and around campfires they taught me much.

To William of Wykeham, who cast his bread upon the waters, I return these crumbs after many days.

J. Eric S. Thompson

Harvard, Massachusetts
June 21, 1954

Preface to Second Edition

In the decade since the above was written, information on the Mayas has grown markedly. Five seasons' work at Mayapán, swan song of the Department of Archaeology of the Carnegie Institution of Washington, liquidated in 1958, showed how low Maya civilization sank in the last three centuries before the Spaniards established their rule. In contrast, work of the Mexican Instituto Nacional de Antropología e Historia at Palenque revealed to us Maya civilization—and particularly its art—at its most brilliant. No research in the Maya area has equaled the present excavations by the University of Pennsylvania Museum at Tikal in magnitude, thoroughness, or careful utilization of every modern technique. The results now appearing in print give a far clearer picture of how a large ceremonial center functioned during the Classic period. Excavations of the Peabody Museum, Harvard University, along the Belize River valley and now at strategic Altar de Sacrificios; of the Tulane University–National Geographic Society's expedition at Dzibilchaltún, in northwestern Yucatán; and of various sites in the highlands of Guatemala have made important additions to knowledge, particularly of the Formative period. The era of discovery is not ended, for in the past ten years almost as many important ceremonial centers have been found in northeastern Petén, south-central Petén, and the area immediately south of the lower Pasión River. Nor must we forget the studies of social anthropologists of Chicago, Harvard, and Stanford on the present-day Mayas of Chiapas complementing those of men such as La Farge, Goubaud, Rosales, and Tax on the modern Mayas of the highlands of Guatemala.

By and large research in the past decade has filled in the canvas; it has not called for painting over the former picture and starting again. The one important exception to that generalization is, I think, the discovery that Maya history is recorded on stelae of the Classic period.

It is good to have the canvas filled in, but now as a sort of *doyen* of Maya research, I am glad I had a minor hand in painting the present picture when I first served under that great academician, Sylvanus G. Morley, at Chichén Itzá forty years ago. Had we then commanded the techniques of today!

J. Eric S. Thompson

Harvard, Ashdon,
Saffron Walden, England

Contents

PREFACE TO FIRST EDITION   *ix*

PREFACE TO SECOND EDITION   *ix*

KEY TO PRONUNCIATION   *xv*

NOTATION OF MAYA DATES   *xv*

I. PROLOGUE
Some Problems Posed   3
Geography and Environment   17
Language and Population   27
Physical Appearance and Psychological Traits   29
Search and Research   32
Dating Maya History and the Carbon–14 Process   40

II. THE RISE AND FLORESCENCE OF MAYA CITY STATES
Populating the New World   42
Beginnings of Civilization in Middle America
     (The Formative Period)   46
The Classic Period: Beginning   57
The Classic Period: Florescence   64
Collapse of the City States   100

III. THE DECLINE AND FALL OF MAYA CIVILIZATION
Wax Moth in the Maya Hive   110
Mexican Intrusion   116
Centralized Government at Mayapán   139
Independent Chieftainships   149

IV. INTELLECTUAL AND ARTISTIC ACHIEVEMENT
Character and Training   156
The Philosophy of Time   162
Intellectual Achievement   169
Inventions and Discoveries   183
Hieroglyphic Writing   189

Literature 200
Artistic Achievement 202
Currency and Commerce 219

v. SKETCHES OF MAYA LIFE
Preamble 223
The Novice 224
The Daily Round 232
The Architect at Chichén Itzá 239
Marriage à la Mode 245
Death and Life 252

vi. MAYA RELIGION
Cosmology 259
The Gods 262
The Soil and the Maize 270
Creation Myths 277
Sacrifices 278
The Priesthood 285
Ceremonies 289
Dances 293
Religion and the Individual 296

vii. MAYA CIVILIZATION IN RETROSPECT
Development 299
Decline 304

SYNOPSIS OF MAYA HISTORY 309

SELECTED READING 311

LIST OF SPECIAL DECORATIONS 316

INDEX 318

Illustrations

PLATES

1. Portraits of Present-day Maya
2. Reconstructions of Maya Cities
3. Reconstructions of Maya Buildings
4. Pyramids and Temples, Tikal
5. Pyramids
6. Architectural Groups
7. Buildings
8. Maya Corbeled Vaulting
9. Stelae
10. Sculpture
11. Stelae
12. Sculpture: Lintels from Yaxchilán
13. Sculpture from Yaxchilán and Palenque
14. Sculpture
15. Sculpture, Dynamic and Static
16. Sculpture in the Round
17. Murals
18. Painted Pottery
19. Modeled Pottery
20. Pottery Figurines
21. Carved Jade
22. Flint and Obsidian
23. Stucco Heads from Palenque
24. Labná
25. Formative Sculpture
26. Sites, Guatemalan Highlands
27. Incense Burners, Palenque, Teapa, and Mayapán
28. Mosaic Mask and Pottery Head
29. Relief Sculpture, Copán

30. Figure with Snake on Vase
31. Written Page and Carved Bone
32. Sculptured Figure, Quiriguá

Figures

1.	Plan of Part of Tikal	*page* 6
2.	Maya "Doodling"	10
3.	Section through Temple of the Cross, Palenque	58
4.	Maya Types of Classic Beauty	61
5.	Plans of Buildings	67
6.	Temple of the Inscriptions, Palenque: Elevation and Section	76
7.	Temple of the Inscriptions, Palenque: Interior of Burial Crypt	78
8.	Interior of Room at Bonampak	82
9.	A Raid on the Enemy	95
10.	Judgment on the Captives	101
11.	Warriors: Mexican and Maya	114
12.	Serpents	122
13.	Elements of Mexican Religion at Chichén Itzá	131
14.	A Noble's House at Mayapán: Plan and Elevation	143
15.	Stelae A and C, Quiriguá	172
16.	The Mechanics of the Maya Calendar	176
17.	Examples of Maya Hieroglyphic Writing	180–81
18.	More Maya Glyphs	193
19.	The Drum and Rattle of the Katun	199
20.	Sculptured Design at Palenque	206
21.	Scene from Stela 11, Yaxchilán	216
22.	Animation in Portraiture of Gods	236
23.	Burials	254–55
24.	Maya Huts	264
25.	Maya Gods of the Classic Period	272
26.	Sundry Art Forms	288
27.	Incised Decoration on Bone	295

Map of the Maya Area   18

Key to Pronunciation

Maya pronunciation of vowels as in Spanish: *a*, between that of *rat* and *rather*; *e*, between that in *pet* and *pray*, but short; *i* as *ee* in *greed*; *o* as in *on*; *u* like our *oo* as in *boo*, but pronounced as *w* before another vowel.

Consonants as in English except that *c* is always hard; *x* as *sh*, so *uix* is pronounced *weesh*. *Qu* is pronounced like *k* before *e* and *i*; Consonants followed by an apostrophe are pronounced with a quick closing of the glottis, somewhat as in military commands—*shun* for *attention*. Final *e* is always pronounced.

EXAMPLES

Quiriguá	Kee-ree-gwa'	Kintun	K'een-toon'
Chichén Itzá	Chee-chen' EE-tza'	Uaxactún	Wash-ac-toon'
Yaxchilán	Yash'chee-lan'	Ahau	A-how'

Notation of Maya Dates

A Maya date in our notation, for example 8.14.10.13.15, represents a Maya record of 8 baktuns (periods of 400 tuns), 14 katuns (periods of 20 tuns), 10 tuns (years of 360 days), 13 uinals ("months" of 20 days), and 15 kins (days) counted from a base 4 Ahau 8 Cumku (p. 177).

The Rise and Fall of Maya Civilization

I. Prologue

The glories of our blood and state
Are shadows, not substantial things;
There is no armour against fate;
Death lays his icy hand on kings:
   Sceptre and Crown
   Must tumble down,
And in the dust be equal made
With the poor crooked scythe and spade.
—James Shirley (1596–1666)

SOME PROBLEMS POSED

The six centuries between the Emperor Constantine's conversion and the death of Alfred the Great, about A.D. 300 to A.D. 900, were dark and bloody for Europe. In the New World they were illuminated by the rise to its highest peak of Maya civilization. During those centuries Tikal, the largest of Maya cities, and scores of other religious centers reflected from pyramids, courts, and temples the fierce light of the Central American sun. Then the balance tipped, as it has done before and will do again. Western Europe passed into the age of faith and beauty, to which the great Norman and Gothic fabrics of Christendom bear immortal witness; the Maya cities were abandoned. The forest engulfed them and with the roots of its giant trees tore stone from stone. Tikal, deep in the forested Petén District of northern Guatemala, suffered its fate impassively for centuries, unvisited save, in recent years, by an occasional gatherer of chewing gum or the rarer archaeologist or curious traveler.

Now the University of Pennsylvania Museum is making large-scale and exciting excavations there, converting the site into a magnificent showplace, and adding each season to our stock of Maya knowledge. A hotel has been opened and tourists flock there in large

3

numbers. Guides escort them around the ruins, imparting much un-related information. This heady knowledge can be imbibed freely by the pilgrim realizing that two hours later, in the modern bars of Guatemala City, he can return to what we call civilization.

Nevertheless, I have an impression that nearly all travelers as well as most readers of books on Maya civilization return from their journeys, physical or mental, curiously unsatisfied. They have been deeply impressed by great architectural wonders and magnificent sculptures erected in this remote area over a thousand years ago by a strange people which unaccountably has disappeared from the stage of history. Yet the story is given as a series of disconnected facts from which they feel remote.

The archaeologist is partly to blame for the frequent failure of the nonprofessional to get a coherent impression of a past civiliza-tion. Because of the nature of much of the material he handles, the excavator is deeply interested in minutiae. Scarcely perceptible changes in the shapes of everyday cooking pots are often of consider-able value in establishing relationships in time and space; the con-stituents of a pottery temper or the manner of drilling holes in stone or shell can be highly significant. Consequently, archaeologists often infer from the particular to the general, and we are apt to fill our reports with detail to support our generalizations. We ape Crivelli in a different medium.

I have tried to avoid that approach. Many subjects which a book of this nature usually covers are hardly mentioned; the reader will have to turn to other sources for detailed information on such mat-ters as the clothing, weapons, slavery, commerce, and farming meth-ods of the Maya. Instead, I have tried to concentrate on material which bears directly on the subject of the book, the rise and fall of Maya civilization and what may have been the causes.

As a prologue, I shall give some impressions of my own visit to Tikal, made long before even an air strip was cleared there to facili-tate the shipment of chewing gum from the Petén forest.

On that visit to Tikal, over thirty years ago, we arrived on muleback after losing our way and spending an uncomfortable night in an abandoned, flea-infested camp of chewing-gum gatherers. There was something Chaucerian about the journey of seven days from that modern Tabard Inn, the ramshackle International Hotel in Belize, up the Belize River two days in a launch, and then five days by mule from El Cayo via another Maya city, Uaxactún. We were in a sense pilgrims journeying leisurely to a great shrine, and, as the mules jogged stolidly through the forest at three miles an hour, we had ample time, denied to the air traveler, for speculation on what awaited us.

On earlier journeys in the rain forest of Central America, the exotic surroundings had excited my interest, but with repetition the novelty had worn off, and the impression of the forest on my mind had become one of overwhelming monotony. On this journey, as on a dozen others, we followed endless, narrow, winding tunnels cut in the forest by chewing-gum gatherers. The trees met far overhead, letting through occasional dapples of sunshine or allowing a fleeting glimpse of blue sky or cloud. Below, the serried tree trunks merged in a dull gray mass, and fallen trees wore the brown of decay. The dense foliage excluded the bright colors one associates with the tropics. Except for a careful eye for an overhanging branch eager to deal one Absalom's fate and a perpetual and largely unconscious struggle between mule and rider, one was free to dwell upon the past, when Maya civilization cut its first teeth on this self-same jungle and partly subdued it on reaching maturity.

The descent of the trail into the great *bajo* of Tikal fetched me back into the present. That low swampland, a lake long before Tikal flourished, is a sea of mud in the rainy season, but it was dry when we crossed it. The few feet of descent brought a complete change, very much for the worse, in the vegetation. Spanish cedars, mahogany, the ubiquitous sapodilla, from the wrinkled trunk of which, when it is slashed with a machete, raw chewing gum drips, and graceful cabbage palms gave place to a low, thorny scrub, from the branches of which numberless stinging ants might descend, like paratroopers, upon the rider who incautiously knocked against trunk or limb. The sun beat down on mules and riders as though in punishment for our hours of playing hide-and-seek with him in the tall forest; the strangely distorted branches of the thorn trees writhed like souls in Dante's hell.

The trail, which had been meandering southward, swung to the west before ascending sharply into rain forest once more. Suddenly we glimpsed an awe-inspiring sight. Four of the great pyramids of

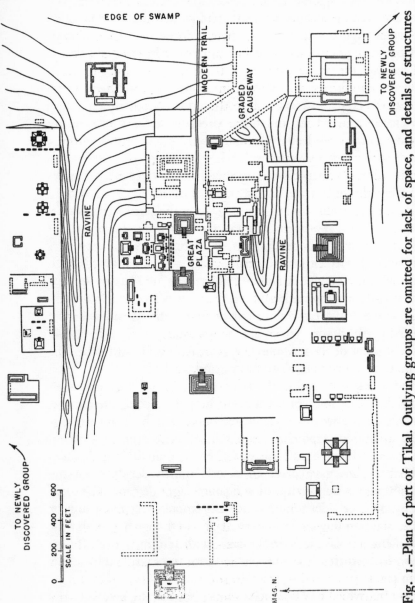

Fig. 1.–Plan of part of Tikal. Outlying groups are omitted for lack of space, and details of structures are simplified. Note the great court with its ranks of stelae, the huge pyramids at the east and west ends, and the "acropolis" with its massed smaller pyramids on the north side. The east-west length is just under three-fourths of a mile. Black rectangles represent stelae. (*After Tozzer and Merwin, with additions.*)

EDGE OF SWAMP

MODERN TRAIL

GRADED CAUSEWAY

TO NEWLY DISCOVERED GROUP

GREAT PLAZA

RAVINE

RAVINE

TO NEWLY DISCOVERED GROUP

SCALE IN FEET

0   200   400   600

MAG. N.

Tikal, clad in foliage and surmounted by ancient temples of lime-stone, grayish white against the sky, rose high above the surrounding treetops, like green volcanoes with summits wreathed in white cloud. The pilgrims were at the gates of their New World Canterbury. Just as Chaucer's riders must have lost sight of the cathedral as they hurried through the narrow streets of the city, so we lost our view of the Maya temples as we plunged into the forest in that abrupt climb from the edge of the swamp to the heart of the city.

The trail ascended for about 150 yards to where it crossed an ancient Maya causeway leading southeastward to an outlying group (Fig. 1). There we were, so to speak, in the outer downtown district. Two hundred yards farther west, our eyes were caught by the great mass, to the right, of one of Tikal's huge pyramids, the blurred out-line of its immense bulk rising through the sea-green foliage like the base of a submarine mountain. To the left were the dispiriting re-mains of two parallel mounds, which, in better days, probably had been the sides of one of those courts in which the Maya played their ball game with a solid ball of rubber a millenium before our western civilization had any knowledge of rubber or rubber balls. Impreca-tions of the muleteer, whose mules heeded only the task of skillfully picking their way across heaps of root-entwined rubble, echoed in another key the shouts of players and watchers and the thud of ball on pad or wall—a brighter wall not then in disrepair.

Beyond that narrow passage between pyramid and supposed ball court the trail enters the great court or plaza of Tikal, great not because of its size, but because, like the Forum of Rome, it is en-closed by great structures raised by the toil of thousands to a glory now passed and knit with a faith which was in vain. We unsaddled and hitched our mules to trees, units in what I would have called the virgin forest which compassed us about, had I not known that the forest had been felled in 1881 by the British archaeologist, Al-fred Maudslay, and again in 1904 and 1910 by expeditions of the Peabody Museum of Harvard University. Each time the tide of vegetation had engulfed the ruins anew; with the years, saplings had grown to giants, anchored to the thin soil and the Maya-built floors beneath by buttressed roots. Lianas—some almost as thick as fire hose —hung from branches or were looped from tree to tree. A troop of spider monkeys chattered high in the trees that swept up the pyramid guarding the west end of the great court, a New World version of Omar Khayyam's "They say the lion and the lizard keep the courts where Jamshyd gloried and drank deep."

We scrambled up the eastern pyramid, clambering over the slides in the great stairway with the aid of some root working to displace yet another stone of the step or some sapling which in years to come would be a giant (Plate 4; Fig. 1). The terraced sides of the pyramid, broken by the actions of roots and rain, were masked by ferns and vines. As we got higher, the cactus-like pitahaya vine with thorny stems triangular in section warned us to climb carefully. The trees thinned out, and we were on the flat crown of the pyramid facing the temple on its summit. We turned to look down the broken stairway we had climbed. The height of the crest of the temple above the level of the court (allowing a few feet for collapse) is almost 160 feet, and each side of the base of the pyramid is a little over a third of a city block in length. So far as we know, there is no natural elevation enclosed in this mass, every cubic foot of which was built without anything that could be termed machinery. The builders were men, and, probably, women and children, who inhabited what is now this forested region twelve hundred years ago; and they erected this vast structure not long after Augustine built the Saxon predecessor of the early Norman church, in turn replaced by the Canterbury Cathedral Chaucer's pilgrims journeyed to see. Gangs brought rock and rubble for the core of the pyramid; they faced the building stone with primitive tools; they cut the wood to heat the lime kilns; they shaped the sapodilla beams for the temple; and, finally, some of them may have given their lives to the building as sacrificial victims at its dedication. I recall no premonition that thirty-four years later University Museum men would find beneath the pyramid a tomb marking its last reconstruction (between A.D. 695 and A.D. 712). The personage lay bedecked with jade and surrounded by his nonperishable treasures, including strange bones incised with designs and glyphs.

From the doorway of the temple, we looked out over the tree-tops whose range of hues was not unlike the contrasting green tones of shoal water. Here and there trees with myriads of scarlet blossoms heightened the effect of a seascape, for they seemed like giant jelly-fish floating on the water's surface. Directly in front, to the west, the gray-white walls of three pyramid-supported temples rose like coral islands above the sea of foliage. A fourth, due south, could be seen by turning to the left. Nearer at hand, a swell in the foliage told of a large building below, not tall enough to break surface. At sunset or dawn deep shadows mapped the contours in better detail.

In ancient times one would have had an uninterrupted view across the city with its clusters of smaller pyramids topped by their temples, its multi-chambered buildings (miscalled "palaces" for convenience), facing courts at different levels, and its endless surfaces of cream-white stucco relieved only by shadow and an occasional building or floor finished with red plaster.

In the great ceremonial court and in various smaller courts stood the stelae, like sentinels, before the approaches to platforms and pyramids. Some of those limestone shafts, particularly at Tikal, are plain. Others are carved with portraits of priest-rulers, often shown impersonating gods, and hieroglyphic texts which record the overwhelming preoccupation of the Maya with the mystery of time and its influences on every side of life from birth to death of high-born and peasant. Dynastic data were inscribed on monuments at some sites, but the evidence for this practice at Tikal is less certain. Every twenty years (every ten or five years at some sites) a new stela rose to carry forward the story. In front of each stood a stone altar, usually uncarved.

Just as we forced our way through the tangled vegetation that crowded the courts and surged up mound and across terrace, so, in ancient times, a late arrival at some ceremony must have shouldered his way through the congregation which, packed in the court, intently witnessed a ceremony held on the top of a pyramid before the temple door. I could visualize the priest-astronomer, anxious to check his theories on the length of the solar year or the lunar month, threading his way from stela to stela to see what calculations his predecessors had recorded in the then distant past, or I could conjure up the acrid, sooty smoke of copal incense rising from clay braziers to a sky then fully visible from the great court.

We wandered through the forest, entering temples, climbing pyramids, and once disturbing a herd of peccary feeding on the cherry-like fruit of the breadnut. As darkness fell after that interlude of dusk so brief in those latitudes, we ate, in the ceremonial court, Maya black beans and canned Chicago pork. The mingling

9

Fig. 2.—Maya "doodling." Designs incised in the stuccoed walls of Tikal rooms probably by bored or inattentive novices. Note litter, standard poles, man tied to a frame being speared, and views of pyramids, apparently with wooden ladders. (*After Maler.*)

of the two foods—one the product of ancient agricultural techniques, the other processed in a modern factory—seemed to symbolize archaeology's task of bringing past and present together.

The rest of the party bedded down in the great court; Agustín Hob, my Maya boy, and I, storm lantern in hand, climbed to one of the Maya palaces on the south side of the court. Passing through a room, the plaster walls of which still showed crude sketches of daily life incised in the plaster a thousand years ago, we slung my hammock, in a second room, from cross-bars of sapodilla wood placed in the vault even before the graffiti were made. Agustín, lantern in hand, returned to the court, and I was left alone with my thoughts.

I thought of those sketches in the adjacent room. One showed a scene of human sacrifice, the victim tied to a frame; another represented a Maya god; several were of temple-crowned pyramids; others were little better than scribbling (Fig. 2). Who had made them? Surely not the Maya priests. My thoughts went back to schooldays and idly and crudely drawn caricatures of schoolmasters, of Dido and Aeneas, and of a football hero making a pass, and then I had the answer. Of course, this must have been the building in which the Maya novices were lodged before initiation at some great ceremony. Tired as I was, I tried to picture those youths of a thousand years ago. Were they full of ideas for setting the world to rights? Did they accept authority, or were they in revolt against their elders? Did they accept the gods without question, or were they skeptical? Surely they complained to each other about the long periods of fasting and vigil. Or did they? What right have we to suppose that they reacted as modern young people would?

Why? How? What? When? Like the soporific rhythm of a Pullman car passing over points and rail joints, the questions repeated themselves as I dozed in my hammock. How did this civilization arise? Why, unlike any other civilization in the world, did it come into being in tropical forest? When did it flourish? What hidden forces made it succeed? Why is it so like, but also so unlike, the ancient civilizations of the Old World? The questions danced across the vaulted room. The sand flies began to bite as a full moon rose behind my head, floodlighting the temple atop yet another huge pyramid to the south. In the immediate foreground its beams strove to penetrate the foliage in the deep gully below, once dammed, probably to serve as a reservoir.

The sybaritic Mr. Keith of *South Wind* remarks in the course of one of his frighteningly long monologues, "I like to understand things because then I can enjoy them. I think knowledge should intensify our pleasures. That is its aim and object, so far as I am concerned." Man is by nature curious, and he is most curious about himself and his surroundings. Knowledge, even when not applied in a utilitarian manner, adds to our pleasure. If on a walk one can identify trees or birds or geological formations, his pleasure is increased.

Knowledge, then, gives pleasure. Any knowledge? Well, hardly. Consider the kind of unrelated scraps of information one gets on a quiz program: the diameter of the moon is 2,160 miles; St. Catherine of Siena was born in 1347; the second largest city in Arizona is Tucson; the tallest Maya stela is thirty-five feet high. All are facts of importance in their own contexts, but without intellectual stimulus if presented as isolated statements worth remembering. If we look at Maya civilization as a jumble of odds and ends, a sort of poking around in the back of an antique shop, we shall get little real satisfaction; we must look at the civilization as a whole to find out why it got where it did, and we should stroll around the gallery of civilizations and take a look at the other pictures. Naturally, this book cannot be a guide to the whole gallery; there is enough behind the eyes of the Maya Mona Lisa to keep our thoughts occupied for the present.

Bare facts by themselves do not fascinate us; they must be clothed with the play and counterplay which produced them. The defeat of the Spanish Armada in 1588 is a bald historical fact. It takes on meaning when it is shown as the culmination of a play of forces and the clash of the opposing temperaments and philosophies of two nations, personified in the characters of Philip the Second and Elizabeth. To understand those antagonisms, one must know the cultural backgrounds, the ways of thought, and the conflicting traditions of the two peoples. One must study Torquemada and Chaucer, John of Austria and Latimer, the choir stalls of Toledo cathedral and the fan vaulting of St. George's, Windsor, and even the dances and field sports of the protagonists. Those are the tesserae of the mosaic of history.

It is not enough then to illustrate Maya civilization with descriptions and photographs of its outstanding accomplishments in architecture and sculpture, astronomy and arithmetic. One must, as far as possible, show in the details of the daily life of the Maya and in studies of their religious conceptions and of their philosophy of life the soil in which those more spectacular manifestations of their culture germinated and grew to fruition.

We shall, unfortunately, never know the Maya as we know sixteenth-century Spain or Elizabethan England, but, in time, by integrating all sources of information, we should have material which will satisfy the man interested in this peak of intellectual achievement in pre-Columbian America, and which will at the same time be of value to the student of comparative history.

The purpose of research in every field, as Lawrence Housman said, is to set back the frontier of darkness. With so many frontiers of darkness, even in the study of man, why choose Maya civilization? To that, I think, the answer must be that Maya civilization not only produced geniuses, but produced them in an atmosphere which to us seems incredible. One can never assume the obvious when dealing with the Maya who excelled in the impractical but failed in the practical. What mental quirks (from our point of view) led the Maya intelligentsia to chart the heavens, yet fail to grasp the principle of the wheel; to visualize eternity, as no other semicivilized people has ever done, yet ignore the short step from corbeled to true arch; to count in millions, yet never learn to weigh a sack of corn?

In its general aspects Maya philosophy closely parallels the Athenian, for "moderation in all things" was the key to Maya living, as it was to life in Athens. Yet to that philosophy the Maya added concepts which are utterly alien to western thought. The great theme of Maya civilization is the passage of time—the wide concept of the mystery of eternity and the narrower concept of the divisions of time into their equivalents of centuries, years, months, and days. The rhythm of time enchanted the Maya; the never ending flow of days from the eternity of the future into the eternity of the past filled them with wonder. Calculations far into the past or lesser probings of the future occur in many a Maya hieroglyphic text. On the stela at Quiriguá a date perhaps over ninety million years ago is computed; on another a date over three hundred million years before that is given. Here the calculation is unquestionable. These are actual computations stating correctly day and month positions, and are comparable to calculations in our calendar giving the month positions on which Easter would have fallen at equivalent distances in the past. The brain reels at such astronomical figures, yet these reckonings were of sufficient frequency and importance to require special hieroglyphs for their transcription, and they were made nearly a thousand years before Archbishop Ussher had placed the creation of the world at 4004 B.C. This was an appraisal of the ages which would have been utterly inconceivable to us even today, had not our minds been conditioned to their vastness by the writings of the astronomers and geologists of the nineteenth century.

Maya interest was not confined to this grandiose aspect of time. Not only the great periods of time, but the very days were divine, for the Maya held, and in some parts still hold, the days to be living gods. They bow down to them and worship them; they order their lives by their appearance. Throughout history man has ascribed favorable or malevolent powers to certain days, but nowhere did those influences attain the importance with which they were invested by the peoples of Middle America. The life of the Maya community and the acts of the individual were rigidly adjusted to the succession of deified days with their varying aspects, for each day was a god who took a lively interest in his duties; happy and sorrowful days succeeded one another. Life passed in this pattern of sunshine and shade was not monotonous. It is not improbable that this strange form of predestination molded the Maya character or, perhaps, was itself a manifestation of that character which recognized man's small part in an eternity not measured by four hundred million years.

There are other aspects of the Maya philosophy of time, such as the strange failure to distinguish between past and future in the prophetic chants. What had gone before and what lay ahead were blended in a way that is baffling to our western minds. Mysticism is not now fashionable, and so writers tend to stress the material side of Maya civilization, but surely it is precisely these (to us) strange aberrations of Maya mentality which pose the most interesting questions.

Why is this Maya mentality so different from ours? Did it produce Maya culture, or did Maya culture produce it? What of its effect on religious conceptions? Can an impractical culture be a successful one by standards other than our own? Did Maya civilization carry within it the seeds of its own destruction? Such, as I see them, are the mysteries that make the Maya a fascinating study.

Cultural behavior—that is, the possible response of civilizations to laws which may govern their growth and decay—has been studied in recent years by writers such as Arnold Toynbee and A. L. Kroeber. To the solution of this problem a fuller knowledge of Maya civilization may make an important contribution.

It is clear that the course of cultural behavior must first be reconstructed from the histories of peoples who have left documentary accounts, for archaeology is the handmaiden of historical research, and a rather flighty handmaiden at that. Unfortunately, civilizations which have left their histories in writing, almost without exception, flourished in the Old World, and with every year it is becoming clearer that in the Eastern hemisphere there were no natural barriers or ideological iron curtains to stop indefinitely the interchange of cultural elements. From the shores of the Mediterranean, across the Near East and South Central Asia, to the Indus and, beyond, to China, there were many two-lane highways carrying inventions, improved techniques, religious ideas, and philosophical reflections. Lesser one-way routes carried many of these elements into the remotest peripheries of Old World civilization. The whole was one loose cultural federation, the members of which benefited, sooner or later, from the advances and discoveries of each unit in it. For the elucidation of laws of cultural behavior this is a most unprofitable situation, for if parallel solutions of a problem or similar mental attitudes appear, for example, in ancient Egypt and in ancient China, we cannot be sure that these did not result from diffusion of ideas, indirectly and perhaps with huge time lags, from one area to the other. Accordingly, only a region which was isolated for many centuries from this great cultural pool can be used to test supposed laws of cultural behavior derived from study of the civilizations of Europe, Asia, and Africa.

The answer, of course, lies in the New World, isolated from the Old for many centuries. Unfortunately, the natives of the greater part of this hemisphere had no writing. One cannot weigh the potsherds and flint points from the archaeologist's shovel against the full range of Athenian or Hindu culture. Even the advanced material cultures of ancient Peru—the incredible textiles of Paracas in the south, the goldwork of inland Chavin, or the magnificent portraiture in pottery of the north coast—tell us relatively little about the mentality and the general philosophical outlook of their makers. Ancient

Peru's nearest approach to writing was the quipu, an elaborate system of knotted and colored cords, which served as mnemonic records of such matters as population, crops, available labor, and tribute. There are details of Inca history, legends, and fairly full accounts of the Inca patrician-communistic state, but this material comes to us transmuted by the Spanish culture of the writers; it is no longer cast in the native pattern, even when, as in one case, the writer was part Inca.

The New World culture to set against those of the old is clearly the Maya, because it alone had a developed hieroglyphic writing. Furthermore, Maya writers of the sixteenth to eighteenth centuries transcribed in the Maya language, using European script, much information on their vanished civilization. Original hieroglyphic texts, greatly expanded by word of mouth, seem to have been the source of part of these transcriptions; oral tradition, principally in the form of historical-prophetic charts within a framework of time, probably supplied the bulk. Hieroglyphic texts carved in stone and written in codices and the colonial transcriptions, together with data on the present-day descendants of the ancient Maya, supply us with a considerable body of material on Maya thought, which can be weighed against that of comparable civilizations of the Old World.

The study of Maya history makes evident the rather obvious deduction that certain moral laws apply just as much to the Maya as to other civilizations. For instance, Maya history underlines the universal truth that good ends can never justify evil means for the simple reason that evil means can only distort and contaminate the end. It also supplies another confirmation of Jesus' saying that those who live by the sword shall perish by the sword. However, there is a big difference between finding new evidences of recognized moral laws and working out patterns of cultural behavior. Whether the pattern will be found is, as I have suggested above, open to question, but, obviously, we must not restrict the search for truth to where we feel confident we shall find it. Were that the attitude of scientists or of scholars in the humanities, there would be little success in conquering the unknown, for success comes to those whom curiosity lures from the traveled highway. The grass is no greener beyond the fence, but it is often fresher. Intensive study of the problem of patterns of cultural behavior may have to wait until more knowledge is accumulated; it will receive little attention in this book. For me, the supreme problems are what made Maya civilization succeed in ways that are not our ways, and how through its study one can bring home the truth our civilization hesitatingly accepts, that for nations and individuals spiritual values are far more important than material prosperity.

Finally, for those not attracted by these problems, there is the excitement of discovery. Archaeologists are forever making discoveries, uncovering evidence, and following clues. We have an affinity with Sherlock Holmes—perhaps with Watson would be nearer the truth—so forward, for, in the immortal words quoted by the sage of Baker Street, "The game is afoot."

GEOGRAPHY AND ENVIRONMENT

At the time of Spanish Conquest the area occupied by the Maya covered all Guatemala except parts of the low coastal strip on the Pacific, sections of western El Salvador and the western fringe of Honduras, the whole of British Honduras, and, in Mexico, the entire states of Yucatán and Campeche, the Territory of Quintana Roo, the state of Tabasco, except for a small area in the west, and the eastern half of the state of Chiapas. The area forms a rough quadrangle with a north-south axis of rather over 550 miles, roughly equivalent to the distance from New York City to about the center of North Carolina. The east-west extension is rather less than 350 miles toward the bottom of the area; about a hundred miles less at the top of the Yucatán Peninsula. The whole region falls within the tropics, with its southern boundary about Latitude 14° 20′ (see map, p. 18).

To the west of the Maya at the time of the arrival of the Spaniards there were groups speaking Zoque, Chiapanec, and dialects of the Nahuatl or Mexican language spoken by the Aztec and other peoples of central Mexico. South and southeast of the Maya were the Pipil, also Mexican-speaking, who occupied sections of the Pacific slope. The eastern neighbors of the Maya spoke sundry languages. Their cultures had been affected to varying degrees by influences from South America.

In cultural but not in physical contact with the Maya during the Classic period when Maya culture was at its height (approximately A.D. 250 to A.D. 900) were three civilizations: that of famed Teotihuacán, about twenty-eight miles northeast of Mexico City; the

17

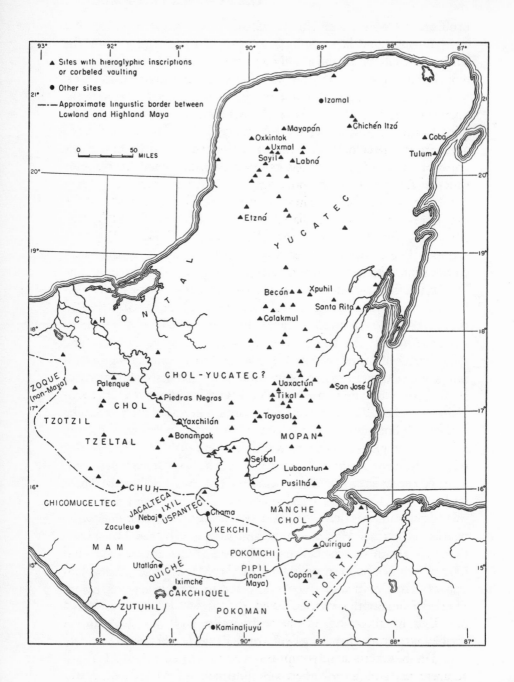

- ▲ Sites with hieroglyphic inscriptions or corbeled vaulting
- ● Other sites
- —·—·— Approximate linguistic border between Lowland and Highland Maya

0 ———— 50 MILES

●Izamal

▲Chichén Itzá

●Mayapán

▲Oxkintok ●Cobá

▲Uxmal

Sayil ▲Labná ▲Tulum

▲Etzná

Y U C A T E C

C H O N T A L

Becán▲▲ ●Xpuhil

▲Calakmul Santa Rita▲

●Palenque ▲Uaxactún

ZOQUE (non-Maya) CHOL-YUCATEC? ▲Tikal ▲San José

▲Piedras Negras

TZOTZIL ▲CHOL

▲Yaxchilán ▲Tayasal

TZELTAL ▲Bonampak MOPAN

Seibal

Lubaantun▲

CHUH Pusilhá▲

CHICOMUCELTEC

JACALTECA IXIL MANCHE CHOL

Nebaj ●Chama

Zaculeu● USPANTEC

KEKCHI

MAM Quiriguá●

Utatlán● POKOMCHI

QUICHÉ PIPIL (non-Maya) Copán▲▲ CHORTI

Iximché

CAKCHIQUEL

ZUTUHIL POKOMAN

●Kaminaljuyú

Zapotec, in Oaxaca, with Monte Albán as its greatest city; and that of north central Veracruz which culminated (but much later, at the close of the Classic period) in the splendid site of El Tajín. The old theory that Maya civilization was a lone cultural peak is now disproved; we now know, for instance, that Teotihuacán strongly influenced almost all Middle America, including the Maya area, in the third to the sixth centuries of our era; that El Tajín style affected Yucatán at a later date; and that Tula in Hidalgo some fifty miles north of Mexico City imposed its culture on the great Maya site of Chichén Itzá around A.D. 1000. Again, the culture called La Venta or Olmec, which flourished in southern Mexico just to the west of the Maya western frontier, radiated influences over nearly all Middle America before the start of the Classic period. Similarly Maya influences affected southern Veracruz in the early Classic period. Such cultural interchanges were unceasing.

In this book *Mexican* serves as a general term for the non-Maya cultures (except the Zapotec) of Mexico. Lack of space precludes frequent reference to the Mexican cultures, but their contemporaneity with, and influences on, Maya civilization must not be forgotten.

The boundaries of the Maya area during the Classic period seem to have been nearly the same as outlined above for the sixteenth century. Possibly the Maya extended a little farther west in Tabasco and Chiapas in early times. In the sixteenth century there was also a Maya-speaking group, the Huaxtec, isolated in northern Veracruz and adjacent parts of northeastern Mexico. How they became detached from their fellow Maya has been the subject of much conjecture. Perhaps they once formed a western extension of the Maya into southern Veracruz, where there are early Maya influences, and were later cut off from the main Maya group and driven northward by entering wedges of non-Maya stock. As the Huaxtec, although Maya in speech, did not share the traits which differentiated Maya from neighboring cultures, their lands will not be considered as part of the Maya area.

Like the early Victorian novel, the government of the United States, or, for those who like an old favorite, Gaul, the Maya area is divided into three parts, the Northern, Central, and Southern areas.

The Southern area, comprising the Guatemalan highlands and adjacent parts of El Salvador, is highly mountainous. Peaks, many of volcanic origin, tower to great heights; towns nestle in mountain-girt valleys or sprawl on plateaus. Plants and animals of temperate climates flourish in this region, which only geographical co-ordinates place within the tropics. The soil, largely of volcanic origin, is fertile; the rainfall is generally adequate; the temperature is never excessively hot or unduly cold. To the north and on the Pacific slopes coffee grows under ideal conditions; wheat and potatoes are raised in the highlands, and on the Pacific seaboard sugar cane and great banana plantations extend for mile after mile. Yet all these crops are of European introduction and for the most part are grown for export. In Maya times the principal crops were maize and beans, squash and sweet potatoes, and, on the Pacific slope, the cacao bean, a most valuable export crop, since cacao was in those days the universal currency of Middle America.

Highland Guatemala with its deep valleys and pine-fringed mountains, its colorful native Maya villages, and its crowning glory, Lake Atitlán, that aquamarine in its chased setting of mountain and volcano, is, indeed, the tourist paradise the folders describe. It must have been even more colorful a thousand years ago.

In terms of native culture, the highlands had other advantages in addition to good soil and climate. Volcanic stone was handy for building, and from it excellent *metates* (rubbing stones for grinding maize) were fashioned. Deposits of obsidian furnished the raw material for sharp knives and spear points, and volcanic tuff, because it will stand relatively high firing temperatures, was a first-rate temper for potters. Iron pyrites served the highlanders for mirrors, and specular hematite was the basis of a much-used red paint. Toward the close of Maya civilization, gold was probably worked from streams and copper perhaps mined.

The commodity which probably contributed most to the wealth of the highland Maya was the highly prized tail-feather of the quetzal, for this bird inhabits only restricted regions of considerable elevation, particularly the northwestern highlands of Guatemala and adjacent areas in Chiapas to the west and Honduras to the east. The birds were trapped and their four long tail-feathers of irridescent blue-green removed. Equally valuable was jade. One ancient work site of the mineral has been found in the Sierra de Las Minas in the northeastern highlands, and no doubt others will be located. Jade was a symbol of wealth but also had religious associations. For instance, a jade bead was frequently placed in the mouth of a dead person of rank. Jades were offered in sacrifice and used in divination.

Despite every advantage of climate and soil, of variety of flora and fauna, of mineral wealth, fairly dense population, and strategic position, the Southern area does not seem to have contributed much to the spiritual advances of Maya civilization. In architecture it lagged far behind the lowlands. Temples were usually of undressed stone crudely laid and had wooden or thatched roofs; corbeled vaulting occurs only in two or three places exposed to lowland influences. In sculpture, after a brilliant start in the Formative period when Maya culture was developing its identity, there is an extraordinary falling off, and sculpture is both crude and uncommon. The same is true of hieroglyphic writing. At the time of writing it looks as though Maya hieroglyphs developed in the Southern area, either in the highlands or on the Pacific slope of Guatemala, and thence spread to the lowlands, where they had their great development. Yet not a single hieroglyphic text of the Classic or post-Classic periods has been found in the highlands, nor is there evidence that the highland Maya were, like their lowland cousins, obsessed with speculation on eternity.

It is hard to say why this great region, materially so advanced, should have been spiritually so impoverished. Earthquakes may have discouraged attempts to equal the architectural achievements of the lowlanders, but that does not explain failure to keep abreast of progress in other branches of arts and science. Beautiful painted pottery was made at one time in the highlands, but, most significantly, only in the northern bastion of the Alta Verapaz, where lowland influence was strongest. Painted stucco decoration was highly developed for a short period at Kaminaljuyú, on the outskirts of the present Guatemala City, but this was at a time when that city was dominated by alien influences, largely from Mexico, but to some extent from the Maya lowlands. This, again, seems significant. It may be that the strong influences from Teotihuacán which affected the Guatemalan highlands in the early part of the Classic period were responsible for the disappearance of hieroglyphic writing among the highland Maya and for the failure of architecture to keep up with lowland advances, for neither feature was well developed at Teotihuacán. On the other hand, we cannot blame Teotihuacán for the highland deterioration in sculpture.

21

Every facet of Maya culture cannot be covered in a book of this size, which, in fact, is directed chiefly to discussion of the outstanding Maya achievements and the groups responsible for them. The Guatemalan highlands, although Maya in speech and in the fundamentals of their culture, receive little space here because generally they are not in the first rank. Neglect of their cultural life here is dictated by lack of space.

The Central area, second in order but first in importance of the three territorial divisions, is that in which Maya culture reached its greatest height, and in this region hieroglyphic texts are most abundant. It comprises the lowland region lying north and northwest of the highlands, and the Chiapas uplands, which geographically might be reckoned a sort of transitional zone but which culturally and linguistically belong with the Central area. On the map (p. 18) the line between the Southern area and the Central area is drawn to include the lowland dialects of Chiapas in the latter. Note that not a single site with a Maya hieroglyphic text on stone or wood occurs south of this line. There are some texts on pottery from the highlands, but except on the edge of the lowland country, these texts appear to be largely ornamental. If one were to mark sites with corbeled vaultings, the same contrast would be almost as sharp. A limited use of corbel vaulting to roof tombs carries a short way over the line into the northern limits of the highlands, but except for such sporadic incursions and freak appearances of vaulted buildings at two sites in southeastern Guatemala, probably an influence from Copán in the lowlands, the corbeled vault appears only in the lowlands and Chiapas.

The Central area is for the most part low-lying limestone country, from 100 to 600 feet above sea level, intersected by rivers and dotted in former times with lakes and ponds, many of which are now swamps as a result of silting.

The great core of this region, embracing the Petén District of Guatemala and the adjacent parts of Mexico and British Honduras, is now largely uninhabited. Within its bounds lie many of the greatest Maya cities, including Tikal, a journey to which opened this chapter. The description of the country on the way to Tikal is applicable to almost the whole area. It is an undulating land of vast tropical forest, with trees up to 150 feet high, interspersed with large swamps. To an observer without botanical training the outstanding features are the single mahogany trees scattered through the forest, the Spanish cedar, the giant ceiba, sacred to the Maya, many varieties of palms, and the sapodilla, from which chicle (the raw product of chewing gum) is bled. Typical, also, are the breadnut tree (not to be confused with the breadfruit tree, but an important source of food for man and beast), occasional rubber trees and vanilla vines, and incredible numbers of aerial plants, bromeliaceae and lianas. Flowers there are, but for the most part they are hardly visible, far above one's head in the treetops. Hibiscus and oleander and the radiant glory of Bougainvillea are marks of civilization; they do not grow in the forest. However, orchids bloom, half-hidden, in the forks of trees. Where the forest is dense, undergrowth may be sparse, but when some giant falls, a tangle of vegetation springs up to fight for its place in the sun.

To raise their crops, the Maya had first to clear this forest with their inadequate stone tools. The large trees could be girdled with fire; smaller trees and saplings had to be cut with stone axes, and anyone who has worked in the woods knows how hard it is to cut small growth even with a steel axe. Saplings give to the blow; they are hard to cut. The task, without metal tools, must have been heartbreaking. Worse still, the land could be cultivated only for a year or two before being left to revert to forest.

There is plenty of life in the forest, but except for insects, birds, and lizards, it is seldom manifest. Jaguars and tapirs are not uncommon, but one seldom sees more of them than their tracks. Deer, peccary, wild pigs, the delicate agouti, and the sloth, as well as two varieties of monkeys, the spider and the howler, are more in evidence. The last fill the forest, particularly at night and at dawn, with their chorus of deep roars.

Parrots are quite common, and there are wild turkeys of the ocellated variety with greeny bronze plumage and peacock-eyed feathers. The curassow, despite its grace, is another welcome addition to the pot. Toucans and red-breasted trogons, first cousins to the quetzal, abound, but the land is too low for the quetzal. Macaws are not very common in most parts; they tend to shun areas under about 1,000 feet.

Rivers include the mighty Usumacinta (a corruption of the

23

Aztec "Place of Small Monkeys") with the sites of Piedras Negras and Yaxchilán on its banks. The Pasión River, with Seibal beside it, and the Chixoy, which rises in the territory of the Quiché Maya in the heart of the Guatemalan highlands, join to form the Usumacinta, and at their junction stands the large site of Altar de Sacrificios recently dug by Peabody Museum of Harvard University. In the swampy stream-cut delta of the Usumacinta and Grijalva rivers, known to the Mexicans as "The Place of Canoes," lived the Chontal Maya, more at home in water than on land. Later they took to the sea and became the great traders of Middle America.

Rainfall is very high, particularly on the southern fringes of the area, where it may reach as much as ten feet a year. There is a dry season from late in January until May, but for the rest of the year the rains pelt down except for a let-up some years in September and October or in December. In the rainy season the swamps and low points become impassable morasses; leather objects grow whiskers.

Groups of chewing-gum gatherers spend the rainy season, when the chicle sap flows, deep in the forest, but their primitive camps are not permanent, and until a few years ago one could travel north from Flores, the tiny capital of the Department of Petén, for 150 miles through the heart of ancient Maya country without striking a single village, or one could follow the Pasión and upper Usumacinta rivers and strike across northeastern Chiapas without encountering more than an occasional hut or a tiny settlement of the almost extinct Lacandón Maya, deep in the forest. The lack of population in this area which once teemed with Maya cities is largely due to the prevalence of malaria and hookworm (both almost certainly introduced from the Old World since the coming of the Spaniards), the lack of roads and natural resources, and difficulty in controlling the forest.

It has been suggested by more than one writer that the climate of the area has changed for the worse since the Maya ruled there, but the arguments advanced are not very convincing. Of interest in this connection is the fact that at Cobá, in Quintana Roo, two great Maya causeways crossing the lake are now submerged below the water even at the height of the dry season, but that is not necessarily evidence of an increase in rainfall, for the lake may have silted or the causeways may have sunk under their own weight. Again, the level of water in an ancient reservoir at another Maya site seems to have remained constant, judging by the steps leading to it. At least, I believe that climatic changes have not been sufficient to have altered significantly the flora and fauna of the region. Sample cores from the bed of Lake Petén carry large quantities of savanna pollen during the Classic period, but I think these may show a change in the direction of the prevalent winds, for there has always been savanna land south of that lake, rather than indicate that the Maya lowlands were savanna land at that time.

The Chiapas uplands present a different appearance, for the country, rising gradually to elevations of about 5,000 feet, is in part plateau covered with pine and savanna or belts of liveoak. There is also a small area to the southeast, in the vicinity of the great Maya city of Copán (elevation about 2,000 feet), which is mountainous, and the same is true of parts of British Honduras. Advanced Maya culture maintained a precarious lodgment in Chiapas uplands and the mountains of British Honduras, but established itself successfully at Copán. Those regions, however, are the exceptions; by and large the Central area is composed of forest-clad lowlands as already noted.

The central core of the Petén and adjacent regions is singularly deficient in natural resources, and the soil is scant except in the valleys. The ubiquitous limestone supplies first-rate stone for building and for sculpture and, in places, holds deposits of flint and chert, good substitutes for the absent, and in some respects more useful, obsidian of the highlands. There is no igneous rock or metal in the region except in a small area of British Honduras, from which granite for making *metates* was obtained on a rather small scale by groups living on the edge of that district. Gold, too, occurs in that area (unlike the Petén, it is mountainous), but not in paying quantity, and there is no reason to believe it was ever worked by the Maya, who for the greater part of their history used no metal. Moreover, in the Classic period the central core of the Petén appears to have been off the most important commercial routes of ancient Middle America, but it did produce the highly prized cacao in some quantity, and no doubt it exported to the highlands other tropical produce, such as parrot, trogon, and toucan feathers, jaguar pelts, logwood dye, chile, copal incense, and smaller quantities of vanilla and rubber. It is probable that other specialties of the region, such as flint points, the hearts of palm trees (a kind of substitute for celery, relished by the Maya despite its bitter taste), painted pottery, and objects of rare wood were also exported. These, however, were far less valuable commodities than those which the highlands could offer. A little of the imported jade was carved and then re-exported. Jade has been reported in the mountains of British Honduras and may have been worked, thereby making the lowlanders less dependent on the highlands for that valuable commodity.

To me, one of the greatest mysteries is why Maya culture should have reached its greatest peak in this region so singularly lacking in natural wealth, where man, armed only with stone tools and fire, had everlastingly to struggle with the unrelenting forest for land to sow his crops. Moreover, when he had wrested the necessary area momentarily from the forest's grasp, he usually found a soil so thin and quickly weed infested that after one or two crops, it had to be surrendered to his enemy, who lost no time in covering it once more with dense vegetation.

Toynbee, in his *Study of History*, has cited numerous examples to show that the conditions under which a civilization will develop and live must be neither too soft nor too hard. His argument is convincing. Yet, in the Maya lowlands, we find conditions so unfavorable that it is not easy to see how Maya civilization could ever have developed there. Can it be that from our western point of view, conditioned by soft living, we overestimate the difficulties? Perhaps to the Maya the obstacles were such as to produce the optimum response; that is, they stimulated him to put forth his best. That might well be the case. On the other hand, if the advocates of a deterioration in climate are right, conditions would not have been so onerous twelve hundred years ago.

The Northern area, the third division, comprises Yucatán and most of Campeche and the Territory of Quintana Roo. As one travels northward from the Central area, the climate becomes drier, until at the extreme northern tip the rainfall is exceptionally low, a scant eighteen inches a year, about one-sixth of that registered for some parts of the Central area. This condition is reflected in the vegetation, which becomes more scrublike as one goes north. The limestone which covers the whole area is more porous than that of the Central area and lets the rain seep through to underground drainage systems, with the result that surface rivers are nonexistent and lakes occur only along fault lines in the eastern part. Much of the country would be quite waterless were it not that in places the surface crust of limestone has caved in, giving access to deposits of water beneath. These natural wells, known as cenotes, a corruption of the Maya word *dz'onot*, together with some artificial wells and catch pools, were, and still are, the sole source of water throughout Yucatán. Yet the country had and now has a considerable population.

This region, like the Central area, is poor in natural resources because there is nothing but limestone country; and in some respects it is even worse off, for some of the products of the Central area, such as cacao, rubber, and vanilla, do not do well in this more arid region. Cotton was an important crop and was widely exported in the form of woven and decorated mantles. The fauna is more restricted. Jaguars are found there, but monkeys, tapirs, and macaws are extremely rare or unknown.

Maya civilization at its height was more advanced in the Central area than to the north, but Yucatán is of prime importance because from there we have the fullest information on how Maya culture functioned at the time of the Spanish Conquest. Alternative names for these three areas are: highland, southern lowland, and northern lowland.

LANGUAGE AND POPULATION

There are fifteen Maya languages or major dialects still spoken and two more are recently extinct. Several have subdivisions which merge into one another. They form a group comparable to the Romance group of languages. Some Maya languages are closer to each other than Spanish is to Portuguese; others stand in approximately the same relationship as French to Italian. Quite possibly we should speak of two Maya languages, a highland and a lowland, and classify the rest as dialects. Maya is not closely related to any other language of Mexico or Central America.

In the Northern area and the north part of the Central area only Yucatec (often called Maya) is spoken. Southwest and southeast of this section, Chontal and Mopan were once spoken, and across the base of the Central area were spread Chontal, two branches of Chol, and lastly the Chorti dialect of Chol around Copán. In eastern

Chiapas are found Tzotzil, Tzeltal, Chaneabal, and Chuh, the last extending into the Guatemalan highlands. All except the last are closely related, and as one travels southward from Yucatán there is a gradual and uniform transition from Yucatec to Tzotzil, the greater the distances apart, the greater the differences. This is strong evidence that no large movements of peoples have taken place for centuries, and that, therefore, Maya classical art and architecture and the considerable achievements in astronomy and arithmetic must be credited to the ancestors of the present lowland Maya.

The same correlation of distance and change holds good also for the highland Maya, the principal groups of which are the Quiché, Cakchiquel, Mam, Kekchi, and Pokoman. The transition is so gradual that it is often difficult to say where one language stops and another begins. As Andrade, the great authority on Maya languages, once put it, one would have to make the linguistic map in blending pastel colors, not in harsh reds and greens and yellows. It is equally clear that in the highlands there have been no marked displacements, although minor changes and expansions are on record.

I should here mention glottochronology, a device claiming to measure the time two related languages have been separated by the percentage of everyday words in a short selection they still share. The method has been severely criticized on the grounds that change in language, where it can be measured—for example, Icelandic—may be at complete variance with the "rule," and that the human factor cannot be entirely eliminated. Glottochronology claims, for example, to have established that Huaxtec separated from Yucatec 2,200 years ago and from Mam 3,600 years ago; that Palencano-Chol, spoken in the area stretching east of Palenque, in the heart of the Central area, separated from Yucatec 1,600 years ago and from Quiché, a highland tongue, 2,600 years ago. Some archaeologists have used glottochronology most uncritically to set up Middle-American chronological charts. Naturally, the longer two languages have been separated, the fewer words they will normally have in common, but that is a different matter from the mathematical precision claimed for glottochronology. It is worth noting that the loss on each side of a single word in the case of the Huaxtec-Yucatec separation would push that back a couple of centuries! Nevertheless, as a rough guide glottochronology is useful.

Maya speech is musical and pleasant. Equivalents of our *d* and *f* are absent, and *r* appears in only one lowland dialect, but glottal stops (a sort of catch of the breath something like the bark of a top sergeant) are frequent. Yucatec is spoken by many whites and mestizos of Yucatán as a second language and is said to be easy to learn. I haven't found it so!

The descendants of the Maya still exist in large numbers in many parts of the lands they formerly ruled, but in some regions they have been absorbed culturally and, to a certain extent, physically into the Latin-American mestizo population. As already noted, the Central area, except for its appendage, the Chiapan uplands, is now largely uninhabited. Karl Sapper nearly fifty years ago estimated that there was a Maya-speaking population of about one and a quarter millions, three-fifths of whom spoke highland tongues. To this total should be added the smaller numbers who have lost their mother tongue and the many of mixed blood.

Estimates on the pre-Columbian population vary considerably. The lowest figures are 1,250,000 for the whole area (Kroeber) and 800,000 for the combined Northern and Central areas (Termer). Morley, on the other hand, estimated the population of the Peninsula of Yucatán alone at over 13,000,000. I have published an estimate of 3,000,000 for the whole Maya area in A.D. 800, the larger part of which would have been in the highlands. This may be a bit low, but reliable data are so scarce that no figure is much better than a "guesstimate."

PHYSICAL APPEARANCE
AND PSYCHOLOGICAL TRAITS

Physically the Maya are fairly homogeneous. Generally speaking the Maya is stocky, with strong muscular development in his legs. He is broad-faced and has prominent cheek bones. Features are soft and both sexes can be described as handsome, but very different in appearance from the conventional idea of the tall, slender Plains Indian (Plate 1). The men look more intelligent than the women. The Yucatec are among the most broad-headed peoples in the world, for the average cephalic index (length of head divided into the breadth) is eighty-five, with examples as high as ninety-three. No other Maya group is quite so round-headed, and in the highlands and the Chiapas uplands there are narrower-headed strains which pull down the average for the group. It is probably significant that the Yucatec are both the most isolated and most round-headed group. The Maya accentuated this roundheadedness by deforming the skull.

Maya of pure blood have straight (or sometimes slightly wavy) black hair and dark brown eyes. The eyelids often show a rather pronounced fold which gives an almond shape to the eyes, also characteristic of the treatment of the eye in Maya sculpture. Many Maya have a fleshy, hooked, or rather aquiline nose, and somewhat drooping lower lip. These are the features which combined with the deformed forehead to produce the type of idealized beauty found everywhere in the art of the great period of the Central area.

By assessing the character and intelligence of the present-day Maya, we can get some idea of those traits in his ancestors who created Maya civilization, and as this civilization was surely a product of lowlanders, let us see what a study of the Yucatec, the best-known lowland group, reveals.

Some years ago Morris Steggerda persuaded a small group of American ethnologists, archaeologists, and missionaries who had had rather close contacts with Yucatec Maya to rate them on certain psychological traits. The majority opinion included these traits: The average Yucatec Maya is socially inclined and likes to work in groups. He has strong family ties, but shows little outward affection. He is not quarrelsome. Though good-natured and sympathetic towards those in distress, he is fond of practical jokes. He is a keen observer, and he has a good memory. He is fairly intelligent, but not particularly inventive or imaginative or inclined to wander. He is fatalistic and superstitious, and not particularly afraid of death. His sexual life is not overemphasized, but he has a strong tendency to alcoholism. He is thrifty and unusually honest. He is exceptionally clean in his person, bathing morning and night, and his wife is a neat housekeeper. Individuals vary in their desire to excel, in their religious enthusiasm, and in their attitude toward change. Murderers and beggars are exceptional in the Maya community.

My own answers agreed fairly closely with those set forth above, except that my observations in remote villages of British Honduras led me to believe that as individuals and as groups the Maya like to move from one place to another. I should also list corporal modesty as a very marked trait and give the Mayas a high rating for industry. I have noticed that unless a Maya has been strongly influenced by Spanish contacts, he is little inclined to sing, and he is still less given to whistling a tune. I should consider the Maya highly religious, rather than merely superstitious, and should say that in his dealings he is formal and, judging by two friendships, one of over twenty years standing, he can develop deep and lasting loyalties. Although generally pacific, he can be savage when aroused or when, under the influence of drink, hidden resentments come out.

I think this estimate would apply pretty well to all lowland Maya groups of the present day, although some are not so clean and pacific as the Yucatec. It probably would have fitted the mass of lowland Maya in pre-Spanish days except in two regards: intelligence and artistic attainment. The lowland Maya of today is fairly intelligent but not exceptionally so, and he shows little artistic inclination. This is a retrogression, attributable perhaps to the submergence of the old ruling class in colonial times, although there were clear signs of a decline in the centuries immediately before the Spanish Conquest. In the Guatemalan highlands and Chiapas uplands fine weaving and brocading of textiles show that the old love of beauty continues where conditions for its survival have been more propitious, and the day may come when the Maya will produce a great modern leader—the great governor of Yucatán, Felipe Puerto Carrillo, was part Maya—as other Indian peoples, notably the Zapotec of Oaxaca, have done in Mexico.

SEARCH AND RESEARCH

Spanish priests and laymen of the sixteenth century were impressed by the architectural triumphs of the Maya cities which even in those days were falling into ruin, but their accounts of Maya civilization as it was when the land was conquered for Spain were hidden in reports for the most part moldering unpublished in Spanish archives or New World friaries. It was not until 1785 that commissions visited the newly discovered ruins of the large Maya city of Palenque and prepared illustrated reports, which, together with samples of Maya sculpture and other arts, were sent to Carlos III and were promptly reburied in the Spanish archives. A copy of one of the reports found its way to London, where it was published in 1822, the first book on Maya archaeology. The author was Antonio del Río, an artillery captain in the Spanish army, who cheerfully told his sovereign: "By dint of perseverance I effected all that was necessary to be done, so that ultimately there remained neither a window nor a doorway blocked up; a partition that was not thrown down, nor a room, corridor, court, tower, nor subterranean passage in which excavations from two or three *varas* in depth were not effected."

As a result of the interest thus aroused, Count Jean Frédéric Waldeck visited Palenque, and stayed there for two years making plans and copying, for the most part with little accuracy, Maya sculptures in that most artistic of all cities. Waldeck was a peculiar character. He had fought in the army of Napoleon in Egypt, and perhaps heard his leader's famed address to his troops in the shadow of the pyramids. Later he served with that eccentric seaman, Lord Cochrane, in the liberation of Chile. At a time when most archaeologists retire, he was starting his field work in the Maya area, at the age of sixty-six, and confounded opinions on the deadly properties of the Central American forest by living to the ripe age of 109. Indeed, his death, in 1875, in a street accident in Paris, is said to have been his own fault; he turned his head to look at a pretty girl. His title was phony and so were many of his drawings. He depicted one Maya figure with a liberty cap and a delightful late eighteenth-century classical pose, and he converted other purely Maya sculptures into most convincing elephants, an artistic aberration which was to have repercussions nearly a century later.

Maya archaeology had gotten off to a bad start—del Río bull-dozing through the ruins (you can see to this day the melancholy results of his artillery tactics at Palenque), and Waldeck with his neoclassicism and elephants. There was to be another queer, although not harmful, chapter.

Lord Kingsborough, an eccentric character of Regency England, was convinced that the ancient peoples of Mexico and Middle America were descendants of the lost ten tribes of Israel, and he devoted the whole of his fortune to "proving" it. Between 1830 and 1848 his *Antiquities of Mexico* were published in nine enormous volumes, each one of which is almost too heavy for the average lady

librarian to replace on a high library stack. These contained reproductions of native codices and sculptures and rare or unpublished accounts of native life, in full or in extract, together with Lord Kingsborough's interpretations to support his views. The set sold at £175, roughly the equivalent of about $3,500 today, and there were, not unnaturally, few purchasers. With his considerable fortune spent in the publication of these tomes, Lord Kingsborough was unable to meet the printers' bills for the final volumes and was cast into debtors' prison, where he died after some time spent under conditions made familiar to all of us by Charles Dickens.

He deserved a better end. Much of the material he put on record was of inestimable value, and, indeed, to this day, his reproductions of two or three of the Mexican codices are the only ones in existence. In the volumes are included new material on Palenque and the first reproduction of the Codex Dresden, the finest of the three surviving Maya hieroglyphic books.

In 1839 an energetic native of New Jersey and graduate of Columbia University, John L. Stephens, decided to see the Maya ruins of which he had read in the accounts of del Río and others. To smooth his way, he got himself appointed special envoy of the United States to what was then the Central American Federation, a position which involved little work, since by the time Stephens reached Central America the Federation was in the last stages of disintegration. He took with him an English friend and accomplished artist, Frederick Catherwood. In this and a subsequent trip to Yucatán, the friends visited, largely on muleback, over forty Maya sites, most of which had not previously been reported. The two books which resulted from their travels—*Incidents of Travel in Central America, Chiapas, and Yucatán* (1841) and *Incidents of Travel in Yucatán* (1843) were best-sellers. In nine months the first book ran through twelve editions, and within a decade the combined sales of both reached some 25,000 copies, an extraordinary popularity for the period. Both books are still read, and have recently been republished in the United States and translated into Spanish.

Stephens gave clear and interesting descriptions of the ruins they visited, free of all the twaddle about Atlantis and Egypt common in the nineteenth century. His accounts of life in Central America a century ago are vivid and delightful. Catherwood's contribution was the excellent illustrations of Maya ruins or sculpture, far superior to any thitherto published. Their accuracy may be judged by the fact that many of the glyphs in his engravings can be read with almost as much ease as photographs. Theirs was a fine team, and their two books are as fresh today as when they were written and illustrated.

With the publication of these travel books, interest in the Maya gathered momentum. To name all who contributed to knowledge of the Maya would be out of place in this book, but a word should be said of the activities of the Abbé Brasseur de Bourbourg, for it was he who brought to light and in some cases saved from destruction several of our best written sources on the Maya.

Most important of these was Bishop Diego de Landa's history

of Yucatán, written about 1560, a mine of information on Maya customs, religious beliefs, and history, together with a quite detailed account of the Maya calendar, illustrated with drawings of the glyphs. This was the indispensable foundation on which to reconstruct Maya hieroglyphic writing, and is as close to a Maya Rosetta stone as we are ever likely to get. Indeed, without this book it is doubtful whether we would have made any progress in glyph decipherment, and we would know very much less about the Maya. Bishop Landa, then a Franciscan friar, who reached Yucatán a few years after the Spanish Conquest, was a man of unquestionable ability. He has been much criticized for his severity in stamping out recrudescences of paganism, but in that he merely reflected the views of his century. Moreover, he had uncovered sickening evidence that the Mayas, although nominally Christians, were still secretly sacrificing children, even in the churches, and, as a result of Christian contacts, had begun to crucify them. He knew that only severity would end such barbarities. Landa, like any modern ethnologist, obtained his material from native informants. Oddly enough, had he not campaigned so violently against Maya relapses into paganism, we might not now have this prime source, for it was while he was in Spain, awaiting trial on charges of exceeding his authority, that he whipped his material into shape to serve as indirect testimony for the defense.

Brasseur de Bourbourg also discovered part of one of the three surviving Maya codices, and saved many manuscripts from destruction when the monastic orders in Mexico were suppressed. On one occasion he purchased for four pesos at a secondhand book stall in Mexico the manuscript of the finest Maya-Spanish dictionary ever made. This is the indispensable Motul dictionary, now one of the treasures of the John Carter Brown Library.

Of the many nineteenth-century explorers, Alfred Maudslay is far and away the most important. The results of his extensive explorations between 1881 and 1894 appear in five superbly published volumes containing a great number of magnificent photographs of stelae and buildings, accurate drawings of hieroglyphic inscriptions, and many maps, plans, and sections. Together with the plaster casts of stone carvings which he brought back to the British Museum for duplication and distribution, his published work formed an incomparable basis for intensive research along many lines. Maudslay set

35

a scientific approach which the twentieth century was to follow and amplify.

Just before the turn of the century individual effort began to give way to the institutional. The Peabody Museum of Archaeology and Ethnology, Harvard University, led the way in 1892, and between that date and 1915 it sent a series of twenty expeditions to explore various parts of the Maya area. Many new sites were discovered, and much fresh information collected. The results—also published with exceptional photographs—added greatly to Maudslay's material.

Maya archaeology seems to attract colorful characters. Much of the exploratory work of these expeditions of Harvard University was done by a single man, Teobert Maler, German by birth but Austrian by naturalization, who came to Mexico in the train of that most pathetic figure in Mexican history, the Emperor Maximilian. After Maximilian's well-intentioned life was brought to a close by a firing squad, Maler drifted to Central America, where he became interested in the Maya civilization. For years he traveled the forests of the Petén and out-of-the-way parts of Yucatán, Campeche, and Quintana Roo, alone except for his native crews, who frequently decamped. He was indifferent to comfort, and would as soon start for the forest at the height of the rainy season as in the dry. He was a first-rate photographer and possessed a rare determination and patience in the face of difficulties, many, alas, of his own making. Later, Maler took it into his head that the Peabody Museum was making huge profits out of the sales of his reports (no archaeological report in history has even yielded a profit!) and refused to have anything more to do with the Museum.

Another strange character was Le Plongeon, who believed the Maya had come from Atlantis and that the Greek alphabet was a Maya hymn recounting the submergence of that mythical land. Some rootlets adhering to a sculptured lintel at Chichén Itzá, where he worked for a long time, were interpreted by him as telegraph wires, and led him to declare that the Maya had a telegraphic system some ten thousand years ago by his dating. He also credited them with the invention of the metric system.

However, students of Maya civilization are not all crackpots;

Förstemann, in Germany, did brilliant pioneering in the deciphering of the Maya codices, and Eduard Seler, another German, made contributions of outstanding importance. Alfred Tozzer, emeritus professor at Harvard, living for some time among the primitive Lacandón Maya, made the first ethnological studies in Central America. On his return to the United States, he directed the teaching of Middle American archaeology at Harvard, where many of the present workers in that field studied under him.

In 1915, the Carnegie Institution of Washington entered the Maya field. For the next following years it had anywhere up to a dozen men in the field studying every aspect of the culture. The program has included large-scale excavation at three types of sites—Uaxactún, north of Tikal, a typical Petén city of the classic period; Chichén Itzá, in Yucatán, where Mexican influences were very strong at a later date; and Kaminaljuyú, on the outskirts of Guatemala City, an important early center of the highlands. The Institution's last work was at Mayapán, capital of the Maya of Yucatán shortly before the Spanish Conquest. In recent years Mexican archaeologists have taken the lead in field work in Chiapas, Campeche, and Yucatán.

University Museum of the University of Pennsylvania started in 1956 a ten-year program at Tikal. Working on a large scale and with the latest methods and techniques, the team has accumulated a mass of new data on Maya life during the Classic period and on the late Formative period which underlies so much of Tikal. Peabody Museum, Harvard, has re-entered the field, with excavation in British Honduras and later at the strategic sites of Altar de Sacrificios and Seibal in the upper Usumacinta-Pasión drainage.

Other research centers—the Middle American Research Institute of Tulane University, the Instituto de Antropología e Historia of Mexico, the British Museum, and the Chicago Natural History Museum—have also contributed greatly to our present knowledge of the Maya. Research has turned from surface exploration to detailed excavation; from the general to the particular. As a result of this intensive work more has been learned and published about the Maya in the past thirty-five years than in the previous century and a half, with the result that now research tends to shift again from the particular to the general. So many have contributed to our present pool of knowledge that I make no attempt in these pages to give credit for each piece of knowledge. The general reader can have little interest in knowing that this grave was excavated by Brown and that by Black, this temple cleared by Gray and that glyph deciphered by Green. The specialist knows to whom the credit belongs.

We should, however, give a line of credit to all gum chewers. To keep the chewer supplied, hundreds of *chicleros* spend every rainy season deep in the forests of Central America bleeding the sapodilla tree for its thick, milky sap, the *chicle* or raw material of chewing gum. Searching for new stands, they frequently come upon Maya ruins hidden in the forest. In the dry season the sap does not run, and the *chicleros* leave the forest for the small towns and villages on its perimeter, but that is the time when the archaeologist is busy (Maler was exceptional). *Chicleros* guide him to new ruins and the chicle contractors' mules carry him there along the temporary trails used for bringing out the gum, which has been cooked to a bricklike consistency.

Synthetic gum is replacing the natural product, and the *chicleros* are pulling out of many parts of the forest, so their aid to archaeology will soon be a thing of the past. Recent trails through the forest are now overgrown; tiny landing strips, recently shipping points for the gum, are reverting to forest. These outposts of our age are being submerged beneath the green tide, as were Maya cities a thousand years ago. Not being built of substantial materials, they will completely disappear in a few years, perhaps foretelling in their extinction the fate of the fretted civilization which brought them into being. Still more recently, an intensive search for oil has further opened up the Petén, but it would seem there is no oil, so again we may see the forest closing in. Still, road building goes on apace, and one can now go by bus to Tikal and by train to Palenque!

Archaeology is not the only key to Maya life. In addition to the three surviving Maya hieroglyphic books (p. 197), we have the so-called Books of Chilam Balam. These compilations by men who wanted to preserve their traditions and their lore are written in the Maya of Yucatán but using European script. Mixed with a hodge-podge of medical recipes, astronomy, astrology, and material on both the Spanish and Maya calendars, is precolonial history. A rather similar urge in the highlands of Guatemala led to the reduction of the myths and history of the Quiché Maya to a book in European script known as the Popol Vuh (p. 277).

There is also much information on the Maya in the writings of Spanish friars and travelers of the colonial period in addition to the writings of Bishop Landa already mentioned. Often these observations of colonial writers can be integrated with archaeological data. Let me digress to supply an illustration.

A Spanish historian reports that in 1696 the nephew of the ruler of the still independent Itzá of Tayasal in the Petén (p. 153) came as a sort of ambassador of his uncle to the Spanish governor of Yucatán and, as a symbol of submission to Spanish rule, offered him his uncle's headdress of bright-hued feathers. We have no indication from any other source that handing over what we might term a ruler's crown was among the Maya a symbol of submission. It looked like the kind of idea the Itzás, who had held out against the Spaniards for 150 years since they conquered Yucatán, might have taken over from their white enemies. Not a bit of it. Two sculptures at Palenque show a personage seated on a throne (of jaguars in one case, of two disgruntled and highly uncomfortable men in the other) to whom a less important person offers a fine headdress with mosaic decoration surmounted by quetzal feathers (Fig. 26*d*). A sentence from the lengthy and dull writings of an eighteenth-century historian explains reliefs carved a millenium earlier at Palenque. Sometimes an odd bit of information remains unexplained: a Franciscan casually mentions the *pechni* rite, in which a victim had his nose squashed and then was put to death. There is nothing in archaeology or other ethnological sources to amplify the information on this strange ceremony, which was important enough to have its name recorded in a history book (*pech* is to squash between two objects; *ni* is nose).

Studies of the beliefs and customs of present-day Maya have been even more useful in reconstructing the past. Much of our knowledge of Maya religion comes from present-day survivals (p. 274), and similarly the role of the ancient Maya calendar in remote Maya villages in the highlands of Guatemala helps in the interpretation of the past. Sometimes it is not easy to separate elements of

Spanish origin from the aboriginal or those that arise from the mingling of the two strains.

DATING MAYA HISTORY AND
THE CARBON–14 PROCESS

The conversion of Maya dates into our calendar in this book is
according to the so-called Goodman-Martínez-Thompson correlation, now accepted by nearly all Maya scholars; the alternative Spinden correlation makes all dates 260 years earlier in our reckoning.

The solution of this problem has depended on many factors:
astronomy, historical evidence from the period of first Spanish contact, pottery, architecture, present-day Maya calendars, the Aztec
calendar, and, more recently, Carbon–14 readings of dated wooden
beams in Maya temples. In the early stages of Carbon–14 research,
when some of the kinks had not been ironed out, readings supported
the Spinden correlation; with refined techniques the situation has
been reversed.

Because of its tremendous importance to archaeology a word
should be said about the radio-carbon process, usually called Carbon
14 or C–14, mentioned above. Carbon 14 is an element in plant and
animal life which starts to be given off when death occurs. About
fifteen years ago it was found that at the end of rather over five
thousand years half of the C–14 content of a dead organism had been
given off. The value of this to archaeology was immediately apparent,
for by measuring the loss of C–14 in a piece of charcoal or wood or
(less reliable) bone in a given deposit, one could date the associated
finds.

Unfortunately things were not as simple as all that. Specimens
could suffer contamination and then would give the wildest readings. Since a tree dies outwards, a sample from the inmost core of a
tree might be a century older than the date of its cutting. Moreover,
the older, solid-fuel process is less reliable than the conversion to
gas process now used. Single C–14 readings were suspect; long series
of samples were far more trustworthy. In 1959 the University of
Pennsylvania laboratory ran thirty-three counts of samples from
ten beams in a Tikal temple. The whole series averaged out at A.D.
746 with a leeway of thirty-four years on either side. These beams

were carved with a Maya date which is the equivalent of A.D. 741 in the Goodman-Martínez-Thompson correlation here followed; the equivalent in the Spinden correlation is A.D. 481. Subsequent readings of Tikal beams have confirmed the agreement with the former correlation.

II. The Rise and Florescence of Maya City States

There is a kind of intellectual remoteness necessary for the comprehension of any great work in its full designs and its true proportions; a close approach shews the smaller niceties, but the beauty of the whole is discerned no longer.—Samuel Johnson, *Preface to Shakespeare*.

POPULATING THE NEW WORLD

The study of archaeology depends to no small degree on the examination of tens of thousands of potsherds, of stone implements, and of the diverse contents of trash heaps. This close approach is essential for reconstructing the framework of history, but it makes dull reading for the average man.

Philip Guedalla, in one of his more *fin de siècle* passages inserted in the baroque façade of his *Conquistador*, gives archaeologists fair warning of this. He writes: "One of the wildest hazards of history is that which dictates to posterity the particular feature by which it recalls a preceding age. Rome, by some accident, is almost all aqueducts in our recollection, Egypt all funerals. . . . Such chance survivals cause the oddest misconceptions, the most lopsided reconstructions of the past; and it is a shade disturbing to reflect that we shall lie one day, beyond all opportunity of contradiction, at the mercy of such hazards."

There is not a little danger that the fate of Maya archaeology might be to emerge as an interminable catalogue of changes in the shapes and designs of pottery, or of minor evolution in types of masonry.

Sherds are essential for reconstructing trade routes and for establishing the contemporaneity of centers of civilization, and Job found them handy for scraping his boils, but to strive for the intellectual remoteness Samuel Johnson rightly advocates requires that detailed discussion be eliminated from the text. With that end in view, specialized information of that nature is rigorously compressed here, or is omitted to leave the canvas free for a picture in broad outline.

Archaeologists agree that America was populated by immigrants from Asia who crossed by the Bering Strait; there is less unanimity as to when the earliest crossings were made, majority opinion favoring about twenty thousand years ago. It is rather generally accepted that these were not large migrations, but infiltrations of small groups over thousands of years, which slowly populated the New World, and the first had the advantage of a land bridge. The earliest firm evidence of man (at Tule Springs, Nevada) carries us back to 11,000 B.C., but more ancient sites will certainly turn up.

The whole problem of early man in America is extremely complex and is still far from being solved. One trouble is that archaeologists, who think in decades and centuries, are in this matter largely dependent on geologists, in whose sight "a thousand ages . . . are but an evening gone." In any case, the matter is not of much consequence so far as Maya civilization is concerned, for there is no reason to believe that the Maya came over with those first Americans; their ancestors were probably late immigrants.

No specialist in the field supposes that America was populated by immigrants from across the Atlantic or from across the Pacific, although the possibility of late influences having reached the New World from Polynesia cannot be ruled out (it is even less likely that at any time voyagers from Peru or elsewhere in Latin America sailed to Polynesia).

The American Indian type is mixed, but Mongoloid features dominate, indicating rather clearly that the majority of the immigrants came from northeastern and eastern Asia. There are, however, other strains. Earnest Hooton, of *Up from the Ape* fame, in describing a series of Maya skulls, remarks that they could be duplicated without difficulty in Pueblo crania from New Mexico or Arizona or from burials of coastal Peru. After noting that cranial deformation is found in the Near East and in the western parts of the New World, but is absent among Asiatics describable as Mongoloids, he continues: "I am inclined to think that the ancestors of the classical Mayas were not very different from the white hybridized type which we call Armenoid—hook noses from Henry Field's Iranian Plateau race, round heads from the good old Alpines—and inspired with similar aesthetic ambitions to improve their head form. Eventually they picked up some Mongoloid features—hair, pigmentation, [high] cheek bones, et cetera."

If Hooton is right—and there are few to challenge him in his field of physical anthropology—it is an exciting thought that the Maya were, so to speak, second cousins once removed to peoples such as the Sumerians, who were busy erecting pyramids, developing astronomy, and adapting and expanding a high civilization about three thousand years before the Maya. Were those parallels fortuitous? Did the Maya and others of their race carry the seeds of such ideas with them when they crossed to the New World? Or can there be something in the Armenoid blood which inclines them to such interests? The trouble is that we have no real evidence as to what group originated such ideas in either hemisphere. The Egyptians may have done so in the Old World, but, for all we know to the contrary, the first pyramid builders and astronomers of the New World may have been a longheaded group with no trace of hooked, beaky noses. About such speculation Hilaire Belloc once wrote some happy lines: "The student should be warned that they are theories, and theories only, that their whole point and value is that they are not susceptible to proof; that what makes them amusing and interesting is the certitude that one can go on having a good quarrel about them, and the inner faith that when one is tired of them one can drop them without regret. Older men know this, but young men often do not."

The first inhabitants of the New World were hunters and wild-plant gatherers, and among the game they hunted was the mammoth. Evidence of the hunting techniques of these groups has turned up in widely separated areas from the U.S.A. to South America, but not so far in the Maya area. This is almost surely because little search for this early culture has been made in that region; one can postulate its former existence from its occurrence on both sides of the area that was later Maya territory.

Considerable evidence of early hunters has been found recently

44

in a district a few miles north of Mexico City, once the swampy fringe of Lake Texcoco. At Iztapan the remains of a young mammoth were found in 1952 with a flint point lodged between two of the ribs and with other implements of flint and obsidian mixed with the bones. The beast had been butchered after apparently being driven into the sticky soil of the so-called Upper Becerra formation, dated about nine to ten thousand years ago. Bones of another mammoth found two years later under similar conditions had clearly been moved around by human agency, and again points were associated with them. Some of the bones showed deep cuts made by the hunters as they chopped up the beast.

At Tepexpan, only one and one-half miles away, and in a similar formation were the remains of a woman of about thirty, the only human so far associable with those early hunters. Her bones did not differ noticeably from those of the general run of present-day Indians of Mexico; there was nothing primitive about her, although she was buried when mammoth still roamed the land.

Excavations in caves in northeastern Mexico and around Tehuacán, about halfway between Mexico City and the western boundary of the Maya area revealed the trash left by these early hunters underlying that of the first agriculturalists; the trash shows, as one would expect, that wild plants and seeds as well as grasshoppers and other insects were far more important constituents of their diet than game.

How and where maize was first cultivated for long attracted the interest of botanists, southern Mexico or the Maya area on the one hand and Peru on the other being the main contenders for place of origin. The very recent finds by the Canadian archaeologist, Richard MacNeish, and his assistants in the caves near Tehuacán mentioned above establish beyond much serious doubt that maize was first cultivated in the former area.

In those dry, well-sheltered caves, strata of occupational deposits lay one below the other, spanning some nine thousand years. The first cultivated plants to appear were maize, squash, and chile, followed by gourds, and later beans, pumpkins, and amaranth. The first ears of maize are only about one and one-half inches long, shorter than ears of wheat, but they revealed precisely those features which botanists had previously predicted would be found in the most primitive maize. The increase from those earliest ears to the ears the

Indians cultivated when the white man arrived is a tribute to their abilities as selecters and breeders. The Coxcatlán complex is the name given to the deposits in which agriculture first appears. Five Carbon–14 dates show it to have flourished from about 5,200 B.C. to about 3400 B.C. Much wild, but a little cultivated, maize was found in the earliest levels of the complex. There is a gradual rise in the percentage of cultivated as opposed to uncultivated plant remains as one works one's way up through time. In the subsequent Abejas phase (3400 B.C. to 2300 B.C.) cultivated becomes commoner than wild maize.

At the same time one must bear in mind the possibility that there was more than one center of plant domestication in the New World. Manioc almost certainly originated in eastern South America, and the great ritualistic importance of amaranth in ancient Mexico has long led me to believe that it had a very early development, perhaps in western Mexico. How long the interval was between those early stages of agriculture and its widespread acceptance in the Maya highlands is, at present, anyone's guess, but from MacNeish's work in caves in Tamaulipas, in northeastern Mexico not far from the Texas border, we know that the time lag in agriculture's being adopted there was not great.

Developed agriculture entails a sedentary life and a far greater density of population, both of which are conducive to cultural progress. Of those early stages in Middle America extremely little is known.

BEGINNINGS OF CIVILIZATION
IN MIDDLE AMERICA
(THE FORMATIVE PERIOD)

It is still not known when pottery, that greatest prop of archaeology (because of its susceptibility to changes in design and its indestructibility), first appeared in Middle America, nor where it originated. The art of pottery making might have been brought by late immigrants from Asia into Alaska, but more probably was developed independently in the New World. Presently, its earliest known appearance is at Tehuacán in deposits dated by Carbon 14 at about 2500 B.C., but considerably later so far as the Maya area is concerned.

Archaeologists of the New World Archaeological Foundation

working near Chiapa de Corzo in central Chiapas, only twenty-five miles west of the present boundary of Maya territory, have found a long sequence of pottery deposits, the earliest of which, Chiapa I, was flourishing around 1300 B.C. according to a Carbon–14 reading. More recently a contemporaneous horizon, named Ocós, has been uncovered at La Victoria, on the Pacific Coast of Guatemala, just east of the Mexican boundary and about 150 miles south-southeast of Chiapa. The region of La Victoria was very probably Maya-speaking at the time of the Spanish Conquest or, at most, a few miles outside Maya territory. What languages were spoken in those two areas three thousand years ago can only be guessed; our only hint is that the boundaries of the Maya area seem to have changed little.

The people of the Ocós horizon almost certainly built temple mounds, evidence that even at that early date communities were well organized and probably beginning to show social stratification, for temple mounds hint at an organized priesthood supported by the group.

Various names—Archaic, pre-Classic, Formative—have been applied to these early cultures. The last is my preference, for it indicates that in its course the features which characterize the subsequent Classic period were taking form. By the middle of the first millenium before Christ, Middle America was quite thickly studded with settlements of the Formative period.

I am inclined to think that small groups drifting across the Bering Strait brought many inventions, perhaps even weaving and pottery, and that the last arrivals who may have left Siberia as late as the beginning of the Christian Era brought with them certain religious concepts which survive in eastern Asia to this day mixed with Hinduism and debased Buddhism. I have in mind such developments as the association of colors and celestial dragons with the four world quarters, ideas which I think are too complex and unnaturalistic to have been evolved independently in both Asia and America.

These views are not orthodox; the generally accepted opinion is that immigrants from the Old World brought a minimum of culture with them, and that practically all Old World inventions found also in the New World were duplicated independently in this hemisphere. On the other hand, some writers have maintained that there is no such thing as re-invention in the New World, but that all such duplications are due to diffusion from Asia. A stand between these extremes seems reasonable.

The traveler of about 2,500 years ago would not have noticed much difference in the way of life of Indian communities in the whole length of a walking tour from what is now Mexico City to what is now Guatemala City—he would have had to walk or be carried in a litter, for there was no beast of burden or other means of locomotion. (He might, perhaps, have sat in a sort of chair, resting against an Indian's back and supported by a tumpline passing across the Indian's forehead, but I suspect that was a refinement of travel introduced into Middle America in Spanish Colonial days.) I am assuming that the journey was by land. He might have made part of the journey by dugout canoe, following the Pacific Coast from Tehuantepec to the Guatemalan border, for that was a frequented route in Aztec times.

What would he have seen? Probably lots of forest once he got off the plateau, and every now and again a small clearing with a few huts in it. In some regions they would have been round and in others rectangular or oval, but all would have been thatched with grass or palm leaves. Inside, he would have seen a variety of articles, such as a grinding stone and muller for the corn, vessels of pottery, gourd, and wood, simple frame-beds with mats resting on the slats, net bags holding maize, woven bags for beans, a fireplace, some little clay idols, a rolled-up loom with a half-finished textile, wooden planting sticks, sticks and pieces of wood for drilling fire, round trays hanging from the roof, perhaps a notched pole serving as a ladder to reach the attic, containers for water and for lime (used in softening the hulls of corn before grinding), and perhaps two or three poncho-like garments used as blankets at night and as cloaks in the early morning, but no spare clothes. Points of obsidian or flint, traps, spears, a dressed skin or two, bags of paint, a couple of dogs, and several children would about complete the picture. He would have noticed clearings near the huts sown to maize, squash, beans, and other crops.

A few miles farther on, the trail might skirt a "city," quite deserted as our traveler passes, for it is not market day and no important ceremony is to take place in the near future. There are fair-sized and sometimes quite large pyramidal mounds at these centers, but the tops support only altars or small thatched buildings. Thus the visitor would travel on, seeing over and over again those little settlements, an occasional village, a ceremonial center, fields of maize or cotton or agave or maguey, meeting hunters now and then or witnessing an occasional religious ceremony or passing through a market in full swing. At journey's end he would look back on what he had seen and realize the general monotony of the picture—just as gasoline ads or filling stations or soda counters from Maine to California are the same despite local differences in slogans and architecture.

Here the vessels might be largely of gourd or wood; there, of pottery. Some villages might use garments of maguey fiber; others (wealthier or near good cotton lands) might have a number of their most important citizens clad in cotton. Here the gods might have one set of names, and there another, but like Judy O'Grady and the Colonel's lady, they would be the same under their skins—the ubiquitous gods of crops and of rain. The pottery vessels might vary in shape and finish from one region to another, but essentially they would show the same mastery of the technique of pottery making. Pyramids from later stages of the Formative period at Teotihuacán, or near Guatemala City, or at distant Yaxuna, in Yucatán, show local differences, but they are essentially the same in concept. Had the traveler turned east at the start of his journey, followed the Gulf of Mexico southward, and then continued across the base of the Yucatán Peninsula as far as Honduras, he would have found that even the pottery was almost the same from Veracruz to western Honduras, and little pottery figures from altars of huts deep in the Petén were in many cases hardly distinguishable from those in huts in the shadow of Orizaba's peak. Everywhere, too, he would have found life geared to the changing aspects of the day gods who ruled in succession the 260-day almanac (p. 175), bringing weal and woe according to each one's nature, from one end of the land to the other.

The above is a very generalized outline. The climb to civilization continued throughout the Formative period. To simplify presentation, archaeologists divide the Formative into Early (1500 B.C. to 1000 B.C.), Middle (1000 B.C. to 500 B.C.), and Late (500 B.C. to A.D. 100), all of which dates are tentative. The progress is well illustrated in and around Mexico City by comparing the Middle Tlatilco horizon with its dead surrounded by their treasured possessions from near and far, which flourished perhaps about 600 B.C., with the vestiges left by the earliest pottery users of the Valley of Mexico.

Middle Formative witnessed the first advances of the culture of La Venta, also called the Olmec culture, which developed in a small area of southeastern Veracruz immediately west of the Chontal Maya and just off the map (p. 18). The Olmec developed an extraordinary skill in working jade and other hard stones, and they evolved a unique art with designs derived from snarling jaguars and human (child or dwarf) forms. At the site of La Venta itself, early levels are dated by the solid (and less reliable) process of Carbon 14 around 800 B.C. However, all the large sculpture is surface material, presumably Phase 4 or later; on rather weak evidence Phase 4 would have ended about 400 B.C. The only sculpture at La Venta with hieroglyphs is not typical and was a surface find.

Information on the late Formative period increases rapidly, but as yet the key problem of La Venta's part in the rise of civilization is open to discussion. Some students see it as a sort of mother culture, from which all others in Middle America derive. The same position was once attributed to the Maya, and the picture of Maya civilization as a solitary peak rising from a swamp of low cultures took a lot of time and effort to demolish. Indeed, the most enthusiastic of the La Venta proponents find its shadow extending as far as Peru; other students see La Venta as one of several foci of incipient high culture throughout Middle America two or three centuries before the Christian Era, influencing and being influenced by its contemporaries. Again La Venta is linked to Middle Tlatilco and there are rock carvings in La Venta style on the Mexican plateau, facts which induce one leading Mexican archaeologist to see the origins of La Venta on the Mexican plateau. We are at a stage where a good series of Carbon–14 readings (as opposed to single samples) from all levels at such strategic sites as La Venta and Monte Albán would give us a much clearer idea of the emergence of high cultures from the Formative period. La Venta is certainly an early—perhaps the earliest—manifestation of advanced sculpture, and it certainly influenced the Classic throughout Middle America, but in other respects it shows no evidence of pioneering. All the great cultures of Middle America had their roots in the Formative, and consequently developed their distinctive personalities about the same time, and throughout their histories had in common so much of their culture and religion.

Certainly among the Maya, in the highlands of Guatemala, on the Pacific Coast, and in the lowlands of the Yucatán peninsula there was a brilliant flowering in that same late Formative period.

Excavation of a very few of the nearly two hundred mounds comprising the site of Kaminaljuyú, now almost destroyed by the expansion of the modern Guatemala City, has produced much information on the late Formative horizon there as well as on the succeeding early Classic period. Kaminaljuyú lies in territory which at the time of the Spanish Conquest was occupied by Maya who spoke the Pokoman branch of the Maya language group, and it is probable that the same people controlled the area nearly two thousand years earlier. Digging has uncovered a series of Formative phases, the earliest of which, Las Charcas, has yielded a Carbon 14 date of around 380 B.C., and the latest, Miraflores, has yielded a series of such readings falling a few decades each side of A.D. 1. Las Charcas is represented only by pottery, but for Miraflores the story is very different.

Miraflores has produced evidence of great building activity. One pyramid, enlarged or reconstructed no less than six times, stood to a height of over sixty feet. It was of puddled adobe with terraced sides faced with adobe plaster and had a single wide stairway. Postholes in summit platforms associated with more than one reconstruction supplied evidence that a building of perishable materials once crowned some of the nested pyramids.

Inside the structure were two tombs which bore witness to the social organization and wealth of the community. To illustrate this there follows a brief outline of Tomb 1 and its contents.

The tomb was made by excavating from the summit a stepped

shaft to a depth of about twelve feet, at the bottom of which was the tomb, a space about eleven feet by ten feet. This had been covered by a log roof, laid after burial, resting on deeply planted posts at each corner of the pit. The interstices of the logs were then filled with reed and the whole covered with mats. The dead chief, painted red, lay on a wooden litter set on the floor of the pit; the rich furnishings for his life in the next world were crowded on and around the litter, filling the whole floor space, and more were laid on the roof after it had been built and on the steps of the shaft. One adult, presumably sacrificed to serve his master in the next world, was laid on the lowest step of the shaft with his legs extending onto the roof of the tomb. At the conclusion of the inhumation ceremonies, the shaft had been filled in and a new floor laid over the summit platform.

The tomb, unfortunately, was looted in ancient times, not long after its owner had been laid to rest, with the result that the large quantities of jade the tomb once surely contained were represented only by a few small, overlooked pieces. Yet, the fantastic number of about three hundred pottery vessels, many imported from distant parts, attests the deceased's importance. Little bowls of gray-green chlorite schist and of white marble, the rotted remains of pyrite-incrusted plaques used as mirrors or ornaments, the dust of what must once have been elaborate cotton textiles, and richly carved wood, obsidian blades, and shells were among the contents. A mask with features in albite set on a backing probably of wood had seemingly once covered the dead chief's face, but had slid off to fall upside down on the floor beside the litter, and in that position escaped the looters' notice. Of particular interest among the furnishings of the tomb was a mushroom-shaped stone rising from a tripod base in the guise of a jaguar or puma, the whole standing some fifteen inches high. Such stones are common in the highlands of Guatemala, and it is virtually certain that they were connected with the cult of vision-giving narcotic mushrooms which survives to this day in remote parts of southeastern Mexico. Two thousand years ago the occupant of this tomb had eaten those mushrooms in the ritual setting of his day and had experienced the color-drenched visions they induce.

Here, then, we have full evidence of a highly developed group with the resources to erect great pyramids, to build up commercial transactions with distant parts, and to support in luxury a ruling caste.

The nature of the burial as well as the presence of the attendant, almost surely sacrificed at his master's burial, point to strongly developed belief in a future life; the beauty of some of the pottery and stone vessels indicate a marked aesthetic taste and the craftsmanship to satisfy it. Excellent sculpture is also found in this Miraflores horizon at Kaminaljuyú and with it occur Maya hieroglyphs, good evidence that these early mound builders were Maya (Plate 25).

The presence of hieroglyphic writing with this late Formative horizon at Kaminaljuyú of around A.D. 1, as well as its presence on Formative sculpture on the Pacific Coast of Guatemala—San Isidro Piedra Parada on the Pacific coastal strip has yielded stelae with late Formative sculpture, a definitely Maya glyph, and a rock-carving in pure La Venta style a stone's throw away, but no evidence whether the last is contemporaneous with the others—raises an important point. For long it was assumed that Maya hieroglyphic writing developed in the Petén, where the earliest certain dates in the Maya calendar have been found. Now, however, that seems far from certain, first because hieroglyphs are associated with late Formative horizons at Monte Albán, in Chiapas, perhaps at La Venta, and, as we have seen, in the highlands and Pacific Coast of Guatemala, in any one of which writing could have originated. Secondly, definite Maya glyphs appear on the late Formative horizon at Kaminaljuyú, but have not yet been reported for that horizon from the Central area, although for the Northern area there is a single sculpture of Formative style carved on a rock at Loltún, Yucatán, and this has a single glyph. This rarity of Formative sculpture at lowland sites may not be as significant as it appears because old sculptures were often broken up and buried or dumped. Fragmentary texts of the Late Formative may lie deep beneath later construction at Tikal or some other Petén site.

In the Maya lowlands as in the highlands, early Formative is represented by little more than monochrome pottery of distinctive forms (a deposit at Dzibilchaltún in northwestern Yucatán yielded a Carbon-14 date of 965 B.C. with a margin each way of two centuries); in the late Formative (the Petén manifestation is named Chicanel) there was a great forward surge shortly before the Christian Era. A rather dense population is indicated by the fact that at almost every excavated site, late Formative debris—for the most part sherds —underlies the Classic period occupation.

The finest surviving building of the late Formative in the lowlands is a pyramid at Uaxactún, deep in the Petén and a few miles north of Tikal, which suffers the unromantic but strictly archaeological designation E–VII sub, bestowed on it because it was found inside Pyramid VII of Group E. For in accordance with a quite general Maya custom, this original structure had subsequently been covered entirely by a larger and higher pyramid, so that the inner and older one nested inside the outer, like the layers of an onion. When the badly damaged outer pyramid was removed, the inner one came to light in not far short of mint condition (Plate 5c).

The square pyramid is only twenty-seven feet high, but its impressiveness derives from the elaborate staircases with their subsidiary flights of steps, the eighteen huge masks flanking the staircases, and the complex arrangement of terraces supporting two platforms, one above the other. The effect is distinctly rococo, although, so far as we know, this is an incipient, not a decadent art. The grotesque masks, each about eight feet wide by six feet high, display a serenity which contrasts strangely with the restlessness of the pyramidal mass. The curled tusks at the corners of the mouths, the eyebrows with accented shagginess, the flat snouts, and the peculiar half-tongue, half-incisor pendent from the upper lip leave little doubt that the jaguar god is here displayed. The masks of the lowest zone, still more highly conventionalized, are modeled so as to give one the impression of staring straight at the muzzle of a being part snake, part jaguar. Some students have seen strong influences from La Venta in these masks, but they are manifestly in the Maya tradition as expressed in the early stages of the Classic period.

The whole surface of the pyramid is covered with a thick layer of light cream stucco, dazzlingly bright, when first excavated, in the clear tropical sunlight. One of the most impressive and touching sights I have ever seen was this pyramid, then newly excavated, bathed in the light of a full moon. The towering trees of the uncut forest surrounding the little court in which it stood created a backdrop of black velvet for its brilliantly stuccoed mass. At a distance it lost its restlessness, and appeared to repose in the peacefulness of age. Few white men have seen or will see this early pyramid in its pristine beauty, for with each rainy season and with the unchecked growth of vegetation more of its stuccoed surface disappears. It can be but a matter of a few years before it is reduced to a shapeless mass.

In the flat, stuccoed summit were four postholes, forming a rectangle about sixteen feet by eleven, evidence that a temple of perishable materials had once crowned the pyramid. Its size, that of an average room, would have permitted ceremonies requiring the presence of six or eight priests.

Excavation at Uaxactún also revealed late Formative platforms about a foot high. The larger are roughly rectangular; the smaller are round or oval, sometimes with a rectangular projection in front so that in plan they resemble squat keyholes. In some cases postholes in these platforms showed that huts of perishable materials had stood on them and, in one case, two postholes were set in the rectangular projection in such a way as to suggest they held posts supporting the thatched roof of a veranda—the American porch has a respectable antiquity. Strangely enough, squat, keyhole pyramids, in plan not unlike these platforms at Uaxactún, were being built at the time of the Spanish conquest in the area around Veracruz, then occupied by the Totonac, a non-Maya people. Maya huts are still built in Yucatán with four postholes but with rounded ends, and round huts are shown on frescoes. So probably these early Uaxactún people had rectangular huts for worship; smaller round or oval ones to live in.

Tikal, with a scantier occupation than Uaxactún in early Formative, is yielding much information on the late Formative. By about 100 B.C. Tikal's great plaza and adjacent north terrace area was about as large as it was at the height of late Classic, around A.D. 700, but building had thrust upward. The north terrace had become in late Classic times a massive platform supporting eight temples, whence its name of Acropolis, and to get at the early material below was slow, difficult, and expensive. A main trench, about 140 feet long, was cut through over a dozen floors to a depth of some sixty feet, bringing to light parts of temples and buildings as well as two very important tombs.

Stucco masks flanking central stairways were reminiscent of those of the contemporaneous E–VII sub at Uaxactún, but at Tikal were polychrome and unfortunately damaged. One such building had supported a stone temple, much of which had been razed by the

Maya in early times to add a new structure. Consequently, it will never be known whether the temple had had a roof of corbeled vaulting as was the common practice in the Classic period (p. 187). However, at the foot of the stairway and of slightly later date was a tomb which was corbel vaulted and closed with a line of capstones in regular Maya style. Architecturally, therefore, Tikal was ahead of contemporaneous Kaminaljuyú, which had not advanced beyond buildings of perishable materials.

In this late Formative vaulted tomb were twenty-six pottery vessels, a splendid jade mask, five inches high with shell-inlaid teeth and eyes, the sting of a ray used by the Maya for drawing blood from the body, and the dust of textile wrappings. The remains were of a man, but the thigh bones and the skull were missing. The person had been placed squatting, with shinbones against trunk, in one of the vessels. Slivers from carbonized pine in a vessel yielded a Carbon–14 reading of around A.D. 1.

An individual also minus thigh bones was found at Uaxactún, again in late Formative times. He, however, was full length. Shinbones were crossed at the ankles in a peaceful attitude, but between the knees was a skull—a trophy or the deceased's—sawed across so that all the facial bones were missing. The right hand rested below the pelvis in a Pickwickian pose. Now sawing off the facial bones of a dead chief and replacing the flesh with features modeled in bitumen was customary among the Cocom in Yucatán at the time of the Spanish Conquest. This burial suggests that some such rite was practiced in the middle of the Petén nearly two thousand years earlier.

A second late Formative burial at Tikal was in a tomb the walls of which were decorated with murals which included glyph-like elements. In this case the personage had his head and thigh bones.

Imports of jade, obsidian, pottery, shells, sting rays, and so on confirm the prosperity and far-flung trade routes of the lowlanders of the late Formative. The huge building programs, notably at Tikal, point to well-organized communities governed by a privileged minority which could command a large labor force. Preparations for a luxurious after-life indicate a high standard of living in this world for that ruling group. Corbeled vaulting, stucco masks, stone temples, and murals mark advances in architecture and art, and for the most part demonstrate the religious orientation of the community. Strange burial rites and the use of sting rays also hint at preoccupation with religion.

There can be little doubt that these lowlanders were Maya. Little pottery figurines of early Formative show Maya-style head deformation and Maya hooked noses. The large stucco masks of Uaxactún are, as noted, in the Maya tradition, as, too, is corbeled vaulting. Well-preserved skeletal material of the Formative is scarce, but at least one skull was that of a very broad-headed person, and,

as has been noted, the lowland Maya of Yucatán are among the most broad-headed people in the world. Moreover, our divisions into Formative and Classic are unrealistic in that they imply sudden breaks. In fact, the transition from Formative to Classic was surely gradual—a flowering after orderly growth, not a new crop.

THE CLASSIC PERIOD: BEGINNING

When precisely does a puppy become a dog, or a kitten a cat? When did Maya civilization earn the right to be credited with an individual personality? Naturally, in such cases of slow growth one cannot define the moment. Some would say that the presence of distinctive Maya glyphs on these monuments plus the use of the corbeled vault marks that attainment; others might equally well argue that until the original art style of the Maya had developed, one could not speak of Maya culture. As William Browne wrote nearly 350 years ago:

> *Where none can say, though he it strict attends,*
> *Here one begins, and there the other ends.*

The division between Formative and Classic has become meaningless now that corbeled vaulting and hieroglyphic writing are known to have begun in late Formative times. As those terms are too firmly established in the literature to be dropped, we are now in

Fig. 3—Temple of the Cross, Palenque. Section to illustrate Maya constructional methods. Wooden lintels and parts of façade restored. (For plan see Fig. 5c.) a, front (south) stairway; b, pilaster separating entrances; c, end wall of front room; d, doorway to rear side room; e, jamb of doorway into shrine room; f, jamb of doorway into shrine; g, end wall of shrine; h, former position of Tablet of Cross with relief and long hieroglyphic text; i, masonry brace across vault; j, capstone of corbeled vault of doorway; k, end wall of sanctuary; l, projecting stones forming steps in interior of roof crest; m, medial ceiling and capping to hold together sides of roof crest. The sloping upper façade, typical of Palenque, is replaced by a vertical upper façade at most sites. (*After W. H. Holmes*).

the ridiculous position of having to correlate the start of the Classic period, once regarded as a great landmark, with changes in shape and color in non-utility pottery which took place around A.D. 200. There is an equally meaningless dating of the start of the Classic at Teotihuacán, falling a little earlier. One must not look on the line between these two periods as something synchronized to the year throughout middle America. It was not a sort of "when father says 'turn,' all turn."

Until recently the earliest surviving dated monument in the Maya lowlands was Stela 9 at Uaxactún. This irregular tapering shaft of limestone, nine feet high, is carved in low relief with a human figure in profile on the front and with hieroglyphs on the back. Glyphs and personage are dreadfully eroded. The former record the Maya date 8.14.10.13.15 in our notation (p. *xvi*) corresponding to April 9, A.D. 328 (all dates are according to the Goodman-Martínez-Thompson correlation). It was still standing, although very much the worse for wear, when the late Maya scholar Sylvanus Morley found it in 1916, nearly sixteen hundred years after its erection.

Actually, we can push the development of hieroglyphic writing as Uaxactún further back toward the beginning of the Christian era. Stela 9 had before it an altar which was the reshaped lower half of another stela (No. 10). Unfortunately, the small glyphs on this surviving fragment are too weathered to be deciphered, and it is not possible to say whether it was placed as the altar of Stela 9 at the time of the latter's dedication. However, Tatiana Proskouriakoff, the outstanding student of Maya sculpture, believes it to be earlier than Stela 9 (she sees in some of the details analogies to those of early stelae of the Pacific Coast), and so it is probable that Stela 10 was reshaped to serve as an altar at the time Stela 9 was dedicated. The Maya broke up and reused some monuments, whereas others, such as Stela 9, were left unharmed. Why some were destroyed and others left, we do not know, but if a stela was in the way of some new construction, so that it would remain, let us say, half buried in a new platform or building, the decision to break it up may have been taken, and that is probably what happened to Stela 10. There is, accordingly, a good chance that this monument carried the stela record at Uaxactún further back toward the beginning of our era.

In the course of the present excavations at Tikal the top part of a stela (No. 29) was found. This carries a date 8.12.14.8.15 in Maya notation, corresponding to July 6, A.D. 292. The human figure on the front of the monument has details definitely in the mainstream of full Classic Maya art. This is the earliest dated monument yet found in the Central area.

Against this earliest known lowland date of A.D. 292, there is a possible date corresponding to A.D. 58 on a stela on the Pacific Coast of Guatemala. This was found at the large site of El Baul. It has an arrangement of bars and dots without period glyphs, resembling the method of dating in the Maya hieroglyphic book called the Dresden Codex. In style it seems to fit about the start of the Christian era or perhaps a trifle earlier, but to get a reading corresponding to A.D. 58, one must make the quite questionable assumptions that it was counted from the same starting point as the lowland calendars, that the year was of 360 days (a 400-day year was used in the nearby highlands of Guatemala and possibly in southern Veracruz) and that the day at the head of the text is the terminal date, whereas normally the opening date is the start of the count. Moreover, eroded numerical bars and dots have to be restored to fit the reading. The stela is very old, but the actual date must remain in doubt. When I stood before this stela on revisiting El Baul in 1964, copal incense and candles were burning at its base; after nearly two thousand years the stela was still receiving Indian prayers and offerings.

On the present evidence the Maya lowlanders received sculpture and hieroglyphs from outside—a bit later they influenced others (markedly at Cerro de las Mesas, in distant Veracruz). However, the lowlanders carried those elements, as well as architecture, to far greater heights than did their neighbors. As the percipient reader will have noted, we archaeologists are a trifle artless; each likes to see his own cultural baby win the prizes.

Dated monuments were a very important feature of Maya ceremonial life and, because of the framework of dates they supply, are of immense importance to the archaeologists. Nearly all ceremonial centers in the Central area endeavored to erect these dated monuments either in the form of stelae or as altars, lintels, boulders, panels, cornices, or stairways. At the very beginning of the Classic period these commemorated odd dates, but soon it became the fashion

Fig. 4.—Maya types of classic beauty. These drawings show the features which constituted the Maya ideal of beauty: artificially deformed head with sloping forehead, almond-shaped eyes, large nose, drooping lower lip, and slightly receding chin. *a*, *b*, Palenque; *c*, Copán; *d*, *e*, Yaxchilán; *f*, water lily motif, Palenque. (*After Maudslay.*)

to set up a monument at the end of every twenty of their years (of 360 days). This period, called *katun*, was of very great importance in Maya life (pp. 166, 198). Some centers (notably Quiriguá and Piedras Negras) took pride in setting up monuments at the end of every quarter-katun (five-year interval) or each half-katun (ten-year interval).

Although the dates given on the monuments—and some monuments may have half a dozen or more—can be read, the meanings of the accompanying hieroglyphs are far more difficult. Certainly astronomical, religious, and probably divinatory elements are involved. For example, information on the age of the moon and on the current lunation is given, and those were no asides, for the Maya priest-astronomers got highly excited about the manipulation and content of lunar and eclipse tables. There are also references to the gods reigning on the day and the night and during the month corresponding to the first date of the inscription, and there are other such references.

Recently, cogent arguments have been advanced for accepting the records engraved on the monuments of some, if not all, lowland sites as referring to lay events, such as the birth or initiation of rulers, their accession and their triumphs in war and captures of prisoners, and even details of wives and children. The case for such an interpretation is good, and has led me to discard the opinion I once held that these records were purely impersonal discussion of problems of astrology, divination, and the luck of the days. Although the general argument for historical records on the stelae is, I think, unanswerable, in small details there is probably room for redefinition. For instance, glyphs now taken to refer to individuals may refer to brothers or fathers and sons. As at present interpreted, one man ruled Yaxchilán for sixty years and was well over ninety when he departed this life. Again, at near-by Piedras Negras, six reigns average out at twenty-nine and one-half years apiece, and at that the average is pulled down by one reign of only five years and another of seventeen. Lives which can be measured averaged fifty-seven years. Yet the eight Aztec reigns prior to the accession of Moctezuma II average sixteen years, and the seventeen reigns covering the third of a millenium between the death of Elizabeth I of England and the accession of Elizabeth II average nineteen years. With these comparisons in mind and considering the shortish lives thought to be the lot of somewhat primitive groups in the tropics, one feels somewhat suspicious of the Maya reigns.

One may, therefore, say that the stelae and other monuments with texts were set up to supplicate the gods, to glorify the rulers of the community, and to give vent to that extraordinary preoccupation with the passage of time.

Before A.D. 450 the custom of erecting dated monuments was, so far as present evidence indicates, confined to half a dozen sites clustered within an area of less than two hundred square miles in the forest land of northern Petén. By the end of the century the custom had spread northward to Oxkintok, in distant Yucatán, and southeastward to Copán, over the border into modern Honduras, and had effected a lodgment in the Upper Usumacinta River at Altar de Sacrificios. It may also have penetrated to Veracruz, thereby accounting for the Maya-influenced stelae at Cerro de las Mesas.

One must not get the impression that the spread of this custom was carried by immigrants, any more than one should suppose that bands of colonists from Chicago carried the custom of erecting skyscrapers to New York, St. Louis, Dallas, and Minneapolis. Maya had surely been living in Copán and Oxkintok long before they started carving stelae or erecting vaulted buildings. These were manifestations of a spreading cult, just as mosques and Arabic script mark the spread of Islam.

Half a century later, that is, by A.D. 550, the dated-monument cult had invaded the middle Usumacinta Valley, establishing itself at the great Maya centers of Yaxchilán and Piedras Negras, and had been accepted at Calakmul, in southern Campeche. By the end of the sixth century the cities of Tulúm and Ichpaahtún, on the east coast of Yucatán, Lacanhá and others in the Chiapas forests south of the Usumacinta, and Pusilhá, in British Honduras, were erecting stelae. The custom was spreading in all directions, just as the erection of skyscrapers did thirteen centuries later, but the absence of the stela cult did not mean that a ceremonial center was not Maya, any more than that a city in the United States without a skyscraper is not American.

About this time there is some evidence of lessening activity. Some centers which had already embraced the stela cult erected no more monuments for a time. Tikal and Uaxactún, which had been foremost in the practice in the fourth century, seem to have ceased to erect stelae. At least, no carved stelae attributable to this period have been found.

THE CLASSIC PERIOD: FLORESCENCE

Around A.D. 650 there was another and far greater wave of activity which with gathering force and momentum rolled forward, only to break against the rocks of dissolution on the far shore of the Classic period 250 years later.

The cause of the quiescence before this renewed activity is unknown, but it is significant that at its close Maya art and architecture had undergone notable changes. Pottery shapes alter abruptly, and so do the designs on them. The principal figures on stelae, which had usually been carved in profile, with the rear foot partly obscuring the front one, are now generally shown with bodies in full view and with feet turned out, although the head may be in profile and the shoulders slightly turned. The disappearance of archaic details is accelerated, and one gets the impression of an emancipation from awkwardness into what would soon be the florescence of Maya sculpture. In masonry there was a shift from large, unfaced stones deeply tailed into the concrete hearting of walls to faced and wellcut stone applied as a veneer to the hearting, a more elegant but less stable treatment. These changes seem to have been roughly contemporaneous, but they did not appear everywhere at the same time.

One may wonder whether such innovations reflect any change of direction in Maya life, perhaps due to external pressure of ideas or even people. The archaeologist, of course, is constantly on the lookout for outside influences, but for that very reason he runs the risk of exaggerating their importance and their effects. In fifteenth-century England the florescence of Perpendicular Gothic produced such novelties as immense windows, fan vaulting, and, of course, a replacement by vertical and horizontal axes of curvilinear patterns not only in architecture but in all ecclesiastical furniture. Yet we know that these profound changes were not due to any extraneous influences, political or cultural. Accordingly, it would be wise, in our present state of knowledge, to abstain from theorizing on the cause of these Maya developments.

Once Maya culture got into its stride again, development was rapid. City after city adopted the stela cult, and the cities vied with one another in erecting temple-topped pyramids and "palaces" and in beautifying buildings and monuments with sculpture and modeled stucco. Hieroglyphic inscriptions have been found at no less than ninety sites. In some ceremonial centers only one inscription has been discovered, whereas at others inscriptions are plentiful. Tikal, with 115 stelae, leads the field, but of the total only 32 are carved. It has also 18 carved and 74 plain altars and texts on wooden lintels. Calakmul comes second with 103 stelae, 73 of which carry these inscriptions. Copan has just over 100 texts. Many are on altars and some on buildings, but none are on lintels. Palenque, Yaxchilán, and Piedras Negras inscribed lengthy texts, but in many cases they occur not on stelae, but in connection with buildings—carved on steps, lintels, door jambs, or panels (Plates 9–15). These numerous inscriptions, taken in conjunction with the huge building programs, indicate the tremendous activity that marked the Classic period throughout the lowlands.

At Tikal in the late Classic the stela cult reached extraordinary proportions: There the close of each of the six katuns (twenty-year periods) ending between A.D. 692 and A.D. 790 was marked by the building of a special court. On its east and west edges were set two rather squat pyramids with the somewhat rare feature of stairways on all four sides, but without any building of a permanent nature on top. In front of the east pyramid was set up a line of uncarved stelae each with its round altar before it. On the south side of the court a long masonry building, invariably with nine doorways, on a low platform faced a large, almost square room on the north side. This must have been palm-thatched if it had any roof at all, for it was too wide to have had a stone vault or flat-beam-and-mortar roof, nor was the debris of such roofs found. Inside stood a stela with altar in front. The stela with one exception recorded the end of the katun which the whole assemblage commemorated. Strangely, with no cross light to bring out the design, the low relief of the carving would have shown up poorly. Yet a great deal of effort must have gone into building these "twin-pyramid complexes" to honor the passage of time—the largest of these courts is nearly five hundred feet wide by over four hundred feet deep. No comparable arrangement has been found at any other Maya center.

Although the stela cult never found favor in the Guatemalan highlands, there is full evidence that the same building boom affected that region, but at an earlier date. In fact, some highland cities, notably Kaminaljuyú, as well as such non-Maya centers as Teotihuacán, La Venta, and apparently Monte Albán, had passed their peaks and were in decline when the lowland Maya were riding on the crest of productivity.

What was a Maya city, and how did it function? First, as I have already said, it was not a city at all in our sense of the word, because it was a ceremonial, not an urban, center, to which the people repaired for religious ceremonies, civic functions, and markets. The stone buildings were quite unsuited for permanent habitation; they had no chimneys and no windows, although some rooms had small vents in the walls. Moreover, they were damp and ill lit. So much was this so that *chicleros* often fail to distinguish between natural caves and partly collapsed Maya buildings, using the same word to describe both, and the Maya word *actun* means both a cave and a stone house.

Inner rooms, illuminated only by the light filtering through a narrow doorway from an outer room, are almost completely without light, and there are many cases where the light has to pass through two rooms to reach the innermost, and at that, the doorways may not be in line (Fig. 5f). In such inner rooms, unless the sun is low and shining through the outer doorway, one cannot see his hand

66

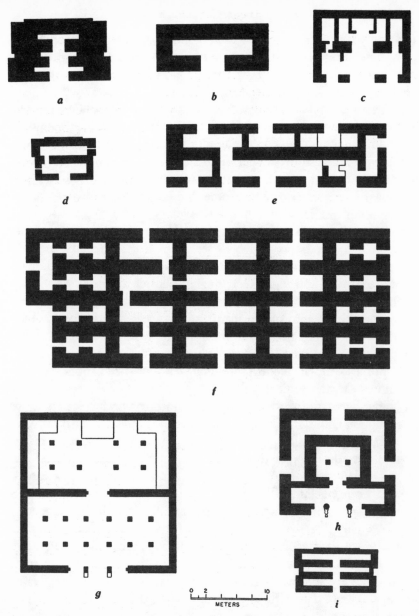

Fig. 5.—Plans of buildings, from the simple to the complex. Note proportion of masonry to floor space in *a*, and how little light reached the
inner rooms of *f*. All are Classic period except *h*, transitional to the
Mexican period, and *g*, typically Mexican Chichén Itzá with columns
permitting much wider rooms. *a*, Temple 1, Tikal; *b*, Nakum; *c*, Temple
of the Cross, Palenque; *d*, Uaxactún; *e*, San José; *f*, Tikal; *g*, Temple of
the Warriors, Chichén Itzá; *h*, Castillo, Chichén Itzá; *i*, Naachtún.

in front of his face. They can never have been inhabited; they can only have been used for storage of paraphernalia or perhaps for secret rites. As each deity or group of related deities had its own insignia, much room would have been needed to store them.

Even the outer rooms would have made poor residences. The absence of chimneys and windows meant that no cooking could be done indoors, and the rooms, besides being dark, were damp. The walls ooze water now in the rainy season, in large part because of damage to roofs from roots, but excavation of buried buildings undamaged by roots reveals the same conditions. Indeed, with cross-ventilation often lacking or poorly developed, one could hardly expect such rooms to be anything but clammy in the rainy season. Finally, in many rooms huge daises or platforms occupy most of the space, so that the actual floor is confined to a small area perhaps three feet wide and eight feet long just inside the doorway. Such arrangements might have been suitable for ceremonies in honor of a god or chief seated on the platform, the select audience standing on the small area of floor in front, but they would have been highly inconvenient for housekeeping.

Burials of men, women, and children have been found beneath the floors of such rooms, and have been cited as evidence that these buildings were residential (the Maya did bury under the floors of their houses), but I think they can best be explained as the bodies of sacrificial victims or perhaps those of families of chiefs and priests buried there because of their rank. There are women and children buried in Westminster Abbey (even an alabaster cradle as the monument to one of James I's children), but to deduce therefrom that Westminster Abbey was a residential building would be erroneous.

Actually, we have good grounds for believing that these platforms were used as daises at important functions, for they surely served in the same way as regular daises which are found in some rooms. A very fine panel from Piedras Negras shows a chief seated on an elaborate dais with various functionaries gathered around, and somewhat similar scenes are depicted on murals at Bonampak, although there the chief is accompanied by his family.

It seems probable that for the long periods of fasting and continence which preceded the most important festivals, priests and novitiates and perhaps civil officials took up residence in these buildings. The uncomfortable conditions, particularly during the rainy season, would have been precisely what was required, for we know from Aztec sources that rugged conditions were a feature of these periods of preparation. One imagines a file of attendants and wives and mothers arriving each morning with drinking water and the rather meager rations for the inmates (In parts of Mexico we are told that the ration was one tortilla! Salt was not eaten during periods of fasting.) and perhaps depositing them at the entrances to the ceremonial center.

The time would pass, slowly no doubt, in long vigils, attending the sacred fires, drawing blood from tongues and ears for offerings to the gods, and burning much copal incense in grotesquely decorated incense burners. The market held every five days might have given a little interest to life, but surely it had to be watched from afar, for there could be no mingling with women during these periods of preparation.

Then would come the big celebration, and at its conclusion a general exodus from temple and palace back to everyday life. The city would lie deserted except for those who swept the courts and buildings or stored the masks and vestments, and for priests on tour of duty. Then at the next market day the city would come alive again. Buyers and sellers, their business done, would come to gaze and make their offerings at humbler shrines; persons of rank, borne in litters, would worship secludedly at the great shrines or gather for a council of state; a game of ball would be going on with many onlookers crowding to see the play; and perhaps dancers decked in fantastic masks would weave their patterns on some sunlit court to the sound of drum and flute.

In support of the above, the great missionary friar Las Casas wrote that the men retired to a special building near the temples to be separated from their wives, to fast and make daily offerings of their own blood for periods of up to one hundred days before a really important ceremony. He also remarks that the market was near the temples. Another friar wrote of the stone buildings in Yucatán: "They seemed in such good condition that it seemed not twenty years that they had been built. The Indians did not live in these when the Spaniards came, for they lived as family groups in straw-thatched houses in the woods, and they [the stone buildings] served them as temples and oratories, and on top of each one, at the highest point, they had their god." Another comment reads: "In all this province of Yucatán there is no town with two houses together. Rather, each is by itself, surrounded by trees, so that a town of fifty houses is spread over at least a quarter of a league." As for dancing, the Lacandón, the only Maya pagan group, until a few years ago visited the old ceremonial centers for worship, and are reported also to have performed ritual dances there.

Moreover, this reconstruction of how a Maya ceremonial center functioned agrees with what some Maya communities do to this very day in the highlands of Guatemala and Chiapas. There the present-day Maya live in scattered settlements covering a wide area, where they have their cornfields and where they carry on their normal activities, but they also have their town centers, to which they repair for important religious functions, Roman Catholic, pagan, and mixtures of the two, and for such civic events as the installation of new communal officers and markets. The modern town, in fact, functions very much as we have supposed the old Maya cities did, save that family houses now invade the center. Between ceremonies the town is largely vacant, as we suppose it to have been in ancient times.

The religious ceremonies have changed; some products now sold in the market may come from New Jersey or Ohio; Brigitte Bardot may be advertised at the local movie house; and marimba music may be blaring from a loud-speaker at the corner of the square. Yet essentially nothing has changed. The continuity of life is one blessed thing archaeology demonstrates.

Modern Maya towns and ancient Maya centers have another feature in common: they are undefended. Here, however, there is not continuity, for in the period of unrest which followed the end of the Classic period Maya cities were surrounded with defenses or were moved to easily defended positions on hilltops or islands or peninsulas of land guarded by deep ravines. The ceremonial centers of the Classic period occupy open sites with no walls or bastions.

One can no more speak of a typical Maya city than one can speak of a typical European city, for there are marked local differences within the Maya area just as there are in Europe. However, all Maya sites have certain features in common, of which the ceremonial court, flanked on all sides by terraces, platforms, pyramids, and temples, and often studded with stelae, was the most important. It vaguely recalls the modern stadium with its stands, both in plan and function, bearing in mind that the court is rectangular, and the spectacles staged in it were primarily religious (Plate 2*b*).

It is only a surmise that the crowds at times sat on the stairways and terraces of pyramids and flanking platforms to watch spectacles in the great court. Recently, on the occasions of an archaeological conference in Mexico, the government of Veracruz staged native dances and the spectacular *Volador* ceremony in the great court of Tajín, and nearly all of us automatically seated ourselves on the steps and terraces of the great pyramid to view the spectacle, so unless there was a religious prohibition, one can be fairly sure that a Maya audience acted as we did. There is more than a hint that the Aztec did the same.

A description of the great court of Tikal and its surrounding buildings, of which we had a glimpse at the beginning of the previous chapter, will serve to give a general idea of all such centers. It is nearly 400 feet east to west, and some 250 feet north to south; that is to say, with space to spare for two parallel football fields, including the ends (Fig. 1). In fact, this is small compared with some courts; that of Yaxchilán is 1,000 feet long, that of Xultún, in northeastern Petén, 825 feet, and that of Copán, 780 feet. In comparison, the Roman Forum was about 420 feet long; the piazza and forecourt of St. Peter's, Rome, have a combined length of 820 feet.

To east and west the court is bounded by two huge temple-crowned pyramids. In the introductory tour we entered the court at its southeast corner and later climbed the eastern pyramid. The pyramid on the west side of the court is quite similar. A wide staircase, now badly ruined, but once with every step plastered, leads to the summit on which stands another massive temple, and above soars its huge roof crest. A single doorway, through which three, but not four, men could enter abreast, leads to a transversal room sixteen feet long but less than four feet wide. Another broad doorway and a step lead to an inner room parallel to the first and of about the same dimensions. A third doorway leads to the back room, also parallel to the others, but not so long, and lighted only by the light entering through the outer doorway (Fig. 5*a*). It seems almost incredible that the Maya should have raised this enormous pyramid and built on it the massive temple with its soaring roof crest to hold three small rooms so narrow that, spirited to New York, they could not be passed off as kitchenettes by the most persuasive real estate man showing them to the least critical tenant. A very rough estimate of the area of the pyramid and stairway alone indicates a volume of about half a million cubic feet of rubble and masonry to support three rooms which have a combined floor space of less than 150 square feet. If one calculates the cubic area of these rooms in relation to the whole bulk of the temple with its massive walls and towering roof crest, the proportions are equally fantastic.

These minute rooms are depressing after the superb grandeur of the terraced mass of the pyramid and the soaring beauty of the exterior of the temple with its lofty roof comb, and they are not typical of Maya architecture. The explanation probably lies in the architect's lack of boldness. He was, one can imagine, not sufficiently sure of himself to erect rooms with thinner walls and consequent increased floor space in view of the tremendous weight of the roof crest which they must support. The collapse of some earlier building with narrow walls may have led to a cautious approach, particularly if, as is not improbable, the collapse of a building might bring the chief architect to the sacrificial block (we know of a drummer sacrificed because he did not keep proper time in beating his drum).

The north side of the ceremonial court is bounded by a large platform on which are four smaller temple-capped pyramids. Behind, to the north of these, the platform rises again to form a small ceremonial court surrounded by five more smallish pyramids, each with its temple towering as high as those of the first tier, or higher. A fantastic sight it must have been to an observer standing in the center of the great court and facing north. On each side of him was a huge pyramid with its temple and soaring roof crest rising like a volcano; before him stood rows of stelae and then that sort of Kremlin with its nine smaller temple-crowned pyramids. Everywhere his gaze would have fallen on acre upon acre of stuccoed surface, like creamy icing over writhing masks of gods on façades and roof crests and smoothly spread on geometric equilibrium of stair and terrace—dynamic and static in silent conflict. His eye would have been caught by doorways of temples, black in shadow or with a gay textile drawn across the gaping mouth.

Behind him, to the south, was another acropolis or second Kremlin, the base of which stands higher than that to the north, for it rises some eighty feet above the level of the court. On it stood nearly a score of buildings of the "palace" type, in contrast to the small temple-topped pyramids of the northern Kremlin. It was in the southernmost of these that I had slept and where several of the rooms are covered with incised scribblings made, I like to think, in moments of boredom by young candidates for the Tikal priesthood.

South of that is a deep ravine, on the far edge of which stands another mighty pyramid with temple on top, and just west of it yet another acropolis-like platform, about 125 feet high, supporting still more buildings. It would be tedious to continue the enumeration of pyramids, platforms, temples, and palaces. Those we have noted are those an observer would have around him as he stood in the great plaza, just as an observer standing at the junction of Broadway and Forty-second Street in New York would see the soaring buildings around him, but would not see those more distant, hidden by the ones nearer to him.

Not all the buildings in a Maya city were of stone. Many platforms and some pyramids, which now have no ruins on their flat summits, once supported buildings with walls of perishable materials and roofs of thatch, and some buildings with stone or rubble walls had flat wood and concrete ceilings or thatched roofs. Huts may have served as clubhouses for the unmarried men, for we know that such buildings existed in Yucatán at the time of the Conquest. Other huts may have been set aside for unmarried girls of noble blood, the Maya equivalent of Rome's Vestal Virgins, who had certain duties, such as sweeping the courts and weaving the elaborate textiles required in religious ceremonies, and who took part in sundry religious observances.

In addition to the types of structures already described, there were various others with specialized functions. Most important of these was the court in which the sacred ball game was played (Plate 6a). The Aztec had special buildings for markets, and it is probable that these occur in Maya cities. A huge rectangle enclosed by vaulted-corridor buildings, now being dug at Tikal, may be one.

At some ruins, including Tikal, elaborate sweathouses have been found. These are provided with a small sweat room, complete with steam-generating apparatus, and a cooling-off room. Many cities have reservoirs, the floors of which are lined with stone or cement. Complex systems of stone-lined drains to carry off water from enclosed sunken courts have been uncovered, and excavation would probably show that they existed everywhere. At Palenque a stream which meandered through the city was diverted to flow through an underground aqueduct with corbeled vault. Parts of this have now collapsed, but through untouched sections four or five men can march abreast. Drains from the acropolis almost certainly discharged into this aqueduct water from courts and roofs. Lower down, where the stream has emerged from its man-made confinement, it is spanned by a vaulted bridge. At Pusilhá, in southern British Honduras, the stone abutments of a large bridge are to be seen on opposite banks of the river.

Palenque also possesses three underground corbeled passages, which lead from a low-lying building on the north edge of the palace acropolis. The most important, some sixty-five feet in length, ends in a flight of stairs which leads through a hole in the floor to a room in the center of the palace building. When not in use, this exit was covered with stone slabs flush with the floor of the room. The other two passages emerge similarly through the floors of the buildings of this palace. Each passage has a jog in it, obviously made for some deliberate purpose of mystification or secrecy, or to shut out light, for not a ray of light reaches the extremities.

One can surmise that these passages might have been used for a little religious hocus-pocus. For instance, there was an extremely important Aztec ceremony in which the gods, who had been absent for some months, were believed to return, the sign of their arrival being a footprint in maize flour sprinkled before the temple. Supposing an analogous ceremony among the Maya, the main buildings of the palace could be inspected by important laymen and seem to be quite empty. Then, entering through the secret passage, the priest who impersonated the god could miraculously emerge from the building, or, unseen, could leave his footprint in the corn flour. These subterranean passages could also have been used in ceremonies connected with the underworlds. The latter explanation is, perhaps, more logical, since there are finely carved decorations within the passages, which would be superfluous in secret passages. Whether they are a

74

remnant of Spanish folklore or not, Central America is riddled with stories of secret tunnels connecting one group of ruins with another, and it is possible that underground passages, such as these, might have given rise to such stories. It has also been suggested that these passages were for defense—a means of taking attackers in the rear, a view which I find hard to accept.

Palenque also boasts a square tower, three stories high, with an interior staircase, each story being roofed, not with the usual corbeled vault, but with a ceiling of wooden beams.

In the later cities of Chichén Itzá and Mayapán there are round buildings said to be connected with the worship of Kukulcán, the feathered serpent god.

Several cities in Yucatán have elaborate gateways often of imposing size, but none has been found so far in the Central area. They could only have served some ceremonial purpose, for the Maya had no wheeled traffic or beasts of burden. Broad roads connect the different sections of certain cities, notably Tikal, Uaxactún, and Oxkintok, and in northeastern Quintana Roo there is an elaborate network of roads, one of which, slightly over thirty feet wide, links the city of Cobá with Yaxuna, a distance of sixty-two miles. Other roads connect Ake and Izamal, and Uxmal and Nohpat. An early writer mentions long roads in Chiapas and southeastern Petén. In the last few years long roads comparable to those of Cobá have been discovered in the northern Petén.

The silhouette of a Maya ceremonial center was strangely like that of a modern American city. In the center, corresponding to our massed skyscrapers with their setbacks to permit light to penetrate to the street level, were the terraced pyramids around the central court. The series of outer rings of structures gradually decreasing in height, with an occasional area of loftier construction, can be equated with the less important business districts of a modern city. Finally, the outer ring of a Maya city, consisting of the thatch-roofed residences of the priests and members of the nobility, correspond to the suburbs of the American city.

To a person not familiar with mediaeval architecture, Gothic cathedrals might seem on first inspection very much alike, but closer study will reveal a bewildering amount of local variation in minor details which serves to counteract the lack of deviation in major

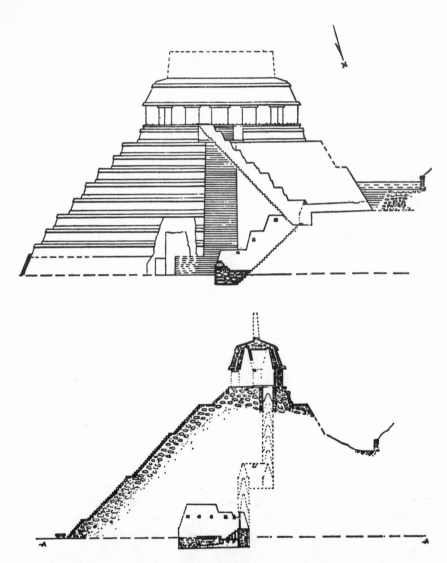

Fig. 6.—Temple of the Inscriptions, Palenque. Elevation and section to show the interior staircase leading from the rear room of the temple to the burial crypt. A light and ventilation shaft led from the stairway landing to the exterior of the pyramid. (*After A. Ruz.*)

aspects from a pattern imposed on the builders by tradition, function, and the laws of stress and gravity. The same is true of Maya ceremonial centers. There is an amazing uniformity in essential features from one end of the Central area to the other, but familiarity with the material brings cognizance of the many local divergences and reveals much charming individuality.

Tikal, in its crowded buildings and soaring pyramids, and even in its sculptural art, has the nervous restlessness of a Tschaikowsky symphony, whereas at Palenque, far to the west, the rhythm of architecture and art flows more peacefully. The restful lines of its stone-sculptured and stuccoed bas-reliefs (Plates 13, 15, 16; Figs. 20, 22) and the less pretentious elegance of its smaller and less numerous buildings with their traceried roof-crests are indicative of a greater cultural self-assurance. They are best translatable in terms of an eighteenth-century minuet. No city is so finely situated as Palenque, for it is built in the foothills of the great mountain range of Chiapas. Steep hills, rising behind, give its buildings a superb background, while from any doorway facing north one has an incomparable view over the plain below, a green carpet which unrolls as far as the eye can see across Chiapas and Tabasco to the unseen Gulf of Mexico, eighty miles away.

Perhaps the most remarkable discovery in the whole Maya area was made at Palenque by the Mexican archaeologist Alberto Ruz. By chance he noticed that a large slab in the floor of the inner room of the building called the Temple of the Inscriptions (Plate 5b) had finger-holes for raising it. It proved to be a trap door, and gave on a narrow vaulted staircase which led down into the heart of the pyramid. This staircase had been deliberately filled in ancient times from floor to capstone with rocks and earth, the removal of which was a slow business. A flight of steps led down to a landing, from which a second flight continued down in the opposite direction until, at a depth of about sixty feet, a passage, blocked with a wall, was reached. A few feet beyond the wall the way was again blocked, this time by a large stone slab. In front of it were the bones of six youths, who may have been attendants slain so that they could serve their master in the next world (Figs. 6, 7).

On removing the slab, the explorers looked down into a large vaulted room, which was a veritable fairy palace, for it was decked

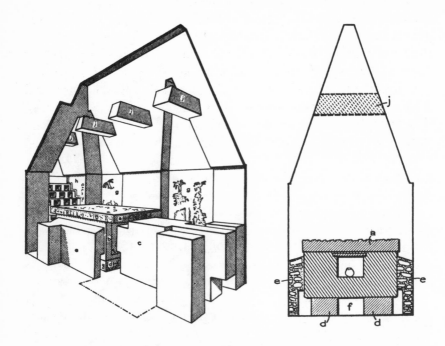

Fig. 7.—Temple of the Inscriptions, Palenque. Interior of the burial crypt. Side and end removed to show arrangement. Length and height of crypt just under thirty and twenty-two feet respectively. *a*, lid over sarcophagus (see Plate 13*b*); *b*, sarcophagus; *c*, masonry supports which probably supported lid before burial when it was slid into present position; *d*, supports for sarcophagus; *e*, buttress supports for sarcophagus; *f*, here beneath sarcophagus were stucco heads (Plate 23); *g*, nine relief figures in stucco on walls; *h*, steps into crypt; *j*, vault crossties of polished black stone. (*Redrawn from A. Ruz.*)

with stalagmites and stalactites formed by water dripping, century after century, from the pyramid above. Around the walls were nine stucco reliefs of gods (the nine lords of the underworld?); the greater part of the floor was occupied by a huge stone sarcophagus, the lid of which (estimated to weigh about five tons) was superbly carved (Plate 13). Glyphs on its side date the burial at about A.D. 700. Inside was the skeleton of a Maya chief decked with jade, and with a composite pearl, over an inch long, as one of the treasures. The chief, forty to fifty years of age, lay full length. A magnificent mask of two hundred pieces of jade arranged mosaic fashion, placed over the chief's face, had slipped to one side; a jade ring was on each finger. Jade necklaces and wristlets brought the count of jade pieces to 978, in Maya values the wealth of the Indies (Plate 28*a*).

The vaulted chamber (its floor was slightly lower than that of the court outside and about seventy-five feet below the floor of the temple above) clearly had been built before the pyramid above, probably during the lifetime of the chief, and we can suppose that the staircase was filled in immediately after the burial.

At the far end of the chamber are heavy masonry blocks which presumably supported the sarcophagus lid until the chief was laid to rest. Then it would have been slid into position (Fig. 7). Naturally the slab had to be in the chamber before the pyramid was built.

In the pyramid of the High Priest's Grave, at distant Chichén Itzá, a vertical shaft, carefully constructed and covered with slabs in the temple floor, leads to a natural cave. On the floor of this were found broken bones, jades, a couple of pearls, and other treasure. The shaft had been deliberately filled in ancient times, and in the fill were several burials, one above the other. These, too, perhaps, were the remains of slain attendants, but the presence of copper bells shows these burials to be considerably more recent than the Palenque burial. There is a similar shaft in one of the pyramids of Mayapán. More such secret burials may be found as time passes.

I had the good fortune to descend that Palenque staircase with Ruz as my guide, but before the hidden chamber was reached. It was an experience I shall not forget. The past was very near, and it required little imagination to reverse the scene around me and picture the ancestors of Ruz' Maya laborers working to fill the staircase. One needed only to substitute pitch-pine torches for flashlights, breechclouts for trousers, and a Maya head-man with artificially deformed head for Ruz.

Yaxchilán and Piedras Negras, on the banks of the great Usumacinta River which divides the Petén from Chiapas, and Copán, southeastern outpost in distant Honduras, share with Palenque the honors in Maya sculpture.

Yaxchilán specialized in carved stone lintels spanning the exterior doorways of temples and palaces (most cities of the Central area used wooden lintels). Some of these are among the finest examples of Maya sculpture in existence (Plates 12–14, Fig. 21), but Yaxchilán's hieroglyphic texts are repetitious, the same phrases appearing over and over again on lintel and stela.

Piedras Negras equaled Yaxchilán and Copán in the delicate delineation of clothing and jewelry and the details of the elaborate headdresses of its personages and in the grace with which the hieroglyphs were carved. Its specialities were stelae with chiefs seated in niches in Buddha-like poses, magnificent wall panels alive with figures and columns of glyphs, and sculptured daises, the last two features in which Palenque also led the way (Plates 3, 9, 10, 14).

Copán, 2,000 feet above sea level, backing (not facing) on the river of the same name, stood high in both science and art (Plate 2). This center appears to have been in the van in solving problems connected with the length of the tropical year, a matter of supreme importance to the Maya for ritual and divination, and there is some evidence that astronomers of Copán either formulated the extremely good eclipse tables used by the Mayas, or were sufficiently intelligent to recognize the brilliance of an outsider's work and embody his ideas in their own system. Yet in art Copán was equal to any other Maya city, and in one respect perhaps ahead of all, for the personages sculptured on some of its stelae stand out from the stone mass of the shafts in a remarkable manner, and the friezes depicting seated individuals reveal exceptional skill in portraiture (Plates 11, 29). In architecture, the inspiring hieroglyphic stairway of Copán stands alone. The riser of each step of this stone stairway is decorated with hieroglyphs, each deeply and carefully carved. The flight of sixty-three steps rises majestically to a height of eighty-six feet above the level of the court. At intervals were seated five figures of gods or priests, each some six feet high, as though guarding the ascent to the temple which once crowned the summit. There is a decorative ramp on each side of the stairway, making a total breadth of thirty-three feet. These ramps, too, are elaborately carved with celestial bird-and-serpent monsters. Of the small temple which once stood at the top nothing remains except fragments of the plaster floor and a number of magnificently carved stones which once formed a hieroglyphic frieze on the inside of the temple at the level of the spring of the vault. The plaster fragments, on being fitted together like a jigsaw puzzle, revealed the original area of the floor!

From the doorway of this temple the Maya had a fine view of the ball court below and slightly to the right, with the stela-studded ceremonial court beyond, or if one turned half-left, he saw the temple, now prosaically named No. 11, with its beautifully sculptured friezes of individuals and mythological beings. The ball court with its sculptured markers set in the playing floor, its stone parrot heads, deeply tenoned three abreast on the side walls, and its vaulted temples on each side, at which the players made their offerings before and after the game, must have been one of the most magnificent in the Central area. One pictures the novitiate, busy with his religious duties on the summit of the pyramid of the hieroglyphic stairway, taking a surreptitious peek at a hotly contested match in the court below when the applause of the spectators advised him of some spectacular play.

This great city, with its magnificent stelae, with the soft beauty of its light-green trachyte stone used in such imposing masses, and with the ornate pomp of its great hieroglyphic stairway, has an emotional magnificence enhanced by the grandeur of the surrounding mountains—"*Each give each a double charm / As pearls upon an Aethiop's arm.*" There is a peaceful splendor here, which, the wickedness of child sacrifice forgotten or forgiven, now evokes the incomparable third movement of Beethoven's Fifth Symphony.

Quiriguá, on the railroad between Puerto Barrios and Guatemala City, lies in a fertile plain on the bank of the Motagua Valley, once rain forest, but in recent years banana land.

Quiriguá has no high pyramid and but few stone buildings, but it is renowned among Maya centers for the loftiness and grace of many of its carved sandstone stelae and for its strange altars, huge boulders shaped as fantastic monsters of the sky, which so harmoniously combine ponderous mass and graceful intricacy of carved de-

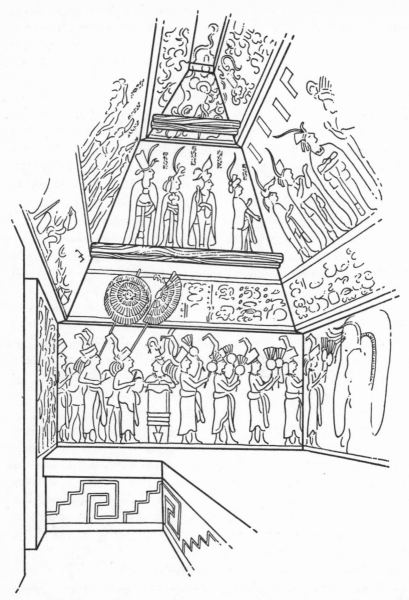

Fig. 8.—Interior of room at Bonampak. This shows the arrangement of the murals, the corbeled vaulting, the tie-poles, the bench which occupies most of the room, and the doorway on the left.

tail (Plates 11, 32; Figs. 15, 22 *b–d*). There is about it a sturdy, likable independence, manifest in its sculptural art and hieroglyphic texts.

Lubaantún, in southern British Honduras, has no stelae or corbeled buildings, yet asserts its individuality in the beautiful stepped effect of its pyramids executed in square blocks of superbly cut crystalline limestone, which has the appearance and most of the qualities of marble. Perhaps in the past they were not so beautiful as when I saw them a few years ago, with their dazzling whiteness partly masked by the deep green foliage and coral flowers of great clumps of wild begonias lodged in the interstices between the tiers. Bonampak, in the forests of Chiapas, is famed for its murals representing dances, ceremonies, and scenes of battle (Plate 17; Figs. 8–10). There, too, I have seen masses of begonias, but of another, white, variety. The roll call of stately cities with their individual characteristics, is not confined to the Central area; in Yucatán and Campeche we find an emphasis on huge buildings of the so-called palace type, often two or three stories high (Plates 6, 7).

Sayil supplies an extreme example of these "apartment" buildings, for its largest building has all together seventy rooms arranged in three stories, the second and third set back, so that the roofs of the first and second floors served as terraces for the occupants of the second and third floors. A great central staircase leads to the third floor. A mass such as this could be awkward and monotonous, but the Maya architects introduced contrasts and variations which give an extraordinary lightness to the bulk (Plate 3). For instance, the second floor has very wide doorways with triple entrances formed by pairs of columns (a feature practically never found in the Central area), in contrast to the single narrow entrances to the rooms of the third floor and to most of those of the ground floor. The façade of the second story is profusely decorated with designs of engaged columns and masks of the rain dragons; the façade of the third story is largely undecorated, but was originally covered with stucco. This is a late classic building of the style called Puuc (derived from a range of low hills of that name in southwestern Yucatán and adjacent parts of Campeche). The masonry, as in all buildings of this style, is massive concrete faced with thin and beautifully cut stone, like tiles bedded in cement.

At nearby Uxmal the same Puuc style with its veneer masonry

occurs, but there the most spectacular building is the so-called *Monjas* or Nunnery. Four ranges of rooms enclose a quadrangle, like a cloister garth, entered by a vaulted gateway in the middle of the south range (Plates 6, 8). In 1843, Stephens described the quadrangle in these words: "We enter a noble courtyard, with four great façades looking down upon it, each ornamented from one end to the other with the richest and most intricate carving known in the art of the buildings of Uxmal; presenting a scene of strange magnificence, surpassing any that is now to be seen among its ruins." A noble flight of stairs flanked by four rooms on each side leads to the second story of the north range. The garth itself is eighty-six yards by seventy-one yards, an area nearly half as large again as a football field. Once more, we see the diversity of decoration. The north range carries frets and masks of rain dragons; the east range has as its motif a lattice pattern derived from the scales of a serpent, on which are superimposed lengthening two-headed snakes with horizontal barlike bodies placed one above the other to form huge *V*'s. On the other façades are such details as writhing snakes, statues of men or gods, little models of huts (Fig. 24f), grecques, and yet more masks. To the east the great mass of the pyramid and temple of the Adivino rises in heavy domination of the scene. The effect should be overpowering, but it is not. The great mass of the Adivino (it is over one hundred feet high), rising like some New World Tower of Babel, together with the size of the quadrangle, emphasizes the lack of height of the Nunnery buildings so that they seem to cling to mother earth. The effect is that produced by a French cathedral on the town huddling around its base, or the buildings of Fountains Abbey beside its soaring tower. There is something of humility in these buildings despite the exuberance of their façades.

The name of "Nunnery" was given to the group in early Colonial times by Spaniards—always more interested in chastity in theory than in practice—on the assumption, surely mistaken, that this building was occupied by the Maya Vestal Virgins. The group is late, dating from the very close of the Classic period or perhaps a few decades later. Some of the rooms are the widest with corbeled vaulting (excluding those with more than one line of vaults owing to the use of interior columns) in the Maya area, reaching a width of some fourteen feet.

Near by is the so-called House of the Governor, a range of rooms over one hundred yards long, overlooking the whole city and standing on a vast platform. It is one of the most imposing buildings in the Maya area and of about the same date as the Nunnery.

For other diversities in architecture one could turn to the Río Bec area, where buildings flanked by high ornamental towers are found (Plate 7), or the near-by Chenes, of Campeche, with façades constructed so that the main doorway is the gaping mouth of a rain monster, his nose above and eyes to each side of the doorway, and the teeth of his lower jaw the sill of the doorway.

One other example must suffice, and for that we shall turn from the lowlands of the Central and Northern areas, and journey to the highlands of Guatemala, outside the area of the hieroglyphic stela and corbeled-vaulting complex.

Kaminaljuyú, on the outskirts of Guatemala City, was—for much of it has been demolished—a most important city in the early Classic period. In addition to the fine tombs of the Formative (p. 52), the site has yielded even more richly stocked tombs of the early Classic period (Fig. 23a) in and under its rather unpretentious pyramids. Among the pottery are a striking hunchback and vessels of "thin orange" ware (Plate 19b,d) traded from central Mexico. Still others show very strong influences in shape and design from Teotihuacán. These foreign influences are reflected also in some of the pyramids, for they have the same sort of horizontal panel framed top and bottom with a molding such as is found at Teotihuacán, but, so far as our present knowledge goes, in no Maya lowland city except Chichén Itzá, where it occurs in buildings of the Mexican period (Plate 6c). The materials of which the pyramids were constructed are also quite different from those of lowland sites. There are no vaulted stone temples, but postholes on the summits of pyramids indicate buildings with thatched roofs. Kaminaljuyú is also remarkable for the extraordinary number of ball courts within its limits.

It is possible that Mexican control of the Maya highlanders was strong enough quite early in the Classic period to lead to the virtual disappearance of hieroglyphic texts and to the failure of the highlanders to accept their lowland brethren's ideas on art and architecture.

Petén cities are built of limestone; dolomite was employed for buildings in parts of the Usumacinta Valley; Copán, as already noted, used a trachyte with a delightful and distinctive green hue; Quiriguá quarried sandstone for its buildings and stelae; and Lubaantún used a crystalline limestone. At Comalcalco, Chiapas, and at near-by Bellote, on the western flank of the Maya area, buildings were of kiln-fired bricks, some of which have simple incised patterns. The use of brick has been explained by the absence in that area of suitable building stone; it is one of the few places in America where kiln-fired bricks were used architecturally. Kaminaljuyú at one time used adobe for its pyramids, but later faced them with pumice set in mud with a very thin outer skin of soft concrete of gravel coated with lime plaster. Some sites expressed their individuality in the shapes of their stelae. Cancuen, for example, erected stelae with castelated tops, a pleasant change from the blunt rounded tops of most Maya centers; Quiriguá had its slender shafts (Plate 11*b*). Some sites, notably Caracol, with easy access to deposits in the Southern Pine Ridge of British Honduras, used slate for stelae, altars, or building stone. At Altar de Sacrificios, a relatively stoneless area, structures of the late Formative period were faced with musselshells incrusted in natural lime deposits, several times their natural size, from the river. These artificial stones of nature's producing were of considerable size. They were set in mud. This choice of material shows considerable resourcefulness by the builders.

It was, however, in planning that the greatest diversity occurred. Although there is great variety in the size of sites, this was not merely a matter of wealth. Some very large sites, such as Holmul, in east central Petén, erected very few or no stelae, whereas others, such as Pusilhá, in southern British Honduras, set up a considerable number of carved stelae, but built only low mounds of boulders and rocks without any attempt to dress their faces. In the case of Pusilhá this is particularly surprising, because a scant thirty miles away, at Lubaantún, which pottery vessels and figurines show to have been flourishing at the same time, one finds the exact opposite—no stelae but beautiful masonry. It is difficult to explain such dissimilarities. There is an abundance of limestone at Pusilhá, such as was dressed elsewhere. Indeed, it was dressed and sculptured at Pusilhá itself when shaped as stelae. As a matter of fact, the difference was one of material rather than of appearance, since the Maya coated the surfaces of all their pyramids, mounds, and buildings with lime stucco, even covering the finest stone, such as the crystalline limestone of Lubaantún or the beautiful green-tinged trachyte of Copán, in this manner. There is, therefore, little doubt that the mounds of Pusilhá were not just heaps of boulders, but were finished off with flat stuccoed surfaces, the interstices being filled with a mortar, now disintegrated, to make a fairly even bed for the application of the stucco coating.

Some cities were concentrated; others were spread out with different groups separated from one another (Plate 2). In some cases hilly terrain may have dictated this dispersal, but in others there appears to be no geographical cause. Orientation of the buildings to the points of the compass is another variable factor.

In addition to the many large sites, the Canterburys, Romes, and Rheimses of the Maya area, there were scores of smaller centers, the equivalent of our small towns or villages. The study of this type of small grouping is important, for it, like Sinclair Lewis' Gopher Prairie, mirrors more faithfully the native culture because it is less exposed to external modifications. Such foreign ideas as do reach that far have been transmitted through the large centers which have first modified and naturalized the exotic. The modern tendency in history is to pay less attention to pomp and circumstance, and rather strive to recreate and stress the cultural and physical background against which the average man played his simple part.

San José, in west central British Honduras, is perhaps typical of the smaller ceremonial center. It comprises four separate small groups of ruins, each consisting of a court flanked by mounds. Three of the groups include pyramids up to forty feet high. There are also a small ball court, a reservoir, one small plain stela, and one fairly elaborate two-story palace with eleven vaulted rooms, several benches or daises, and an interior staircase. The next most pretentious structure has six rooms arranged in two parallel rows with a seventh transverse room at one end; all are corbeled (Fig. 5e). Another building is a mixture of corbeled and non-corbeled rooms. The pottery shows a continuous occupation of the site from the Formative period through the Classic period, and probably into the first stages of the Mexican period. The uncovering of burials revealed for the most part skeletons laid on their sides with knees flexed and doubled up so that they are in front of the trunk. With them are usually some of the deceased's possessions, not the best to be had, but such as one would expect to find around a member of the bourgeoisie of a small provincial center who distrusted ostentation and the ways of "furriners."

Nevertheless, San José was not entirely a backwater, as a considerable number of trade pieces attest (Fig. 22a). These include certain pottery jars with a slatelike slip imported from Yucatán, spindle whorls from Veracruz, shells from the shores of the Pacific, obsidian, from Ixtepeque volcano or some other source in the Guatemalan highlands, jade from some unidentified source, copper objects perhaps from Mexico, coral from the Caribbean, marble vessels probably from Honduras, and large quantities of painted pottery, certainly not of local manufacture. The San Joséans did not produce any sculptured works, but they adorned their buildings with designs in stucco, and clearly were acquainted with Maya hieroglyphs because they decorated the front of one dais with glyphs of the same material. Not unnaturally, they were a bit behind the times. This shows in their architecture, for the type of masonry they were using at one time had already gone out of date elsewhere. There is a little evidence pointing to the practice of human sacrifice, both of adults and of children, but this, so far as the evidence goes, was on rather a limited scale, in keeping with the provincial character of the site.

One or two of the smaller buildings may have served as permanent residences, but in other respects San José was a small-scale ceremonial center, of which there must be literally scores in the Central area and perhaps hundreds in the whole Maya area.

Recent surveys of house mounds scattered over the surrounding country, notably that of William Bullard on the eastern Petén, give a good insight into the distribution of the surrounding populace which sustained the ceremonial centers.

Of the huts nothing remains, for they were of perishable materials, probably almost replicas of those the Maya use to the present day. However, the stone and rubble platforms on which they stood remain. These are of all sizes, but thirty feet long by twelve feet wide and one to three feet high are typical dimensions. These platforms, in turn, may stand on two or three sides of a small artificial court. House sites, Bullard notes, often appear in small clusters of five to twelve, suggestive of hamlets, in an area of about ten to twenty acres. These clusters in turn coalesce to form a zone, to which a minor ceremonial center pertains, although this often is not in the center of the zone, but to one side or isolated, because ceremonial centers usually stood on a hilltop. San José is too large to fit into this category of minor ceremonial feature. Moreover, it possessed features such as ball court and stela not normally associated with this type of minor ceremonial center.

The zones, each with its minor ceremonial center, come together to form a district, which, in turn, maintained a major ceremonial center of the type discussed above. Districts varied in size. Bullard suggests an average of nearly forty square miles.

The arrangement here of a number of zones, each with its small ceremonial center, combining to support a major ceremonial center reminds us of the situation at Tenochtitlán, the ancient Aztec capital, on which Mexico City now stands. There the great ceremonial center, in which great national ceremonies took place, was surrounded by twenty districts or precincts, each occupied by a different *calpulli*, a sort of clan with a geographical basis. Each "clan" had its own administration, controlled its own lands, had its own small religious center, where the tribal and clan deities were worshiped, and had its own officials to run the various local affairs. The "clans" were grouped in four "quarters," and each "clan" had representation in its quarter and in the over-all tribal organization, both lay and religious. We have no information on any division into quarters in the Maya area, but there does seem to be a certain parallel between the probable arrangement in the Maya lowlands in Classic times and the situation among the Aztec at the time of the Spaniards' arrival, although one must bear in mind that the former was rural, the latter largely urban.

In connection with the area of a district, the late George Brainerd noted that computations of time and labor required to construct Maya ceremonial centers demonstrate that at a density of thirty persons per square mile, which was what it was in Yucatán a few years ago and somewhat less than it was estimated to be at the time of the Spanish Conquest, a population drawn from a radius of a few miles would have sufficed to build any ordinary-sized ceremonial center. Naturally, he took into account that the work of building and enlarging almost never ceased from the day a ceremonial center was started until it was abandoned.

A recent survey of an area around Tikal led to the conclusion that there were at least 1,948 presumed house mounds (excluding kitchen and family temple mounds and such like occupied at the height of the Classic period) in an area of 6.2 square miles. Allowing 5.6 persons per household, this produces a minimum population of 10,800, or no less than 1,724 souls per square mile.

However, one overlooked factor would reduce this enormous concentration. Late Classic, represented by the Tepeu 1 and 2 pottery types, endured for a couple of centuries, and it is impossible to conclude that all mounds containing those pottery types were occupied at the same time. One mound may have supported a house in, say, early Tepeu 1, but may have been abandoned at the close of the phase (although, in fact, pottery phases don't close abruptly; like old soldiers, they merely fade away). Indeed, in almost any modern Maya village, one sees decaying houses abandoned a decade or two before, but excavation would not reveal that all the houses in the village were not in use at the date of the latest. Moreover, Bishop Landa tells us that a hut was abandoned on a death in the family. Whether that custom applied to the Petén is not known; it did not apply even in Yucatán to stone buildings, but stone buildings represent a large investment in wealth, whereas a thatched hut, such as the mounds around Tikal largely supported, is built in a few days. Yet another point: abandonments may have been more frequent in ancient times, when the people lived scattered over the countryside, than in present times, when because of concentrations by the friars, settlements are in villages, in which building land is not so available; a good site in a village is not willingly abandoned.

The area around Tikal, greatest of Maya centers, must have had a large population, but surely not as great as this estimate produces.

As to the political organization of the Classic period, I suspect that the provinces into which Yucatán relapsed after the fall of Mayapán (p. 139) were in existence long before the rise of Mayapán and continued to reflect more or less the set-up of the "districts" controlled by each major ceremonial center. As found by the Spaniards, the head chief, a personage of immense authority (a cloth was held before his face so that an interceder might not see his face) was called *halach uinic*, "real man," and associated with him was a high priest, *ah kin Mai*, religious leader of the whole province, although the *halach uinic* was ex officio also a religious leader. Both offices were hereditary. Each town under the *halach uinic*, presumably corresponding to the zone of the smaller ceremonial center, was ruled by a chief called *batab*, "axe-bearer," assisted by a council. Among the members of the council were the *ah cuchcabs*, "office-bearers of the township," who probably ruled over small areas equatable with Bullard's hamlet. The *halach uinic* undoubtedly had a council which included his *batabs* to advise him, but our information on the political organization is very scant. The *halach uinic* appointed the *batabs*, the succession was frequently, but not always, in the same family. *Halach uinics* and *batabs* were supported by taxes paid by their subjects and from the produce of lands they controlled. Possibly a man of humble birth might rise to the rank of *batab*, although that clearly was not easy; he could not rise to become *halach uinic* or chief priest. As in central Mexico, the organization was partly autocratic, partly democratic.

In the past few years social anthropologist students of present-day Maya groups in Chiapas have seen the Maya political system of the Classic period as ancestral to that which obtains in the present-day Maya communities, whereby an able and ambitious man can rise from a humble position to the highest rank in the village organization. That the ancient Maya city was essentially a democratic organization is a pleasant thought, especially to Americans whose faith in the general acceptance of democratic institutions by non-Europeans has been so rudely shattered in recent years, but I doubt its validity. The essential democracy of Maya village life today may well parallel that of ancient times, although in its socio-religious pattern it has been at the same time profoundly affected by the impact of the Spanish system of democratic religious societies—confraternities and sodalities. However, it is very dangerous to go a step further and assume that it reflects the pattern of regional (national) religious and political organization of a thousand years ago. As a matter of fact, one cannot make that assumption even today, for the supra-village organization of Guatemala and of the states of Mexico, being in non-Indian hands, is beyond the reach of the ambitious village leader. That is because the specialized knowledge he has acquired to rise in the village is useless to him outside it, and he has not acquired the informed background necessary for him to operate on a wider political horizon. I think the same barriers to progress must have existed in ancient times.

All available data from Spanish sources picture the Maya chief rulers, secular and religious, as members of a small hereditary group, and the same is true of other peoples of Middle America. For instance, the rulers of the Aztec and of neighboring centers such as Texcoco, Culhuacán, and the like were drawn from a single "royal" family. Moreover, the same sources inform us that only a limited number of the nobility and the high priesthood had mastered the hieroglyphic writing. Even assuming that such barriers to progress did not exist, it is hard to believe that an honest Maya son of toil, on rising to the highest rank, could in late middle age learn to read and write, to calculate heliacal risings of Venus, and to work out the dates on which solar eclipses might occur. Such knowledge would have had no place in his rise to the top of his village shamans, but it was an essential requisite for high priesthood. The wrong sort of knowledge which is an obstacle to the rise of the present-day Maya leader higher than his local community similarly held back his ancestor of the Classic period. Apart from such considerations, the dynastic information, particularly at Piedras Negras, uncovered by Miss Proskouriakoff, indicates rulers coming to power seemingly in their twenties and once at about thirteen. Such ages indicate a hereditary system, no log cabin to White House romances.

There is linguistic evidence in Yucatec-Maya for a former system of cross-cousin marriage; that is to say, a man married his father's sister's daughter, although "sister" probably was used in a wider sense than we use it. There is incomplete evidence for a system of totemic clans among the almost extinct Lacandón Maya, with marriage with a person having the same totemic animal forbidden. Prohibition of marriage with a person of the same name in Yucatán is perhaps indicative of a former clan organization there, but the whole system had clearly disintegrated before the coming of the Spaniards. In parts of the Guatemalan highlands the clan organization, with marriage only outside the clan and usually with each clan occupying a single locality, was not in a state of disintegration. Conceivably, in view of the geographical clans of the highlands of Guatemala and elsewhere in Middle America (e.g., the Aztec), Bullard's hamlets of the Classic period contained the residences of members of the same clan, but that is pure speculation.

Presumably land was not privately owned but was alloted by the community; consequently, one must not regard the nobility as holding all the wealth with the farmers a poverty-stricken group. Also, a successful jaguar hunter, for instance, could presumably trade his pelts for fine polychrome dishes; a farmer with skill in, say, gourd painting or working tortoiseshell or who had a wife who was an outstanding weaver could similarly acquire wealth, and by correct expenditure work his way up the ladder of officeholding in his community. Wealth also was affected by local resources. A good share of the wealth cacao growers produced surely remained in their hands. The contents of burials along the middle reaches of the Belize River, a known center of cacao orchards, seem to bear this out, for they are of above normal wealth.

Beside nobles and commoners, there seems to have been a smallish middle class recruited from the latter and including artists, craftsmen—makers of idols, for instance—and the religious and political functionaries of small towns and villages. At the time of the Spanish Conquest slaves were numerous, and presumably they existed during the Classic period and probably even in the Formative. They were drawn from the children of slaves, commoners captured in war or enslaved for debt or some civil crime. For some offenses, e.g., theft, a slave could be redeemed by payment of the debt. Sometimes the community redeemed a slave who was mistreated. There was also a little-understood system of indentured labor.

There remains the problem of relation between one city state and another. We have a picture of great numbers of cities and towns flourishing during the Classic period (A.D. 200–A.D. 925) and showing marked diversity in terms of space and time. Here is no slavish copying, but a virility which finds expression in experiment and diversification, yet—and here I am speaking of the lowland area—retaining a marked similarity.

Does this unity with local diversification indicate a system of city states, such as existed in Greece or mediaeval Italy, with political independence but a fairly uniform culture and a common language, or does it point to a single state? Frankly, the answer must be largely guesswork, although there are factors which can influence the conclusion.

In favor of a fair degree of unity is the fact that the language was practically the same throughout the lowland area, for the differences between lowland languages and dialects a thousand to fifteen hundred years ago must have been less than they are today, and there seems little doubt that a Chol would have understood a Yucatec, or a Tzotzil a Chorti, certainly as easily as a Neapolitan understands a native of Turin. Sculpture and name glyphs of gods demonstrate that religious concepts must have been fairly uniform throughout the area (information for Yucatán not as full as it might be), at least so far as the hierarchic cult is concerned, although the religious ideas of the peasants may have shown some variation from region to region. The whole philosophy of time—a hierarchic trait, with the more abstract implication of which the peasants surely were unacquainted—was found from one end of the Maya lowlands to the other, as the glyphic inscriptions demonstrate.

The absence of fortifications, the fact that most classic centers are in open country, and little evidence of warfare (the Bonampak murals of fighting [Fig. 9] rather clearly show a raid, not regular warfare) argue for an assumption of prevailing peace during the Classic period, as does the incredible building activity which apparently was carried on uninterruptedly throughout the period. Such evidence as there is of warfare is largely confined to the southwest of the Maya area, not too far removed from non-Maya peoples such as the Zoque and Chiapanec, and is strongest for the last decades of the Classic period. I rather doubt that the Maya of the Classic period used wooden fortifications (long since perished) in view of their long tradition of masonry construction, which, after all, is fire resistant.

Hieroglyphic texts show that new ideas flowed freely from one city to another. Thus a new method of computing moons appeared at Copán in A.D. 682, and spread rapidly to almost all important cities in the Central area. About A.D. 700, Copán appears to have produced the most up-to-date computation of the length of the tropical year (all specialists in the field do not accept this interpretation of the hieroglyphic calculations, but I am satisfied that it is correct), and recorded it on a number of monuments. The sides of one altar commemorating this achievement are carved with the figures of sixteen persons

Fig. 9.—A raid on the enemy. Part of a mural at Bonampak (about A.D. 775), with scene showing the head chief and his assistants leading a raid against a neighboring village. The head chief, with jaguar tunic and stabbing spear, has taken a captive (grasping by the hair symbolizes capture). Note flexible shield and grotesque headdresses. Lower part of design damaged. (*After Antonio Tejeda and Agustín Villagra.*)

who face inwards toward the date in question. Teeple, who first advanced the explanation that this was a computation of the length of the solar year, speaks felicitously of this "group photograph of the Copán Academy of Sciences taken just after their sessions."

Twenty years later, another altar was dedicated commemorating that anniversary of the original computation, and on it are carved twenty persons facing inwards toward the date. More than half of them wear masks of animals or represent gods. One of them is disguised as a bat. Unfortunately, we know the ancient names of very few Maya cities or linguistic groups, but it is worth recalling that *Tzotzil,* the name for one of the big linguistic groups of Chiapas, means "bat." It seems, therefore, not too impossible that membership in Teeple's Copán Academy of Sciences was not confined to priest-astronomers from Copán, but was composed of representatives of the whole Maya lowlands, and among those present was a representative of the Tzotzil. In that case, and admittedly the case is not too strong, we have possible evidence of lowland unity.

Other lines of evidence indicate, at least, friendly relations between cities. Cities developed certain glyphs of their own and used them frequently, but sometimes these local glyphs were borrowed by other cities. For instance, one glyph which originated at Piedras Negras subsequently was adopted by Palenque. Also, influences in both architecture and sculpture passed from one region to another. Petén architectural concepts spread to the Usumacinta, and sculptural treatment typical of the Northern area appears at Yaxchilán, together with a northern method of recording dates.

Against these factors must be set hierarchic traits which have local distribution. In parts of Campeche and Yucatán the method of recording month positions was one day less than in the standard practice, as though Texas wrote Monday, March 15, when all the rest of the country recorded the date as Monday, March 16. In view of the tremendous role of the Maya calendar in the life of both the group and the individual, that deviationist policy is significant. Moreover, the clauses in hieroglyphic writing varied from city to city. Palenque, for instance, used the same combinations of glyphs over and over again, but no other Maya city employed them. Each had its own clauses which Palenque and other large cities ignored. It is now known that these include names of rulers and what seem to be names of cities or city states.

There is good evidence of regional styles of sculpture and glyphs which point to cities having areas of influence. Yaxchilán, for instance, strongly affected the sculpture, architecture, and hieroglyphic writing of Bonampak. Yaxchilán's "emblem" glyph figures in Bonampak's hieroglyphic texts, and that strongly hints that the latter was part of the Yaxchilán "city state." A word on "emblem" glyphs is in order.

Henry Berlin recently was able to show that each of the really important Maya centers had its own distinctive glyph with certain affixes which were the same whatever the emblem glyph might be. Pretty clearly the emblem glyph must be a transcription either of the name of the ceremonial center or of its ruling family or something along those lines. Because of uncertainty about its exact meaning, Berlin called it the emblem glyph.

Now whereas large sites such as Palenque, Copán and Piedras Negras each has its own emblem glyph (Fig. 18a–f), and a large and a near-by smaller site may share an emblem glyph, e.g., Yaxchilán and Bonampak, and Piedras Negras and the somewhat insignificant El Cayo, the same emblem glyph is shared by both Tikal and a group of fairly large and approximately equally important sites in the Río Pasión (upper Usumacinta) Valley. Such an arrangement suggests that we may be dealing with some sort of a grouping of ceremonial centers in that area as a single unit.

I am inclined to think of the Maya lowlands during the Classic period as a loose federation of autonomous city states, the government of which was largely in the hands of a small caste of priests and nobles, related by blood and dominated by religious motifs. It is quite likely that, as in central Mexico, the rulership of each city state was dual: One chief was the civil ruler, but also with priestly functions (the *halach uinic;* the best Maya dictionary translates this as both governor and bishop); the other devoted the whole of his time to priestly and astrological duties. The ruling class would have been a small quasi-religious minority, holding the peasant masses in subjection by its claim to know how to satisfy, please, and, perhaps, control the gods by magico-religious processes. Withal I suspect the rule was

97

fairly benevolent except for the constant call on the people for labor for bigger and better pyramids, temples, and "palaces." Perhaps the closest parallel to this theocracy was the benevolent Jesuit rule of the Guarani in seventeenth-century Paraguay.

Perhaps we can assume that relations between city states of the Classic period were, on the whole, quite friendly. Presumably their rulers were related; certainly they shared the same upbringing, education, taste in art, and religious beliefs. That does not necessarily lead one to conclude that relations were always cordial. I think one can assume fairly constant friction over boundaries sometimes leading to a little fighting, and occasional raids on outlying parts of a neighboring city state to assure a supply of sacrificial victims, but I think the evidence is against the assumption of regular warfare on a considerable scale. Conceivably there was one supreme ruler over all the city states, but we could probably assume that larger cities tended to dominate the smaller ones. For instance, one imagines the high priest of Tikal being held in high regard by the peoples of neighboring city states, such as Nakum and Yaxha, because of the magnificence of his seat of office, and one supposes that a raid by Tikal on some outlying settlement in Nakum territory would have been endured without thought of retaliation, but the Maya motto was "live and let live," and somehow I don't see too much bullying of a small city state by a big one, although affection for the Maya may have influenced that opinion.

It is barely possible that Tikal was the seat of a supreme ruler of the Central area. The site is enormous, yet there are other ceremonial centers in the vicinity (Uaxactún twelve miles, Nakum fourteen miles, and Yaxha seventeen miles distant) to compete for labor. Moreover, it is difficult to account for Tikal's grandeur. There is little natural wealth, and the scant limestone soil and abundant swampland are unsuitable for growing cacao, the chief lowland wealth, nor, so far as is known, are there good flint beds in the vicinity. Also, the site is on no obvious trade route. Yet the fact that Pasión sites used Tikal's emblem glyph hints at their subservience to that distant metropolis.

The evidence of Bonampak's ties to Yaxchilán seems to show that a city state could consist of more than one city. The fact that boundaries between styles of architecture or of glyphic writing do not seem to correspond to linguistic areas has some bearing on the problem. Thus, we have every reason to believe that both those who built in Río Bec style (Plate 7*b*) and those who used Puuc style (Plate 3*a*) spoke the same Maya language, Yucatec. Similarly, peoples of such Petén cities as Tikal or Uaxactún almost certainly spoke a dialect somewhere between Yucatec and the Chol-Chontal dialects which were probably current in Yaxchilán, Piedras Negras, and Palenque, where local styles in art and architecture prevailed. Copán spoke a variant of eastern Chol, differing mainly in the substitution of *r* for *l*. Minor differences corresponding to dialectical variations probably appeared in the arts and crafts and the religious concepts of the peasant villagers, not in the manifestations of the hierarchic cult.

One has then a picture of this whole lowland area, excluding savanna, swamp, and other sections unsuited to settlement, studded with countless ceremonial centers, varying in size from those comprising four thatched hut-temples atop simple platforms enclosing a court scarcely fifty feet in each direction to vast masses of platforms and pyramids, palaces and temples, rising jaggedly like granaries in Iowa or grouped with the architectural harmony of an Andalusian city. The country around, one visualizes as a patchwork of forest, cleared acres, and land reverting to forest, with the first the dominant factor, and here and there the thatched huts of the peasants grouped in fours and fives in clearings shaded by fruit trees. As to the ceremonial centers, they might well be empty, but should you return tomorrow, you would find them filled with crowds present for some ceremony or for market; and visiting them again a month hence, when the corn needs little attention, you might see files of men, women, and children carrying rocks and earth for the enlargement of a pyramid, and masons and carpenters busy laying yet more stone walls or stairways or cutting lintels or cross-ties for yet another temple.

I would suppose that some of the nobility, including the chief ruler and high priest of each city state, lived in an outlying group of the ceremonial center, but not in the "down-town" part. Apart from wishing to avoid the discomforts of the windowless stone-built and stone-roofed "palaces," they would surely have wished to get away from those sun-seared acres of plastered courts to some spot where they could enjoy shade trees and perhaps a flower- or shrub-filled patio or garden—everywhere in Middle America there was a love of flowers, and they were used even in sacrificial offerings. Presumably a part of the priest nobility lived in or near the smaller ceremonial centers, as the *batabs* did later in Yucatán and as the distribution of larger (presumed) house mounds in the Central area suggests. So one would have a situation such as obtained in Europe until recent years, with most of the aristocracy scattered over the countryside, or as in present-day New York, with most members of the Harvard, Yale, and Princeton clubs forming a local aristocracy in the communities of Long Island and Connecticut, but going to the ceremonial center of Wall Street to carry out their religious (?) obligations to Mammon and attend the markets.

Through the seventh, eighth, and part of the ninth century the pace quickened; more and more buildings were added, more and more stelae were erected. Quality also improved. Masonry was better, buildings more spacious, pottery finer, stelae more elaborate. Sculpture? Growing sensitivity and inspiration and then a touch of flamboyancy. Art students tell us that the last is a signal that the style has run its course and the seeds of decay are planted in the art, and perhaps also in the culture that gave it birth.

COLLAPSE OF THE CITY STATES

Certainly for the Maya that was true. Toward the close of this florescence Maya cities were bright-hued as autumn foliage, and then the leaves began to fall. One by one, activities at the various cities ceased; no more stelae were erected, no more temples or "palaces" were built. In some cases work ceased so suddenly that platforms built to support buildings were left uncrowned, and at Uaxactún the walls of the latest building were left unfinished. We can best date the cessation of effort by the dates of the last hieroglyphic inscriptions.

Copán ceased to erect hieroglyphic monuments in A.D. 800, the year Charlemagne was crowned in Rome; Quiriguá, Piedras Negras, and Etzna (in Campeche) followed suit in A.D. 810; Tila gave up in A.D. 830; Oxkintok's last date is A.D. 849; Seibal, Jimbal (an outlying part of Tikal), Uaxactún, Xultún, and Chichén Itzá kept going until A.D. 889 (the last perhaps a little later). La Muñeca, not far

Fig. 10.—Judgment on the captives. Part of a mural at Bonampak, a sequel to the raid (Fig. 9). A captive in fear before the head chief, a dead man in a posture worthy of Michelangelo below, and captives from whose fingers blood drips. The head chief is decked in jade and wears the same jaguar tunic as in the previous scene. (*After Antonio Tejeda and Agustín Villagra.*)

north of the border between Campeche and Petén has a stela which probably commemorates A.D. 909, and possibly the same date may be recorded on the latest stela at Naranjo. Just possibly a crude stela at San Lorenzo, near La Muñeca, carries a Maya date (10.5.0.0.0. in Maya notation) equivalent to A.D. 928, the latest of all. Five years later the Magyar hordes were turned back at the battle of Unstrut, and European civilization was saved.

The latest known date at Palenque (except for one inscribed on a pot) is A.D. 784, but as Palenque dates occur largely on wall tablets or stuccoed on pilasters, it is possible that still-buried tablets or stuccoed glyphs now destroyed carry the count forward. Yaxchilán inscriptions still cannot be dated in every case, but the Yaxchilán-Bonampak region probably was active until about A.D. 810.

A number of these very late stelae are in degenerate style, and a few show Mexican influence (Toltec type of sandal and style of representation on the latest stela at Seibal; a god with spear and spear-thrower emerging from a sort of sun disk, reminiscent of Toltec treatment at Chichén Itzá, on the latest stela at Ucanal), both of which facts have a bearing on the collapse of these cities of the Classic period.

For many years it was believed that for some reason or other the Maya of the Central area abandoned their cities and migrated north to Yucatán and south into the highlands of Guatemala, in both of which regions they established Maya culture, which subsequently blossomed forth into a renaissance. More recent archaeological work has shown that thesis to be untenable; both regions were flourishing centers of Maya culture all through the Classic period. For the cessation of activities in the various ceremonial centers a number of theories have been advanced, none of which has much to recommend it.

It has been suggested that Maya methods of agriculture (cutting and burning forest for one- or two-year plantings and then allowing the clearings to revert to forest for some ten years) were so wasteful that in time and with an increase of population lack of food would have forced migration. To refute this theory, one can note that the soil around Quiriguá, frequently fertilized by floodings of the Motagua River, is very rich, yet Quiriguá was one of the earlier cities to cease functioning.

The explanation has also been offered that repeated clearing of forest was followed by the appearance of grass, which gradually covered the land, producing savannas which the Maya, having no plows or even spades (the shallow soil in many parts would make such implements unusable even if the Maya had possessed them), were unable to break up to plant their crops. This explanation, strongly advocated by my late colleague, Sylvanus G. Morley, was advanced by agronomists of the United States Department of Agriculture. It it quite neat, but I am not certain that it is tenable. It is true that grass will appear in cleared forest land if those patches are kept free of trees and shrubs for several years, but the Maya abandoned their clearings after one or two seasons' use, and in that short time grass cannot establish itself. I have noticed that verges of roads cut in the forests and used for several years to extract mahogany are often of grass, but when those roads are abandoned, they revert rapidly to forest. Some years ago I was in Chichanha, an important Maya town in southern Quintana Roo until its abandonment in 1852. During its occupation the main plaza and the streets must have been under grass, as in any other Maya town. Yet, when I visited the town, it was entirely covered with deep forest, to a layman indistinguishable from the surrounding virgin forest. In fact, it was not until I saw the walls of houses and gardens and then the ruined church that I realized that I was riding down former streets and across what had once been an extensive plaza. Thus forest will quickly displace grass, even when, as in the plaza of Chichanha, it had been established for very many years.

The botanist Lundell has modified this theory, supposing that it applies only to regions where the soil is deep, such as the savannas of Campeche and south of Lake Petén. These are bottom lands and not too extensive. The fact that large Maya sites are not found on or even contiguous to them gives little support for the theory that their growth caused the desertion of the Maya centers. There are no savanna lands around the great concentration of ceremonial centers in the northern Petén, or around Quiriguá with its deep soil, or along the Usumacinta. I suspect those savannas were formed long before the Classic period reached its peak.

Sample cores recently taken from the bottom of Lake Petén show a high percentage of savanna-type pollen during the Classic period, of forest-type pollen in the post-Classic period. The choice of that lake was unfortunate, for, as noted, there is much savanna land, probably natural, not man-made, south of the lake. Shifts in the prevailing winds could explain the pollen shift.

A most diverting theory has recently been advanced. It was noted that in two quite small Maya villages near Lake Petén the death rate among girls is higher than among boys, and the explanation offered is that girls suffer neglect because they are of less economic importance. The figures, multiplied ten thousandfold and shifted backward a thousand years, are advanced as the cause of the end of the Classic period; a woman shortage brought the end. The advocate forgot the law of supply and demand. Had there been a girl shortage through neglect, the price of brides would have risen, stimulating parents to give their daughters greater care and so end the shortage.

The abandonment of the cities has also been attributed to the incidence of malaria or yellow fever, but both of those diseases are almost certainly of Old World origin, introduced to the New World by the Spaniards. Hookworm is a serious destroyer in this region at the present time, but that, too, is a post-Columbian importation. Moreover, all these explanations call for a gradual death of Maya culture in city after city, but the building already mentioned at Uaxactún with its half-built walls suggests a sudden catastrophe.

I think the fundamental mistake has been to assume that the whole area was abandoned because activities ceased in the great ceremonial centers. As a matter of fact, we know that there was a considerable population in the region in the sixteenth century. There was a heavy population around Copán in early colonial days, and Cortés, in his march across the peninsula, came across quite a number of settlements. Friars and military groups in the sixteenth, seventeenth, and eighteenth centuries reported many other groups, although smallpox and other newly introduced diseases had carried off large numbers of inhabitants. Clearly the population of the Central area at the time of the Spanish Conquest was considerably smaller than it had been eight hundred years earlier, but it is incorrect to suppose that this vast area had been a vacuum for hundreds of years. This later population might have descended from groups subsequently filtering into the region, but it is more reasonable to assume that they are the descendants of the original peasant population of the ninth century.

It is not illogical to suppose that there was a series of peasant revolts against the theocratic minority of priests, "squarsons" (a term for that phenomenon of eighteenth-century English life, the squire who was also the village parson), and nobles. This may have been caused by the ever growing demands for service in construction work and in the production of food for an increasing number of nonproducers. Exotic religious developments, such as the cult of the planet Venus, adopted by the hierarchy may have driven a wedge between the two groups, making the peasants feel that the hierarchy was no longer performing its main function, that of propitiating the gods of the soil in whom, alone, they heartily believed. I am rather dubious of physical invasion and conquest of the Central area, but there may well have been ideological invasions, as foreign ideas on very late stelae would indicate. Whether degeneracy in art—and it is apparent only in a few cities—reflects a moral weakening in the hierarchy is a question which probably can never be answered. Huxley, I think, showed that Italian art was at its purest when morals were at a very low level. (In our age both seem to have hit bottom together!)

It is suggestive that the collapse of the stela cult seems to have started across the base of the Peninsula of Yucatán, the region most easily invaded by the revolutionary ideas or perhaps even armies of non-Maya peoples or of the nonconformist Maya of the Highlands, and its last stronghold was in the very remote region of northern Petén and southern Campeche. This, however, was only a general tendency. Around Comitán, in the Chiapan highlands, which was certainly an outpost of the stela cult on the frontier of the hierarchic empire, monuments continued to be erected until the middle of the ninth century, and there was another holdout in the middle Usumacinta Valley. However, all sorts of local circumstances may account for these, just as they account for the present distribution of kingdoms in modern Europe.

The gradualness of the collapse over the whole area argues against the view that there was strong central authority and in favor of the city-state theory. In my opinion, and it is one on which I would not stake heavily, in city after city the ruling group was driven out or, more probably, massacred by the dependent peasants, and power then passed to peasant leaders and small-town witch doctors.

The building program and the erection of stelae ceased abruptly, but the people still repaired to the ceremonial centers for certain religious services and perhaps for markets, but the buildings, no longer kept up, gradually fell into disrepair. Vegetation began to invade the courts and terraces and to lodge on the roofs of buildings.

There is some evidence for these assertions. Excavation at Uaxactún revealed that after the buildings had been abandoned, burials were still made in the city. One body was placed in the debris of a collapsed room; another lay on an accumulation of dirt in a corner of a court; another (a child) was on a dais or bench, with a few stones and much charcoal placed around it and with a covering of dirt and fall from the roof. In two cases the skulls were deformed, indicating that these were not post-Columbian burials. The child had a piece of jade in the mouth (a common Middle American practice) and two jade beads. As children were commonly sacrificed, the presence of the child with jades and charcoal in this abandoned room would strongly suggest that it had been brought there to be sacrificed. Burials have also been found in collapsed rooms at other sites, notably a burial with pottery of post-classical types at Copán.

As buildings began to collapse, doorways were slovenly blocked to shut them off, and refuse containing broken pottery and bones is found overlying thin deposits of debris from disintegrating vaults and walls. Shaped spindle-whorls, unknown in the Classic period of the Petén, occur both at Uaxactún and San José in thin deposits of dirt above the latest floors. A bow was found on the floor of one room at Uaxactún below about eight feet of collapsed masonry.

Such data indicate visits to the sites after their abandonment, half-hearted attempts to keep them in service by blocking off collapsed rooms, and probable use of the buildings for human sacrifices. It is, I think, a fair assumption that these activities can be attributed to the peasant population after the massacre or expulsion of the hierarchy. The jades might have been loot, for peasants would not have owned such valuables; the crude masonry of one of the blocked doorways at Uaxactún suggests that the work was done after the last of the masons working for the hierarchy had joined the great majority. At Tikal broken stelae were reset, even upside down.

Accumulating evidence at a number of Petén and British Honduras sites now rather strongly suggests that the last part of what had been regarded as late Classic pottery, the so-called Tepeu 3, is in fact post-Classic and represents casual use of the ceremonial centers in the way described above after the ruling group had been massacred or expelled. Twenty-five years ago I suggested that this late ceramic material be reassigned to a post-Classic horizon to account for the surface finds at San José and Uaxactún, but then I could find no colleague to support the idea.

Altar de Sacrificios, strategically placed at the confluence of the Pasión and Chixoy rivers, which join to form the Usumacinta, supplies very interesting evidence of post-Classic occupation. The ceremonial center is covered with a blanket of figurines and untempered pottery of the types named Fine Orange Y and Fine Gray. These are nonlocal wares originating from somewhere along the bottom of the Gulf of Mexico, where potters for centuries fabricated these wares of the same untempered clay but varying shapes and designs from center to center and generation to generation. The little figurines are of particular importance because they portray individuals lacking the Classic Maya features of retreating forehead (head deformation), curved nose, receding chin, and elaborate coiffure. Instead, nose and forehead are straight, chin is prominent and hair straight and shoulder-length. The fact that these figurines do not conform to the idealized style of Maya beauty may indicate that their makers were not Maya. Unfortunately, we cannot be certain, for around the estuaries of the Usumacinta and Grijalva rivers, the home of the Chontal Maya, many of the clay heads are not in Classic style. Moreover, on the walls of a tomb at Comalcalco, on the western edge of Chontal territory, there seem to be portraits of chiefs of both types. One may also suggest that if the Maya ideal of beauty was associated with the hierarchy—and there are arguments for that view—it might well have lost its popularity when the priest-nobles were liquidated.

In connection with the Altar de Sacrificios enigma, it may be relevant that very late stelae at Seibal carry portraits of non-Classic Maya type (Plate 9b), and in one case the hieroglyphs are non-Maya. Seibal lies about forty miles east of Altar de Sacrificios, but perhaps four times that distance by canoe following the twistings of the Pasión. Here, apparently, we are dealing with replacement of Maya rulers by foreigners in the last century of the Classic period who maintained the stela-raising Maya rite, but modified the art style and had heretical

107

ideas about hieroglyphic texts. This regime at Seibal seems to have ended at about the close of the Classic period. Similarly, the intrusion at Altar de Sacrificios must have been quite short, for no sherds of the widespread and highly prized effigy plumbate pottery occur. This unusual pottery (p. 209) was being traded far and wide around A.D. 1000. Invasion, I think, was a minor factor in the collapse of the ceremonial centers, except that a usurping group would be an added reason for revolt.

At Piedras Negras a magnificent dais (Plate 14a) had been deliberately smashed. This destruction might have been the work of invaders, but, equally well or better, it could have been an act of vengeance or spite by revolting peasants, since the dais was the seat of former rule—a sort of razing of the Bastille. It is also possible that the damage is more recent and is attributable to superstitious fear. Modern Mayas believe that stelae, incense burners with faces on them, and suchlike relics of the past house evil spirits which, coming to life at night, cause death and sickness, and they frequently destroy them out of fear (the beautiful murals at Santa Rita, in northern British Honduras were destroyed by Indians probably for that reason, almost as soon as they were uncovered and before they had been completely copied). However, the fact that the figures of gods on the Piedras Negras stelae were not likewise destroyed perhaps indicates that the damage to the throne was inflicted neither by invaders nor by superstitious Indians, but by revolting peasants who attacked the symbol of their civil bondage, but respected the images of their gods.

In Yucatán the epilogue to the fall of the great cities was somewhat different, as we shall see in the next chapter.

In all probability the causes of the collapse will never be surely known, and writers will be speculating on the matter long after this book shall have been forgotten.

Shelley a century and a half ago summed up a like situation in an Old World setting:

> *And on the pedestal these words appear:*
> *"My name is Ozymandias, king of kings:*
> *Look on my works, ye mighty, and despair!"*
> *Nothing beside remains. Round the decay*
> *Of that colossal wreck, boundless and bare,*
> *The lone and level sands stretch far away.*

III. The Decline and Fall of Maya Civilization

Vain the ambitions of kings
Who seek by trophies and dead things
To leave a living name behind,
And weave but nets to catch the wind.
—John Webster (1580?–1623?)

WAX MOTH IN THE MAYA HIVE

In *Actions and Reactions* Kipling published a short parable, "The Mother Hive," the story of the moral and physical degeneration of a hive. Working bees lay eggs; wax moths get into the hive; misshapen oddities are born in increasing numbers; the young bees refuse their duties; circular cells are built; for a time the hive is without a queen. Finally the apiarist and his son open the hive and destroy its contents, except for a very small band of the old good stock which escapes to swarm on a near-by branch, ready to start again.

" 'Why this isn't a hive! This is a museum of curiosities,' said the voice behind the Veil. It was only the Bee Master talking to his son. 'Can you blame 'em, father?' said a second voice. 'It's rotten with wax moth.' . . . 'Aren't you confusing *post hoc* with *propter hoc?*' said the Bee Master. 'Wax moth only succeed when weak bees let them in.' "

Kipling addressed his parable to Edwardian England. For him the key to that moral disintegration was overpopulation; the remedy, emigration. Yet the parable can be applied to any culture, including the Maya, in process of degeneration.

The uncouth oddities and the circular cells of the Maya hive are plain to see, as are its combs riddled with the tunnels of the wax moth. We can only guess at the weaknesses that allowed these conditions to develop and lowered the guard so that the wax moth could enter, the wax moth of Central America being the new concepts and influences of a morally weaker culture which originated in central Mexico. Kipling was not the first to employ this simile of the wax moth; centuries earlier the Maya thus stigmatized those interlopers who imposed these lower standards on them.

Brief mention has been made of the degeneration of sculpture which is visible in the closing days of the Classic period in the Central area. The evidence for this degeneration and the appearance of new concepts is far stronger in Yucatán than in the Central area, which, with the abandonment of the great ceremonial centers, passes from history. For Yucatán there is considerable archaeological evidence for continued, but reoriented, activity, and this is supplemented by historical data.

During the Classic period the Northern area, comprising Yucatán and most of Campeche and Quintana Roo, had developed its own ideas in architecture and sculpture. In architecture the local styles, such as Puuc, Chenes, and Río Bec, differ from architectural styles of the Central area to about the same degree that Perpendicular Gothic of England differs from the contemporary Flamboyant Gothic of France. That is to say, both used the same general principles and concepts, but each had its local character. Yet the unity derived from a common heritage far outweighed regional divergences. In sculpture there is a considerable body of low relief in the Classic tradition, although displaying fairly marked localisms, but there are also other styles with little in common with typical work of the Central area (Plate 15*a*), and yet other carvings which are quite foreign to Classic treatment. Miss Tatiana Proskouriakoff, who has made a special study of this subject, remarks of Yucatecan sculpture that it is "essentially heterogeneous and seems to represent an imperfect fusion of several independent styles." Some sculptures—notably a series of dwarflike figures with distended stomachs which have parallels in the art of southern Veracruz—indicate the presence of non-Maya influences in Yucatán during the Classic period. The little dwarflike figures in their very freakishness seem to reflect an unbalanced culture. Perhaps it is a subjective approach, but a lot of these odd sculptures convey to me messages of cultural unhealthiness or restlessness.

There is, too, a not inconsiderable body of phallic sculpture in Yucatán which probably made its appearance at the close of the Classic period and continued into the Mexican period. The dating of this intrusion is not too secure, but phallic symbols are numerous at Uxmal, which did not long survive the close of the Classic period, and appear in one building of the Classic period at Chichén Itzá. This is the more remarkable in that Maya sculpture of the Central area is entirely free of any such concept. Such ideas are strongly developed in southern Veracruz, and it is rather clear that it was from that region that the cult reached Yucatán. It continued during the Mexican period, and the fact that it was a foreign idea and distasteful to the Maya is brought out in passages in the books of Chilam Balam.

The acceptance of such concepts, even if a minority looked on them as not consonant with the old Maya ideal of moderation in all things, is, I think, symptomatic of a sick culture; the country was ripe for a change.

While Maya civilization had ripened in the sun of the Classic period, its cultural cousins, descended from the same ancestral Formative period, had also blossomed. Great centers such as Teotihuacán, near Mexico City, Monte Albán, standard-bearer of Zapotec civilization in Oaxaca, and various regional cultures in different parts of Veracruz state had developed along their individual lines the common heritage, but giving it a less spiritual, though more successfully material, aspect. As we have seen, strong influences from Teotihuacán, as well as secondary impulses from Monte Albán, had made themselves felt at the highland city of Kaminaljuyú, but at that time the cultures of Mexico had, like the classic cities of the Central area, a dominantly religious setting. Subsequently there seems to have been a shift to a more secular society, which later developed strongly militaristic tendencies. So far as we can now tell, the abandonment of the great ceremonial centers of the Maya Classic period is partly paralleled in Mexico. The sites themselves were not abandoned in most cases, but there was a shift in emphasis from the building of religious structures, such as pyramids, to the erection of large secular edifices, in the form of residential quarters comprising rooms surrounding small patios. This type of structure had existed in the first half of the local equivalents of the Classic period, but, to judge by murals which often adorn its walls, it had housed priests or leaders in a dominantly theocratic organization. Later the building of temples and pyramids yielded first place to secular construction. This shift seems to have been accompanied by a cultural orientation toward warfare as a leading activity in the culture, and to have started about A.D. 400, before the Maya, to the south, had reached the peak of their Classic period. Kaminaljuyú and Teotihuacán were of secondary importance in the late Classic period.

Warfare throughout Meso-America appears to have had its origin in the need for getting captives to sacrifice to the gods. The sun in particular had to be nourished with blood, preferably human. Each evening, after crossing the sky, the sun descended to the underworld, the land of death and of the gods of death, and, traveling across it from west to east during the night, he reached the east in time to rise again each morning. During his nightly passage through the underworld, he took on the qualities of death, so that when he emerged from the underworld at sunrise, he was in part a skeleton and could only recover his body and strength by quaffing blood, preferably human. Successful warfare insured a plentiful supply without depletion of the tribal man power. At the same time it developed, at the expense of the priesthood, a dominant warrior group. Warriors earned special privileges, not only in this world but in the next, as saviors of their people through their ability to keep the gods powerful and friendly.

It is not easy to weigh the motives for any action. To say that the capture of prisoners was the sole object of war in Meso-America would be untrue; the conquest of territory and the imposition of tribute were also important factors in Aztec times and perhaps before, but those may, I think, be regarded as secondary developments which became important after warfare had become a national industry. In any case, the Mexicans were convinced that war did pay, economically and spiritually. They trained young men for warfare; graded their young warriors and gave them privileges according to how many enemies they had captured; and organized military orders

Fig. 11.—Warriors: Mexican and Maya. Itzá warriors with spear-throwers, darts, and round shields (*a* and *b*); a Maya warrior with less efficient
spear and flexible shield (*c*). The warrior in *b*, with his headdress with
bird effigy, his breast ornament, back shield, and non-Maya features,
duplicates figures on buildings at the distant Toltec city of Tula, north of
Mexico City. *a*, from a mural; *b*, *c*, low-relief carvings. All from Chichén
Itzá, about A.D. 1100.

of knighthood. The chief of these were the orders of Eagles and Jaguars, so named because those creatures symbolized the sun in the sky and in the underworld respectively.

Our knowledge of Mexican militarism is derived largely from eyewitness accounts of Spaniards who had known the Aztec military machine or had gotten their material from sixteenth-century informants, but there is good reason for believing that militarism was well developed in central Mexico nearly half a millenium before, for the Toltec of Tula then had the orders of Jaguars and Eagles, and sculptures and murals there bear witness to the importance of militarism.

When Mexican groups moved into Yucatán with their vastly superior military training, organization, and even weapons, there could be little doubt of the outcome, particularly in view of the break-up of the old Classic culture and hierarchy. The Mexicans went into battle with sheaves of darts hurled by means of a mechanical arm, called a spear-thrower (Fig. 11*a, b*); the Maya used a stabbing spear, apparently hurling a volley of these, and then closing in for hand-to-hand fighting (Fig. 11*c*). The Mexican spear-thrower and dart gave their users the advantages of longer range, greater penetration, and vastly superior fire power. It was a New World precedent for Hitler's blitzkrieg against the Polish army of 1939 with its dependence on cavalry.

Probably the Mexican conquest did not achieve totality so far as area was concerned because of the numerical weakness of the invaders, but its influences were spread wide. Accordingly, this period is called the Mexican period.

We have gotten ahead of our story; it is necessary to go back to the end of the Classic period in Yucatán, and give such details as we can about these events and what led up to them.

Most of the Maya cities of Yucatán and Campeche seem to have been abandoned at the same time as those of the Central area or not long thereafter. This is almost certainly true of the great number of sites with Puuc architecture, such as Labná, Sayil, Kabah, and a score of others, and is probably true of the cities with Chenes and Río Bec architecture. So far as the Puuc sites are concerned, excavations have not brought to light pottery of types known to have been used during the Mexican period. The only exception to this rule is Uxmal, where small quantities of sherds attributable to the Mexican period have been found, and where, too, Mexican motifs are more apparent than at any other Puuc site. Uxmal, too, it will be recalled, shows evidence of phallic worship, probably brought from the Gulf of Mexico and adopted by the Mexicans. Alberto Ruz found refuse including two plumbate sherds of export type and other late pottery above the patio floor of the Monjas at Uxmal. This indicates occupation—perhaps reoccupation—in the tenth or eleventh centuries, probably tenuous control by later arrivals, perhaps the Xiu. The latest date at Uxmal, painted on a capstone in the Monjas, probably records A.D. 909. The latest dates at neighboring Puuc sites are A.D. 849 at Oxkintok, a few miles to the northwest, and A.D. 869 at Labná.

At Kabah two door jambs, which bear a date perhaps corresponding to A.D. 879, show figures with spear-throwers and close-fitting jackets of Mexican type. These are probably indicative of the infiltration of Mexican ideas into Yucatán before the main invasion, since the building in which they occur is of typical Puuc style, referable to the Classic period. Norman architecture, it will be recalled, reached England before 1066.

MEXICAN INTRUSION

The big invasion of foreigners and foreign ideas occurred in the century following the end of the Classic period. They derive from Tula, the capital of the Toltec, in the state of Hidalgo, north of Mexico City, and are most apparent at Chichén Itzá. The shortest line by land between these two sites is not less than 800 miles, somewhat less than the distance between New York and Chicago. To us, living in the age of airplanes and the Twentieth Century Limited, that is a matter of a few hours travel; to the peoples of Middle America in the tenth century the distance was immense, for the only form of transportation was shanks' mare or, for members of the aristocracy, a litter (part of the journey might have been accomplished in dugout canoes). Moreover, much of the intervening territory was hostile. Not only were the inhabitants unfriendly, but swamp, forest, and mountains were physical barriers. Yet there are the closest resemblances in the sculptural art, the architecture, the planning, the religious symbolism, and even the details of costume, ornaments, and weapons of the two cities (Plates 6*c*, 8*c*; Figs. 11–13). The extraordinary fact is that nowhere between central Mexico and Yucatán have buildings or sculptures in this distinctive style been found, although it is still possible they may turn up somewhere in southern Veracruz or coastal Tabasco.

Sixteenth-century Spanish accounts and the Maya books of Chilam Balam are at variance concerning who introduced Mexican culture and when. Here we will not list all the possibilities, but follow the interpretation I consider most reasonable, remembering that other interpretations have been proposed and yet others will be advanced before the problem is finally, if ever, solved.

Chichén Itzá, it should be recalled, was a Maya city of some importance during the Classic period, as many buildings in the Maya tradition (Plate 7*a*), sculptures in the Yucatecan classic style, and hieroglyphic texts bear witness. The dated monuments connected with these buildings cluster around the Maya equivalent of A.D. 889, which is approximately the end of the Classic period in the Central area. There is a dubious date of A.D. 909 on the façade of the round tower called the Caracol, which appears to be one of the latest buildings in Maya style (Toltec ornaments were later added to it). There is a transitional building in the inner temple of Kukulcan (inside the later pyramid of El Castillo; Plate 5*a*), which is in Maya style but with certain Mexican motifs, and then come the mass of Toltec buildings. As there are cases in which a Toltec house or wing has been built on to a Maya structure, but no example of the reverse process, it is clear that the Mexican style is later than the Maya. There are also cases of stones in Maya style being reused in Mexican buildings; for example, part of a Maya hieroglyphic stone lintel was recarved to serve as the tail of that typical Toltec feature, a feathered-serpent column, but the reverse is unknown. There is, accordingly, incontrovertible evidence that Mexican architecture is later at Chichén Itzá than the Maya style, and therefore its introduction dates sometime after A.D. 889 or perhaps 909, the latest dates associated with Maya architecture.

From various sources we learn that the Itzá who were foreigners and spoke broken Maya, settled at Chichén Itzá and also that Kukulcan, who was a Mexican leader, seized Chichén Itzá. Bishop

Landa, our best Spanish source on Maya life, says, "The Indians are of the opinion that with the Itzá who settled Chichén Itzá there reigned a great lord called Cuculcan [Kukulcan] . . . and they say that he entered from the west, and they differ as to whether he entered before or after the Itzá, or with them." As, however, a Maya prophecy speaks of both Kukulcan and the Itzá coming again to Chichén Itzá in a katun 4 Ahau, and as in Maya opinion history always repeated itself, it would at first seem that Kukulcan was the leader of the Itzá invasion which seized Chichén Itzá in the Maya katun 4 Ahau which ended in A.D. 987, and introduced Toltec religion, Toltec architecture, and Toltec art.

The problem remains who was Kukulcan and who were the Itzá. Kukulcan (*Kukul*, feather or quetzal; *can*, snake) is the Maya form of the Mexican Quetzalcoatl (*Quetzal*, the quetzal bird, the feathers of which were valued highly in ancient Middle America; *coatl*, snake). Quetzalcoatl was a ruler of Tula who was subsequently deified as god of the planet Venus and as a god of vegetation. Driven out of Tula by the machinations of his rival, the god Tezcatlipoca, he made his way to southern Veracruz or Tabasco, and embarking on a raft, was lost to view. According to another version, on reaching the sea, he made a pyre and cremated himself on it. Then, eight days later (the period of invisibility at inferior conjunction), he reappeared as the planet Venus at heliacal rising. Owing to the abbreviated method of dating used in central Mexico, the date of the expulsion of Quetzalcoatl is not certain, but Mexican archaeologists tend to favor A.D. 978 or a few years later.

That certainly rings the Maya bell (Katun 4 Ahau corresponding to A.D. 967–987), but before we become too sure, it is well to recollect that Quetzalcoatl was also the title of the Mexican high priest, and Quetzalcoatls seem to be as frequent in Mexican history as Roosevelts or Adamses in American public life. It seems almost too good to be true that the historical Quetzalcoatl and his Toltec followers, fleeing Tula, conquered Chichén Itzá. Moreover, other parts of the Maya area have traditions concerning the arrival of Quetzalcoatl.

Aside from the problem of the identity of Kukulcan, there is the mystery of who were the Itzá. Were they Toltec followers of Quetzalcoatl-Kukulcan, or were they some other group, perhaps even a Maya people from Tabasco, such as the Chontal, who had adopted the Quetzalcoatl cult and Toltec culture? At least, Itzá seems to be an old Maya name, for it is recorded for regions far from Yucatán. The terms "foreigners" and "those who speak our language brokenly" could well refer to a Chontal Maya group.

The Book of Chilam Balam of Chumayel has an account of the arrival of the Itzá and the places they passed through after they arrived at Polé. This was a small port in northeastern Yucatán from which people crossed to the island of Cozumel. This account is of interest in several respects. First, there is no mention of Kukulcan during the migration or subsequent events at Chichén Itzá. Secondly, we can deduce that the Itzá were seafaring because they came by sea and to a port by no means the nearest to their point of departure (murals at Chichén Itzá show warriors in canoes off a seacoast village as the marine life shows [Plate 17a]). The Chontal were the great seafarers and traders of Middle America, whereas the Toltec were landlubbers. Thirdly, it reminds us of an old belief in Yucatán that invasions came from both the east and west coasts. Finally, the landing place is of interest in view of the control, at least in later times, of the island of Cozumel by Chontal Maya.

All things considered, I incline to the idea that the Itzá were Chontal Maya who had come under strong Mexican influence in their homeland at the bottom of the Gulf of Mexico, that they invaded Yucatán and from the east coast established themselves at Chichén Itzá before the arrival of the feathered serpent cult, possibly in the year A.D. 918 (one source places the Itzá seizure of Chichén on the date 2 Akbal 1 Yaxkin, whereas another says it was in a Tun [year] 11 Ahau, a combination which gives A.D. 918). I would suppose that they erected the inner Castillo building at Chichén Itzá, which is not pure Maya yet shows no evidence of plumed serpent rites. Later, I think, Kukulcan and some followers arrived in Katun 4 Ahau (A.D. 967–87), and the two groups were welded together, perhaps not a difficult job in view of the strong Mexican strain in Itzá culture. The transformed culture was markedly Toltec in religion, architecture, and social organization and outlook. Because there are influences from Mexico, particularly Veracruz, which are not derived from Tula, it seems best to refer to this period as Mexican rather than Toltec, and to bear in mind the likelihood that the Itzá were at Chichén some sixty years before the official opening date of the Mexican period. Moreover, as Kukulcan traditionally entered from the west, both invasions are accounted for.

The Mexican period of Chichén Itzá lasted for two centuries (i.e., from *circa* A.D. 987 to *circa* A.D. 1185) according to the Maya chronicles; it profoundly altered the Maya way of life. How much territory was ruled by Chichén Itzá at that time is not known; native sources speak of the whole country's being under the domination of Chichén Itzá, but Toltec art and architecture are not widespread outside the capital. We read of the Itzá conquest of cities such as Izamal and Mayapán. Maya sources speak also of a triple alliance between Chichén Itzá, Mayapán, and Uxmal, which lasted for the two hundred years (A.D. 987–1185) of Itzá rule at Chichén Itzá. Yet archaeology shows that Uxmal was deserted during the greater part of those two centuries and Mayapán was of little importance.

This is an interesting example of how archaeology can be used to check Maya accounts, which, as they have come down to us, are not too reliable. A good deal of Maya history was incorporated in prophecies because of the Maya belief that what happened in a certain twenty-year period (the katun) would repeat when that twenty-years repeated. Each katun bore the name and number of the day on which it ended. On account of the construction of the Maya calendar, the katun had to end on the day Ahau, and as the attached numbers ran 1–13, a day such as 4 Ahau would repeat as the closing day and therefore the name of a katun after 260 Maya vague years (actually 256½ of our years because this type of Maya year—the tun—consisted of only 360 days). Again, because of the construction of the Maya calendar, the number attached to the day Ahau which ended each successive katun dropped by two, so that the katuns were named in this sequence: 11 Ahau, 9 Ahau, 7 Ahau, 5 Ahau, 3 Ahau, 1 Ahau, 12 Ahau (1 plus 13 minus 2 equals 12), 10 Ahau, 8 Ahau, 6 Ahau, 4 Ahau, 2 Ahau, 13 Ahau, and after that the count started again with 11 Ahau.

Eighteenth-century Maya antiquaries, trying to write the history of their people at a time when all the old knowledge was passing away, sought to disentangle these references to events which fell in certain katuns and to restore the events to their proper sequence. It is as though in the year A.D. 2500, with nearly all knowledge of

European and American history lost, someone tried to reconstruct it from a couple of notebooks which contained abbreviated entries such as: Battle of Waterloo, '15; Surrender at Yorktown, '81; Defeat of the Armada, '88; Lincoln assassinated, '65; Fall of the Bastille, '89; Kaiser flees to Holland, '18; Battle of New Orleans, '14.

The historian might will decide that the surrender at Yorktown and the defeat of the Armada fell in the same century, the seventeenth, and, linking the Kaiser's flight to Holland with the Battle of Waterloo, place both events in the twentieth century, whereas the battle of New Orleans he might associate with the French and accordingly place it in the eighteenth century. The Maya antiquarians of the eighteenth century had the same problem, save that instead of having to figure out the century, they had to place events in cycles of 260 years. Their answers were not always right. The triple alliance, if such ever existed, probably fell not in the eleventh and twelfth centuries, where they placed it, but in the eighth and ninth, late in the Classic period, when Uxmal flourished; or else the alliance did start when the Itzá conquered Chichén Itzá, but lasted but a few decades, not two centuries. Only those arrangements will meet the archaeological evidence that Uxmal was abandoned in the tenth century or very shortly thereafter.

The Mexican invaders introduced new religious cults, the most important of which was the worship of Quetzalcoatl-Kukulcan, the feathered-serpent god. Everywhere on these new buildings is displayed the feathered snake, its plumed body terminating at one extremity in exaggerated head with open jaws ready to strike, at the other end the warning rattles of the rattlesnake (Plates 8c, 14c; Figs. 12a,c,d, 13b). Plumed serpents writhe on low-relief sculpture, the focus of lines of warriors who pay their god homage; they descend on balustrades which flank steep staircases; they rise behind warriors or priests performing human sacrifice; with head on ground and tail in air they serve as columns in triple doorways; in pairs they pugnaciously face one another with open jaws across cornices of altars, or in more friendly fashion intertwine their bodies to form guilloches reminiscent of Jacobean furniture. The repetition is excessive and monotonous; one is reminded of those Hitler youth rallies with their unending *heils* and swastikas, save that the Chichén artists were not so unimaginative. At Tula the feathered serpent is equally domi-

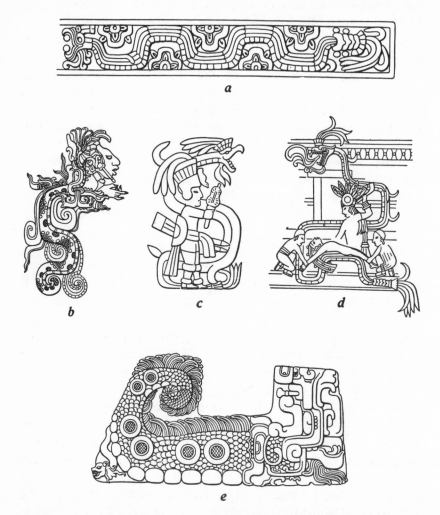

Fig. 12.—Serpents. All are feathered except *b* (Classic Period, Yaxchilán). *e*, one of the rare feathered serpents of the Classic Period (Copán, about A.D. 800). *a*, *c*, *d*, Mexican period, Chichén Itzá (about A.D. 1100); note rattles. In the scene of human sacrifice (from a mural) the victim rests on a coil in the snake's body. His arms and legs are held by attendants; the priest is about to cut out the heart. The warrior in *c* is a typical Toltec Itzá.

nant. Feathered serpents are rare in the art of the Classic period of the Central area, but there are one or two outstanding examples at Copán, which, most significantly, were carved just before the abandonment of that city (Fig. 12e). At that, the treatment is entirely different from that customary at Tula and Chichén Itzá, and one may doubt that they represent the same concept. Other gods came to Chichén Itzá from Tula. Tezcatlipoca, the all-powerful deity who overthrew Quetzalcoatl, is there, but with a far less formidable role; Tlalchitonatiuh, "sun at the horizon," god of the warrior cult, had considerable prestige to judge by the number of times he is represented (Fig. 13c); and Chicomecoatl, "seven snake," a corn goddess, is represented, as in Veracruz, as a headless figure from whose neck seven snakes radiate fanwise. There are, too, representations of the Mexican rain gods, the Tlalocs, but these foreign gods were unable to displace their well-loved Maya counterparts, the Chacs. A Mexican sun god peers earthward from countless solar disks and an earthmonster of Tula origin displaces his less stereotyped Maya cousin.

With these manifestations of a new religion, aggressive militarism is intimately associated. We have already discussed the rise of warfare as the servant of a distorted religion; it remains to note its impact on Maya civilization, for which the best evidence is the art of Mexican Chichén Itzá.

In sculpture and mural one finds line upon line of proud warriors, who face toward an altar where sacrifice is made to the feathered serpent or who receive the surrender of defeated Maya (Plates 8c, 14c). The two groups are recognizable by differences in their costume, and by such details as spear-throwers, the identifying bird on the headdress and the pectoral or helmet ornament, seemingly a conventionalized butterfly, which are worn only by the Mexicans and occur with equal frequency in the art of Tula (Figs. 12c, 11a,b). From every side of countless square temple columns a tall warrior with his weapons gazes vacantly to left or right. Despite minor differences in costume, all look as though they came from the same mold; one almost expects to turn round and find Russia's leader taking the salute before Lenin's tomb. We are no longer dealing with a theocracy, but with a society in which the soldier dominates the priest who had called him into being.

That is not all. On friezes around pyramids and platforms jaguars, pumas, and eagles, symbolizing the military orders, offer the hearts of sacrificial victims to Tlalchitonatiuh, the rising sun (Fig. 13*b,c*), and walls, carved with lines of human skulls impaled on poles grimly recall that Mexican barbarity, the *tzompantli*, "the skull rack," on which the heads of sacrificial victims were placed to the honor of blood-thirsty gods and the glory of the warrior caste. It is, indeed, a sad change from the Classic period, when the current of life flowed more gently.

That these ideas were foreign is demonstrated by the fact that Mexican terms for some of them were adopted by the Maya, presumably because the Maya lacked words for such concepts foreign to their culture. These borrowed words throw light on the new social organization introduced under inspiration from Tula.

With the shift from a theocracy to one in which lay influence, with a strongly militaristic cast, was dominant, we find the following words of Mexican derivation: *tepal* or *tepual*, "lord," and *macehual*, "common people"; *tecpan*, "large community structure" or "royal palace"; *tenamitl*, "fortified or wall town"; *tepeu*, "greatness," "glory."

Now it is obvious that the Maya had rulers long before the Mexican transformation, but, in view of the other terms introduced, we are justified in assuming that the change in rulership was sufficiently marked to necessitate a new word to describe it. The adoption of the term *tecpan*, which describes both a community structure and storehouse for weapons and also the residence of the ruler, as well as the newly adopted words for "fortified town" and "glory," similarly mark the shift from the old pacific and essentially introvert position of moderation to the militaristic and extrovert attitude of the belligerent Mexicans.

Even in words for weapons we can see some new introduction, for the Maya took over Mexican names for "shield" and "banner." They had, of course, shields before the Mexicans arrived and a Maya name for them, so it is probable that the Mexican term refers to some new type of shield introduced by the invaders. The term for "banner" almost certainly refers to the little flags the Mexican warrior wore on his back when he went into action, a custom unknown to the Maya of the Classic period. The Maya also took over the Mexican name for a tight-fitting sleeveless jacket which was sometimes worn by fighters, and they borrowed Mexican armor, a thick-quilted garment of cotton, which was so efficient against native weapons that it was used later by the Spaniards.

In the highlands of Guatemala there was a marked shift after the close of the Classic period from open ceremonial centers to easily defended sites, such as hilltops or tongues of land surrounded on two or three sides by deep ravines. The same thing happened in the Northern area. For instance, Mayapán, which was to become the capital of Yucatán after the decline of Chichén Itzá, is surrounded by a massive stone wall, now in a bad state of collapse, which has a circuit of over five miles and six main gateways.

Tulúm, on the east coast of Yucatán and an important city after the Mexican invasions of Yucatán, has a wall on the land side, enclosing the city on three sides for a distance of nearly eight hundred yards, the fourth being protected by cliff. The walls are ten to fifteen feet high and as much as twenty feet thick, and are pierced by five narrow gateways. These are much better preserved than the ones at Mayapán, and some were clearly made with an eye to defense. In one case the doorway leading to the narrow passage is only four feet high, so that an attacker had to stoop to enter the passage and, coming from daylight into semidarkness, would clearly be at considerable disadvantage. Xelhá and Ichpaatún, also on the east coast, are similarly defended by stout walls. Xelhá, important in the Classic period, was reoccupied in Mayapán times; Ichpaatún and Tulúm were coeval with Mayapán. The evidence indicates that the walls date from the time when Mayapán was dominant. The absence of a city wall at Chichén Itzá supports this view. The process of militarization, then, would have been lengthy, with walls of stone a late consequence of much earlier changes in the pattern of life. "The evil that men do lives after them."

We know from early Spanish accounts that some Maya cities were on islands in lakes and that others were surrounded by palisades. One Maya town was protected by a living wall of maguey. Cortés, on his famous march, passed several fortified Maya towns in north-western Petén, one of which he described as follows: "The town is situated upon a lofty rock, having a great lake on one side and on the other a deep stream which empties into the lake; there is but one accessible entrance, and all is surrounded by a deep moat behind which there is a palisade, breast high; and beyond this palisade there is an enclosure of very thick planks, two fathoms high, with loop-holes at all points from which to shoot arrows; its watch towers rise seven or eight feet higher than the said wall which was also provided with towers, on the top of which were many stones with which to fight from above." (MacNutt translation.) It is interesting to recall that at Tulúm there are small temples at the corners of the walls, from the flat roofs of which the walls could be defended.

In 1934 a Carnegie Institution expedition, under the leadership of Karl Ruppert, discovered in southeastern Campeche a fair-sized Maya city, named Becan, which was surrounded with an artificial moat. This varied in width from ten to over eighty feet and in depth from seven to thirteen feet, and was spanned by seven stone cause-ways either ten or fifteen feet wide. In his report Ruppert notes that there is some evidence that the moat may never have been finished.

Becan is a counterthrust to the argument I have been develop-ing that large-scale warfare and fortifications are due to Mexican influences, for the recognizable architecture at Becan is of the Río Bec type which surely flourished in the second half of the Classic period. It is, of course, possible that the moat was added at a later date or that some buildings, now collapsed, may have belonged to the Mexican period (Toltec-type buildings at Chichén Itzá have structural faults which caused most of them to collapse), but it is rather more probable that the moat was built at the very end of the Classic period when influences from Mexico were already be-ginning to make themselves felt, for there are slight grounds for supposing that northeastern Petén and adjacent parts were the last stronghold of the hierarchy. The possibility that the moat was never completed (its bottom in one part is some sixteen feet higher than where the moat joins a swamp, the probable source of water; some of the causeways are still solid so that water could not circulate from one section to another) lends support to the thesis that this was a last project of the Classic period never completed because of the overthrow of the hierarchy which had initiated the work.

The picture we have, then, is of a complete reorientation of life. Alien gods and an alien ruling class impose a new way of life on the Maya of Yucatán and of the Guatemala highlands; the old agricul-tural life of the peasant continues as before, but now supports new masters who, from regarding warfare as a means to an end, have inevitably found that the means are far more important than the end; warriors organize to serve the gods, but the latter in turn become patrons of warfare.

If the theory that the peasants overthrew the old theocracy because of the burdens it imposed on them is true, we can rest assured that the revolt did them no good; the new rulers set them to work to build new buildings to the honor of the new gods and to the glory of their followers. The chastisement shifted from whips to scorpions.

Parts of Yucatán which did not come under foreign rule were forced to adopt militarism in order to survive. Only the Central area seems to have been generally unaffected by the change, because, apparently, the region was too isolated to invite conquest. There, in the apparent absence of a strong ruling caste, construction of cities seems to have ended. However, as we have noted, the country was not unpopulated. In British Honduras, where archaeological activity and modern road building have been more intensive than in other parts of the core of the Central area, some evidence of a later occupation has come to light: finds of metal (unknown during the Classic period), types of pottery vessels and figurines which are subsequent to the great abandonment, and, at Santa Rita, in the extreme north of the colony, brilliant murals with marked Mexican influence. There was post-Classic activity at Tikal and Topoxte.

We have vivid accounts of Maya reactions to their conquerors, for these, somewhat garbled and partly made to apply also to their Spanish conquerors, survive in the native Maya books, called the books of Chilam Balam. The Maya were particularly shocked by erotic practices introduced by the Itzá, apparently as part of the cult of Quetzalcoatl-Kukulcan. One passage (translation by Ralph Roys) refers to the Itzá in these words: "Their hearts are submerged in sin. Their hearts are dead in their carnal sins. They are frequent backsliders, the principal ones who spread sin, Nacxit Xuchit in the carnal sin of his companions, the two-day rulers. . . . They are the unrestrained lewd ones of the day, the unrestrained lewd ones of the night, the rogues of the world. They twist their necks, they wink their eyes, they slaver at the mouth, at the rulers of the land, lord. Behold, when they come, there is no truth in the words of the foreigners to the land. They tell very solemn and mysterious things, the sons of the men of seven-deserted buildings, the offspring of the women of seven-deserted buildings." *Nacxit* is a name for Quetzalcoatl-Kukulcan. In fact, elsewhere in these books he is called Nacxit Kukulcan in a passage which refers to him as ruler of Chichén Itzá and speaks of the introduction of violence and of sin.

An old song about the Itzá invaders (they are called the Putun people, an old term for the Chontal) appears in the Book of Chilam Balam of Chumayel. Parts of it, as translated by Roys, read: "A tender boy was I at Chichén, when the evil man, the master of the army, came to seize the land. Woe! At Chichén Itzá heresy was favored. *Yulu uayano.* Ho! 1 Imix was the day when the ruler was seized at Chikin Ch'en. . . . We were like tame animals to Mizcit Ahau. An end comes to his roguery. Behold, so I remember my song. Heresy was favored. *Yulu uayano! Eya!* I die, he said, because of the town festival. *Eya!* I shall come, he said, because of the destruction of the town . . . ."

The italicized words are probably Mexican exclamations. *Mizcit* is almost surely the Mexican *mizquitl*, the mesquite bush. A man with that name should be from northern Mexico; mesquite, I believe, does not grow far south of the region of Tula, but many Chontal acquired Mexican names by contacts or intermarriage. Heresy (the original word is a corruption of the Spanish term) must refer to the introduction of a new religion by the invaders; the word is used elsewhere to describe paganism.

The Mexican invaders evolved at Chichén Itzá a new architecture. Basically it was the style of distant Tula, but the Maya corbeled vault was retained. The ritualistic needs of the Maya of the Classic period had called for small narrow rooms which imposed an atmosphere of secrecy (Plate 8*b*; Fig. 8). One passed from a narrow outer room to an inner room, and then sometimes to another inner room or, as at Palenque, to an enclosed shrine in the second room (Figs. 3, 5*c*). Dividing walls were added to rooms to make them smaller, or the doorway to an inner room was not in line with that of the outer room, so that light was deliberately cut off (Fig. 5*d,f*). These are calculated steps to attain privacy and seclusion; mediation between gods and men clearly did not require the presence of many priests within the sanctum. The Maya of the Puuc region had used columns in their outer doorways for perhaps two centuries before the Mexicans came to Chichén Itzá, and a sort of colonnade had developed in cities of the Central area by decreasing the wall space between doorways until the remaining sections of wall had become wide piers. Nevertheless, they never placed columns or piers in the walls dividing an outer from an inner room, clearly because that would nullify the mystery of what went on in the inner room, not because they lacked the intelligence to repeat on the back wall of a room the piercing they had done on the front wall, or feared the extra weight a medial wall must sustain. Exceptionally, two inner rooms at Sayil have columned doorways. The outer rooms perhaps were added later.

Mexican religion, as practiced at Tula and as introduced at Chichén Itzá, clearly was less sacerdotal; the warriors as providers of sacrificial victims shared with the priests an intimacy with the gods; the latter were no longer remote mediators between gods and men. There is a parallel, which must not be carried too far, to this development in the differences between Roman Catholic or Orthodox churches and those of advanced Protestantism. The sanctuary, with its screen or gates, or the separated monastic stalls, together with Lady chapel and side chapels, respond to functions of those churches which have priests; they disappear in Protestant churches where the priest is replaced by a pastor. Instead, we find a large uncompartmented interior dominated by a central pulpit in replacement of the sanctuary. The Classic Maya temple corresponds to the former interior; the Toltec temple to the latter.

The Mexican invaders achieved the spacious interiors they desired by replacing the interior walls of the Maya temple by lines of columns, on which were strung beams which in turn supported corbeled vaults (Plate 8c; Fig. 5g). Usually, short walls partly separated the inner part of the hall from the outer. The builders presumably did not expect their structures to last forever, and so they saw little objection to resting the vaults on wooden beams, usually of sapodilla, the hard wood which yields chicle, but the result was that in time the beams decayed, and the whole roof collapsed. There is not one building of this type of construction now standing at Chichén Itzá, whereas several of the older buildings, erected in the old Maya style, are still intact. Atmospheric conditions surely affect the time a wooden beam will last in Central America; wooden lintels over a thousand years old have survived at Tikal, but at Palenque

I have seen sapodilla beams, placed in position some twenty years ago, already decaying and ravaged by termites. That some of the beams in Mexican buildings decayed before Chichén Itzá was abandoned is shown by sections of walls added in ancient times.

The civic or ritualistic needs of the Mexicans at Chichén Itzá also called for long colonnades, which sometimes were independent of other buildings and sometimes stood before them. These were built on the same principle as the temples in that spaciousness and light were achieved by replacing walls with columns on which beams rested. They stand on low platforms about six feet high and have back and side walls as well as short antae on the front, almost surely added to brace the end walls, but the rest of the front is open. (Plate 6c).

The north colonnade at Chichén Itzá is the most grandiose of these structures. The east end of it was apparently torn down in ancient times, and the part excavated by Carnegie Institution is some two-thirds of the total length, which was in the neighborhood of 425 feet. The interior width is 45 feet, and the roof was formed of five parallel vaults, resting on five lines of columns and the back wall. A large area such as this would hold several hundred people, but except for one dais, in front of which was placed a statue of a reclining god of the type called Chacmol, there is no sign of religious usage (Plate 8c).

I am inclined to think such colonnades were primarily for lay functions, such as meetings of the members of the military orders of Jaguars and Eagles. I call them lay functions, but they were also religious, perhaps reflecting the religious origin of the orders, as in the case of the Knights Templar. In the case of this particular colonnade, its association with the military orders is, I think, proved by its sculptural decoration. The fronts of the antae carried ornaments apparently depicting shields; the back of the platform carried a frieze of jaguars, eagles, pumas, and the like, offering human hearts to the rising sun (cf. Fig. 13c), symbolizing the purpose of the military orders named after those animals. Moreover, the dais or altar was carved with a procession of warriors, around which writhe feathered serpents, and more of those representations of Kukulcan adorn the balustrades of the staircase in front of the building. The frequent representations of these symbols of the fighting orders show the

a

b

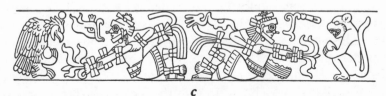

c

Fig. 13.—Elements of Mexican religion at Chichén Itzá. All date from
A.D. 1000 to A.D. 1200.

a: The four Bacabs, set at the four sides of the world to hold up the sky. Each wears
his insignia—a turtle shell, a spider web, and two kinds of shell. They wear special
loincloths and are usually bearded. From columns in the Castillo.

b: Scene of Itzá sacrifice to the sun god, who emerges from the jaws of a rattlesnake. The victim is held by four youthful chacs. They, the high priest, and attendants (some omitted in this drawing) wear Toltec costume. Almost surely a sacrifice
of the orders of Jaguars and Eagles. From a gold disk recovered from the sacred
cenote.

c: Warriors, in guise of eagle and jaguar, symbols of the Toltec military orders,
offer hearts of sacrificial victims to Tlalchitonatiuh, the Mexican god of the rising
sun. From frieze, Temple of the Warriors.

extent to which Mexican Chichén Itzá was dominated by this military complex.

The same kind of temple with interior columns, the same long colonnades, the same processions of warriors with almost identical clothing and weapons, the same feathered serpents, and even the same statues of the recumbent god occur at distant Tula. The stone there is different, the carving is rather more crude, there are no masks of the Maya rain god, and the people of Tula did not use the corbeled vault, but in most other respects the two cultures are as alike as two peas.

Carvings in some of the buildings of Mexican Chichén Itzá show victories over Maya neighbors (probably the greater part of Yucatán never was conquered by the Mexicans). Groups of dejected Maya, easily recognizable by their distinctive costumes and attributes. (Fig. 11c), appear before their conquerors with left hand on right shoulder, sign for peace or surrender. Gold disks dredged from the cenote of sacrifice at Chichén Itzá again show the defeated Maya submissive before their Toltec conquerors.

Presumably the invaders were not sufficiently numerous to keep the area in subjection without local support, and of this there is some evidence in sculpture. It is to be doubted that the invaders made any effort to convert the peasants to the new worship, which may have been regarded as something exclusive and not to be shared with the lower-class natives. They did, however, accept old Maya deities—the masks of the rain gods on their buildings is evidence of that—and they seem to have accepted the old Maya priesthood, for indubitable Maya priests are carved and painted in their temples (the masks of the old Maya rain gods may have been given prominence to conciliate the conquered). It may be significant that in the Temple of the Chac Mool, which lay beneath the Temple of the Warriors, the figures carved on the columns of the outer room are Mexican warriors, while those on the columns of the inner room, or sanctuary, are priests, for the most part Maya (two or three of them do not show head deformation, a Maya practice, and therefore may be Mexicans despite certain Maya details).

The Maya, like the Chinese, seem to be able to absorb and redefine in terms of their own culture foreign ideas and foreign concepts. Just as they have Mayanized Christianity, blending it with native concepts, so they were able slowly to Mayanize their Mexican conquerors and the religion they introduced. There were obviously no limits to a people who in time seem to have identified a Protestant buccaneer as a reincarnation of Kukulcan come to restore liberty.

So far as we can tell, these Mexican or Mexicanized conquerors gradually became Yucatec Maya in speech and outlook, retaining only the boast of their descent from Mexican warriors. The same thing happened in the highlands of Guatemala, for at the time of the Spanish Conquest the ruling families of the Quiché and Cakchiquel were in every respect Maya save for their proud claim that their ancestors came from Tula. A somewhat similar fate overtook the Norman conquerors of England. Yet, these Itzá, as well as the Xiu, who conquered the people of Uxmal shortly before (or after?) that city was abandoned and set up their capital city at near-by Maní, were still regarded as foreigners centuries later when the Spaniards arrived. The Maya books of Chilam Balam disdain them as foreigners, as those who "speak our language brokenly."

The Itzá, of course, gave their name to Chichén Itzá (it means "at the rim of the well of the Itzá"). The name of the city used before their arrival is not surely known, but it may have been Uucyabnal. This could be translated "seven great owners," and reminds one of the seven deserted buildings, from the women of which the Itzá were descended. The invaders presumably married native women. Chichén Itzá was famed as a center of pilgrimage for hundreds of years. Indeed, surreptitious pilgrimages thither continued until some time after the Spanish Conquest.

The focal point of these pilgrimages was the sacred cenote, into which sacrifices, both of persons and valuables, were cast to propitiate the rain gods. When this cult began is not surely known. Some carved jades dredged from its muddy bottom are certainly of Classic workmanship. One, carved at Piedras Negras, bears a Maya date equivalent to A.D. 706, and a jade bead, almost surely carved at Palenque, bears a Maya date equivalent to A.D. 690. The problem is whether these jade objects were kept for several centuries as family heirlooms or as temple treasures and then thrown into the cenote, or whether the cenote cult was already active during the Classic period. Personally, I am inclined to think it was in full swing before the Itzá arrived, but received fresh impetus under the Itzá. Sacrifice to large sheets of water was a widespread and ancient custom in America, yet it may be significant that the Classic Maya buildings at Chichén Itzá are farther away from the cenote than those of the Mexican period. Recently aqualung enthusiasts have recovered large numbers of offerings of pottery vessels from Lake Amatitlán, in the territory of the Pokoman Maya of the Guatemala highlands, and also from Lake Petén. In both cases there were vessels of the Formative period, evidence of the antiquity of such rites.

The sacred cenote (there is another at Chichén Itzá which supplied the city with water and, in later centuries, archaeologists with a bathing pool) is about two hundred feet in diameter, the level of the water is about sixty-five feet below the surface of the ground, and its depth is about seventy feet. A Maya road connects the great court on which stands the temple of Kukulcan (usually called the *Castillo*) with the cenote. However, I have suspected that this causeway may be older than the great court, and excavation might show that it passed beneath the court to join one of the causeways on the far side. The ruined foundations of a temple stand at the edge of the cenote, and it was almost certainly from here that the sacrifices were thrown in.

Dredging of the cenote by Edward Thompson brought to light large quantities of offerings. These include huge quantities of jade, in most cases deliberately smashed, gold disks, copper bells, copper soles for sandals, wooden spear-throwers, idols and labrets of the same material, balls of copal incense, into some of which jades had been pressed, while others had a core of rubber, idols shaped from copal and rubber, pieces of textiles and basketry, as well as skulls and bones. Recently, the Mexican government has recovered more material, including rubber idols, from the cenote by suction, but the scheme entailed much breakage and has been abandoned.

Spanish accounts tell of virgins being cast into the well, a detail which has caught the public imagination. Lurid pictures of fair damsels plunging into the pool are common. Actually, of the identifiable remains, thirteen are of men; twenty-one of children ranging in age from eighteen months to twelve years, and of these half were under six years old. Only eight are of women, seven of them over twenty-one, past the normal age of marriage.

The percentage of children was probably far greater than the 50 per cent of the identified remains because children's skulls are more easily broken than those of adults. This high percentage is understandable, as throughout ancient America where human sacrifice was common, children were offered to the rain gods, and the cenote cult was dedicated to the rain gods.

It seems to me most plausible to suppose that the Mexicans chose Chichén Itzá as their principal city because the cenote cult had already given the center renown throughout Yucatán. There must have been some attraction which caused the Mexicans to pick distant Chichén Itzá rather than one of the larger Puuc cities, and I think it was the cenote cult.

The conquerors also settled at Cozumel, Izamal, Motul, and Mayapán, according to various sources. It is, I think, highly significant that Cozumel was the shrine of the moon goddess, Ixchel, which also drew pilgrims from all parts of the country. Landa compares the pilgrimages to Chichén Itzá and Cozumel with the Christian pilgrimages to Rome and Jerusalem. Furthermore, Izamal, as the home of Kinichkakmo, a manifestation of the sun god, and of Itzamna, one of the greatest of Maya gods, was also a most important shrine. To these places came immense concourses of pilgrims, many of them from quite distant parts. As Itzamna and Ixchel were purely Maya deities, it is logical to suppose that these pilgrimages were in full swing long before the Mexicans came on the scene. Indeed, Izamal's architecture shows that its greatest period fell in early Classic times. Thus the Itzá controlled the three greatest religious shrines in Yucatán of which we have knowledge, and all dedicated to the most important gods of the Maya pantheon. Their conquest must have been deliberate, the outcome of a policy. By seizing these three shrines of the old faith and the old regime, the Itzá could keep a tight control over the old Maya priesthood, and at the same time gain the prestige and the revenue of the pilgrim traffic; by accepting the old Maya gods, they could, perhaps, conciliate the Maya peasant.

According to native sources, Chichén Itzá, Mayapán, and Uxmal together ruled Yucatán for two centuries, clearly those (A.D. 987–A.D. 1185) of which we are speaking. This is difficult to believe: as already noted, Uxmal had surely been abandoned for the second time by the late eleventh century and Mayapán was of little consequence before the close of the twelfth century. There had been an earlier city at or near the site of Mayapán, for its buildings became a quarry of finely dressed stone of Puuc style for late comers, but not a single building of the earlier city survives. The carved stelae of Mayapán perhaps came from the earlier city, but the style is late; none can be dated. I think that the best guess—and it can be no more than a guess—is that Uxmal soon dropped out of the picture and the third place in this triple alliance was taken by Izamal. Thereby, the triple alliance became an all-Itzá affair.

After two hundred years, war put an end to the alliance. Choosing again between conflicting versions, I think the explanation given below best fits the facts, although quite different reconstructions have not a little in their favor, and in the opinion of some students the incidents now to be related should be brought forward another two and one-half centuries.

The central character in this turning point in Maya history was a certain Hunac Ceel, also called Cauich. His first appearance on the Maya—or perhaps we should say Maya-Mexican—stage was at that most dramatic moment, a sacrifice to the rain gods at the sacred cenote of Chichén Itzá. It was customary to draw out at midday anyone still alive or one of several victims still alive (the old accounts are not too clear about this), and the rescued victim then gave a message from the rain gods as to whether the year would be one of rain or drought. Hunac Ceel Cauich was present at one of these sacrifices, and when no victim survived to bring back the prophecy, he dived into the well to get it himself. The dramatic story is given in Maya in the Book of Chilam Balam of Chumayel, and, as translated by Ralph Roys, reads:

"Then those who were to be thrown arrived; then they began to throw them into the well that their prophecy might be heard by their rulers. Their prophecy did not come [i.e., all were drowned]. It was Cauich, Hunac Ceel Cauich was the name of the man there, who put out his head at the opening of the well on the south side [the sacrificial temple stood on the south rim]. Then he began to take it. Then he came forth to declare the prophecy. Then they began to declare him ruler. Then he was set in the seat of the rulers by them. Then they began to declare him head-chief. He was not the ruler formerly."

Hunac Ceel, as Roys has remarked, was "evidently of the stuff of which rulers are made, a man with sufficient courage and force of character to shape his own destiny." He was head-chief of Mayapán, of which city, one suspects, he was a native, perhaps the son of a chief of that town. Evidently he became head-chief of both cities, and proceeded to make Mayapán the principal city in the alliance. A certain Chac Xib Chac was the ruler of Chichén Itzá, and if, as seems to be the case, this incident is subsequent to Hunac Ceel's plunge into the sacred cenote, we must assume that he governed Chichén Itzá for Hunac Ceel. The ruler of Chichén Itzá, presumably Chac Xib Chac, stole the bride of Ah Ulil, the head-chief of Izamal, during the wedding festivities, and because of this, Hunac Ceel, supported by a group of Mexicans, drove the ruler of Chichén Itzá and his followers from the city.

This Maya version of the Helen of Troy theme refers to the treachery of Hunac Ceel, but of what precisely this treachery consisted we do not know. Did Hunac Ceel side with Izamal against his own subordinate, or, by appearing to support Chac Xib Chac, did he maneuver so that a split occurred between Chichén Itzá and Izamal, and then throw his support to Izamal, perhaps the weaker of the two? We can only speculate, but it does not seem unreasonable to suppose that Hunac Ceel doubted the loyalty of Chichén Itzá and, fearing that his subordinate there was plotting with Izamal to overthrow him, smashed that potential threat by some fancy double-crossing. Whatever actually happened, Chac Xib Chac was "trampled upon," as the Maya book puts it, and the Itzá were driven from Chichén Itzá. Izamal disappears from history at the same time. Hunac Ceel, having disposed of Chichén Itzá with the aid of the brideless ruler of Izamal, turned on his ally, and defeated him, apparently in the determination to eliminate all rivals. There is a laconic and obscure statement that the sons or son of holy Izamal were given in tribute "to feed and nourish Hapay Can." Hapay Can, "sucking snake," is the name of a Maya deity, and as sacrificial victims nourished the gods, one can be reasonably sure that Izamal had to supply sacrificial victims, presumably because of its defeat, to nourish this god.

There is archaeological evidence of the destruction and looting of Chichén Itzá. For instance, in the case of the Temple of the Warriors and its surrounding colonnades, sculpture had been toppled down from the top of the pyramid under circumstances which ruled out natural decay and collapse, and there was evidence that this destruction took place before the buildings began to collapse. The Maya customarily placed dedicatory offerings under altars. Looters, searching for such a cache, had dug a hole through the red stuccoed top of the altar in the colonnade at the foot of the stairway to the Temple of the Warriors. Later someone had filled in the hole and resealed it with white stucco before the roof of the colonnade collapsed. The looters had been successful, for in the debris thrown back into the hole, in addition to fragments of the original red stucco of the pierced surface, was part of the pottery vessel, originally at least fourteen inches in diameter, which had held the offering. Later, pilgrims and squatters had strewn large incense burners and red-slipped dishes of the subsequent Mayapán period over the debris of collapsed vaulted roofs of temple and colonnade. In fact, the sacred cenote continued to draw pilgrims until the Spaniards succeeded in suppressing the cult around A.D. 1560. There is evidence that Chichén Itzá had largely reverted to forest by the time the Spaniards arrived, although the approach to the sacred cenote and two or three of the adjacent structures were kept cleared.

There is much evidence of a hand-to-mouth existence at Chichén Itzá in those three hundred years between the expulsion of the Itzá group by Hunac Ceel and the coming of the Spaniards. Buildings fell into semiruin and were abandoned or shored up with emergency walls. In a corner of one colonnade a small makeshift room had been constructed, and built into the crude walls were sculptured stones robbed from the façade of the building and even from the dais or altar! Clearly these last dwellers at Chichén Itzá had little interest in the glory of their predecessors. As already noted, the east end of the great colonnade which flanks the south side of the Temple of the Warriors was without much doubt torn down at this time, and the stones in all probability were used to build mean little buildings, of which over fifty are scattered haphazard in the adjacent court, for these contain many reused column drums.

There is evidence that the decay of Chichén Itzá must have started almost as soon as Hunac Ceel triumphed. In debris formed by the partial collapse of the round tower called the Caracol was found intact a vessel of the ware called plumbate which had obviously been deposited after the building had started to fall. Plumbate pottery was carried in trade all over Middle America during the eleventh and twelfth centuries, but early in the thirteenth century its export and probably its manufacture ceased. We can, therefore, be reasonably certain that buildings at Chichén were falling into ruin about A.D. 1200, which is approximately the date of Hunac Ceel's conquest of the city.

CENTRALIZED GOVERNMENT
AT MAYAPÁN

With the defeat of the Itzá group at Chichén Itzá and the apparent elimination of the Itzá group in control of Izamal, Hunac Ceel and the Itzá of Mayapán appear to have gained complete control of northern Yucatán, and probably of the once populous Puuc region as well, although the ceremonial centers of that region had long been abandoned.

For the next two and one-half centuries (approximately A.D. 1200–1450), Mayapán controlled Yucatán, both politically and, through its domination of Chichén Itzá and Izamal, in religious matters. The rulers of Mayapán kept a tight control of Yucatán by the simple expedient of making the head-chiefs of the various city states reside in Mayapán. The emphasis was definitely on centralized government, and the head-chiefs can have had no encouragement to advocate states' rights. At this same time powerful rulers in Western Europe had a similar policy, customarily retaining the sons of rulers as hostages for the good behavior of subordinate or rival kingdoms.

How many Maya states were controlled by Mayapán at this time (approximately A.D. 1200–1450) is not certain, for we do not know the exact boundaries of Mayapán's rule, but the number was probably just about one dozen, and the total area about equaled that of Massachusetts and Connecticut together; but one must think of those states with their seventeenth-century communications, not as they are today.

Architecture and pottery show many sites on the east coast of Yucatán, including walled Tulúm, and as far south as Santa Rita in northern British Honduras had their greatest expansion during Mayapán's dominance. Even in the Petén, core of lowland Maya Classic, buildings and pottery related to those of Mayapán occur, notably on the little island of Topoxté in Lake Yaxhá (note the defensive position). At Tikal there is evidence of late intrusions probably of this same period and conceivably the work of Itzá pilgrims from Tayasal (p. 153). Also on the Tabasco plain various centers flourished at the same time as Mayapán.

The ruins of Mayapán are extensive. Mention has already been made of the great wall which surrounds the city, and within which, according to Bishop Landa, the head-chiefs of the states had their residences. A careful map made in 1950–51 by Morris Jones of the United States Geological Survey reveals the remains of some 3,600 structures, the vast majority of which are rather clearly residential. Indeed, there are very few buildings which can be regarded as definitely religious in function. Most of the latter form a small ceremonial center surrounded by residential mounds. Even if one assumes

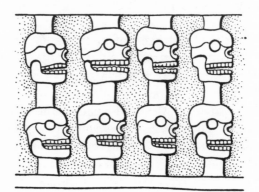

that not all the structures were in use at the same time, a conservative estimate would place the population as not less than 10,000.

Here, then, we have a remarkable shift from the old ceremonial center, never permanently inhabited, to regular populated cities.

This, of course, marks the next and inevitable stage in the change from a fairly peaceful theocracy to a warlike lay autocracy. Once a state decides to live by the sword and to rule its neighbors with the sword, it must seek to increase and concentrate its population to carry out that policy, and there must be a shift from a predominantly agricultural economy. In this connection it may well be significant that Mayapán is situated in a most infertile region and the city is literally built on rock. Rock ledge covers the surface everywhere, and pockets of soil are rare. The surrounding country is largely of the same nature, and no honest farming community would deliberately choose such territory for settlement.

The group that made Mayapán the capital clearly did not have a farmer's outlook. To them the richness of the soil was not of great consequence because they expected to get their bread not by the sweat of their own brows but by that of their tributaries. Intimidate your neighbors by the might of your military organization, and you can be assured of plenty in return for a minimum of effort. This seemingly rose-strewn path has been traveled countless times by militaristically organized groups and by aggressive dictatorships in the course of world history, but always the roses show their thorns, the trail becomes worse and leads sooner or later to the abyss. Power corrupts and weakens its holders; every culture and every dictatorship must live by the sweat of its brow if it is to survive, for that is its essential sacrifice. The Mayapán regime was no exception.

Mexican Chichén Itzá had marked a decided falling off from the artistic attainments of the Classic period, and the almost complete absence of hieroglyphic texts during that period is evidence that there was an intellectual retrogression. The showy, but unstable, architecture of Mexican Chichén Itzá is yet another indication of the deterioration in values which accompanied the militaristic order. There is an even sharper decline in the arts with the rise of Mayapán. The temple of Kukulcan at Mayapán, although it stands on a fairly large pyramid, is a doll's size reproduction of that at Chichén Itzá and definitely lacked a vaulted roof; the round temple, now a mass of rubble, similarly cannot have held a candle to the Caracol at Chichén Itzá. Moreover, the religious buildings at Mayapán are few in number.

In view of the great concentration of power at Mayapán, with labor presumably available from the subordinate states, the paucity of temples there is surely significant. It wasn't that the rulers of Mayapán could not erect a grand ceremonial group, but, rather, that they were not interested in doing so. Religion had lost its predominant place in the culture; warfare introduced to bring man closer to his gods had become the master. The Itzá had journeyed far through time and space to learn that the end never justifies the means, but is itself warped and shaped by them. The Spaniards in their relations to the Maya were to repeat that mistake in the sixteenth century. Indeed, the same false doctrine has been embraced over and over again down the centuries, and has countless followers to this day, particularly east of the Oder.

The architecture of Mayapán reveals a sad degeneration from that of Mexican Chichén Itzá. The tile-like veneer of the Temple of the Warriors, the great ball court, the Temple of Kukulcan, and other buildings of the great Mexican period at Chichén Itza—which was used by earlier builders in that locality—is unknown in the period of Mayapán's dominance. Instead, undressed rough blocks of stone were everywhere used. They are unbelievably crude, and would make one think of developmental stages in stone architecture were it not known that they represent decadence. The Mayapán masons covered up these stone chunks with heavy overlays of stucco to produce whitened sepulchers, like heavy make-up to hide wrinkles.

There are many short colonnades at Mayapán, for the most part crude and puny imitations of the colonnades at Chichén Itzá, but, unlike those of the great period at Chichén Itzá, they are often not attached to any temple, but stand alone. The column drums in those buildings at Chichén Itzá are carefully cut, whether they are round or square; at Mayapán they are pieces of rocks of varying height roughly pecked to an approximation of roundness. Imagine seven or eight gladioli corms stacked one on top of the other, and you have a Mayapán column in miniature. The spaces between the uneven drums were filled with small rocks, spalls, and mortar, and the application of a thick coating of stucco hid the transgressions, but it was jerry-building of the worst kind.

The colonnades, unlike those of the early Mexican period at Chichén Itzá, lacked corbeled vaulting. In some cases the roofs appear to have been of mortar laid over a flat wooden roof; in others, judging by the paucity of debris in the collapsed buildings, thatching was probably used. The function of these smallish colonnades is conjectural; they may have been buildings for civil administration or men's houses. Some probably were for the warriors of the orders of Jaguars and Eagles.

The many house mounds, evidence that Mayapán was a true city, vary in size and complexity from the very simple single room with a single course of stones forming the bases of its perishable walls to the imposing stone buildings which housed the nobility.

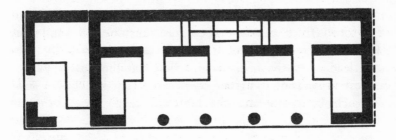

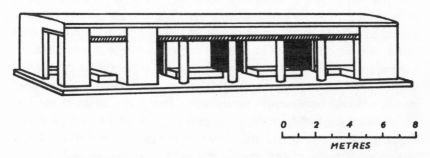

0   2   4   6   8
METRES

Fig. 14.–A noble's house at Mayapán. Plan and elevation of stone building with beam and mortar roof (structure Q–208) burned at destruction
of Mayapán. Exact height is uncertain, perhaps two or three feet higher.
Note shrine with altar occupying central rear room.

One such noble's house I excavated at Mayapán consisted of a long front room with three smallish rooms behind, and another, of medium size at one end (Fig. 14). The front room, a little over fifty feet long by eleven feet wide, was really a sort of enclosed portico or verandah, for the front was open except for four stone pillars and short end walls which carried the roof. The back wall was pierced by three doorways leading to the back rooms. Between the doorways and against the end walls of the front room were four benches of solid masonry, each about eighteen inches high and faced with well-dressed stone slabs robbed from earlier buildings. There is little doubt that these served both as beds and as seats or couches on which guests and host sat tailor-fashion or with one leg dangling over the side like persons are shown in reliefs and frescoes (Plate 18c). A large bench occupied much of the end room. Perhaps occupants of it had complained of a draft, for the open space at the foot of the bench had been walled up at some time or other.

The center back room had been the family shrine, and against its back wall stood a small altar. There is evidence that in this late period family ancestor worship became very important, and a residence of the nobility had its own little chapel, either in a back room, as here, or in a detached building. The roof had been of large wooden beams supporting smaller transversal poles; over these and squeezed into the chinks between the poles was a layer of pebbles in mortar. Often there is a family ossuary beneath the floor in this type of residence which was opened for the insertion of a new body as necessary, but no such convenience was found in this particular building, although several burials of children were under the floor. It is probable, but the evidence was inconclusive, that near-by buildings in the group were for servants and for a kitchen. Maya kitchens were and still are usually in detached buildings, nowadays a thatched structure behind the house.

A family could have lived very comfortably in this home. The wide openings on the front and the high ceiling kept the front room cool in summer, and as the building faced south, the worst effects of the cold "northers" in winter would have been avoided. Arson and pillage brought a sudden end to this pleasant life.

Masses of charcoal into which the timber of the roof had been turned lay on or just above the plaster floor of the main room under

a: Tzotzil, Chiapas. (*Photography by Giles G. Healey.*) *b*: Lacandón
man. (*Photograph by Giles G. Healey.*) *c*: Chol. (*Courtesy Middle
American Research Institute, Tulane University.*) *d*: Yucatec woman.

PLATE I.—Portraits of Present-day Maya

a

b

a: A part of Uaxactún with the "palace" in foreground in its final form. *b*: Copán. The great court with stelae in left foreground. Center foreground, the ball court with hieroglyphic stairway. Copán River in background. (*These, like all the restorations drawn by Miss Tatiana Proskouriakoff, accurately incorporate all archaeological data. Guesswork is minimal.*)

PLATE 2.—Reconstructions of Maya Cities

a

b

a: The "palace" at Sayil, Yucatán, Puuc style of about A.D. 850. Much of the original is well preserved.   *b*: A part of Piedras Negras at its peak, about A.D. 800. Note lines of stelae. (*Courtesy University Museum, Philadelphia.*)   (*Drawings by Tatiana Proskouriakoff.*)

PLATE 3.—Reconstructions of Maya Buildings

a

b

a: Temple on east side of great court, height about 158 feet. Note stumps of smashed stelae on left.   *b*: Temple on west side of great court, height about 145 feet, with two other temples in background rising above tree-tops.   (*Courtesy British Museum and Peabody Museum, Harvard University.*)

PLATE 4.—Pyramids and Temples, Tikal

a: El Castillo, Chichén Itzá, the so-called Temple of Kukulcan. Early Mexican period, about A.D. 1000. *b*: Temple of the Inscriptions, Palenque, A.D. 692. Inside is the secret stairway leading to the burial chamber beneath the center. *c*: Pyramid E–VII sub, Uaxactún. This stuccoed pyramid is of the Formative period, about A.D. 325. Note stela in front of main stairway. A later pyramid which encased this one was removed, revealing the earlier building in almost mint condition.

PLATE 5.—Pyramids

a

b

c

a: The ball court, Copán, as it is now. Note central playing alley with three markers, the sloping sides, and the temples on each side.   *b*: The "nunnery" quadrangle and the Temple of the Adivino, Uxmal, about A.D. 900. (*Drawing by Tatiana Proskouriakoff.*)   *c*: Temple of the Warriors, Chichén Itzá, after excavation; colonnade in front. Typical architecture of the Mexican period, about A.D. 1150.

PLATE 6.—Architectural Groups

a

b

a: Temple of Three Lintels, Chichén Itzá, a pre-Mexican building of the Classic period, about A.D. 875. The lattice pattern represents the markings on the bodies of snake monsters; the corner masks represent the heads.   *b*: Temple at Xpuhil, Quintana Roo, in Río Bec style, about A.D. 875. The towers take the form of miniature temple-topped pyramids, but the steps are too narrow to climb and the temples, with their roof combs, are dummies. (*Drawing by Tatiana Proskouriakoff.*)

PLATE 7.—Buildings

a　　b

c

a: Gateway of quadrangle of the "nunnery," Uxmal, looking out (cf. Plate 6*b*). Note tenoning of vault stones and line of capstones. (*Courtesy Middle American Research Institute, Tulane University.*)　*b*: Interior of a room of the "nunnery," Uxmal, about A.D. 900.　*c*: North colonnade, Chichén Itzá, showing how wide rooms were attained in the Mexican period by resting the vaults on wooden beams supported by columns. Note dais or altar and the reclining figure of the kind called Chacmol, a Mexican deity. About A.D. 1150. (*Drawing by Tatiana Proskouriakoff.*)

PLATE 8.—Maya Corbeled Vaulting

a   b

a: Stela 13, Piedras Negras, A.D. 771. (*Courtesy University Museum, Philadelphia.*)   *b*: Stela 10, Seibal, A.D. 849. Erected some sixty years before the collapse of the Classic period, it displays late mannerisms and incipient decadence. Both personages wear short skirts of jaguar skin. (*Courtesy Peabody Museum, Harvard University.*)

PLATE 9.—Stelae

a

b   *c*

a: Incised panel, Bonampak, showing offerings to personage on dais. Style is early, perhaps about A.D. 600. *b*: Part of Stela 40, Piedras Negras, A.D. 746. The maize god scatters corn. Note maize headdress and seed bag in left hand. *c*: Part of Stela 51, Calakmul, A.D. 731.

PLATE 10.—Sculpture

a   *b*

a: Stela H, Copán, A.D. 731. An approach to sculpture in the round.
b: Stela F, Quiriguá, A.D. 761, height twenty-four feet. Note treatment
of plumage on side, shield, and elaborate sandal heels. (*Courtesy British
Museum.*)

PLATE 11.—Stelae

a

b

a: Kneeling person makes blood offering. The cord, set with thorns, is passed through a hole in his tongue. The blood spatters on paper in the basket. Note diagonal effect produced by spear and glyph panels countering the kneeler. *b*: Kneeling person offers vessel with blood-spattered paper to god emerging from the jaws of the serpent. Both lintels from the same building, about A.D. 750. (*Photographs courtesy British Museum.*)

PLATE 12.—Sculpture: Lintels from Yaxchilán

a

b

a: Top of Lintel 26, Yaxchilán. Person on right holds jaguar head. Note head deformation, typical Maya eye, receding chin, and jacket of man on left. A.D. 720. (*Photograph by Giles G. Healey.*) *b*: Part of design on lid of newly discovered sarcophagus, Temple of the Inscriptions, Palenque, probably A.D. 692. Reclining or falling figure on the headdress of a terrestrial monster. Behind rises the base of a world-directional tree with grotesque face on it. Note elongated hand and foot. (*Photograph by Don Leonard.*)

PLATE 13.—Sculpture from Yaxchilán and Palenque

a

b

c

a: Back of a dais or altar, Piedras Negras. The design represents the head of a dragon monster with human figures looking out of the eye sockets, A.D. 786. (*Courtesy University Museum, Philadelphia.*) *b*: Front of Lintel 39, Yaxchilán. The reclining figure holds a double-headed serpent with head of long-nosed god in each mouth. A.D. 780. (*Courtesy Peabody Museum, Harvard University.*) *c*: Dais or altar, Mercado, Chichén Itzá, Mexican period, about A.D. 1150 (cf. Plate 8*c*).

PLATE 14.—Sculpture

a

b

a: Dancing figures on Stela 9, Oxkintok, Yucatán. A regional style, A.D. 849. *b*: Classic Maya profile, Ruz Tablet, Palenque, about A.D. 725. (*Courtesy Instituto Nacional de Antropología e Historia, Mexico.*)

PLATE 15.—Sculpture, Dynamic and Static

a: Stucco head, Palenque. Classic type of beauty, about A.D. 700. (*Courtesy Instituto Nacional de Antropología e Historia, Mexico.*) *b*: Grotesque head, Copán, about A.D. 800. *c*: Façade ornament, Uxmal. Tattooed head in snake's jaws, about A.D. 900. *d*: Façade ornament, Chichén Itzá. Head in snake's jaws. Mexican period, about A.D. 1150.

PLATE 16.—Sculpture in the Round

a

b

a: Temple of the Warriors, Chichén Itzá, Mexican period, about A.D. 1150. Soldiers in canoes in foreground; village behind. Note trees, feathered serpent, and women tending pot on fire. *b*: Bonampak, about A.D. 800. Trumpeters and masked dancers to left; musicians beating turtle shells, an upright drum, and men with rattles to right. (*From water colors by Ann A. Morris and Antonio Tejeda F.*)

PLATE 17.—Murals

a: Masked and winged dancers. Note elongation of arms and legs and elimination of bodies. Copán, about A.D. 800. *b*: In the same tradition as *a*. Man with jaguar mask bows before occupant of house or temple. El Salvador, about A.D. 800. *c*: Naturalistic treatment. Two kneelers before individual on dais. Note feather cloak, shield, basket, and jaguar cushion at back of dais. Near Flores, Petén, about A.D. 750. (*From water colors by Antonio Tejeda F.*)

PLATE 18.—Painted Pottery

a

b

c

d

a: Vessel of plumbate ware. This,
the only glazed pottery in ancient
America, was traded far and wide. About A.D. 1000. b: Vessel of thin
orange ware from a tomb at Kaminaljuyú, about A.D. 550. This ware was
also traded widely, but at an earlier date. c: The jaguar god of the
underworld is seated on the rim; the bust of a youthful god is on the
front. Hun Chabin, Comitán, Chiapas, perhaps about A.D. 800. d: Vessel and lid representing a hunchback, about A. D. 550. Painted in pastel
colors after firing. From tomb at Kaminaljujú. (a and d from water
colors by Antonio Tejeda F.)

PLATE 19.—Modeled Pottery

a: Seated woman, Palenque, about
A.D. 750. Note delicate treatment
of features. (*In Museo Nacional de Antropología, Mexico.*) *b*: Seated
man, Simojovel, Chiapas, about A.D. 750. (*In Museo Regional, Tuxtla.*)
c: Woman with child and dog, Xupa, Chiapas, about A.D. 750. (*Courtesy Middle American Research Institute, Tulane University.*) *d*:
Seated woman, Cobán, Alta Verapaz, Guatemala, about A.D. 750. Note
width of face. (*From a drawing by Antonio Tejeda F.*)

PLATE 20.—Pottery Figurines

a

b

a: Perhaps the finest known jade, about A.D. 750. Found by A. Ledyard Smith, of Carnegie Institution of Washington, with other jades and pottery in a cache at Nebaj, Guatemala. *b*: Said to have been found at Teotihuacán, but clearly of Maya workmanship, about A.D. 800. It is nearly six inches tall. (*Courtesy British Museum.*)

PLATE 21.—Carved Jade

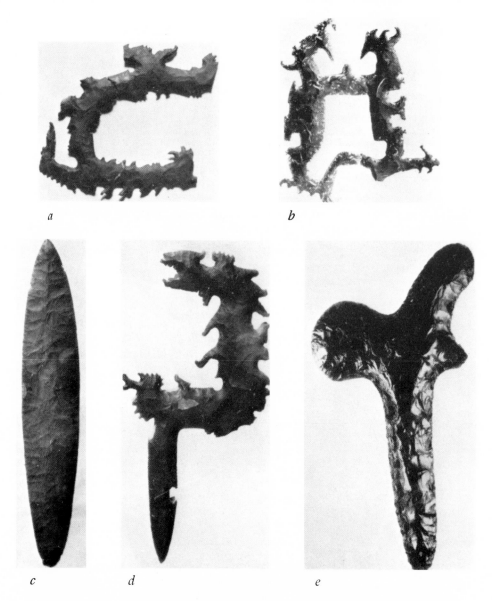

a: Eccentric flint representing a man with elaborate headdress and blade in his hand. Width, nearly six inches. Copán, about A.D. 750. *b*: Eccentric flint with profile head at each corner, slightly over one foot high. From beneath a stela dated A.D. 746, at El Palamar, Quintana Roo. *c*: Flint blade nearly eighteen inches long. From beneath stela dated A.D. 780, at Quiriguá. *d*: Flint dagger, the handle perhaps representing a plumed serpent, nearly nine inches long. From beneath a stela dated A.D. 790, at Quiriguá. *e*: Obsidian axe for ceremonial use, almost one foot high. Base of the haft once covered with pink stucco. About A.D. 950. San José, British Honduras. (*Courtesy Chicago Natural History Museum.*)

PLATE 22.—Flint and Obsidian

a   *b*

Two stucco heads recently found beneath the slab (Plate 13*b*) over the tomb in the secret crypt beneath the Pyramid of the Inscriptions, Palenque. This superb example of Maya modeling dates from about A.D. 690. (*Photographs by Señora Carmen Cook de Leonard.*)

PLATE 23.—Stucco Heads

a

b

a: Arch at Labná.   *b*: Reconstruction of the palace.   (*Drawing by Tatiana Proskouriakoff.*)

PLATE 24.–Labná

Part of late Formative (Miraflores) stela from Kaminaljuyú, Guatemala highlands, about A.D. 1, with glyph in top left corner. Deity holds up axe-like object. The trident element obscuring eye is the god's identifying attribute which appears also in later lowland sculpture.

PLATE 25.—Formative Sculpture

a

b

a: Chutixtiox, Department of El Quiché, on top of steep hill and surrounded on three sides by the Río Negro. The only easy access (left background) was defended by a wall. The acropolis with ball court attached in center foreground. Site is proto-historic, approximately A.D. 1300–A.D. 1520. *b*: Chalchitán, Department of Huehuetenango. The ball-court group, part of this large, undefended site built chiefly during the Classic period before the rise of militarism, but also occupied in the post-Classic period. (*Restoration drawings by Tatiana Proskouriakoff.*)

PLATE 26.–Sites, Guatemalan Highlands

a: Large pottery incense burner with head of jaguar god of the under-world and number seven wearing mask and bird headdress. Palenque, about A.D. 700. *b*: Crude factory-assembled incense burner from Maya-pán, about A.D. 1400. *c*: Burner with seated figure on mask. Teapa, Tabasco, about A.D. 700.

PLATE 27.—Incense Burners, Palenque, Teapa, and Mayapán

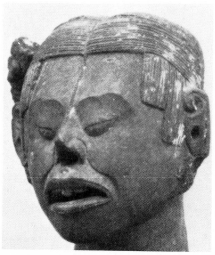

a   *b*

a: Mosaic jade mask which once covered the face of the chief buried in the crypt of the Temple of the Inscriptions, Palenque. (*After A. Ruz.*) *b*: Pottery head of woman (?) with filed teeth. (*Museo Regional, Tuxtla.*)

PLATE 28.—Mosaic Mask and Pottery Head

Youthful head with rings around eyes, but not to be regarded as Tlaloc.
Relief from façade of building, Copán. Height, approximately 22 inches.
(*Courtesy British Museum.*)

PLATE 29.—Relief Sculpture, Copán

Superb example of late Classic figure-painting from a burial at Altar de Sacrificios. The person wears a pair of tailored snakeskin trousers. Tailoring is very uncommon among primitive peoples. The closed eye and mark on cheek suggest that the man may represent the god Xipe Totec. About A.D. 750. (*Courtesy Peabody Museum, Harvard University.*)

PLATE 30.—Figure with Snake on Vase

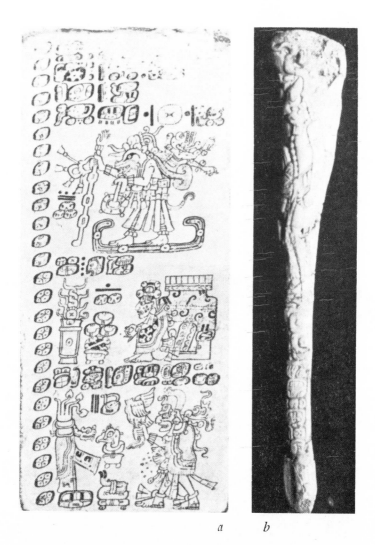

a   *b*

a: Page of Codex Dresden with ceremonies for a new year starting with
day Lamat. Top, a world-directional god called Bacab disguised as an
opossum (the Bacabs were called opossum actors) brings in the death
god on his back. Center, the death god in his temple. Bottom, a priest,
impersonating the god Itzamna, offers a beheaded turkey to the holy
acante post set up for the new year. This last is expressed rebus fashion
as *acan*, a plant with heart-shaped leaves, *can*, "snake," to confirm the
acan reading. The wood sign (*te* or *che*) is on the bark of the post, the
ku, "god" or "divine," inside indicates that the post is of the holy cedar
(*kuche*) wood. The post is set on the rock pile. Turkey tamales and
haunches of venison also are offered.   *b*: Carved bone with bearded
figure and glyphs. Copán.

PLATE 31.—Written Page and Carved Bone

Front end of huge boulder, Altar P, at Quiriguá, carved as a double-headed celestial dragon. The personage is seated in the monster's open mouth. Panels of glyphs decorate its open jaws. One pair of its teeth project on each side of the person's headdress, a second pair touch his arms, and a third pair, set in the monster's lower jaw, are on each side of the person's crossed legs. A.D. 795. (*Courtesy School of American Research, Santa Fe, N. M.*)

PLATE 32.—Sculptured Figure, Quiriguá

or mingled with the pebbles and mortar of the topping. A breach in the plaster top of the family altar was evidence of looting. A small stone idol and two rather fancy pottery jars which may once have stood on or before the altar were beneath the debris. As it would have been almost impossible for the roof timber to have caught fire accidentally, it seems a fair conclusion that the building was sacked and deliberately burned when, as history tells us, Mayapán was looted and destroyed about A.D. 1450. In the debris were two small polished celts of greenish stone, valuable in Maya eyes. I think they must have been tucked away in some obscure place and so overlooked by the looters.

There is a very marked degeneration in sculpture and in pottery at Mayapán paralleling that in architecture. As noted (p. 123) the reliefs of Mexican Chichén Itzá lack the beauty and spontaneity of Maya carving of the Classic period, but the worst one can say is that they are dull and repetitious; in contrast, sculpture of the subsequent period at Mayapán is downright bad and pitiably crude.

Pottery is extremely dull. That made locally is of poor workmanship and none is polychrome. I except the bright paints of incense burners discussed below, for they were added after firing and rub off easily. Very little pottery was imported. During the domination of Chichén Itzá large amounts of untempered pottery of the types of Fine Orange ware archaeologists call X (different from the Type Y of Altar de Sacrificios, p. 107) were imported. They are gay and attractive, with pleasing shapes and designs. With them came the strange glazed pottery called plumbate from the Pacific slopes of western Guatemala (p. 209). On the other hand, by the time Mayapán had risen to power, plumbate was no longer made, and only a very thin trickle of Fine Orange reached Mayapán, and this (Type V) was largely undecorated and of dull shapes. Stone tools, too, show little craftsmanship, and are far inferior to the splendid flint work of the Classic period.

The degeneration in all the arts in this last period of Maya history is really heart-breaking. I feel it is a manifestation of great cultural dislocation resulting from a shift from a hierarchic to a secular and militaristic culture.

In one respect Mayapán was ahead of the Classic period—it had metals, although in limited quantity. No metal is associated with the

145

Classic period, but large quantities of gold and copper ornaments have been dredged from the sacred cenote at Chichén Itza. The gold almost without exception came from Panama and Costa Rica (one piece from even more distant Colombia) as designs, processes, and content of the gold show, and it is reasonable to suppose a brisk sea trade from the late tenth to the twelfth century between the isthmus of Panama and Yucatán. I would suppose that this was through the efforts of the Chontal Maya, the great sea traders of Middle America, to which group I believe the Itzá once belonged. That this trade was brisk during the Itzá rule at Chichén is demonstrated by gold disks from the cenote with embossed designs of Itzá defeating the Yucatec Maya. The disks were imported in blank (there is no metal in Yucatán), not made locally from melted-down discards. Later (about A.D. 1200), when Mayapán became dominant, this trade with the isthmus had fallen to a trickle. Carnegie Institution's five seasons' work at Mayapán produced only five minute broken fragments of gold.

The use of copper, on the other hand, seems to have increased. A great deal of copper comes from the cenote at Chichén Itzá, but the conditions under which it was found are of no help in dating it. Most of it was cast in central Mexico, and on stylistic grounds is thought to date to a large extent from the Mayapán period. The only datable find of copper at Chichén Itzá comes from the burial shaft of the High Priest's Grave and is dated (A.D. 1300–1450) by accompanying red Mayapán-period pottery.

A fair number of copper bells (worn as tinklers on arms and legs), finger rings, and tweezers for removing hair from the face were recovered from burials at Mayapán, but copper is still rare. One reason for the comparative scarcity of copper objects and the almost complete absence of gold at Mayapán is that, unlike the Maya of the Classic period, the rulers of Mayapán did not supply the burials of their leaders with plentiful offerings for the next world. This shift may be connected with the rise of secularism.

Turquoise, rated almost as valuable as jade, and excellently made beads of rock crystal appear for the first time in the High Priest's Grave, at Chichén Itzá. The accompanying pottery shows that these burials were made after the fall of Chichén Itzá, although the building dates from early in the Toltec period. They probably represent an Itzá exile brought back to rest in his ancestral home.

The bow and arrow, certainly the most radical of the innovations, appeared in the Maya lowlands during the domination of Mayapán, introduced by Mexican mercenaries in the pay of the rulers of that city. This weapon probably reached the New World from Asia, but for some reason diffused slowly southward. It is not pictured in the many representations of Mexican warriors at Chichén Itzá, but once accepted by the Maya, it came into general use for both hunting and warfare. In fact, it may have led to a decrease in certain varieties of game, for prior to its introduction, the Maya had depended on traps and spears (clay pellets shot from blowguns were used against small birds) for their supply of game.

Three features point to the decline of religion and rise of secularism at Mayapán. Firstly, the best masonry is in the residences of the nobility, not in the temples. Beautifully dressed stone of Puuc style from the site which preceded Mayapán is frequently reused in private homes, but crude stonework of the Mayapán period was thought good enough for many of the temples. Secondly, each important residence had its family oratory, either in a special room of the house or in a near-by building, and there is archaeological and literary evidence that these shrines were primarily for ancestral cults (with family ossuaries before the altar) and for the worship of deities who had gained the devotion of the family. Such private cults were elements of family aggrandisement and flourished at the expense of organized communal religion. There is some evidence for family shrines in the Classic period, but not on this scale.

Thirdly, Mayapán's temples and shrines are strewn with the fragments of large incense burners, of highly porous coarse pottery and up to eighteen inches high. Each had on its front, in relief, the full-length figure of a god painted, after firing, in brilliant colors. The heads, arms, legs, and sandaled feet were made in separate molds. They were assembled before firing and small details to indicate the costume or attributes of the required god—many of these also made in molds—were added. For example, faces came toothless from the mold, but, if one was making a portrait of the old god, it was a simple matter to add in appliqué a tooth at each corner of the mouth, the conventional attribute of that god. If the facial characteristics were unusual, for instance in figures of the god Xipe, a special mold was used. This is, of course, mass production and the assembly line, so that one can say that Mayapán anticipated Henry Ford's contribution to modern culture by some six centuries. Technically, the process was a step forward; aesthetically, it was outrageous. In spite of their brilliant colors, these figures are lifeless, as is inevitable with mass-produced art. Religion had sunk low when the principal gods could be treated in that off-hand manner. (Plate 27*b*).

Sting-ray spines were used for drawing blood from the body in auto-sacrificial rites. Seven seasons' intensive work at Tikal produced 239 complete and fragmentary spines plus 112 imitations in bone; five years' excavation at Mayapán on a smaller scale produced sixteen fragments and one possible imitation in bone. The comparative figures perhaps may be interpreted as additional evidence for the decline of religion in the Mayapán period.

Sooner or later centralized dictatorships fall and the militaristic super-state dissolves into its component parts. Power corrupts and produces mental sluggishness. The descendants of Hunac Ceel, with the family name of Cocom (the name of a climbing plant with yellow flowers), maintained themselves in power for some 250 years (approximately A.D. 1200–1450) by their system of centralized government with the head-chiefs of states in residence at Mayapán. Presumably states dared not revolt with their leaders held as permanent hostages. Moreover, the Cocom consolidated their "empire" by matrimonial alliances with the ruling families of subordinate states. No state by itself could overthrow the Cocoms, since the latter, in addition to their own men, had the support of a considerable body of Mexican mercenaries. The Mexicans were, and still are, tougher and more warlike than the gentle and pacific Maya, but as time passed, those Mexicans had been Mayanized, as had the Itzá before them, and they had probably grown soft. They were known as *Ah Canul*, a Maya word which signifies protector—"bodyguard" might be a fair translation in terms of our culture.

Possibly their "barracks" at Mayapán are to be identified with two groups of residences built around a central patio in a manner reminiscent of central Mexico. These groups were rather easily put in a state of defense (assuming some perishable battlements, access would have been only by a long tunnel passage), and were joined by a special road.

The revolt against the Cocoms was engineered by a certain Ah

Xupan, who belonged to the important Tutul Xiu family, also claiming Tula ancestry. The Tutul Xius claimed to have been the rulers of Uxmal, but there is good archaeological evidence that Uxmal was abandoned before the Tutul Xius, who apparently were also of Mexican descent, appeared on the scene, or, at least, very soon afterwards. However, the ruined city was within their territory, and that probably gave the Tutul Xius extra prestige, of which they were not slow to take advantage. Ah Xupan urged the revolt on the grounds that the Cocoms were seizing many Yucatec Maya and selling them as slaves to "foreigners," that is, to Mexico and Honduras.

INDEPENDENT CHIEFTAINSHIPS

The revolt was successful; Mayapán was sacked and the ruling Cocom and all his sons, except one who was away on a trading expedition to Honduras, were slain. With the fall of Mayapán (within four or five years of A.D. 1450) centralized government ended, and the Cocom empire dissolved into its component parts, the dozen or so regional states each with its head chief. There is archaeological evidence pointing to the sack of Mayapán. Other buildings besides the residence described above had been set afire. Everywhere, to our intense disappointment, looters had broken into altars in search of offertory caches, and smashed incense burners were scattered everywhere. Most dramatic was the finding of seven skeletons, apparently flung down on the floor in front of a building so that they lay alternately head to foot. Large flint blades were in the rib cases of two of the individuals, and another blade rested against the pelvis of a third. One cannot say positively that these seven died in the battle, but it is a distinct possibility.

The end of Mayapán's hegemony accelerated the cultural decline which had continued almost uninterruptedly since the end of the Classic period. Religious influence, which had grown less through those centuries, sank to a new low. Pyramids were no longer constructed; stone temples gave place to thatched huts. Perhaps indicative of this decline is the possibility that the ancient ball game ceased to be played. Although in Toltec Chichén Itzá at least six courts were in use, not a single court has been identified in all the length and breadth of Mayapán, and there is no account of the game's being played in Yucatán at the time of the conquest (Landa, with his full account of Maya life, makes no mention of it).

Archaeological remains at the capitals of the various states which succeeded Mayapán are meager in the extreme. Ancient pyramids and stone temples in the vicinity may have been used by some towns, but we read of annual repairing and refurbishing of the temples, indicating that for the most part they were of wattle and thatch. The construction of wide, carefully surfaced roads between cities seems to have ceased at the close of the Mexican period or earlier (I do not refer to the intra-city roads, of which there is one at Mayapán less than 400 yards long). Just as Roman roads continued to be used for centuries, so these ancient Maya roads were still traveled by the pilgrims to the great shrines, such at Izamal, but they probably were not kept in repair.

Constant warfare between the states which inherited the Cocom "Empire" prevented any attempt to arrest the cultural decline. There are parallels between this situation and the cultural decline and internecine warfare of England after the Roman withdrawal. Maya culture for several centuries had lived by the sword with its attendant cultural retrogression. Now it was perishing of the same disease.

A remarkable parallel to this sequence is discernible in the history of the highlands of Guatemala at the same period. There, at the close of the Classic period, militarism, probably introduced by groups also influenced by Tula, radically affected the local civilization. After a time, as in Yucatán, one group became dominant and imposed its rule on its neighbors. This was the Quiché, living to the north of Lake Atitlán, whose chiefs likewise boasted descent from ruling families of Tula, although, like those in Yucatán claiming Mexican ancestry, they had become completely Maya in outlook and speech. They, too, imposed the cult of Quetzalcoatl, the feathered serpent, on the conquered Maya.

For some time the Quiché seem to have been overlords of their neighbors, the Cakchiquel, the Zutuhil, and parts, at least, of Mam territory. They and the Cakchiquel expanded southward from their highland homes into the foothills and coastal belt of the Pacific at a time when the two nations seem to have been allies. The Cakchiquel conquered territory to the southeast at the expense of the Pipil, a Mexican group long established there; the Quiché took over territory to the southwest at the expense of the Zutuhil and probably the Mam. These conquests were of great economic consequence, for they involved some of the land best suited to cacao cultivation in the whole Maya area. It was the Maya equivalent of conquest of a region of extensive gold mining. Later, the incipient Quiché empire, beset by revolts, collapsed at about the same time as Cocom Mayapán fell. There followed an intensification of intertribal warfare, which, as in Yucatán, ended only with the coming of the white man.

The upsurge of militarism at the close of the Classic period in the highlands led to a move from open to easily defended sites on hilltops and spits of land surrounded by canyons. The Spaniards gave the impression that these cities they encountered and overcame were urban centers, but obviously they were ceremonial centers. Zaculeu, the capital of the Mam Maya in western Guatemala, which was excavated and restored under the auspices of the United Fruit Company, is an interesting example of the defended ceremonial center. It covers an area of only three acres, most of which is occupied by courts and their flanking buildings, and obviously there was no room for an urban center. It is surrounded by canyons on three sides, and breastworks and revetments defended the fourth side, a narrow neck of land to the north, some four hundred feet wide. Alvarado's attack by the narrow neck of land was repulsed by the Mam, and in the end it was hunger that forced the defenders to surrender. Utatlán and Iximché, capitals of the Quiché and Cakchiquel Maya respectively and both flourishing at the time of the Spanish Conquest, occupied similar positions with canyons on three sides. Iximché had a ditch and rampart to defend the narrow neck of land.

To this pattern belongs Chutixtiox, in Quiché territory about twenty-five miles north of Utatlán. This is a large and, because of its isolation, a far-better-preserved site of the late post-Classic or proto-historic period (approximately A.D. 1250–1525). It stands at the southeast end of a three-hundred-foot-high ridge surrounded on three sides by the winding Río Negro. Terraces add to the natural strength of the position (Plate 26a) and the Mayas had dug a deep gap across the only easy approach, at the northwest end; this presumably was spanned in time of peace with a removable wooden bridge.

An enclosed ball court is in the foreground, and behind rises a sort of acropolis with main pyramid, and to the right, with back to the observer, a colonnaded building with beam and mortar roof. The plaza floor is paved; the buildings are of rough stones and slabs laid in mud and thickly plastered. Many structures were thatched; the roof of the main temple is conjectural. Chutixtiox in its spectacular mountain setting left me with an indelible impression of its rugged majesty when I, in the company of that great Maya scholar Ralph Roys, climbed its flanks in the year of Pearl Harbor. In places the plaster on the walls was almost as fresh as when the last Maya chief left, and the mountain wind, as then, still blows where it listeth.

Chalchitán, just halfway between Zaculeu and Chutixtiox and now in the territory of a group speaking a Maya language akin to Mam, is an undefended valley site occupied from early Classic or perhaps Formative times into the post-Classic. The restoration (Plate 26b) shows one part of the site with ball court in foreground, small altar shrine in the court, and, in rear, a small structure with central ramp and balustrades, very typical of highland architecture. The ball court had jaguar heads projecting from the side walls, their locations corresponding to those of the rings of ball courts in central Mexico and Yucatán. This type of ball court is early post-Classic. The density of ball courts in the highlands of Guatemala is phenomenal; A. L. Smith lists 132, about the equivalent of giving Brooklyn ten first-class ball parks.

There are good reasons for believing that one structure at Chalchitán, not illustrated, had human skulls set in one of the walls.

Excavation has recently been carried out by the Guatemalan authorities at Iximché, which has suffered much as a quarry for builders in near-by towns of colonial and modern times. Fair-sized pyramids, various small religious structures, two ball courts, and what appear to be colonnades are spread around several loosely connected courts. Here, again, there could have been no city in our sense of the word. Iximché recently yielded the largest haul of gold yet found in the Maya area excluding that dredged from the cenote at Chichén Itzá. This came from a tomb which potsherds in the fill date as less than a century before the Spanish Conquest. With four badly damaged skeletons, one apparently a chief, the other three probably servants sacrificed when their master died, were ten small jaguar masks of gold, forty gold beads, a gold head circlet or crown, a copper ring and copper nose ornament, a little jade, turquoise from a mosaic design, and an engraved shell bracelet. The Cakchiquel certainly gave a member of the nobility a better send-off than did Mayapán, destroyed probably a decade or so before this burial. They were also a bloodthirsty lot: a recently discovered offertory cache comprised forty-eight decapitated human heads.

The Spaniards, under the infamous Alvarado, subdued Guatemala in 1525; the final conquest of Yucatán took place sixteen years later. In both regions Maya betrayed their fellows. In Guatemala the Cakchiquel fought with the Spaniards against their old enemies, the Quiché and Zutuhil; in Yucatán, the Tutul Xius, who had won the everlasting enmity of the Cocoms for the betrayal at Mayapán, threw in their lot with the Spaniards. The same thing happened in Mexico, where the powerful Tlaxcalan joined Cortés in fighting the Aztec. Clearly there was no feeling of racial solidarity in Middle America, and there was also a failure to foresee that by such actions the Indians were hastening the day of their own enslavement. The Spanish Conquest was inevitable, but it would have been delayed, especially in the case of Mexico, except for native aid. Perhaps these betrayals were ignoble clamberings aboard the bandwagon (the Tlaxcalan won some privileges for their aid), but there were to be no seats or even holds for them in the Spanish coach of state.

The Petén and northeastern Chiapas, core of the Central area, were not conquered by the new rulers for another 150 years because of the impenetrability of the forest and lack of natural resources of interest to Colonial Spain. At Tayasal, a small island in Lake Petén, in the heart of this country, had settled the remnants of the Itzá driven from Chichén Itzá, and there in their isolation they retained their independence and their old ways until their conquest in 1697.

It is interesting to reflect that many of the thirteen colonies had struck deep roots before this last Maya citadel fell. The temple-topped pyramids of Maya tradition yet reared themselves heavily from the earth of the tropics at a time when graceful steeples were rising, with the yeast of Wren's inspiration, in a more temperate climate to the north. Maya priests were not a whit less austere than their fellow clerics in New England.

Moreover, there is a bond between hanging witches and human sacrifice, for both were performed for the supposed good of the community at the expense of the individual. If anything, the Maya position was a shade more ethical: witches were the victims of hysteria, whereas humans sacrificed by the Maya died in an orderly manner to keep man's bargain with the gods.

Unfortunately, no one who participated in this conquest of Tayasal has left any detailed account of life in this Maya fossil. Curiously enough, there is a record of a red-headed man, married to an Itzá woman, living on Tayasal just before its conquest. He had a book with him—the Bible?—and in all probability was an Englishman from the old buccaneer settlement of Belize. When one recalls that the writing of books on native life was for long a leading British occupation, one regrets that this sojourner among the Itzá never returned to civilization to indulge in the national pastime; his observations would have been of inestimable importance.

This picture of the last six centuries of Maya history is somewhat disheartening. It is the story of a series of declines in art, architecture, and religion, due primarily to the deviation into militarism. Jane Austen, in *Sense and Sensibility*, gave the only civilized verdict on such developments: "I have more pleasure in a snug farmhouse than a watch-tower . . . and a troop of tidy, happy villagers please me better than the finest banditti in the world."

The Maya, as has been pointed out, had the ability to absorb their foreign conquerors and to modify to their own taste new concepts forced on them. By the time of the Spanish Conquest the cult of Quetzalcoatl had almost ceased, and among present-day Maya, who still worship the old Maya rain gods, there is no recollection of that deity, or of other importations from Tula, such as Tlalchitonatiuh and Tezcatlipoca. The military orders of Jaguars and Eagles are not mentioned by Spanish eyewitnesses of Maya culture. It is for this reason that I have called this second Mexican period in Maya history the period of Mexican absorption. Yet warfare flourished to the end despite the generally pacific attitude of the Maya. There must have been just enough Mexican blood in the ruling families to resist that last stage in Mayanization; they never learned that "the paths of glory lead but to the grave."

Why there was no revival in the arts is hard to say—Greece had its Byzantine revival and Italy its long renaissance with Canaletto and Tiepolo (born respectively the year of the fall of Tayasal and the year before) as its last fruits. Warfare does not account for this lack of a rebirth, for art development can coexist with intensive military campaigns. Except for the weaving and embroidery of textiles in the Guatemala highlands and one or two minor handicrafts, art has not smiled again on the present-day Maya. This divorce from beauty does not seem to be due to Spanish domination, for the independent Lacandón Maya and the semi-independent Maya of Quintana Roo are still less artistically inclined. Perhaps the answer is that after the Classic period the Maya never recovered an enthusiastic faith to bring into being a revival of their old brilliancy.

In conclusion, I would again point out that in details this brief sketch of Maya history may not be correct, for there are alternative arrangements, particularly in the dates of the principal events in the history of Chichén Itzá, and we still do not know what was happening in other cities of Yucatán during the Itzá domination of Chichén Itzá. As long as that problem is unsolved, no reconstruction of Maya history can be certain. However, the melancholy picture of decline and fall is correct in its main outline whatever reconstruction is accepted. Once Maya civilization was forced to use the wrong means to placate the gods, the end was inevitable.

In this and the previous chapters we have followed the poorly marked path of Maya civilization along its stages: the Formative period, its prenatal existence (perhaps 1500 B.C. to approximately A.D. 100); the Classic period, its growth and its glory (approximately A.D. 100 to 925); the Mexican period, its submergence beneath Mexican-Toltec domination and the rising tide of warfare (A.D. 925–1200); the period of Mexican absorption, its transformation into small-scale universal states and the gradual reassertion of Maya values (A.D. 1200–1450); and a final sub-phase of Balkanization among the weak successor states to centralized government, which ended with the Spanish Conquest (A.D. 1450–1540). It is a steep rise, a lengthy section of plateau, and then a down gradient which grows precipitous as the end comes in sight.

IV. Intellectual and Artistic Achievement

A man with a deep sense of continuity sees himself not as an accidental unit doomed to vanish in a few years but as one of a great procession, influenced and helped by those who have gone before him, responsible in his turn for giving help and encouragement to those who will come after.—Robert Gordon Menzies, *Character and Training*.

CHARACTER AND TRAINING

In the first chapter were given the results of a kind of poll on the character—psychological traits—of the present-day Maya of Yucatán. This, in brief, revealed the Maya to be exceptionally honest, good-natured, clean, tidy, and socially inclined. In my own opinion, the lowland Maya could also be described as deeply religious. They take pride in their work, especially in the care of their fields, but there is no marked desire to get ahead, or even to keep up with the Joneses. That trait, I think, stems from a characteristic feature of the Maya outlook on life, the attitude of live and let live. No one, they feel, should strive for more than his fair share, for that can be attained only at one's neighbor's expense; consideration for others is all important.

This attitude applies not only to one's fellowman, but even to animals. A hunter should shoot only what he needs; he should not slaughter game indiscriminately, an attitude inculcated in folk tales and embodied in prayers. The hunter asks the gods of hunting to send him what he requires, and usually points out that he is in need of the food; *otzilen*, "I am poor or afflicted," is the term he uses, but as money plays only a small part in Maya economy, the expression really means that he needs food. There is also a realization that if hunters indulge in wholesale slaughter, the entire community will be the loser because game will become scarce; it is a kind of voluntary enforcement of game laws. In contrast, the Spanish-speaking *chicleros* have no such restraint or thought for the future. I have seen a *chiclero* cut down a wild cherry tree to get a few handfuls of fruit, rather than climb the tree. The punishment of the indiscriminate slaughterer is brought out in folk tales, the recital of which teaches the moral code of the group to the young. The hunting gods have servants who care for wounded animals; the bee god is at hand to mend the wings and legs of bees damaged when men break into the hive to get the honey. The hunter apologizes to the deer he has shot for taking his life and, as in his prayer, concludes with the word *otzilen*, "I had need." Nevertheless, the Maya in practice is not kind to animals—kindness to animals is a rare feature of civilization—and more than half starves his dog so that he will be a good hunter. Rather, I think, his attitude comes from the ingrained conception that one should not take advantage of others, whether human or animal.

The Maya apologizes to the gods of the earth when he cuts the forest to make his cornfield, burns the dry brush in the clearing, and disfigures the landscape. A prayer of this type collected in southern British Honduras reads in part: "O God, my mother, my father, Lord of the Hills and Valleys, Spirit of the Forests, be patient with me for I am about to do as I have always done. Now I make my offering to you that you may know that I am troubling your good will, but suffer it, I pray. I am going to dirty you [destroy your beauty], I am going to work you that I may live." There is beauty in this apology for disfiguring the land, but the essential point is that justification has to be offered for destroying vegetation and for "disfiguring the face of the earth god," as one prayer has it. The earth and all vegetation are living sentient beings.

This constant endeavor to be fair-minded comes out in the incident given in the day in the life of a hunter in Chapter V below, in which the Maya chief strives not only to see both sides of the case he is trying, but also to make each party see the other's point of view. It is based on actual observation in a Maya village in southern British Honduras. The Maya trying the case was more interested in an amicable settlement of the case and in making sure that both plaintiff and defendant saw each other's point of view. His approach seemed an epitome of the whole Maya attitude of reasonableness and restraint.

Maya philosophy is best summarized in the motto, "Nothing in excess," which was inscribed over the temple of Delphi. Harmonious living, moderation, and a full comprehension of that spirit of toleration for the foibles of one's neighbors contained in the expression "live and let live" characterize the present-day Maya. The development of a somewhat similar philosophy has been considered one of the great achievements of Athenian culture, and rightly has been put before material progress.

The surviving books of Chilam Balam reveal unconsciously that the preceding paragraph not only applies to the present-day lowland Maya, but also summarizes Maya outlook in the past. This is particularly apparent in descriptions of the two occasions when the Maya felt the impact of alien ideas and ways of living: first, when they were conquered by the militaristically minded Itzá; second, when the imposition of Spanish rule required tremendous physical adjustments. Both conquests were accompanied by great bloodshed and cruelty, but it is highly significant that it was the disappearance of harmonious living, not the temporary slaughter and cruelty, which impressed itself on the Maya to such an extent that generations later it was still a major theme in the books of Chilam Balam. One passage contrasting life before and after the Itzá conquest in the Book of Chilam Balam of Chumayel has been translated by Ralph Roys as follows:

In due measure did they recite the good prayers; in due measure they sought the lucky days, until they saw the good stars enter into their reign. Then they kept watch while the reign of the good stars began. Then everything was good. Then they adhered to the dictates of their reason; in the holy faith their lives were passed. Then there was no sickness. . . . At that time the course of humanity was orderly. The foreigners [the Itzá] made it otherwise when they arrived here. They brought shameful things when they came. They lost their innocence in carnal sin. . . . This was the cause of our sickness also. There were no more lucky days for us; we had no sound judgment. At the end of our loss of vision and of our shame everything shall be revealed. There was no great teacher, no great speaker, no supreme priest when the change of rulers occurred at their arrival. Lewd were the priests . . . .

The mention of carnal sin and lewdness refers to certain erotic practices introduced by the Mexicans which were the very opposite of the Maya concept of purificatory rites before interceding with the gods. The Maya clearly attributed the subsequent outbreaks of sickness and general disaster to these erotic practices imposed by the conquerors. Maya contempt for these orgies of the Itzá, so contrary to the whole Maya spirit of moderation and decorum, is brought out in one passage from the same source already quoted (p. 127). Another of a similar character but even more forceful reads in the Roys translation: "They twist their necks, they twist their mouths, they wink the eye, they slaver at the mouth, at men, women, chiefs, justices, presiding officers . . . everybody, both great and small. There is no great teaching. Heaven and earth are truly lost to them; they have lost all shame . . . understanding is lost; wisdom is lost. . . . Dissolute is the speech, dissolute the face of the rogue to the rulers, to the head chiefs."

Absence of sound judgment, of wisdom, and of orderliness are emphasized; blame for the lack of great teachers and men of vision is laid on the immoderate and shameful conduct of the Itzá.

Of the changes resulting from the Spanish Conquest the Maya scribe writes:

Before the coming of the mighty men and Spaniards there was no robbery by violence, there was no greed and striking down one's fellow man in his blood, at the cost of the poor man, at the expense of the food of each and everyone. [And elsewhere] It was the beginning of tribute, the beginning of church dues, the beginning of strife with purse snatching, the beginning of strife with guns, the beginning of strife by trampling of people, the beginning of robbery with violence, the beginning of debts enforced by false testimony, the beginning of individual strife, a beginning of vexation.

There had been tribute before the Spaniards came, but it had not been onerous, and violence was not unknown, but what an indictment of our civilization! The early Spanish settlers in Yucatán exploited the natives who were allotted to them as tributaries and plantation laborers. The Franciscan friars could only partly alleviate the harsh conditions, and the Spanish crown, which was strongly opposed to exploitation, was too remote to check the rapacity of the settlers. Yet the Maya complaint is not primarily directed against exploitation, but against violence, greed, and lack of consideration for others.

Maya character was also regulated by discipline aimed at teaching obedience and self-control. The German ethnologist, Karl Sapper, who lived for some years among the Kekchi Maya, remarks on the strictness with which Indian children are brought up. He notes that there is a consistency in their training and that discipline is not relaxed when the child is out of sorts or ill. The child impressed by the absolute obedience which his parents and the adults around him accord to a tribal elder finds it easier to submit to the control of his parents. Again, when he notices that conversation is largely carried on by the old people and that visitors are greeted in order according to their rank and age, he learns to follow the example of the young adults in remaining silent, to respect and obey his elders. He also learns to hide his emotions under an outward calm. Indeed, Indian children seldom cry.

In ancient times training must have been much more strict, particularly in the schools and seminaries. We know little about how these functioned in the Maya area, but, to judge from the full information on analogous institutions among the Aztec, the young men had a far from easy time, and the girls in their own educational establishments did not fare much better.

Discipline continued through life. Before great religious festivals and important stages in the agricultural year, such as cutting forest, burning, and sowing, there were periods of fasting and continence. These are still followed by the Maya, and, as it is believed that failure to adhere to the rules will bring misfortune to the whole group, the individual is strengthened in his group loyalty, which, in turn, fortifies him to fulfill his obligations. Generally the period of continence lasts thirteen days, a Maya "week," but before great festivals men in some parts of the Maya area moved into the men's houses for three, four, or five Maya "months" of twenty days each, and there fasted, drew blood from their bodies to offer in sacrifice, and abstained from washing. The Kekchi to this day maintains continence for forty days before the annual pilgrimage to a certain cave which is peculiarly sacred, and various forms of fasting were practiced in all parts of the Maya area.

Another feature of Maya culture which helped to develop a sense of duty to neighbor and community was group labor. For clearing forest land, for building houses, and for other such activities the Maya worked, and still work, in teams of a dozen or more. A helps B and C to clear their cornfields, and they return the service by helping him to prepare his land. A co-operative housebuilding for a young couple about to marry is described in Chapter V. We teach team spirit by means of sports; the Maya made it a feature of their lives.

Thus upbringing, the practice of self-restraint, co-operative work, and the inculcation of the spirit of moderation produced a tranquil Maya character which was essentially introvert, but of a disciplined rather than an individualistic nature. This character has, of course, molded Maya civilization, and that civilization, once established, helped to keep the pattern before succeeding generations. Our knowledge of early Maya history lacks detail, but there are incidents which show this spirit at work:

As already noted, after the overthrow of Mayapán, the Ah Canul, the Mexican mercenaries who had sustained the power of the tyrannical Cocom, were not massacred—a not unusual fate in civilization on or above the Maya level. They were not even expelled from the country, but were assigned territory in Yucatán in which to settle, and were accepted into the Maya family of chiefdoms, apparently on terms of trust and friendship.

Early in the seventeenth century two friars visited the still independent Itzá of Tayasal. On a conducted tour of the city one of them on a sudden impulse smashed the chief idol in its temple and then exhorted the enraged Itzá to accept Christianity. After resting in the guest house, the two friars visited the Itzá head-chief and told him of the incident. He, of course, already knew all about it, but showed no outward sign of anger and did not once refer to the matter in the subsequent conversation. Far from suffering the death which in Maya eyes they must have merited for this sacrilege, the two friars were permitted to remain on the island and to say their daily masses in public. The only outward manifestations of anger were a refusal to supply the friars with men to accompany them when they finally departed and a shower of stones and some jeering as they set out. How many other people would have displayed equal moderation in those circumstances?

As we shall see, Maya character, with its emphasis on moderation, discipline, co-operation, patience, and consideration for others, made possible outstanding achievements in the intellectual field.

THE PHILOSOPHY OF TIME

So far as this general outlook on life is concerned, the great men of Athens would not have felt out of place in a gathering of Maya priests and rulers, but had the conversation turned on the subject of the philosophical aspects of time, the Athenians—or, for that matter, representatives of any of the great civilizations of history—would have been at sea. No other people in history has taken such an absorbing interest in time as did the Maya, and no other culture has ever developed a philosophy embracing such an unusual subject.

Time has been the subject of many similes and metaphors in the history of man. In our own civilization the most familiar symbol is that of Father Time with his scythe. He reminds us of the brevity of our span of life but fails to convey the idea of the eternity of time. A better picture is that of the poet which compares time to an ever flowing stream, but the concept is narrowed to the experience of the individual when Isaac Watts conceives of this stream as bearing its sons away. These and other metaphors reflect the attitude toward time in our own culture; time is regarded not as an abstract, but rather according to its effect on us as individuals. It is as though we, the self-styled lords of creation, were surprised and a trifle offended at having to bow to the passing years.

For the Maya time was an all-consuming interest. Every stela and altar was erected to mark the passage of time and was dedicated at the end of a period. It is as though we set up a monument at the end of every five or ten years, and inscribed on it the date—Sunday, December 31, 1950; Saturday, December 31, 1960, etc.—together with information on the age of the moon and the gods then ruling. It was once believed that Maya hieroglyphic monuments—about 1,000 with glyphic texts have so far been found—deal only with the passage

of time, data on the moon and the planet Venus, calendrical calculations, and material on the gods and rituals involved in these matters;
but evidence now shows that historical events are also recorded. The
three surviving hieroglyphic manuscripts are largely filled with
divinatory almanacs giving information on the aspects of the gods
of days, such as which are favorable or unfavorable for sowing crops
or hunting. There are also passages on astronomical matters, but,
again, with emphasis on the gods.

In Old World cultures the days may be under the influence of
gods or planets—witness our own Saturn-day, Sun-day, Moon-day,
etc. Among the Maya the days themselves were divine, and still are
in remote villages of the highlands of Guatemala in which the old
Maya calendar still survives. Each day is not merely influenced by
some god; it is a god, or, rather, a pair of gods, for each day is a
combination of number and name—1 Ik, 5 Imix, 13 Ahau, and so on—
and both parts are gods. The Maya still speak of a day as "he," and
often prefix the masculine *ah* to the name to emphasize that the day
is a living god. The personified days were vastly more important
in the life of the Maya, from prince to peasant, and played a much
greater part in shaping the culture than any astrological or divinatory mechanism of ancient Europe or the Near East.

The Maya conceived of the divisions of time as burdens carried
through all eternity by relays of divine bearers. These bearers were
the numbers by which the different periods were distinguished. The
burdens were carried on the back, the weight supported by tump-
lines across the forehead. In terms of our own calendar it is as though
for December 31, 1972, there were six bearers: The god of number
thirty-one with December on his back; the god of number one
carries the millennium; the god of number nine bears the centuries;
the god of number seven, the decades; and the god of number two,
the years. At the end of the day there is a momentary pause before
the procession restarts, but in that moment the god of number one
with the burden of January replaces the god of thirty-one with his
December load, and the god of number three relieves the god of
number two as bearer of the year (Fig. 17).

This theme appears in the most elaborate hieroglyphic inscriptions, which show the various gods of numbers at the moment the
journey is done. One god raises his hand to the tumpline to slip it

off his forehead, whereas others have slipped off their load, and hold them in their laps. The night god, who takes over when day is done, is in the act of rising with his load. With his left hand he eases the weight on the tumpline; with his right hand on the ground he steadies himself as he starts to rise. The artist conveys in the strain reflected in the god's features the physical effort of rising from the ground with his heavy load. It is the typical scene of the Indian carrier resuming his journey familiar to anyone who has visited the Guatemalan highlands.

The Maya transcriptions of the Colonial period bear out the picture supplied by the hieroglyphic texts, for they contain many references to this conception. We read of the bearers' letting fall their burdens of time; of tying on their burdens; of taking the road; of the resting places, that is, the ends of periods; and of events happening during the journey of such-and-such a year. This imagery differs strikingly from any picture of time our civilization has produced, in that the passage of time is not portrayed as the journey of one bearer and his load, but of many bearers, each with his own division of time on his back. Mystically, too, the burden came to signify the expected good or ill fortune of the year according to the benevolent or malevolent aspect of the bearer god, and the priests were kept busy with the complex task of weighing the conflicting weal and woe of the various periods of time. The burden of one year was drought, of another a good harvest. The day with which a new year started was its bearer, and was called the year-bearer. Actually only four day-names could occupy that position. Thus if the year began with the day Kan, one could look forward to a good crop because Kan was merely an aspect of the maize god; if the day Muluc was the year-bearer, good crops would also be expected since Muluc was the rain god. On the contrary, the influences of the day gods Ix and Cauac were malevolent, so years which started with them would be disastrous.

A too literal acceptance of predestination will soon affect the welfare of the whole community, for there is not much point in sowing a large crop if drought is certain to destroy it. Moreover, priests soon expose themselves as poor prophets if they cannot hedge on their predictions, and they can hardly justify public support unless they claim the power to modify fate. Rites of expiation and hedging were inevitable, and the latter gave the priest every incentive to juggle with the influences of the many gods marching on the journey of time and to master astronomy for astrological ends; the more factors that could influence the predictions, the more complex the problem grew and the greater the dependence of the group on the priest's specialized knowledge. It was in the attempts to find a key to the conflicting influences of the gods of many cycles of time that the Maya had their greatest intellectual successes.

The search for the factors that influenced each day and each year was perhaps mundane; the Maya idea of the eternity of time was noble. In the Maya scheme the road over which time had marched stretched into a past so distant that the mind of man cannot comprehend its remoteness. Yet the Maya undauntedly retrod that road seeking its starting point. A fresh view, leading further backward, unfolded at the end of each stage; the mellowed centuries blended into millennia, and they into tens of thousands of years, as those tireless inquirers explored deeper and still deeper into the eternity of the past. For them time receded in endless vistas of hundreds of thousands of years; the resting places, those annual stages of the bearers of the burden of time, mounted to millions and even scores of millions. In the introductory chapter I have already cited one inscription that probes 90,000,000 years into the past, and another which sweeps back some 400,000,000 years. The accompanying glyphs record that the starting point of those calculations were thousands of millions more years in the past. Indeed, we can feel rather confident that the Maya had concluded that time had no beginning.

Time, in the conception of the Maya, sweeps forward, too, but surviving calculations carry us only a paltry four millennia into the future. Evidently, future time was of less interest than time past, probably because the Maya were much more interested in the past than in the future on account of their belief that history repeats whenever the divine influences are in the same balance. Apparently, the Maya, like the Aztec, believed the world would come to a sudden end, presumably when an overpowering combination of evil influences marked the termination of a time period. If, therefore, the priest, by probing the past, could find precisely the same combination of evil influences that he knew was to mark the end of an approaching time period, he could be sure that, as they had not destroyed the world in the past, they would not now destroy it. In all probability, then, this great Maya conception of the eternity of time evolved from the dominance of superstition and astrology in Maya life.

The idea that, given the same influences, history would repeat itself had two interesting consequences: it tended to confound the future with the past, and it introduced a conception of cycles of time which partly conflicted with the imagery of time as an unending march by its bearers into the future.

The period of time which most concerned the Maya was the katun, a span of twenty tuns (approximate years, each 360 days). Because of the peculiar construction of the calendar, katuns could end only on the day Ahau (each was named by the day on which it ended) and at each repetition the attached number decreased by two, so that the succession was 13 Ahau, 11 Ahau, 9 Ahau, 7 Ahau, 5 Ahau, 3 Ahau, 1 Ahau, 12 Ahau, 10 Ahau, 8 Ahau, 6 Ahau, 4 Ahau, 2 Ahau, and then 13 Ahau repeated. Thus a katun of a given name repeated every 260 tuns (approximate years; 257 of our years), and as the ruler of each katun wielded the same influences each time a katun returned, history was expected to repeat itself in cycles of 260 years. Accordingly, if the priest looked up what had occurred at previous appearances of a given katun, he had a picture of what would happen when that katun returned. Details would vary, but in broad outline events would follow the established pattern.

The Maya prophets were as pessimistic as Jeremiah; direful predictions vastly outnumbered those that were favorable. We find, for instance, the following: 13 Ahau, "There is no lucky day for us"; 11 Ahau, "Niggard is the katun; scanty are its rains . . . misery"; 7 Ahau, carnal sin, roguish rulers; 5 Ahau, "Harsh his face, harsh his tidings"; 10 Ahau, "Drought is the burden of the katun." For only three katuns were the prophecies good.

Katun 8 Ahau was a katun of fighting and political change; therefore, at every repetition of katun 8 Ahau such changes could be expected. An interesting example of this fatalism occurs in connection with the last days of Tayasal, the independent Itzá chiefdom which held out against the Spaniards until 1697. Andrés de Avendaño, a Franciscan of outstanding ability who had mastered the intricacies of the Maya calendar, visited Tayasal in 1696 and in a conference with the Itzá chieftains persuaded them that only four months were lacking to the time when, according to their ancient prophecies, they would accept Christianity and, of course, submit to the Spanish crown. Avendaño, who tells us that he was thoroughly acquainted with the old katun prophecies, clearly pointed out to the Itzá that katun 8 Ahau, the katun of political change, was about to start, and the time for acceptance of Christianity had come. The Itzá agreed to submit at the end of the four months lacking until the new katun began. As a matter of fact, Avendaño was about a year out in his calculation; katun 8 Ahau started in July, 1697; the defeat of the Itzá and their submission to Spanish rule came four months before the start of the katun, in March, 1697. The Itzá, who had a great reputation as warriors, put up very poor resistance. It is possible they did not fight well because they knew resistance against the power of the incoming katun was useless.

The extraordinary feature, however, is that in these prophecies past and future become one. Spanish rule coalesces with the foreign yoke of the Itzá; Christian worship introduced by the Spaniards is identified with the worship of Kukulcan, an alien cult imposed on the Maya six hundred years earlier; and, apparently, the impact of an obscure pirate, who seems to have had a hide-out in northeastern Yucatán, led to the identification of the Roman Catholic church with the hated Itzá, and of Protestantism with the old Maya religion. Present and future events blend with past history because they are really one, for both result from the same divine "burden" of the katun. The cross of Christendom is the tree, conventionalized in art as a cross decked with vegetation, on which the quetzal bird perched; the bearded Spaniards are the Toltec invaders because their leaders, too, were bearded; the house of Montejo, the conqueror, which stands on the south side of the great plaza in Mérida, is the "house to the east" of katun 11 Ahau, during which Spanish rule was firmly imposed on Yucatán; and the measuring of the great cathedral of Mérida raised by the Spaniards is mystically the measuring of time by the pacing of its bearers through eternity. I do not believe that any other people in history has evolved a similar conception of the compartmentalized identity of past, present, and future.

The divine bearers in relays carry time forward on its unending journey, but at the same time there is this cyclic aspect represented by the recurring spells of duty for each god in the succession of bearers. We might picture the course of the katuns as a giant track, the circuit of which requires 260 years, but the image would be only partly correct. The round of the katuns was only one of the very many cycles of time; every period larger than a day, together with the lunar month and the synodical revolutions of planets, as well as the groups of gods who ruled the sky, the earth, and the under-world, had their individual cycles. That is to say, all were members of relay teams marching through eternity. The Maya wished to know which gods would be marching together on any given day because with that information they could gauge the combined in-fluences of all the marchers, offsetting the bad ones with the good in an involved computation of the fates and astrological factors. On a successful solution depended the fate of mankind.

I suspect the problem was in a secondary sense a challenge to the intellect—a sort of tremendous anagram which had a particular appeal to the Maya with his deep regard for orderliness. A compre-hension of the harmony in the universe and its rulers was the key to methodical living.

The general problem that faced the Maya might be expressed in terms of our modern civilization in this way: In the speedometer of your automobile you have a mileage gauge, which also records tenths of a mile. Suppose you have installed also gauges which re-cord the distance you drive in furlongs and chains, in kilometers, in Roman stadia, in Russian versts, in Spanish leagues, and other meas-ures of distance. Now suppose only the mileage gauge is illuminated at night, and, furthermore, that you, a very superstitious driver, fear that you will be in danger if several of the dials show your unlucky number, five, at the same time. On the other hand, when the gauge registers a group of sevens, your luck is in. You must calculate when the fives will appear on the gauges during your night journey so that you can then drive with great caution; and also discover when the sevens will be in position, so that you can speed to make up time lost during the dangerous period.

The problem that the Maya priest had to solve was along these lines, but considerably more difficult because some of the factors he used were tricky. Solar and lunar reckonings and the synodical revolutions of planets are not easily reduced to order or to round numbers. The tropical year is approximately 365.2422 days long;

the lunation is slightly over 29.53 days; the synodical revolution of Venus is 583.92 days; the sidereal year is a shade under 365.2564 days. Such cycles had to be brought into relation with one another and, above all, into relation to the sacred divinatory almanac of 260 days. There were other Maya time counts which had to be taken into account: the tun, an approximate year of 360 days; the vague year of 365 days; the cycle of nine nights, over each of which in turn a god ruled; and a cycle of seven days, the components of which were probably ruled by earth gods. These were the Maya equivalents of the gauges on our modern car.

The Maya had no knowledge of handling fractions and they had no decimal system. Moreover, they did not use leap years, but made marginal calculations to take care of the discrepancies between counts of solar years and of their vague years of 365 days. Handling these figures, therefore, was a difficult business. That was not all. Each lunar month in the series and each division of each revolution of the planet Venus had its divine patron, and the influences of all those gods had to be taken into consideration. The Maya priest-astronomer was anxious to find the lowest common multiple of two or more of these cycles, or, to state it in the Maya pattern of thought, how long would be the journey on the road of time before two or more of the divine carriers reached the same resting place together.

INTELLECTUAL ACHIEVEMENT

It was in the solution of these problems that the Maya had their most outstanding intellectual successes. It is an arid subject which cannot be presented without recourse to arithmetic and a little of the simplest astronomy, but if you will bear with me I am sure that you will applaud the Maya successes in the light of the obstacles they overcame with native perseverance and patience.

Without going too deeply into the subject, let us see how the Maya solved the problem of bringing the Venus cycle with its average length of 583.92 days into relation with the year and the 260-day cycle. Every Maya cycle had its re-entering point in terms of the 260-day cycle: that of the katuns was the day 13 Ahau; that of the moon, 12 Lamat; and that of the Venus calendar, the day 1 Ahau. That was *the* day of Venus, the resting point at the end of the great cyclic journey, the god most closely identified with the planet. Indeed, 1 Ahau was another name for the Venus god. It was the day of heliacal rising after inferior conjunction when Venus reappears as morning star.

After observing the heliacal risings of the planet for many years, the Maya almost surely concluded that the synodical revolution of Venus averaged 584 days. The next questions they wished to answer was how many synodical revolutions of the planet will there be before Venus will once more appear as morning star on the day 1 Ahau. We would find the highest common factor which is 4, divide that into one of the numbers, and multiply the other number by the result. The answer is 584 divided by 4 equals 146: 146 times 260 equals 37,960. The gods of the Venus and 260-day cycles therefore will reach the same resting place on the march of time after 37,960 days, which is 65 Venus revolutions and 146 rounds of 260 days. The Maya worked out the problem by a more involved system of multiplication tables. They also knew that this was also the equivalent of 104 of their vague years of 365 days, so three of the marchers reached the resting place at the same time. However, things were not as simple as that.

As actually the synodical revolution of Venus averages not 584, but 583.92 days, an error of 5.2 days (0.8 times 65) will have accumulated after 65 revolutions calculated at 584 days; and when the resting place is reached, heliacal rising of Venus will not theoretically fall on 1 Ahau. (Theoretically because 584 days is the average length of the synodical revolution of the planet; in practice the revolution can vary from 580 to 588 days). That wobble must have made it difficult for the Maya to realize that their figure of 584 was too great, and centuries of observation may have been needed before they approximated the required correction of 5 days in 65 revolutions of the planet. How to deduct those days was a problem, for if they subtracted 5 days from any of the formal positions of heliacal rising, they could not reach 1 Ahau as the new base; only the deduction of 4 days or a multiple thereof would lead back to 1 Ahau.

In the end they solved their problem very neatly by making a correction of four days at the end of the sixty-first Venus year. As the sixty-first Venus year would end on the day 5 Kan, four days after 1 Ahau, the subtraction of four days leads back to 1 Ahau

(61 times 584 equals 35,624. 35,624 minus 4 equals 35,620 equals 137 times 260). The corrected Venus cycle and the 260-day almanac will now reach their resting place together after that interval, but the 365-day year is put out of step, for 35,620 is not divisible by 365. Moreover, the correction is of 4 days whereas it should be 5.

The Maya got round that difficulty again with great ingenuity. At every fifth cycle they made a correction of 8 days at the end of the fifty-seventh revolution, and that, too, led to the day 1 Ahau. That is to say, after 301 Venus revolutions they had made corrections amounting to 24 days (four corrections of 4 days and one of 8 days). Actually, the correction should have been 24.08 days.

An error of 0.08 day in the course of 481 years is a really great achievement. One must remember, too, the condition under which Maya astronomers worked. Early morning mist is frequent in the rain forest of the lowland Maya country and much cloudy weather is to be expected during the long rainy seasons. Knavish weather must have frustrated observation of heliacal risings time after time.

There are only five inferior conjunctions of Venus in eight years, and so in the thirty years of his manhood (the Maya are not long-lived) a priest-astronomer might under ideal conditions observe about twenty heliacal risings. In reality, bad weather would reduce that number to about ten. Moreover, the Maya reckoned heliacal risings as coming four days after inferior conjunction, and it requires very sharp eyes to distinguish the planet then when it is still so very close to the sun. If the observer missed seeing the planet on the fourth day, his calculations might be thrown out a day. Also, he had to work out the planet's deviation from the average of 584 days between heliacal risings and take that into his calculations.

Under those adverse circumstances it must have required many generations of observers to reach the final accuracy of the Maya—an error of one day in slightly over 6,000 years. The two requisites for success were boundless patience and close co-operation between astronomers of sundry cities and different generations. The Maya character and upbringing surely contributed to this result, supplying the essential elements of perseverance and teamwork. The end was less praiseworthy. The Maya believed that the morning star was very dangerous at the time of heliacal rising; it was essential to know beforehand the exact date so that effective measures could

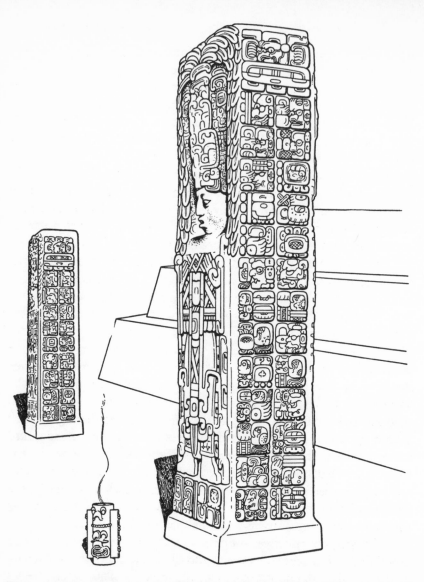

Fig. 15.–Stelae A and C, Quiriguá. In typical fashion chiefs are carved on the fronts and backs and glyphs on the sides of these two monuments, both dedicated in A.D. 775. The nearer text (somewhat simplified for clearer reproduction) records the usual starting point of the calendar, probably a recreation of the world, written 13.0.0.0.0 4 Ahau 8 Cumku (3113 B.C.). Copal is still burned before stelae by the Maya. The incense burner is a British Honduras type of approximately correct date; no Quiriguá incense burners of that date have been found.

be taken by the priesthood to save those in peril. Astronomy was the handmaid of astrology.

The results of these centuries of observation, of deduction, and of improvement on older formulae are given in six pages of the Maya hieroglyphic codex known as the Dresden (it is in a Dresden library). The pages were first identified as tables for the planet Venus over sixty years ago by Ernst Förstemann, librarian at Dresden, who began to study Maya codices as a hobby; the complex system of corrections was solved by John Teeple, a chemical engineer, who took up Maya studies to while away time on the long train journeys his professional work entailed. As in the case of the Maya priest-astronomers, one took up the torch where the other had dropped it.

A second intellectual feat of the Maya priest-astronomers was the construction of a table for predicting when solar eclipses might be visible. Here again patience, co-operation, and deduction were required. The Maya certainly had no knowledge that a solar eclipse can occur only at the new moon's falling within about eighteen days of the sun's crossing the moon's path (the node), an event that takes place every 173.31 days (the eclipse half-year). They could not have known this because they never realized that the earth revolved around the sun. However, by keeping lists of the positions in their sacred almanac of 260 days, they finally realized that eclipses fell within three segments of slightly under 40 days apiece in a doubled sacred almanac, that is to say, a period of 520 days. That is so because three eclipse half-years (3 times 173.31 equals 519.93 days) are only 0.07 days less than two rounds of the sacred almanac. By noting the center points of each of those three segments, they had discovered the nodes without, however, knowing what the node was.

Thus by calculating forward in multiples of six moons, they could find whether the date reached fell within the correct segment of the 520-day double almanac. If it did, they knew an eclipse might occur on that date; if the date reached fell beyond the segment, they knew there could not be an eclipse at that point, and so subtracted one moon from the total to reach a position within the segment. In that way they were able to work out the correct sequence of several possible eclipses at intervals of six moons and then one after five moons.

The results of these observations and of the reasoning from them are presented in this same hieroglyphic Dresden codex as a table giving sixty-nine dates on which solar eclipses would occur for a span of nearly 33 years (11,960 days), after which the table could be used again.

The astronomical knowledge of the Maya and their lack of any information on the nature of the earth or the paths of eclipses prevented them, of course, from knowing which eclipse would be visible in the Maya area or, indeed, from realizing that on every date which they had picked a solar eclipse would be visible somewhere in the world, although probably not in the Maya area.

About one eclipse in four or five is visible in some part of the Maya area, so that a Maya priest-astronomer in the course of his working life of some thirty years would not observe over a dozen solar eclipses, perhaps not that number in view of the many cloudy days. With such limited data no one man could have realized the association of eclipses with the doubled sacred almanac. We must postulate an accumulation over several generations of notes on observations, and finally the genius who experimentally plotted the recorded eclipses not on a single, but on a doubled, sacred almanac and found the key to predictions. Many solutions seem quite simple once they are published, as does this one of using the double sacred almanac, but the unknown Maya astronomer, roughly a contemporary of Charlemagne, who took that step, made a brilliant discovery. One must admit this was not a search for truth for truth's sake. During solar eclipses fearsome beings descended to earth, endangering mankind; foreknowledge of the times of possible eclipses allowed the priests to take counteraction to save mankind.

The really outstanding successes of the Maya in determining the average length of the synodical revolution of Venus and in constructing tables of possible dates for solar eclipses were equaled by the accuracy with which they learned to measure the length of the tropical year.

In addition to the tun of 360 days and the katun of 20 tuns, the Maya had a year of 365 days which ran concurrently with the 260-day sacred almanac, and was divided into 18 "months" of 20 days, and a final period of 5 days, which was considered as in a way outside the year. This last was a time of extreme danger when all kinds of evil might be expected to afflict man, and while it lasted the people abstained from all unnecessary work, fasted, and were continent.

174

The interlocking parts of the calendar are shown in Figure 16 as engaged cogwheels. The smallest carries thirteen numbers which represent gods and accompany the twenty day names. Cog 13 engages Cog Ahau; the following day will be 1 Imix, the starting point of the 260-day almanac. As there are only thirteen cogs on the number wheel, but twenty on the day-name wheel, the next time Ahau comes round full circle, its number will be 7, and it will be followed by 8 Imix, 9 Ik, etc. The name wheel will have to make thirteen revolutions before cogs 13 and Ahau are again engaged. That round of 260 days is the sacred almanac. On the right is part of a larger wheel of 365 cogs, representing the year of eighteen months of twenty days each and the five odd days that end it. The day 13 Ahau is locked with day 18 of the month Cumku. Eight days later, after passing through the five unlucky days of Uayeb, 1 Pop, New Year's Day, will be reached, and the two wheels at the left will have moved eight cogs to reach 8 Lamat. The whole date, therefore, will read 8 Lamat 1 Pop. As 5 is the only common factor of 365 and 260, the year wheel will have to rotate 52 times before 13 Ahau again falls on 18 Cumku. This period of 52 years of 365 days is called the Calendar Round. There were, therefore, 18,980 different combinations of day name, number, and month position in the Maya calendar.

At the top left a large sprocket moves the 20-day month wheel one position every time the day-name wheel completes a revolution. Similarly, at every complete revolution of the month wheel, a tun (360-day) wheel (not shown) would be moved one position, and so on up the scale of Maya time periods until after 8,000 of their years of 360 days, the pictun wheel would move one cog.

A Maya would not approve of this illustration, for to him it is not a matter of a complex machine, but of series of gods who take it in turn to rule the world. The gods of 4, 7, 9, and 13 are kindly disposed toward man; those of 2, 3, 5, and 10 are malignant. Ahau is not just the name of a day—he is the sun; Imix is the earth god; Kan the friendly corn god; Cimi, the feared god of death. For a good harvest plant corn on 8 or 9 Kan, but don't marry a man born on the day Oc (day of the dog), for he will stray from home too often. The days are live beings. Bearing that in mind, let us return to its mechanics.

No leap days were added to keep the vague year of 365 days in

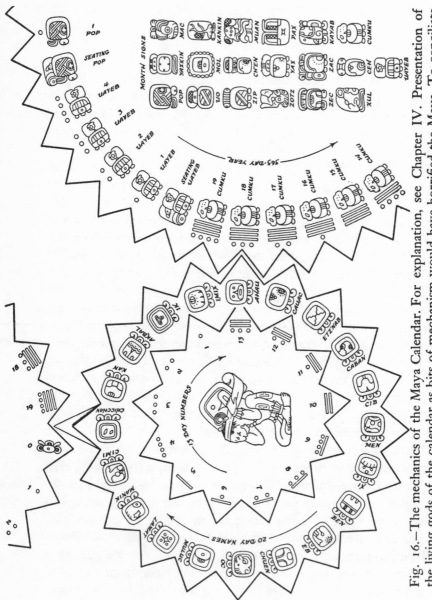

Fig. 16.—The mechanics of the Maya Calendar. For explanation, see Chapter IV. Presentation of the living gods of the calendar as bits of mechanism would have horrified the Maya. To conciliate them, the day 13 Ahau is presented in Maya style in the center of the wheel. The god of the number 13 prepares to set down the load of Ahau at the end of his day's march.

step with the solar year, but the deviation was carefully reckoned and many Maya calculations treat the correction needed to wipe out the accumulated error in my opinion; others feel that the dates in question are historical. However, a date of solar significance might well have been chosen for the enthronement of a chief in that time-conscious culture. I assume below that such was the case. Compare this with the act of consulting the astrologers for a lucky coronation day in the Old World.

Suppose in our calendar we had no leap days. We have added 46 leap days to our calendar since July 4, 1776, but had we done as the Maya did, and added none, we would celebrate July 4 this year when the sun rises where it normally appears on May 19. With the passing of centuries we would find July 4 falling in midwinter. Similarly, in the course of nineteen centuries the feast of Christmas would be celebrated on every day of the year if its position three days after the winter solstice had been retained, and we should now be celebrating it in early April. Easter, governed by the spring equinox, would fall around July; Independence Day would come between Christmas and Easter. The situation would be anarchical.

The Maya, with their orderly nature, being opposed to such chaotic conditions and wishing to know the correct solar influences, calculated the error accumulated by their calendar. The base of the calculation was a certain date corresponding to 3113 B.C. in our calendar, from which normally dates were reckoned. This was a fictitious starting point, which in a general way corresponded to the *ab urbe condita* of the Roman calendar; it perhaps marked the last creation of the world (the Maya believed that the world had been created and destroyed several times, and that we are now in the fifth [?] creation). The actual date was a day 4 Ahau falling on the eighth of the month Cumku, which ended a group of 13 periods, each of 4,000 approximate years. The position 4 Ahau 8 Cumku repeats every 52 years, and it seems that at each repetition, the Maya calculated and recorded on stelae the accumulated error (Fig. 15).

One anniversary fell in January, A.D. 733. On a monument erected in A.D. 731 at Calakmul the error is calculated one year before for this anniversary. Our Gregorian calendar would have inserted 932 leap days in the 3,845 years which had elapsed since that base date. By subtracting 730 to represent the two complete years of 365 days, the actual rectification amounts to 202 days. The Maya correctional date occupies the month position 7 Mol, which is 201 days before 8 Cumku. The Gregorian calendar adds 24.25 leap days per century, a shade too much because the solar year calls for a correction of just under 24.22 days per century, which would mean a total correction (excluding complete years) of 201.2 days. The Maya calculation is a fifth of a day less than is called for, but a day better than our own Gregorian calendar. Actually, as the Maya did not use fractions, it hits the nail right on the head. The next anniversary of the original 4 Ahau 8 Cumku fell in A.D. 785. This time Quiriguá carved the correction on a monument, and gave the correctional date as the month position 15 Yax, which is 212 days after 8 Cumku. The solar correction for this interval of 38.98 years after subtracting two whole years would be 214 days; Gregorian would be 215 days. Thus the Maya is two days short of the solar correction. Most Maya calculations of the accumulated error at the height of the Classic Period run one or two days less than the solar year calls for, whereas in the Gregorian system the correction would be a day too much.

Expressed as figures, this makes dull reading, but remember that a mistake of one minute in measuring the length of the year produces an error of over two and one-half days in calculations, such as those of the Maya, spanning nearly 3,900 years. How did they achieve such precision? So far as we know, they had no exact means of measuring parts of a day, although there is a little evidence that day and night may have consisted of nine "hours" apiece. Their "hours," however, seem to have been rough divisions with such names as "sun comes out," "sun now far away," "a little to midday," "noon," etc.; they were surely not accurate time counts in turn divisible into some native equivalent of our minute. It is, therefore, obvious that the Maya could not set up lines of sight and measure accurately the interval from one equinox to another; all they could have done to gauge the length of the year would have been to reckon how the sun slipped back in terms of days. Careful and patient observation over hundreds of years, transmission of data from one generation to another, and flexible minds willing to discard inaccurate calculations were the essentials of success. These are precisely the qualities requisite for the other achievements in astronomy already discussed.

The cipher (nought) and place numerations are so much parts

of our cultural heritage and seem such obvious conveniences that it is difficult to comprehend how their invention could have been long delayed. Yet neither ancient Greece with its great mathematicians nor ancient Rome had any inkling of either nought or place numeration. To write 1848 in Roman numerals requires eleven letters— MDCCCXLVIII. Yet the Maya had worked out a system of place-value notation while the Romans were still using their clumsy system. The Maya system resembles our own, but differs from it in some respects: numbers are placed in vertical, not horizontal, lines; the space fillers corresponding to our cipher mean completion and normally does not stand for zero or nothing; the system is vigesimal (count by twenties), not decimal.

The completion symbol most commonly used is a shell, although there are other forms (Fig. 17, Nos. 1–5). The vigesimal system seems to us at first somewhat complicated, but it is really almost as simple as the decimal system once it is well mastered. The Maya used dots for numbers one to four, and a bar for five. Thus four is written as four dots; nine as a bar and four dots; twelve as two bars and two dots (Fig. 17, No. 1).

Whereas in our decimal system the addition of noughts at the end multiplies the total by ten, hundred, thousand, etc., in the Maya vigesimal system, the sequence runs 1, 20, 400, 8,000, 160,000, 3,200,000, 64,000,000. These higher numbers were used with sufficient frequency to pass beyond the state of mathematical concepts and to require names. Indeed, Maya terms for all of these multiples, and also for that of the next highest unit, corresponding to 1,280,-000,000, are known, and glyphs for six of them as used in counting of approximate years have been identified (Fig. 17, Nos. 19, 20, 21, 26–29).

The number 400 would be expressed as one dot for four hundred, a shell in the second place to indicate that the count of the twenties was completed, and a shell in the first place to mark that the count of the units was also complete. The number 953 would similarly be written two dots (2 times 400 equals 800), two dots and a bar (7 times 20 equals 140), and two bars and three dots (2 times 5 equals 10 plus 3). This and other examples are illustrated in Fig. 17, but note that the system used for calendrical computations is different, as explained below.

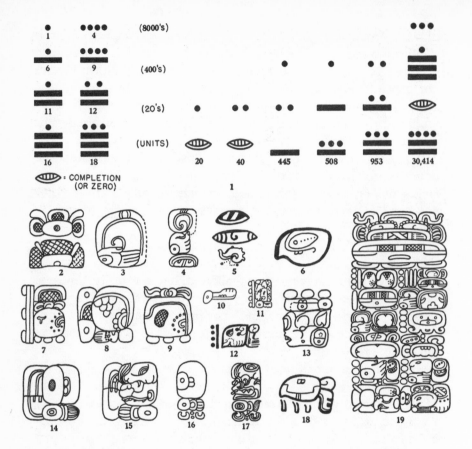

Fig. 17.–Examples of Maya hieroglyphic writing. 1: Bars and dots system of writing numbers. 2–5: Symbols for zero or completion. 6: Sign for 20. 7–9: Month sign Ch'en to show how the hatched element, representing black, can be at left of, above, or inside the main element. 10: *te*, sign for wood or tree. 11, 12: Glyph of the god Bolonyocte, composed of number 9 (*bolon* in Maya), the *Oc* sign, and *te* element. 13: Month position 3-te Zotz'. 14, 15: Count forward to. The head of the xoc fish represents "count" (also *xoc* in Maya); or the water sign, the fish's environment, can be substituted. Element to left means "forward"; that below, "to." 16, 17: Count backward to. Forward sign replaced by element beneath. 18: Fresh maize. 19: An Initial Series date at Quiriguá stating that 3,965 tuns (or vague years), no months, and no days have passed (A.D. 795 in our calendar). The sun god is lord of the night, the moon is three days old, and four moons have been counted. The day is

4 Ahau. 20, 21: The two longest calculations into the past, dates ninety and four hundred million years ago, are recorded. 22, 23: Death signs. 24–29: Glyphs for day, twenty-day month, tun or vague year, 20 tuns, 400 tuns, and 8,000 tuns. 30: Severe drought is the prospect for the year. 31: Drilling fire with sticks. 32: Very lucky. 33: Misfortune. 34: Rainy skies. 35: Seed. 36: Fainting spells. 37: Moon goddess. 38: Maize god. 39: East. 40: West. 41: Red world-direction tree. 42: The numbers 1 to 13 were gods, and at times the Maya carved or painted the head of the god to represent his number. Here in sequence are the heads for 1 through 10, 19, and completion. The Maya used "teens" as we do. The head for 19 combines the jaguar features of the god 9 (spots and hair around mouth) with the death symbols of the god of 10 (fleshless jawbone).

The Maya bars and dots look rather clumsy, and, in contrast, it happens that this particular number, 953, can be expressed rather simply in Roman numerals—CMLIII. However, if you look at Figure 17, No. 1, you will see that 953 is the sum of the two numbers to its left, 445 and 508. The bars and dots are easily added together in this system of place notation; the Roman equivalent, CCCCXLV and DVIII, are less easily summed to reach CMLIII. Once you have a cipher and a concomitant system of place notation, problems of simple arithmetic become infinitely easier, and it matters little whether the system is decimal, duodecimal, vigesimal, or quinary.

This was a discovery of fundamental importance. That it was not an obvious one is shown by the failure of any people of our Western world to make it. Even the great philosophers and mathematicians never found this simple way of lightening their laborious calculations. Indeed, it was not known in Europe until it was passed on to our ancestors, after the Maya Classic period had ended, by the Arabs who had learned of it from India.

Although elaborate multiplication tables and calculations employing the Maya cipher and place notation have survived, all of them concern the calendar; no Maya enumerations of such mundane matters as sacks of maize, army effectives, or counts of cacao beans (the principal currency of Middle America) remain. The calendrical computations are somewhat more involved because they employ a system, roughly comparable to fractions, to take care of periods of less than an approximate year. Just as we normally count time in years expressed in the decimal system and add the months and days in separate decimal counts, as 1/12/1970, so the Maya computed elapsed time in approximate years of 360 days expressed in the vigesimal count, and added the months and days in separate vigesimal counts, more or less comparable to a fractional reckoning. The unit for computation was the year of 360 days, known as a *tun* (Fig. 17, No. 26), divided into 18 "months" (Fig. 17, No. 25) each of 20 days (Fig. 17, No. 24).

The greater part of Maya culture—religion, social organization, agricultural plants and techniques, weapons, and the range of household utensils—was common to all the advanced peoples of Middle America, for one must not forget that great centers such as Zapotec Monte Albán, Tajín, probably Totonac, Teotihuacán, and the cities of coastal Veracruz were at least part contemporaries of the Maya Classic, although Teotihuacán fell early and Tajín rose late. All drew inspiration one from another, just as did the peoples of western Europe in mediaeval times and during the Renaissance. We cannot tell who first introduced such techniques as pressure flaking of flint or obsidian, working jade with the tubular drill, cultivating cotton, or applying polychrome designs to pottery. Most of the luxuries and amenities of life seem to have appeared in the Formative period; others, such as metallurgy, the hammock, cultivation of manioc (cassava), and perhaps batik work on cloth and pottery, reached Middle America from South America.

Nevertheless, we can be almost certain that the purely intellectual discoveries noted above were made by the Maya. So far as we know, no other people in Middle America used tables comparable in accuracy to those the Maya developed to predict possible solar eclipses and to compute the synodical revolutions of Venus, nor, so far as we know, did any other people in Middle America measure the length of the tropical year with the skill the Maya attained. The other peoples of Middle America were not preoccupied with time as were the Maya and, therefore, lacked the stimulus to explore such fields. Indeed, the Aztec had no method for fixing a date except within the fifty-two-year cycle they shared with the Maya and other peoples of Middle America.

It is just possible that the people of La Venta, the so-called Olmec, invented the symbol for nought or completion, since they also used bars and dots in place numeration. However, it is far from certain that they used place numeration before the lowland Maya did (there is no symbol for nought in the few surviving La Venta texts). Furthermore, there is no definite evidence that the Olmec had glyphs in the Formative period.

INVENTIONS AND DISCOVERIES

A number of important inventions and discoveries can be placed to the credit of the peoples of Middle America, but in no case can we be sure which particular group should have the honor for them. Among these is the manufacture of rubber and its use in a number of specialized articles: rubber balls used in playing the ball game, rubber-soled sandals, rubber-proofed rain capes, and poultices of rubber, copal wax, and tar. A brilliant blue pigment of turquoise tone, now known as Maya blue, was much used by the Maya in painting murals. Its composition still defies investigators. As this color was used extensively by the Maya during the Classic period, but is unknown or very rare in the coeval cultures of Middle America, its discovery may be attributed to the Maya with some assurance. Logwood dye, indigo, cochineal, and a purple obtained from a shell fish are pigments discovered by natives of Middle America, but of these only the first can probably be credited to the Maya.

No race has equaled the American Indian in the number and variety of wild plants brought into cultivation, but, again, it is difficult to say where any one plant was first cultivated. As has been noted, the beginnings of cultivated maize have been found in caves not far west of the Maya area (p. 45). Three important food plants may perhaps be credited to the Maya—cacao, the papaya or *pawpaw*, and the aguacate.

Our words cacao, cocoa, and chocolate come from the Aztec, but the cacao tree does not grow on the Mexican plateau, and the Aztec names may have been derived from the Maya (*chacau haa*, literally "hot grated [drink]"). As the tree is probably native to the damper parts of the Maya area and has a relative, *Theobroma bicolor*, which grows wild in many parts of the Maya lowlands, it is at least probable that the Maya were the first to cultivate it. Cacao beans served as currency throughout Middle America (their handling probably accustomed the Maya to large numbers). Indeed, it is only in the last century that they have ceased to be used in market transactions.

The pawpaw or papaya grows wild in much of the Maya area, although the fruit of the wild variety is small and hardly edible. The cultivated fruit is probably a result of Maya industry. The same is true of the aguacate or avocado pear, which is native to Central America and northern South America. Aguacate is the Aztec name, but its use in the Maya area is very ancient, as dialectical variations of its name demonstrate.

All the peoples of Middle America were enthusiastic farmers and keen observers of nature, so it is probable that the Maya acquired more cultivated plants from their neighbors than they gave in exchange. Certainly they received many of their basic foodstuffs from the peoples of the Formative period.

An interesting case of inventiveness is reported, although not on the best authority, of the Xinca, a small non-Maya group in south-eastern Guatemala. They had a mechanical stone-thrower for use in war. A transverse bar rested on two forked posts, and from this hung a rope, to the end of which was attached a beam in horizontal position. The rope was twisted, and, on release, untwisted, rotating the beam, which in turn hit the topmost of a pile of stones, sending each stone flying with great force toward the enemy. One supposes that aim was not too accurate. As the Xinca had borrowed much of their culture from their neighbors, Maya and Pipil, this device may have been a Maya invention, although that it not very probable, for the Maya were not mechanically minded.

A peculiar weapon of the highland Maya was the hornet bomb. Hornets' nests were hurled at the enemy, but we have no information on methods of keeping the hornets peacefully in their nests before the ammunition was used against the foe; the danger of premature explosion must have been considerable.

In road building the Maya did not equal the Inca, but they seem to have been ahead of their Middle American neighbors. The finest Maya road now known connects the city of Cobá in Quintana Roo with a small site called Yaxuna, a few miles south of Chichén Itzá. The road is sixty-two and one-half miles long and averages thirty-two feet in width. For the greater part of its length it is a little over two feet high, but in crossing swampy depressions, its height increases, in one case to slightly more than eight feet. Walls of roughly dressed stone form the sides; large boulders topped with smaller stones laid in cement compose the bed, and the surface, now badly disintegrated, was of cement or stucco. A sort of platform forty feet long and sixteen and one-half feet high covers the road just before the road reaches the outer suburbs of Cobá, and it seems probable that processions halted there to make sacrifices before entering the city. Other mounds and platforms scattered along the road indicate former settlements, but none is of much importance.

Cobá itself is the hub of a series of roads, of which the next most important runs to a fair-sized ruin called Kucican, about five miles south-southwest. Near the beginning, the road, there thirty feet wide and about three feet high, crosses an arm of Lake Macanxoc. A detour of perhaps a quarter of a mile would have avoided the lake, but this was not made (conceivably the lake is now larger than in ancient times, and this arm was not originally part of it). The road protrudes well into the lake from the northern shore, and a short distance from the southern; lines of reeds mark its course for some distance where each end disappears into the water. At various points in the first two miles, side roads lead off to small groups of ruins, and one of these also cuts across another arm of the lake. The road passes through one small group of ruins, a gateway with rectangular pillars at each end marking the entrance and exit. At another point the road intersects another at a sharp angle. A short distance before reaching Kucican the road is several yards high, and at one point a vaulted passage pierces the roadbed, an underpass by which alone one could pass from territory on one side of the road to that on the other, for the high vertical walls could not be scaled.

The building of these roads entailed tremendous labor and not a little engineering knowledge. In swampy sections, the engineers had to be sure that their foundations were deep and secure (there are no detours to avoid swampy sections); the lack of any evidence of subsidence demonstrates that they solved the problem. The tracing of the routes must have presented problems, too. The road from Cobá to Yaxuna follows these directions: start to mile 4, 279°; mile 4 to mile 10, 269°; mile 10 to mile 15, 260°; mile 15 to mile 20, 270°; mile 20 to mile 40, 260°; mile 40 to mile 62 (Yaxuna), 264°. Distances are to the nearest mile; degrees are magnetic. Since three of the changes of direction coincide with archaeological ruins, we can feel fairly certain that the road was planned to link these various cities. Yet there are two sections of twenty and twenty-two miles respectively without any change of direction. At night, with bonfires burning on pyramids at the termini, an engineer at the halfway mark might be able to lay out his line, but with the thick forest around him, the task cannot have been easy. In solving the problem, the Maya demonstrated ingenuity.

These Maya roads were constructed during the Classic period. Shorter ones connecting outlying parts of Uaxactún and other Maya cities of the Petén have been found, and aerial photographs of the Petén, made some years ago in an aerial survey for oil, seem to indicate in the north of that uninhabited land a great road comparable to the Cobá-Yaxuna road. There were roads of sorts in other parts of Middle America, but none comparable to the finest built by the Maya. Yet the Maya had no wheeled traffic or beasts of burden to use these magnificent wide roads.

In architecture the Maya were far ahead of their neighbors in Middle America and showed more engineering skill than the ancient Peruvians. Inca buildings are made of beautifully fitted stonework, but their erection called for neatness, not for engineering.

The religious buildings of the contemporaries of the Maya in Middle America were largely of perishable materials in the Classic period; later they were of stone with roofs which were thatched or were formed of flat beams on which rest poles to support a layer of small stones imbedded in mortar. The high-pitched roof of thatch was far commoner than the flat roof. Both these types were used by the Maya, but the commonest type of roof for ceremonial structures was the corbeled vault, in which the two legs of the vault draw together until the space between can be bridged with capstones (Plate 8; Figs. 3, 7, 8).

In the earlier Maya buildings walls and vaults were constructed of large stones (so-called block masonry) usually tenoned into the hearting and set in mortar with a fairly liberal use of spalls. The hearting was largely stone with only a moderate amount of mortar. At a later time (end of the Classic period) this type of masonry had evolved to the use of solid concrete faced with a veneer of thin well-cut stones. The vault stones often are provided with a cut-away tenon (called a boot-shaped vault stone) to hold it in position against the pull of gravity, but facing stones of walls do not have these tenons and are true veneer. The concrete is a mixture of lime, *sascab* (a friable marl with a high preponderance of calcium carbonate) used in place of sand which is very rare in the Maya lowlands, and lumps of limestone. Concrete construction produced far stronger buildings than had been possible with the old type of masonry.

In building the two inclining walls of a corbeled vault, the Maya had to study problems of stress and strain and the tensile strength of concrete. Newly laid mortar could crush under the weight of the overhanging soffitt and be squeezed out at the vault face, causing the vault to collapse. Concrete, on the other hand, would distribute the weight more evenly over the whole thickness of the vault.

The Maya architect seems to have been fully aware of the importance of the mechanical principle of stability, but to have been hampered by the weakness of his cement until it had time to harden. He got around that problem in two ways: by building his walls to a given height and allowing them to set before continuing the construction (there is plenty of archaeological evidence for this practice), and by setting wooden crossbeams at intervals to help hold apart the two legs of the vault until they were bridged with capstones (Fig. 8).

A detailed description of Maya architecture would be out of place in this book, and I must confess to a complete ignorance of theories of stress. The point, however, that I would make is this: the Aztec and other peoples of Middle America, as well as the Inca, built by the simple process of laying one stone directly on another; the thrust was only vertical, and they needed no engineering knowledge to raise such buildings. The Maya, in choosing to use the corbeled vault, took up a challenge which could only be met with intelligence and experiment.

Earl H. Morris, who was in charge of excavation and reconstruction at Chichén Itzá for several seasons, writes: "With the beginning of the vault, in most cases a decidedly ticklish procedure was at hand, which needed a clear understanding of the principles of balance and a meticulous observance of plan for its successful accomplishment." And of the vaulting at the Temple of the Warriors: "When one visualizes a rib of masonry 91.40 meters in length, as was the case in the North and West Colonnades, balanced upon a row of slender round columns that were not even monolithic in character, one can but regard this type of construction as one of the boldest architectural experiments ever attempted. Surely architects and masons alike must have sighed with relief when at last capstones were laid to bind rib to rib."

Why, one wonders, did the Maya use the corbeled vault instead of thatching their temples or covering them with flat beam-and-pole roofs, so much simpler to construct and permitting much wider rooms? In several English cathedrals a somewhat similar situation obtained: wooden roofs of the Norman period were replaced with the ribbed stonework of the Gothic arch, despite all the accompanying difficulties of lateral thrust. The answer must be that no effort can be too great in building to the glory of God or of gods; man's creations are sanctified by overcoming difficulties. Furthermore, as I have already remarked, it is probable that the Maya favored small dark rooms for their ceremonies; large light rooms would have detracted from the atmosphere of mystery. They could have kept the corbeled vault and still had larger and lighter rooms by resting the vaults on columns instead of solid walls, but it was not until the Toltec reached Chichén Itzá with their less mystical approach to religion that this style of building was employed.

It is remarkable that the intellectual successes of the Maya were not (from our point of view) practical; they were the outcome of spiritual needs. The Maya astronomer strove for knowledge, not as an end in itself, but as a means of controlling fate, a kind of astrology. There was, he felt, an orderliness in the heavens to which the gods conformed; once that was learned, he could predict the future through exact knowledge of which gods held sway at any given time, and influence it by knowing when and whom to propitiate.

The great roads were not built for practical ends, for the Maya had no beast of burden or wheeled vehicle; they were surely for spiritual purposes—as a setting for great religious processions. The corbeled vault was not employed for utilitarian purposes, but almost surely as an embodiment of sacrificial effort. Even the Maya blue pigment was primarily for painting murals to the glory of the gods. In the field of everyday living I can think of no discovery of a practical nature attributable to the Maya.

HIEROGLYPHIC WRITING

Middle America is the only part of the New World in which a system of embryonic writing developed. The Aztec and other peoples of Mexico had books, but in them the information is largely in the form of picture-writing, and the glyphs that are scattered through them or carved on stone are with few exceptions pictorial. The day signs—snake and house, for example—are illustrated by pictures of those objects, and even rebus writing appears to have been somewhat rare before the arrival of the Spaniards. (Rebus writing is the system in which one writes a sentence such as "I can see Aunt Peg" by drawing an eye, a can, waves, an ant, and a peg. That is, one reproduces the sound, not the meaning). Aztec glyphs consist almost entirely of calendar signs and glyphs for persons and towns, and as individuals and towns usually were named after animals or objects, their depiction was simple.

Maya hieroglyphs were sculptured or, more rarely, incised on stone stelae, altars, ball-court markers and rings, steps, panels, walls of buildings, lintels of stone or wood, and wooden ceilings. They were modeled in stucco; incised on personal ornaments, such as jade and shell; and painted on pottery, on murals, and in books. They are far more numerous and more complex than those of the Aztec.

The earliest glyphs may correspond to highland Maya speech. For instance, the day Jaguar is called Ix or Hix in Yucatec, a meaningless word, but in Kekchi, a highland Maya tongue, Hix is still the name for jaguar. The sound values of many glyphs probably correspond to lowland Maya of about A.D. 200 ancestral to, and fairly closely resembling, the still nearly related Chol, Chontal, Chorti, and Yucatec. Still others, confined to the codices, are of later origin and correspond to Yucatec of just before the Spanish Conquest. An example of this last is the glyph for severe drought, *kintunyaabil*, the parts of which correspond to Yucatec speech (Fig. 17, No. 30, left).

I believe that the Maya had neither an alphabetic nor a syllabic writing except insofar as most Maya words are monosyllables. There is a considerable use of a simple phonetic writing which might be described as an advanced form of rebus writing in that the picture has become so conventionalized that the original object is no longer recognizable. For instance, the curious object in Figure 17, No. 10, is the symbol for tree, *te* in Maya. We find it combined with the symbol for red, as the red tree of the East in Codex Dresden. The sound *te*, but totally unconnected with the idea of tree, was also affixed to number in counting months. In hieroglyphic texts the same symbol is used. Figure 17, No. 13, records the third (ox) day of the month Zotz' (bat)—oxte Zotz'. Again, an important god was called Bolon Yocte, and his name may mean something like "nine paces there." His glyphs show the number nine, the glyph for oc, 'dog,' and the *te* sign (Fig. 17, Nos. 11, 12) although neither dog nor wood have anything to do with his name.

Similarly, *u* means "moon" in several Maya languages, but it is also the possessive "of." The lunar glyph may refer to the moon, but it is also used as the possessive, and even can stand for the number twenty (Fig. 17, No. 6). An example of old-fashioned rebus writing is supplied by the Maya sign for "count." In Yucatec the word *xoc* means "to count," but it was also the name of a mythical fish which dwelt in the sky and to which worship was made. As the Maya had difficulty in rendering an abstract idea such as "count" in glyphic form, they turned to rebus writing and used the head of the *xoc* fish as the glyph for *xoc* "count" (Fig. 17, Nos. 15, 17).

Ideographic glyphs were used rather extensively by the Maya. For example, the head of the *xoc* fish was not easy to carve and might be confused with the head of some other fish or of some animal— there are many animals in Maya mythology which no zoologist would recognize. The Maya, therefore, often substituted for the picture of the fish an ideograph, the symbol for water, apparently with the idea that water, as the element in which fish live, recalls the *xoc* fish. The symbol for water was a jade bead, because water and jade were both precious and green (Fig. 17, Nos. 14, 16). Thus jade equals water equals *xoc* fish equals *xoc* to count. The system is extremely complex.

A good example of an ideogram is the frequent combination of the seed glyph (Fig. 17, No. 35) with the earth glyph to form the sign for milpa, cornfield (Fig. 18*h*). However much the name for milpa might differ from one Maya language to another, the combination of the two signs seed and earth would always be recognizable as corn- field. In the picture which accompanies the glyphs (Fig. 18*h*) the rain god with planting stick in hand is walking on the cornfield glyph. Metaphorgrams are another feature of Maya writing and pictures. The vampire bat, common in the Maya lowlands, supplies a glyph which is combined with that for sacrifice, apparently to indicate human sacrifice or a sacrifice involving blood, a natural metaphor in view of the blood-sucking of the vampire. Again, the bat rests head down. A rare glyph is the inverted head of a bat. This, used only with the katun glyph and its number, indicated that that particular katun had come to rest, that its journey in the unending march of time (p. 163) had ended. What a striking and obvious metaphorgram for the abstract idea of rest. A Maya metaphor for drought was *cim cehil*, "the deer die." We find a picture of a dying deer in one scene and the drought glyph (Fig. 17, No. 30) is in the text which the picture illus- trates. "The deer die" is a metaphor for severe drought, because, as

Yucatán lacks streams and ponds, the deer die of thirst in time of extreme drought. "Maize in bud" was a charming Maya metaphor for a youth of marriageable age. Glyphs of sprouting maize in contexts treating of marriage seemingly are metaphorgrams for these youths.

A knowledge of Maya thought processes is often necessary to understand Maya glyphs: a divinatory almanac running across Codex Dresden pages 31–35 has four similar scenes of Chac, the rain god, seated on a coiled snake enclosing a deposit or reservoir of water. From other sources we can be pretty sure that these are the water deposits from which the rain gods dip water to sprinkle on the earth in the form of rain. The glyph denoting these water deposits is a spiral with the number nine attached. A spiral is a common water symbol throughout Middle America. Special ritual water is called *zuhuyha*, *zuhuy* meaning uncontaminated, virgin, fresh; *ha*, water. However, *bolon*, the term for the number nine, is to this day used by the Maya in the sense of uncontaminated, fresh, etc.; that is, it is a synonym for *zuhuy*. The glyph 9 spiral therefore means fresh, uncontaminated water.

The chain of Maya imagery which leads to the equation nine equals fresh, uncontaminated, is as follows: The god of number nine is the Chicchan snake god, whose symbol (normally worn on his forehead) is the yax sign. *Yax* signifies green, but it is also used in Yucatec in the sense of new, fresh, first, first time, first born. Through the latter meanings *yax* equates with *zuhuy* (for example *zuhuy akab* is the start of night, nightfall, *akab* being night, but *yaxokinal*, "newly set the sun" is practically a synonym). A parallel in our culture would be a sketch of a military figure standing in a boat or of a hand thrust into a wound (Mediaeval attribute of doubting St. Thomas) instead of writing Delaware or Missouri. It is because such thought associations lie behind many glyphs that I see little hope that computers can help, a matter shortly to be discussed.

A remarkable feature is that many, particularly calendric, glyphs have two quite distinct forms, which may be used indiscriminately. One is a head form; the other is a symbolic or ideographic form, usually some attribute or element, often highly conventionalized, which recalled the glyph to the reader. It is as though one were to write "St. Peter" or, instead, draw a picture of crossed keys. For example, the day Cimi, "death," could be carved or painted either

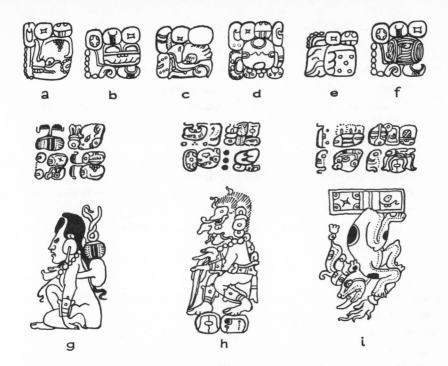

Fig. 18.—More Maya glyphs. a–f, Emblem glyphs of Copán, Yaxchilán, Palenque (2), Piedras Negras, and Tikal and the Pasión confederation. g–i, Divination passages in Codex Dresden. Glyphs read top line left to right, then bottom line same fashion. g. Glyph 1, "Skin diseases allied to smallpox" (*Kak*) are Glyph 3, "the divine fate" (*cuch.*) which Glyph 2, "the moon goddess, Zac Ixchel" has in store for us. Glyph 4: meaning unknown. Here is double use of rebus writing or punning. The fire symbol *kak* stands for *kak*, skin disease, and *cuch*, load carried on back, stands here for *cuch*, fate, in both the glyphs and the picture. h: Glyph 1, meaning unknown; Glyph 2, "in the corn field or milpa"; Glyph 3, "the yellow Chac"; Glyph 4, "Very good tidings" or "great abundance." The picture shows Chac, the rain god, with planting stick in hand, standing on the glyph for cornfield. This is an ideograph combining the glyphs for seed and earth. i: Glyph 1, meaning unknown; Glyph 2, *pek* sky. Glyph 3, sign for god with "woe to" prefix; Glyph 4, woe to the maize seed. *Pek* is the usual Yucatec name for dog, but it also means rains of little value, rainless storms, and by extension is a symbol for drought. As this text is in a weather almanac and the maize-seed glyph is in the context, we can be certain here that this again is rebus writing; *pek*, dog, is used for *pek*, rainless storms. The dog carries a lighted brand, a symbol of drought or great heat, confirmation of the proposed interpretation of the passage.

as a head of the death god or as a symbol resembling the percentage sign, which was an attribute of the death god often painted on his body or clothes (Fig. 17, Nos. 22, 23). To the initiated that symbol stood for the death god, just as the crossed keys recall St. Peter to the devout.

Most glyphs are compounds, consisting of a main element to which are attached various affixes. A prefix occurs to the left of, or above, the main element; a postfix is to the right of, or below, the main element. The choice of position for either a prefix or a postfix usually depended on artistic considerations, which generally meant a question of how best to fill the available space; but, with few exceptions, a prefix could not appear as a postfix or vice versa without changing the meaning of the glyphic compound. The glyph for "count" supplies a good example of a compound. The main element, as noted, is the head of the *xoc* fish or the sign for water, its counterpart; the affixes are adverbs and a preposition, and change the meaning. The little torch-like element which occurs as a postfix in all examples (Fig. 17, Nos. 14–17) represents the locative preposition *ti* "to," "at," or "from"; the prefix to the left or above is the symbol for "forward"; the third affix, never present when the "forward" prefix is given, is a postfix indicating "backward." Thus, the affixes alter the sense. In one case (Nos. 14, 15) the whole signified "count forward to"; in the other case (Nos. 16, 17), "count backward to [or from]." Such variability, for there are eight ordinary combinations of these elements, does not make the interpretation of the glyphs any easier, but all boil down to "add" or "subtract."

Identified affixes include adjectives, adverbs, prepositions, and relationship terms, but Maya writing is so fluid that an affix can change places with a main element or it can be "infixed" in the main element; that is, the affix can be omitted and its outstanding characteristic added as a detail in the interior of the main glyph (Fig. 17, No. 9). Similarly, two glyphs can be fused into one by combining the essential elements of both in a new glyph.

The Maya wrote simple sentences, but I rather doubt that they had affixes to express pronouns and tenses. Actually, verbs are rather weak in the Maya language; they can be described as verbal nouns. Thus we find in the divinatory almanacs sentences which can be tentatively translated as, "His influencing the maize, the death god. Heaped up death," or as we might say, "The death god now rules the growing maize. Much death will be the result." Three divinatory passages in Codex Dresden with translations are in Figure 18*g–i*.

Most of the glyphs are still undeciphered, and, in the absence of an alphabet, progress is slow. There is no key or Maya equivalent of the Rosetta stone, save for the little information Bishop Landa gave us on the glyphs of the calendar. The decipherment of new glyphs does not appreciably simplify the task of tackling the remainder, as in a crossword puzzle or in a writing which employs an alphabet.

Maya glyphic research is now at an uncertain and frustrating stage. Recently, several students have claimed to have found the key to decipherment, but they agree on neither method nor results; for a common glyphic element there are as many decipherments as would-be decipherers. It is claimed that Maya writing is partly syllabic and alphabetic, a view I find hard to accept. However, an electronic computer in remotest Siberia has now been brought into action to substantiate that claim, but a computer is like a sausage machine— what comes out at one end depends on what was fed in at the other. Here is one result of its highly publicized work: scenes on page 20 of the Maya Codex Madrid show gods seated or kneeling, each in a sort of wooden cage, the crosspiece or roof of which they support with upraised hands. According to the computer, the accompanying glyphs tell us that brick-making is the activity shown. Apart from the fact that the pictures contain nothing remotely resembling brick-making, only in the region of the Grijalva-Usumacinta delta, home of the Chontal Maya, were bricks used (there is no building stone in the area). The Siberian group accepts the view that the language of the surviving Maya books is Yucatec Maya, and, indeed, there is overwhelming evidence that Codex Madrid did not come from the delta area. The Yucatec-Maya word *hi*, which the Russians say corresponds to one of the glyphs, does not mean clay, as they claim, but means the arenaceous temper mixed with the clay; the word *kak*, which they give as the translation of another glyphic element means "fire," not "bake," as they inform us.

Something is awry when the computer comes up with a reading "quartz-sand fire," which we are told means to bake bricks, and this is offered as the interpretation of scenes totally unconnected with brick-making in a book composed by a branch of the Maya who never made bricks. "Decipherments" of this kind serve only to illustrate how needful it is to know something about Maya ethnology and linguistics before undertaking glyphic research. One person informed the world with exemplary modesty that he had deciphered the glyphs after only two months' study, whereas his predecessors, he added, achieved little or nothing in the best part of a century. Another, with equal disdain of the efforts of others, although willing enough to take their decipherments without giving credit, solved the problems thanks to a Marxist-Leninist approach.

We are back where we were nearly a century ago, at the start, when a rash of decipherments, each lot more fantastic than its predecessor, brought the subject into disrepute and led to the virtual abandonment of glyphic research for several decades. In a very different category and one productive of important results is the work on texts of the Classic period which treat of lay activities.

Most Maya glyphs are composed of several elements, a main sign and variable affixes. One common glyphic sign is found as a main element in combination with nearly eighty different arrangements of affixes or infixes. Some of these affixes may be variants of one another, thereby reducing appreciably the total of different meanings. Furthermore, affixes can not only become main signs or vice versa, but they can have both personified or symbolic forms. Moreover, as the Maya abhorred exact repetition, the sculptor (and, to a lesser extent, the scribe) often introduced every permissible variation when it was necessary to reproduce the same glyph several times in a text. In a recently compiled catalog I list 492 main signs and 370 affixes. Subsequent research will show some to be merely variations, reducing the total to perhaps 750.

In some inscriptions, principally composed of dates and calculations, most of the glyphs can be read; in others, which appear to deal with history or ritualistic matters, the percentage of deciphered glyphs is quite low; in a few texts not a glyph can be translated.

In many cases we know what the main element of a glyph signifies, but we cannot decipher the affixes; in other cases the reverse is true. The matter is further complicated by the different meanings an element can have; for instance, the glyph for *tun* (Fig. 17, No. 26) can mean the approximate year of 360 days, or it can mean "end," or it can serve as an intensifier as in the glyph for severe drought, *kintunyaabil—kin*, "sun," *tun*, "intense," *yaabil*, "for the [whole] year" (Fig. 17, No. 30), or means stone or rock ledge.

So far as is known, the hieroglyphic texts of the Classic period deal in part with the passage of time and astronomical matters, the gods associated therewith, and, probably, the ceremonies appropriate for these occasions. Recently, Miss Proskouriakoff has established that passages treat also of rulers, with dates which probably mark their births, their accession to power, and anniversaries thereof. Name glyphs of rulers, even of women, are given, and we are in a fair way to working out dynasties. Henry Berlin has identified glyphs which are probably those of city states.

In the historical fragments which survive in the colonial transcriptions called the Books of Chilam Balam, there is singularly little stress on the doings of individuals, and that only when individual behavior affected history.

Maya hieroglyphic writing was perfected primarily to record the passage of time, the names and influences of the reigning gods of each of its divisions, and the accumulated knowledge of the priest-astronomers which had a bearing on those subjects. Its use for other purposes was a secondary development. Again, Maya ingenuity was directed by an end which we would regard as impractical.

Hieroglyphic writing was also set down in books composed of a single sheet of paper up to about eight inches high and several yards long. This was folded like a screen, each fold forming a page about six inches wide, both sides of which carried writing. Because of the screenlike construction, the text on the whole of the front is to be read before one passes to the back. The contents are divided into what we might term chapters, which occupy a varying number of pages. The material for the paper was a fiber obtained from a variety of the wild fig tree. This fiber was pounded as though to make bark cloth, and, when reduced to a clothlike consistency, was covered with a thin sizing of lime to supply the writing surface. (Plate 31*a*).

Only three of these books have survived, and they are known by the names of the cities in which they now rest. Codex Dresden, a beautiful example of Maya draughtsmanship, is a new edition made probably about A.D. 1200 of an original executed during the Classic period. It treats of astronomy (the eclipse and Venus tables) and divination. Codex Madrid, of crude workmanship, almost surely is not earlier than the fifteenth century. It treats of divination and ceremonies connected with various crafts and rituals of general importance, such as those at the new year. Codex Paris, also late and not of very good workmanship, illustrates on one side ceremonies and probably prophecies in connection with the endings of a sequence of katuns and tuns. Divinatory matters fill the reverse side. Early Spanish writers speak of codices which treat of history. None of these have survived, but it is possible that the prophecies from the sequence of katuns in Codex Paris are also historical in that Maya prophecies are projections of the past into the future.

The count of the katuns and their historical and prophetic functions survived the influx of Mexican ideas into the Maya area and, in fact, were still going strong at Tayasal, the Itzá stronghold, at its capture by the Spaniards in 1697. Landa discusses them at length: "They had a certain way of counting time and their affairs by ages . . . of twenty years . . . they call katuns. . . . with them they keep tally of their ages marvellously. . . . This was the learning in which they placed most faith. . . . They worshiped these katuns . . . and governed themselves by their superstitions and deceptions"

As noted, much of this lore survives in the books of Chilam Balam of colonial times, and the prophetic material in Codex Paris, referred to above, is surely post-Mexican. A sequence of gods (many of them very Mexicanized) ruling over tuns (360-day years) and a fragment of what seems to have been a count of katuns and half-katuns were painted on the walls of a buried building at Santa Rita, northern British Honduras, dating between A.D. 1250 and A.D. 1500.

These illustrate how archaeology and the colonial written sources complement each other. In one scene (Fig. 19) a Maya merchant god, recognizable by his Pinocchio nose, braided carrying-strap on head, and (in the original) his blue and red coloring, shakes a rattle and beats an upright drum (compare with the drum on the Bonampak mural, Plate 17*b*.) Beneath is the glyph 7 Ahau, probably to indicate that this scene is referable to a katun 7 Ahau. Now in the books of Chilam Balam the drum and rattle of the katun is a stock phrase, and in a prophecy for katun 7 Ahau itself we find "at that time the drum below, the rattle on high [resound]." Moreover, in one series of katun prophecies, Ek Chuah, chief god of merchants, is named as

Fig. 19.—The drum and rattle of the katun. The god of merchants, recognizable by his pinocchio nose, tumpline, and coloring, holds his rattle aloft and beats the drum. The glyph 7 Ahau, at left bottom of drawing, names the katun. This was Katun 7 Ahau, ending in A.D. 1342, and is probably the date of this design, taken from a mural at Santa Rita, British Honduras. (*After T. Gann.*)

patron of katun 7 Ahau. One could hardly find a better example of one line of research authenticating the other.

Between the earliest surviving record of a katun count (there were surely earlier ones which have not survived) and the last to be counted at Tayasal 1,340 years elapsed—quite a span for that one brand of "superstitions and deceptions."

It is highly probable that the katun prophecies as preserved in the Books of Chilam Balam were memorized songs or poetic recitations such as we know were presented in public. The keys to them were the short glyphic texts such as the pages of katun prophecies in Codex Paris and Codex Dresden (page 60). These would have been expanded to long recitals, but they functioned, so to speak, as prompt books should the verse get corrupted.

The details of the Maya calendar with its meshing of concurrent cycles into the great "long count" recording the lapse of time are too involved to be summarized here. For a fuller discussion of the matter the reader is referred to Sylvanus G. Morley's *An introduction to the Study of the Maya hieroglyphs* and, as a more advanced course, to the writer's *Maya Hieroglyphic Writing: Introduction.*

However, in carving the Initial Series, as the long count is called (Figs. 15, 17, No. 19), Maya sculptors did justice to the honor in which time was held. The roll call of the periods has a grand cadence, which in itself is a prayer and a noble oblation to the divine powers. Because it embodied a living creed, it was carved with the same faith, humility, and loving patience that guided the hands that embroidered the magnificent vestments of mediaeval Christendom. It is the opening movement of the symphony of time, a treasure in history's store of beauty.

LITERATURE

A few Maya songs have survived, but a fuller appreciation of Maya literature is to be had from the Books of Chilam Balam, which contain many oral traditions and songs of ancient times. These are often antiphonal in the sense that the second line or sentence answers or expands or is a variation of the first, an arrangement familiar to us from its frequency in the Old Testament. Typical examples are: "The fan of heaven shall descend; the wreath of heaven, the bouquet

200

of heaven shall descend. The drum of the Lord 11 Ahau shall resound; his rattle shall resound." "They shall find their harvest among the trees; they shall find their harvest among the rocks, those who have lost their harvest in the katun of Lord 11 Ahau." "The hills shall burn, the ravine between shall burn. The fire shall flare up at the great *sucte* tree. It shall burn at the sea, on the beach. The squash seeds shall burn, the squash shall burn, the *macal* [an edible tuber] shall burn." And "They moved among the four lights; among the four layers of the stars. The world was not lighted. There was no day: there was no night, there was no moon. Then they perceived that the dawn was coming; then dawn came."

Compare these with "They shall roar together like lions: they shall yell as lions' whelps" (Jer. 51:38); or "He shall come down like the rain upon the mown grass, even as the drops that water the earth" (Ps. 72:6).

This antiphonal character of Maya verse is, I feel fairly certain, present also in the hieroglyphic texts. Glyphs which seem to be redundant probably represent this responsive quality. The prayers of present-day Maya similarly display literary qualities of a high order, and tend to have this same form of antiphony.

Sometimes the Maya played on the sounds of words. For instance, note the contrasting *c'alab* and *c'ilab* in this line: *bal cin c'alab ca bin c'ilab uinic ti be*; or *zilic* and *tz'ilic* in this: *hex u zilic u pice: u tz'ilic u pach*.

The story of the creation of the *uinal* or twenty-day period is a good example of Maya literature and, likewise, a pleasant example of the personification of the divisions of time and of their march through eternity. The creation starts with the day 12 Oc and is completed forty days later, on the day 13 Oc. *Oc* means "footstep," which is most appropriate for the journey of time. In Maya belief the world was in darkness for a long time before the creation of the sun. The days, therefore, came before daylight. The original, in the Book of Chilam Balam of Chumayel, has been translated by Ralph Roys. Very slight emendations have been made:

This is a song of how the *uinal* came into being before the dawn of the world. Then he began to march by his own effort alone. Then said his maternal grandmother, then said his maternal aunt, then said his paternal grandmother, then said his sister-in-law: "What shall we say when we see man on the road?" These were their words as they marched along, when there was as yet no man. Then they arrived there in the east and began to speak. "Who has passed here? Here are footprints. Measure it off with your foot." So spake the mistress of the world. Then he measured the footsteps of our Lord, God the Father. This was the reason it was called counting off the world by footsteps, 12 Oc. This was the count, after it had been created by the day 13 Oc, after his feet were joined evenly, after they had departed there in the east. Then he spoke its name when the day had no name, after he had marched along with his maternal grandmother, his maternal aunt, his paternal grandmother, and his sister-in-law. The *uinal* was created, the day, as it was called, was created, heaven and earth were created, the stairway of water, the earth, rocks and trees; the things of the sea and the things of the land were created. . . . The *uinal* was created, there was the dawn of the world; sky, earth, trees, and rocks were set in order; all things were created by our Lord, God the Father. Thus he was there in his divinity, in the clouds, alone and by his own effort, when he created the entire world, when he moved in the heavens in his divinity. Thus he ruled in his great power. Every day is set in order according to the count, beginning in the east, as it is arranged.

The story has beauty and simplicity, and its imagery is in keeping with Maya philosophy.

ARTISTIC ACHIEVEMENT

During the Classic period there were at least four great cultures—Teotihuacán, Monte Albán (the Zapotec), Tajín, and Remojadas—full or part contemporaries of the great Maya florescence, and each with its distinctive art style. All five peoples were at almost the same cultural level, as least in the field of everyday living; they grew the same staple crops and followed the same system of agriculture so far as differences in climate permitted; they worshiped tribal gods who were as close to one another as the Greek and Roman pantheons; and they shared the same ideas on cosmology and the creation. Yet each had its own style of sculpture and representation in painting, each so distinct from any of the others that it is immediately recognizable.

Despite considerable trade between these centers of Middle America, one region had very little influence on the sculptural style of another during the peak of the Classic period. Some representations of the Mexican rain god Tlaloc in Teotihuacán style appear on sculptures of the early Classic period at lowland centers, notably at Copán and Tikal. It is in pottery that Teotihuacán artistic influence is most apparent, particularly in the squat cylindrical jars with covers and three feet. These were coated after firing with thin plaster-like stucco, on which were painted in pastel tones seated personages. Some were imported; others are local copies. They have been found in tombs at Kaminaljuyú and, recently, at Tikal, and date to the first stages of the early Classic period. They almost duplicate finds at Teotihuacán. It is not until the very end of the Classic period, when the abandonment of the great cities was near, that exotic elements became frequent in Maya art and reached considerable importance in Yucatán. Nevertheless, all of these art styles of Middle America had their roots in the Formative period; the divergences partly reflect tribal character and environment.

Maya religious sculpture is one of the great glories of pre-Columbian America, but the newcomer to the field may have difficulty in appreciating it because its conventions are quite different from those of Western art. Similarly, Japanese art met with little enthusiasm when first brought before Western eyes. The primary interest of the Maya artist lay in exactly reproducing the attributes of each god and in conforming to the traditional style of presentation. The necessity of introducing so much symbolism led to over-elaboration of certain aspects and to consequent distortion of proportions and failure to allow the design to stand forth against a plain background. Thus, in Maya sculptures the head, with its elaborate headdress, may occupy over one-third of the total height of the figure because these were the vehicles principally employed to convey full identification of the deity portrayed and of the "aspect" it was desired to present (Plates 9, 11). At first this disproportion strikes our Western eyes as uncouth and lacking in aesthetic sensibility, but as we grow accustomed to Maya conventions, we come to accept them as natural.

The principal personage on a Maya stela is a typical product of convention. He may have one of three positions: full face with feet turned out so that they are almost in a straight line, heel to heel; or the head in profile and the body full face; or the whole figure in profile (Plates 9–15). These stiff and awkward postures must not be considered symptoms of immaturity. They surely were demanded by tradition and represent a rigid adherence to a style of religious portraiture evolved before Maya sculptors had mastered the art of foreshortening. This is not surprising, for religious art throughout the ages has tended to adhere to the canons of past usage. That the Maya were perfectly capable of foreshortening and of giving tremendous vitality to their subject matter is seen in the subsidiary figures on monuments or in the more secular art of the murals (Figs. 10, 19, 22). The artist had to treat the chief impersonating a god with restraint and in the traditional static manner; he was not stifled by religious convention in carving the subsidiary figures, and so could lavish all his skill upon them. He makes them clamber around entwined snakes or peer like startled fawns from behind a cornstalk (Fig. 25a). In mediaeval art we find the same situation: the saint is conventionally posed in his niche; demons and representatives of the European bestiary riot on hidden misericords.

The Maya sometimes introduce humor in their art. Note the look of surprise on the face of the long-nosed god of Figure 27. He seems to be saying to his *alter ego*, "What a fish and a half you've brought me." At Copán a giant jaguar guards each flank of a flight of stairs. The jaguar has always had a largely undeserved reputation for fierceness, with many apocryphal stories of attacks on lonely travelers. The artist must have decided to debunk the dread creature. He carved each with one paw on hip, the other pointing to the steps —like a glorified Mickey Mouse in duplicate ushering folk into Disneyland—and each is given a little loincloth like a lady's maid's apron in movieland and ridiculous pompoms and flares at the end of its tail. "Who's afraid of the big bad wolf?" is clearly the theme.

Maya sculptors seldom failed to achieve an effective balance in their compositions, although occasionally the symmetry was a little too patent, as in the tablets at Palenque, where a central motif is flanked by individuals of almost equal size, and they, in turn, by columns of glyphs of the same length and breadth. Generally, however columns of glyphs are used to counter disharmonic groupings. Where a smaller figure faces a larger one, a mass of glyph blocks above the former restores the balance. Many sculptures have a subsidiary quality of diagonalism which is produced by the two-headed dragon element, called the ceremonial bar, which many personages carry at a cant across their breasts. This introduces a secondary axis; the headdress with its sweeping feathers and massed masks at the top right corner and a kneeling captive in the bottom left corner often counter it (cf. Plate 12a.). Differences of size do not indicate perspective, but rank and sometimes actual size—in representations of adolescents, for instance. The person on the left in Figure 20, for example, is probably a youth.

Depth was sometimes achieved by combining high with low relief, so that the principal figure stands out against a background of low relief or of incised work, and a three-dimensional quality was achieved in low-relief sculpture by allowing details of the design to overflow the frame. The Maya obtained some fine effects by the manipulation of the plumage of headdresses. This is noticeable in their treatment of the long quetzal feathers they prized so highly, particularly in the way they broke long sweeps by carving one or two feathers with a forward swirl, as though ruffled by a breeze (Plates 9, 12a; Figs. 4d, 13b).

Maya sculptural portraiture with its static quality and its innate conservatism conveys a message of calm self-assurance; it clearly reflects the temperament of a group that had chosen a philosophy of life in which moderation, orderliness, and dignity were dominant. It contrasts strongly with the restless art of the Mexican period, as exemplified by Itzá sculptures at Chichén Itzá. Never ending lines of warriors, as awkwardly grouped as figures on an old-style fashion plate, face in toward an altar, or sun disk, or feathered serpent. There is an incredible stiffness in their poses, and a depressing monotony in their dress and weapons (Plate 14c). Feathered serpents, sun gods peering down from sun disks as they hungrily await their sustenance of human hearts and blood, feathered dragons, and supporters of the heavens are repeated *ad nauseam* (Figs. 12a,c, 13).

Fig. 20.—Sculptured design at Palenque. A shield with the face of the jaguar god of the interior of the earth is supported by crossed spears. Two crouching figures with the features of the same god support what is probably the surface of the earth. The scene is flanked by Maya priests standing on subordinate figures. The accompanying hieroglyphs (not shown) indicate that the relief was probably erected in A.D. 692. (*After Maudslay.*)

The creators of mediaeval Christian art worked to the greater glory of God and to instruct the people in the fundamentals of the faith and in the lives of the saints; stained-glass windows, sculptures, and paintings were the catechisms and Bibles of the unlettered. Maya sculpture and painting, however, were not for the instruction of the layman, since they served largely to adorn the temples and other religious buildings to which the public did not have access. Much of the symbolism on the façades of temples could not have been made out by a person standing in the court, and because of lack of space, if for no other reason, we can be sure the peasant was not allowed to ascend to the temples. Moreover, many of the sculptural representations, such as those of the Venus god, were of an esoteric nature and almost certainly had little meaning to the peasant whose interest and affection were centered on gods of the soil. We can, therefore, feel reasonably sure that such manifestations of art were for the delectation of the gods and of the hierarchy.

In contrast to sculptural representation, Maya murals of the Classic period have remarkable animation. The artist, unshackled by the conventions of the stela cult, reveals his mastery of problems of grouping and of difficult techniques, such as foreshortening. Scale is not important; a man may be taller than a hut, and in one case marine shells are more than half the size of trees. Perspective was handled by an upward continuation of the scene to indicate distance. The figures discard their stiff poses; the movement and chatter of life are reproduced with amazing charm and vivacity. On the murals of Bonampak one feels that the warrior on the point of thrusting with his stabbing spear is a man one would not like to encounter with no better weapon; the prisoner, whose hair is grasped by the chief (symbol of capture throughout Middle America), obviously lacks the will to fight (Fig. 9). In the adjacent mural the dead man sprawls on the steps of the high platform in a natural posture which is not unworthy of the brush of Michelangelo (Fig. 10). The terror-stricken prisoner pleads before his captors in a scene which with stark realism contrasts pride and abjection. Nowhere in the New World is there anything comparable to these murals painted about A.D. 800 in a small temple at Bonampak, a relatively unimportant city in the forests of Chiapas. Why the walls of this temple in a city which was probably a dependency of Yaxchilán were ablaze with color and life, whereas the walls of most Maya temples in far more important cities were covered with unpainted plaster, is a mystery we are never likely to solve.

Mural painting is not common in the Maya area. There are some interesting scenes at Uaxactún, and on a late building at Santa Rita, British Honduras, and at Tulúm (one mural there has a black background, giving an effect of negative painting). There is a scattering of others at Palenque and two or three sites in Yucatán. The last include murals at Chichén Itzá of the Mexican period, which are interesting in their subject matter (Plate 17a), but lack the vivacity of the murals of Bonampak or Uaxactún, or what remains of scenes of everyday life at Palenque. Pigments so far identified are: red and pink, red iron oxide; yellow, hydrous iron oxide, much the same as ochre; black, carbon; blue, unknown; green, a mixture of yellow and blue.

With the murals should be studied pottery vessels painted with life scenes. There again the scenes are animate. Consider, for instance, the striding figure with spear in hand on a vase from the Alta Verapaz, or the attendant on another vessel from the same region. The first is aquiver with life; the second watches with intent concentration the scene before him. Enjoy the qualities almost of abstraction in the plunging jaguar, or the gentle satire in the scene representing the chief being carried in his litter, for with his treatment of the arms holding the upraised fan, the artist hints at pomposity (pp. 3, 41, 110, and 223; Plate 30).

In modeled pottery (largely used for incense burning) Maya artists achieve another triumph. Consider the "Punch" (he is humpbacked) from an early classic burial at Kaminaljuyú (Plate 19d). Tremendous vitality is achieved by the treatment of eyes and the lines around the mouth. It is difficult to realize that this caricature left the potter's hands nearly 1,400 years ago. The two figures on a vessel from the Regional Museum of Chiapas represent a combination of modeling and appliqué. Arms, legs, and ornaments are stylized, in contrast to the refined treatment of the faces. (Plate 19c).

Pottery figurines, many of which are hollow and made to serve as whistles, also bear witness to the heights reached by Maya plastic art (Plate 20). Some are portraits in the sculptural tradition, but others are vivid scenes of everyday life—for the man the excitement of hunting, for the woman the dull tasks of grinding corn and tending children. These were made in pottery molds and belong to the late Classic period; simple handmade figurines were common in the first stages of the Formative period.

Changes of shape, decoration, and temper in pottery are among the most important tools of the archaeologist in reconstructing history, but they make dull reading for the non-ceramist. In general, the sequence runs thus: Formative period, of excellently made monochrome wares (two-color and occasional polychrome decoration in the Guatemala highlands); early Classic period, polychrome wares in the Petén; late Classic period, life scenes (Plates 18, 30) and also geometric designs; very late Classic, carved pottery which was often made in two-piece molds (Fig. 22*a*); Mexican period, great falling off in pottery, which was largely monochrome; period of Mexican Absorption, pottery continues to degenerate. Generally speaking, Yucatán and the Guatemalan highlands, excluding the northern parts adjacent to the Central area, produced little polychrome pottery at any time.

Trade in pottery was brisk between various parts of the Maya area and also with non-Maya regions. Such commerce was active even in the Formative period. Burials at Kaminaljuyú of the early Classic period contained many trade pieces from central Mexico (Plate 19*b*) as well as a few from the Petén.

In late Classic times there appears a remarkable pottery, called plumbate, the only glazed ware in Middle America. At that time it was made only in simple forms and was traded over southern Guatemala and adjacent parts of Chiapas. There seems no doubt that it was manufactured in only one place, almost surely near the present boundary of Guatemala and that part of southern Chiapas called Soconusco. From the fact that some later forms of the ware depict not Maya, but Mexican, gods, we can be reasonably sure that the makers were not of Maya speech. Early in the Mexican period (*circa* A.D. 1000) new forms of plumbate, often with figures of gods and animals (Plate 19*a*), became extremely popular, and were traded as far north at Tepic, in northwestern Mexico, and as far south as Nicaragua. Many pieces reached Yucatán, and others traveled as far as Tula and central Veracruz, but the larger part was sent to areas nearer the center of manufacture, such as the Guatemalan highlands and western El Salvador. Plumbate pottery ceased to be traded about A.D. 1200; no pieces are found associated with Aztec deposits, and pottery is not even mentioned in the Aztec list of tribute paid by Soconusco. Plumbate ware, apart from its technical qualities (it was fired at much higher temperatures than the calcite tempered wares of the Petén which disintegrate at temperatures of over 600 degrees) is for archaeologists an "index fossil," for it places pottery of local types, artifacts, or buildings with which it is clearly associated somewhere in the eleventh or twelfth centuries, and establishes contemporaneity for local horizons in distant cities.

Another archaeological index fossil is a pottery called Thin Orange, which has been found at Teotihuacán, Kaminaljuyú, Monte Albán, and other sites, and was manufactured around Ixcaquixtla in southern Puebla, central Mexico, in the early Classic period. It, too, is completely absent in later horizons (Plate 19*b*). It must not be confused with Fine Orange ware from the bottom of the Gulf of Mexico, which was traded very widely from late Classic times onward with varying shape and decoration (pp. 107, 145).

Objects sometimes or invariably made of pottery included idols, incense burners, braziers, drain pipes, boxes to hold offerings (rare), drums, flutes, whistles, earplugs, beads, perhaps net sinkers, stamps, molds, griddles, and, of course, vessels of all kinds.

Gourds are still used extensively by the Maya. Semicircular ones (tree gourds sliced in half, with the pulp removed) are used as drinking cups; large gourds with a cloth over the mouth keep newly made tortillas hot for serving. In Yucatán queer eight-shaped gourds are carried as canteens by means of a cord twisted around the waist of the gourd and passed over the man's shoulder.

In the Guatemalan highlands gourds are painted or decorated with designs in poker work or blackened with soot and then varnished, all of which techniques are probably pre-Columbian. Painted gourds were used in sixteenth-century Yucatán, and probably some were lacquered, a process known to the Maya, but none have survived.

Of carved wood, the finest survivals are the magnificent sapodilla lintels and ceilings of Tikal and Tzibanche. The delicacy with which the hieroglyphs and religious scenes are worked is truly amazing. A few fragments of carved wood, such as spear-throwers, dredged from the sacred cenote at Chichén Itzá, only serve to make us realize what a treasure of art has been lost to us through the action of time and climate.

Except for a few dispiriting fragments, principally from the cenote of sacrifice at Chichén Itzá, where the mud had preserved them, no Maya cotton textiles have survived. This is most unfortunate, as stelae and murals show persons wearing fabrics with very beautiful designs (Plate 12). Not one fragment of a feathered cloak has been preserved, and the magnificent plumage of headdresses is known only in relief sculpture and paintings. It is a pity that in the Maya area there is no arid region comparable to the coast of Peru which would have saved such treasures. The archaeologist who comes upon an important Maya tomb rejoices in the jades, shellwork, and painted or carved pottery, but he is depressed at the thought that these represent but a small proportion of the owner's possessions. The textiles and elaborate headdresses, the featherwork, the carved boxes and lacquered gourds, the leatherwork and the fine basketry, the shields and the stools, and all the other household possessions and personal treasures are no more. A wealth of artistic treasure has turned to dust. Nevertheless, we need not complain; in sculpture and mural the Maya have left us a greater legacy of beauty than most peoples achieve in the whole range of arts and crafts.

Designs on *huipil* blouses used by present-day Maya women of the highlands look like embroidery, but generally are brocade work; that is to say, they are worked into the warp as the textile is being woven. This technique is probably ancient. So, almost certainly, is that of tie-dyeing, a process in which the thread or the finished cloth is firmly tied at intervals so that when it is dipped in dye, the wrapped sections remain untouched. Tapestry work was probably as common among the Maya as it was in ancient Peru. Quilting was certainly practiced, and a muslin was made in early Colonial times in the highlands of Guatemala and is still woven by the Kekchi Maya. Early Spanish writers report that feathers were woven into garments worn by members of the nobility, and this is confirmed by many Maya sculptures.

Weaving to the Maya woman was a sacred undertaking, just as the working of his land was to her husband. Indeed, women of the Guatemala highlands still offer a prayer before starting to weave a new textile. It was not chance that the moon goddess, the special patroness of women, was credited with the invention of weaving. Weaving, too, had a communal or social aspect, for Yucatec women met to do this work in a building set aside for that purpose.

Sisal fiber (the modern henequen) and the related *ixtli* (fiber of one of the aloes) were extensively used for rope, nets, and carrying bags, as well as clothing. Peasants probably wore little else, for there are hints that the wearing of cotton garments was a prerogative of the ruling class. Bark cloth, sometimes with designs painted on it, was also used. The inner bark of certain trees, particularly the wild fig, was immersed in water and then pounded till soft and flexible. Holes that developed were mended by placing patches over them and pounding the cloth afresh. Bark cloth is still made by the Lacandón. Stone pounders believed to have been used in its preparation are frequently encountered.

Maya skill and artistry are well illustrated in the carving of jade. That intractable material so highly prized by all peoples of Middle America presented a challenge to the Maya craftsman which he was not slow to accept, for some of the low-relief designs on jades are among the most beautiful products of the lapidary's skill to be found anywhere in the world (Plate 21). The people of La Venta culture also worked beautiful jade, but their best products are in the round and usually without any detail of costume or headdress, whereas the finest Maya work is in low relief with intricate treatment of accessories.

The production of a jade pendant must have required infinite patience and labor. Sawing with a thin wooden implement and quartz sand and drilling with both solid and tubular drills, perhaps of hard wood, seem to have been the two preliminary methods. Tubular drill marks in the back of a jade head from British Honduras show how the area was hollowed: cones were drilled and removed and then the intervening masses broken away (Fig. 26a). Final carving and polishing must have presented even more difficult problems. Most jade was from highland mines, but design or glyphs show that many pieces were carved in the lowlands.

The Maya, overfond of painting the lily, often covered jades with a red powder, obtained from cinnabar. The finest carved jades have been found in the Alta Verapaz, Chiapas, and the Petén, but in Yucatán they are quite scarce except for those (ceremonially broken) which have been dredged from the sacrificial cenote at Chichén Itzá. Most of these had been imported.

Disks with mosaic designs picked out in contrastingly colored fragments of turquoise and jade have been found in offertories of the Mexican period at Chichén Itzá, and a necklace of turquoise beads came from a burial there of the Mayapán period. Another grave, at Zaculeu in the western highlands of Guatemala, shown by the presence of plumbate pottery to be of the Mexican period, had many tiny pieces of turquoise, presumably once a mosaic. These dated finds, together with the absence of turquoise from sites of the Classic period, bear witness that this stone came into use in the Mexican period; Aztec tribute lists indicate that it was mined in northwestern Oaxaca and central Veracruz. Jade mosaic work was common in the Classic period, particularly for masks (Plate 28). Eyes were generally of shell with pupils of obsidian.

Vases of *tecali* (Mexican onyx) from the Puebla-Veracruz area and marble vases with beautiful designs from the eastern frontier of the Maya in Honduras were imported.

The finest flint points of the Maya about equal those of ancient Egypt (Plate 22c). Both peoples obtained those extraordinarily thin leaf-shaped blades with their beautifully rippled surfaces by gentle pressure, not by blows. Inserted in wooden hafts, these blades made excellent daggers or spear points, but the most interesting examples of flintwork are the so-called eccentric flints (Plate 22a, b, d), frequently found in offertory caches beneath stelae or temples (often in groups of nine). They may be of non-naturalistic shapes, such as crescents or rings, or, more rarely, they are of life forms. The latter include alert dogs, well-executed but slightly impressionistic representations of scorpions, and full-length human figures. Profiles of gods chipped on the sides of flints in the idealized style of Maya beauty bear witness to the craftsman's thorough mastery of his material. These objects can have had no utilitarian purpose; their ceremonial use is unknown.

Flint occurs abundantly in limestone beds in the lowlands, but it is rare in the highlands. In compensation, the highlands yield plentiful supplies of obsidian, which is not found in the lowlands. Thin blades of obsidian, approximately of the size and shape of the blade of a penknife, were struck off oval cores by pressing with a stick or antler at the top. These blades were ready for use as they sprang off the core, and needed no retouching, for both edges were exceedingly sharp.

The volcanic glass, for such is obsidian, is so fragile that these blades were quickly blunted through accidental chipping of the edges. In the highlands used blades could be discarded in rapid succession, for they could be quickly replaced; in the lowlands they must have been used with more care since they had been brought long distances by traders; there are huge deposits at La Jolla, about twelve miles from Guatemala City, and at Ixtepeque, Jutiapa, towards El Salvador. Obsidian disks, about three inches in diameter were set in the facings of the stepped terraces of Kaminaljuyú pyramids, a striking decoration not yet found at any other Maya site.

Large pieces of obsidian, like flints, were fashioned as leaf-shaped points by pressure flaking. Obsidian was also worked into "eccentric" shapes. Portraits of gods and geometric designs engraved on obsidian have been encountered at Tikal and Uaxactún, but as yet at no other Maya site. The finest obsidian piece yet found in the Maya area is in the form of a handled axe, nearly a foot long (Plate 22*e*). The handle had been partially covered with painted stucco. As a weapon it would have been absolutely useless, since with one hard blow it would have shattered, but as it was in an offertory cache, we can be reasonably sure that it was designed only for ceremonial use.

A special obsidian with green tinge was much prized because blades struck off its cores had less longitudinal curve. It is exceedingly common in the Valley of Mexico, and that area may have been the source of the pieces found in all parts of the Maya area in increasing quantities from early Classic times onward. Its extreme rarity at Mayapán (only three fragments in over 1,700 preserved) is significant.

Pentagonal and hexagonal pieces of iron pyrites were carefully fitted together on a sandstone or slate backing, which was usually circular, to form mirrors. These were probably worn as ornaments, for they are provided with holes for suspension, and it is known that mirrors were worn on the back of the belt by the Huaxtec and other peoples of Mexico.

Iron pyrites were also fashioned as beads and were occasionally used in place of jade or obsidian as decorative fillings of human teeth.

As already emphasized, metals came into use only at, or immediately after, the close of the Classic period, and then only to a limited extent. Even at the time of the Spanish Conquest, centuries later, metal objects were still remarkably scarce in the lowlands, for all had to be imported. Apart from the finds in the cenote at Chichén Itzá, they could almost be held in two hands. How much knowledge of metal-working existed among the lowland Maya is uncertain. They certainly knew how to emboss metal. Thin gold disks embossed with scenes of Itzá triumphs (p. 123; Fig. 13*b*) must have been local products, and from the cenote at Chichén Itzá were recovered two or three copper disks, all apparently once decorated with a gold wash. These were without much question embossed on the east coast of the peninsula of Yucatán, for designs are very close to those of murals at Santa Rita in northern British Honduras, part of the ancient Maya province of Chetumal. A small copper mask of a merchant god in lowland style is the best evidence that the lowland Maya knew how to cast metal.

Copper bells, previously mentioned, are far the commonest objects in metal. For the most part they appear to have been imported from Mexico. They were cast, and from Spanish sources we know that the Mexicans used molds of charcoal mixed with clay which could be easily cut. Clappers are usually pebbles just too large to slip through the narrow apertures at the base of the bell. Usually the bells are pear-shaped, an inch to two inches long, or button-shaped; many are decorated with simple designs, and all have small loops at the top. Numbers of these bells were attached by the loops to anklets and wristlets to jingle when the wearer walked or danced. Eight hundred of them, perhaps cached by a trader for safety, were found in a cave in Honduras.

Copper celts were used to a limited extent at the time of the Spanish Conquest and had a secondary use as a form of currency. A few, broken and discarded, have been found in open country, confirming Spanish accounts that they served for felling trees to clear land for planting. Copper tweezers, seemingly used to pluck hair from face and body and apparently imitating bivalve shells, occasionally appear. A copper fishhook has been found in Honduras, and gold fishhooks are said to have been used. Only one copper arrowhead has been reported from the lowlands. It was on the floor of a

Fig. 21.—Scene from Stela 11, Yaxchilán. Three persons, probably prisoners to be sacrificed, kneel before a richly clad individual who wears a
mask of the long-nosed god. Note the elaborate headdress, the pectoral,
belt, and kilt of jaguar skin. His name is Bird-Jaguar. As interpreted by
Miss Proskouriakoff, the stela was erected to mark his accession as ruler
of Yaxchilán at the age of forty-three in A.D. 752 (9.16.1.0.0).

very late building at Chichén Itzá. An interesting discovery in western British Honduras comprised some shell beads, the bores of which were lined with copper tubing.

Finds of metal are also infrequent in the Guatemalan highlands. Most spectacular are two gold disks with embossed heads of the Mexican rain god, Tlaloc, and the head of a bird (from Zaculeu) cast in copper and painted red, blue, and green, a most unusual treatment. We are told that Alvarado, ruthless conqueror of Guatemala, cut gold earplugs from the ears of three Quiché noblemen!

Gold jaguar masks and beads from a tomb at the old capital of the Cakchiquel have been mentioned (p. 152).

On the whole the Maya were not much interested in decorating shell. There are a few pieces competently incised with hieroglyphs, simple scenes, or geometric designs, there is one charming design from the very beginning of the Classic period, and a superb piece of carved mother of pearl which was found at distant Tula, but is clearly of Maya workmanship. Shell was cut and drilled to serve as earplugs, beads, and pendants, for inlay work, and as ornaments on clothing. Pearls, never in large numbers, appear rather rarely in caches and burials. The spiny *Spondylus* shell of the Pacific was highly prized, and beads cut from it so as to show the pink color served as currency. Pairs of these shells, used as jewel boxes and holding jades, sometimes occur in offertory caches beneath stelae or temple floors. Conch shells, with the tops sliced off, were used as trumpets. *Oliva* shells with the spiral tops cut off and with suspension holes, drilled or sawed across, are common in burials. They were attached to clothing so that they knocked together and emitted a rattling sound. They are thus shown on many stelae.

Bone was used for such implements as awls and needles and could be carved or engraved. A deer tibia found at Copán is carved with a ceremonial scene involving two personages, one of whom is bearded and stands on a glyph of the planet Venus. Below are six glyphs (Plate 31*b*). This carving shows highly sensitive workmanship. The greatest haul of worked bone came from the recently discovered burial beneath the great Pyramid I at Tikal. This richly stocked vaulted tomb contained, in addition to twenty pottery vessels, a magnificent pectoral collar of 114 jade beads and other treasures, a pile of some 90 worked bones, of which 37 are engraved with scenes or hiero-

glyphic texts or both. Nearly all the bones are so worked that identification is often impossible. Some are definitely animal, but one
appears to be human. Most remarkable are scenes in which gods and
anthropomorphic animals are paddling in canoes or even standing
in the water holding fish, one figure with a creel containing a fish
strapped on his back (Fig. 27). Another scene shows a god paddling
at stern and another at bow with five animal deities seated on the
bottom of the dugout between them. This is very true to life, for
passengers normally sit on the bottom of a dugout to keep it on an
even keel, if one may be allowed the Irishism.

The incised human skull from an early Classic burial at Kaminaljuyú (Fig. 26b) is unique. It was probably a trophy of the dead
occupant of the tomb. A treasure of the Peabody Museum, Harvard
University, is an incised peccary skull with seated human and animal
featured gods as well as a short hieroglyphic text and three peccary
treated in a very naturalistic manner. This piece was found at Copán.

Sting-ray spines often occur in burials; they were used for drawing blood from the body in auto-sacrificial rites. Their presence may
indicate that the occupant of the tomb was a priest or priestess. With
a burial of a woman at Altar de Sacrificios were ten sting-rays, four
of which were delicately incised with hieroglyphs. Indeed, the custom of incising tiny glyphs on these sting-ray spines, only about half
an inch wide, appears to have been rather common. That sting-ray
spines were regarded as fairly valuable—catching the fish could be
dangerous and there was the cost of transportation from the coast—
is indicated by the finding at Tikal of over one hundred imitations
in bone and two apparent imitations in wood.

Working in tortoiseshell must have been an ancient art, although
no good examples have survived. A colonial report of two centuries
ago speaks of the work in tortoiseshell done by the Maya of Yucatán.
The carapaces had several uses: in the salt workings of Mujeres Island,
off northeastern Yucatán, they were used as salt vats; everywhere they
served as musical instruments, and thus beaten with antler are shown
in the orchestra of Bonampak (Plate 17b); occasionally they served
as covers of votive cache containers.

Arts and crafts fell upon evil days at the end of the Classic
period, for, with the overthrow of the hierarchy, the artist was without an employer. I like to think of the high priests and rulers of the

Classic period as New World patrons of the arts, but in the Mexican period there can have been no Lorenzo the Magnificent. The same decadence is apparent in the intellectual life of the Mexican period, for the conquests in astronomy and arithmetic belong exclusively to the Classic era. From Maya writings in the Books of Chilam Balam one gets the impression that those who held to the old Maya way of life had to go underground during the rule of the alien Itzá and their successors.

Decadence is most marked during the period of Mayapán's domination and in the century before the Spanish Conquest. Excavation at Mayapán has brought to light only sculptured stones which are crude in design and execution. The pottery vessels are almost entirely monochrome and usually of a coarse red ware. The polychrome vessels of the Classic period, with their painted scenes, had no successors in the warrior state. Architecture was showy, but workmanship was poor.

CURRENCY AND COMMERCE

In case the artistic and religious side of Maya life has received overemphasis, let us glance at the Maya as a man of business.

Throughout Middle America the principal medium of exchange was the cacao bean, with beads of spondylus shell and jade as secondary exchange units. Cacao beans made an ideal currency. Inflation was automatically controlled because if the value of the cacao dropped as a result of overproduction, more beans were taken out of circulation to make chocolate, the appetite for which was insatiable throughout Middle America. It conformed to the law that the cheaper a desired product, the greater the demand. Secondly, insect pests and decay made hoarding impossible; the beans shriveled and lost value. Moreover, only certain localities were suitable for production. The tree grows well only in rich soils with heavy rainfall and very high temperatures. Consequently, orchards were largely confined to the coastal strip of Veracruz and the isthmus of Tehuantepec, the Pacific Coast of Guatemala and El Salvador, and the Caribbean Coast and estuaries of Honduras, British Honduras, Guatemala, and Tabasco. The highlands of Guatemala and all the interior of Mexico had to import their supplies in trade or tribute, and Yucatán had to import about 90 per cent of its needs.

The cacao tree produces from its trunk pods, each of which contains a variable number of seeds, usually called beans, which are the raw material of chocolate. Cacao is in all probability a Maya word which has reached us through Aztec, and that would suggest that the Maya first cultivated the tree. Indeed, there is a wild variety, from which the cultivated tree probably came, found throughout the forests of the lowland Maya area.

Price depended on distance from the orchards. A load (like our bushel, a capacity, not a weight, measure) was 24,000 beans (3x8,000; 8,000 is the fourth unit in the vigesimal system: 1, 20, 400, and 8,000 [Fig. 17, No. 1]). Shortly after the Spanish Conquest a load was worth about $9.50 on the isthmus, but nearly double that in Mexico City. That works out at about 650 beans for 25 cents, but the purchase value of the silver peso was then very high. Maya Indians bringing provisions to Mérida in 1553 earned only twenty beans for a long trip, but in Mexico the pay for a long trip was one hundred beans per diem. In Nicaragua, one Spanish chronicler tells us, a rabbit cost ten beans and the hire of a prostitute eight to ten beans, so the Aztec laborer in Mexico City could have wine, women, and song on his daily earnings; the poor Maya in Mérida would have had to cut down on all three items. Cacao remained a currency among the Maya of the Guatemalan highlands until about the start of the present century. In many parts of the Maya area the price of a bride was customarily paid in cacao, and this custom survives in an attenuated form to this day.

Because of its high value, there was regular counterfeiting of cacao money. The skin of the bean was carefully lifted, the flesh removed and replaced with a wax or earth substitute or pieces of avocado rind were inserted beneath the skin of the bean to give it a well-filled look. Such counterfeiting is reported from Nicaragua and the Valley of Mexico; in my mellower moments I would admit that the Maya probably practiced the same falsification.

Traffic in cacao and other commodities gave rise to a wealthy merchant class. Much of the trade in the Maya area was by canoe and was in the hands of the Chontal Maya, whose home in the maze of streams and stretches of swamp at the mouths of the Usumacinta and Grijalva rivers had made them expert canoemen. Indeed, their territory was called by the Aztec *Acallan*, "land of the canoes." Their dugout canoes, capable of holding forty or more people (a capacity equaled by the canoes of the Zutuhil Maya on Lake Atitlán, highlands of Guatemala, to this day) maintained a service which girded the whole peninsula of Yucatán.

Goods brought overland from the highlands of Mexico were embarked in Tabasco and carried right round the peninsula to the north coast of Guatemala and Honduras, where the Chontal Maya had trading stations comparable in many ways to such places as Shanghai a few decades ago.

Columbus, on his fourth voyage, encountered near the Bay Islands in the Bay of Honduras such a canoe, almost surely of Chontal-Maya registry. It was described as being the length of a galley and eight feet wide with a matting shelter amidships, inside which were the women and children and the merchandise so that neither rain nor sea water could wet anything. Presumably there were forty or more souls aboard, for the women and children must be added to the up to twenty-five men reported to be aboard. The cargo included cotton mantles, *huipils* (blouses) and loincloths, all with multicolor designs, *macanas* (wooden swords with pieces of flint or obsidian glued into slots down each side), little copper axes and bells, plates and forges to melt copper, razors and knives of copper, and hatchets of a sharp bright-yellow stone with wooden hafts and large quantities of cacao.

It is a fair assumption that this canoe was on its way from Tabasco to the north coast of Honduras and Guatemala. The copper material would have come from mainland Mexico; the textiles, a speciality of Yucatán known to have been shipped to Honduras, had probably been obtained in trade en route and would be exchanged for more cacao at the trading station of Nito in Honduras. The cacao had probably been acquired along the British Honduras coast and would be disposed of in Yucatán on the return route. This canoe was clearly the predecessor of the tramp steamer of the turn of this century.

Salt from beds along the north and northwest coasts of the Yucatán peninsula was also shipped far and wide. In the late sixteenth century, salt was going by sea from Campeche to Amoyoc, not far south of Tampico, about six hundred miles, and I suspect that this was a pre-Columbian canoe route, for Amoyoc was of scant importance in colonial times. Cacao, of course, went from Tabasco and the Pacific Coast of Soconusco and Guatemala to Mexico, and less bulky material such as quetzal feathers, hummingbird skins, and amber went to Mexico from the Maya area. Late in the sixteenth century Indian merchants were still going from Cholula to the Pacific Coast of Guatemala for cacao. Gold came from Panama, and recently there was excavated in Costa Rica a slate disk with Maya glyphs clearly engraved within a metaphorical stone's throw of Tikal. Middle America was a network of trade routes for every product from metates to live iguanas.

The present-day markets of highland Guatemala are enchanting, colorful, and thought-provoking, but they are but pale shadows of the markets in pre-Columbian times when they held the wealth of the Indies garnered from every corner and clime of Middle America.

V. Sketches of Maya Life

We have as short time to stay, as you,
We have as short a spring;
As quick a growth to meet decay
As you, or any thing.
                    We die
As your hours do, and dry
                    Away
Like to the summer's rain,
Or as the pearls of morning dew
Ne'er to be found again.
—Robert Herrick, *To Daffodils*

PREAMBLE

In this chapter I have brought together a series of miniatures of Maya life, each in a fictional setting, in an effort to give quickening color to the dead past. I submitted one of these sketches to a well-known anthropologist who was inexpressibly shocked at the mingling of fiction with science; the deep impress of the typed words on the sheet of paper showed how upset he was that science should be draped in such intangibles as thought processes not susceptible to tabulation or graphing. If I shared his belief that archaeology is a science, I might feel a trifle uneasy, but, regarding archaeology as a backward projection of history, I see no reason why such reconstructions should not be used. Thomas Carlyle might have been hard put to it to give chapter and verse for thoughts he attributed to the chief actors in *The French Revolution*, but those thoughts gave life to the panorama of action he painted. Other historians have used the fictional approach in varying intensity, and with such precedents there can be little need to justify my approach.

The characters in these sketches are purely fictitious; their actions are largely derived from information we possess on Maya life. Some incidents are drawn from Aztec or other Mexican sources, but the religious ideas of the peoples of central Mexico seem to have been so close to those of the Maya that there is, in general, justification for supposing that certain of their rites were prevalent also among the Maya, although chance has decreed that no record of them has survived. To illustrate what I mean, the incident in "The Novice" in which Ah Balam and his young friend are the front and hind legs of a celestial dragon is my invention. The grounds for it are these: 1. Celestial dragons are important Maya deities and occur everywhere in Maya religious art. 2. Among the Aztec, men dressed up as celestial dragons to participate in certain ceremonies. 3. The Maya wore masks to impersonate gods. 4. It is reasonable to assume, in view of points 1–3, that the Maya also impersonated celestial dragons in their ceremonies. Again, in this story offerings are deposited beneath the stela at a certain point in the ceremony. The depositing of the offering is fact; the moment in the ceremonial context is fiction.

In thought processes I have tried to keep as close as possible to Maya mentality as revealed in sixteenth- and seventeenth-century sources, and as observed by me while living among the Maya of British Honduras—a good deal of "The Daily Round" is based on such observation. I suppose it is impossible to avoid projecting one's own personality into fictional characters, but the reader, forewarned, can make his own reservations. Because the settings vary in time and space, continuity of characters had to be sacrificed.

Finally, it should be noted that there are anticipatory references to certain ceremonies or customs detailed later in the book.

THE NOVICE

Young Balam ached all over. His tongue was swollen; the lobes of his ears, his arms, and other parts of his body were tender from drawing blood from them continuously. Also he was hungry and worn from lack of sleep. For eighty days, from 13 Xul, all through the months Yaxkin, Mol, Ch'en, and over half of Yax, he had fasted, tended the temple, kept vigils, and made sacrifices of his own blood. In another three or four hours all this would be ended, for by then he and everyone else in the world would have been destroyed, or he would be sitting down to a feast, the anticipation of which kept coming to him when his thoughts should have been on more serious matters. Still, it was difficult not to look forward to turkey and veni-son stewed with sweet potatoes, when for so long one had eaten nothing but very skimpy tortillas, and drunk only weak corn gruel.

It was now about three hours before sunset of the day 4 Ahau 13 Yax. The fifteenth katun (twenty-year period) of Cycle 10 (9.15.0.0.0, 4 Ahau 13 Yax) would end at sunset. This was three-quarters of the way through Cycle 10 (we speak of this as Cycle 9, but to the Maya it was Cycle 10), and the day was the lucky 4 Ahau. That alone was of good augury, but Yax was the month of the planet Venus, and that baleful god would be visible at sunset, blazing high in the evening sky. In another four months he would be lost in the sun's rays before reappearing as morning star. Everyone knew that the world would be destroyed at the end of a katun; the real ques-tion was whether this particular one was the appointed one; favor-able and unfavorable factors seemed about equally balanced. Extra care in the performance of every bit of the ritual might save the day.

The first of the big ceremonies was about to start. Today, as on every day 4 Ahau, the fire-walking ceremony was to be held, and, in addition, persons were to be sacrificed to the god Venus, since he was the patron of this month in which the katun closed. Balam should get a ringside seat at these ceremonies since he was to be the front legs and head of the sky monster of the east.

From the building where they were living during this period of fasting and preparation, he and his fellow novitiates had seen fire set to the great pile of wood stacked in the court before the temple of the rain gods, and the heat from the blaze had been terrific. Now the attendants had just finished spreading the glowing embers with long poles of green wood to form a field of fire. Inside the temple, the four priests who were to walk the fire had completed their prayers and offerings of copal incense and *balche* (a mead drink). As Balam and his friends watched, they came out one behind the other, stooping as they emerged so that their high masks and headdresses would not catch against the lintel of the doorway. Slowly they descended the steep stairway.

At the head of the little procession came the high priest, dressed in red as the red rain god of the east, but with his headdress, en-shrining the long-nosed mask of the rain god Chac, bedecked with a mass of quetzal plumage, green to represent the greenness of young corn and the new leaves on the trees, verdure which the rains would bring. Behind him in order followed the Chacs of the north, west, and south, all wearing similar headdresses, but dressed respectively in white, black, and yellow. Each carried in his right hand an axe with stone blade set in a wooden haft, the end of which curled up to form a snake's head. Each had in the left hand a zigzag stick symbolizing the lightning, and, slung from one shoulder, a calabash of water, from which the rain gods sprinkle the rain.

At the edge of the field of glowing embers, the little party halted, and sandals were removed. The high priest took a bowl of burning copal and a gourd of *balche* from an attendant, and turning to the east, offered both to the red Chac. Then picking up an aspergillum formed of the rattles of rattlesnakes, he started without hesitation to walk across the carpet of live coals, dipping the aspergillum in the bowl of *balche*, and sprinkling the embers with it as he advanced. Reaching the far side, he paused a moment and then started on the return journey. Safely back at the starting point and seemingly unharmed by the fire, he offered copal and *balche* once more to the east, and then drank the *balche* remaining in the gourd.

In turn the impersonators of the white, black, and yellow Chacs went through the same procedure. Balam watched the performance of the white Chac with particular attention. This priest was unpopular with the young men training for holy orders, and Balam found himself half wishing that he would slip and get badly burned. He put the idea away, for it was not seemly that such thoughts should occupy one's attention on such a solemn occasion, and such a misadventure would mean the failure of the ceremony, with the consequence that the dissatisfied gods would deny the people rain.

Balam could not wait to see the conclusion of the ceremony, for he had to make ready for his part in the ritual to mark the end of the katun. Inside the hut the four great frames of wood, covered with bark cloth and bedecked with plumage to represent the sky monsters, had been placed ready to mount. Balam moved to the red one, which he and his friend Tutz were to wear. He put his feet in the forelegs of the monster and thrust his head through the throat and into the open jaws, taking care not to scratch himself against the huge fangs. Tutz did the same for the rear part of the monster. Poles resting on the shoulders of the young men held rigid between them the creature's long body.

The master of ceremonial paraphernalia inspected the two youths and, satisfied, placed masks on both of them. That of Balam had slits for his eyes so that he could see where he was going; Tutz was not so lucky. His mask was put on front to back, for it must appear as emerging from the rear head of the monster, whereas Tutz faced front, and eyepieces would have been useless to him. They would only have given him a close-up of the monster's rear throat.

At a signal from the master of the paraphernalia, the four pairs of young men lined up in single file, Balam and Tutz with their red monster of the east heading the line. Their movements had been rehearsed several times, and Balam knew exactly what to do when the order to start was given.

The four monsters emerged one after the other from the hut, and, crossing the court down a corridor kept clear of squatting onlookers, they passed slowly up the great stairway of the pyramid of the Temple of Venus. At every few paces the bearers made short barking noises to represent the alligator's call. Arriving at the platform before the temple on the summit, Balam and Tutz wheeled to the east, and the other monsters placed themselves on the north, west, and south sides of the open spaces. As they faced in, Balam had a splendid view of the proceedings; Tutz, of course, was unable to see anything, and soon began to find the weight of the frame on his shoulders and the heavy mask on his head irksome.

The high priest and his three assistants had doffed their costumes of rain gods and now were inside the Temple of Venus, praying to him to spare the world from destruction. Attendants led up the stairway five young men who were to be sacrificed on the stone block standing before the temple. The victims appeared resigned; they had been given quantities of *balche* to purify them, and, incidentally, to give them courage. Furthermore, they firmly believed that they would be united with the gods to whom they were about to take the messages of the people.

Balam gazed at them curiously. Three of them did not have Maya features and were probably Olmec or Zoque slaves purchased some time ago from merchants from the Gulf of Mexico. Balam knew the fourth, a young man who had grown up as a slave in his father's household, a rather stupid youth who had been the butt of many a practical joke. There had been no need to convince him that his sacrifice was for his own glory; his simple faith had required no strengthening, and he seemed to anticipate with a subdued zeal his coming honor. The occasion had given him a dignity he had never before enjoyed. Terror was in the dark eyes of the fifth victim, a sculptor who was to pay with his life for a mistake he had made in copying the work sheets for the glyphs on the stela about to be dedicated.

As the priests issued from the temple at the conclusion of their prayers, attendants brought forward one of the foreigners and placed him on the sacrificial stone. Two junior priests, called Chacs, held his feet; two, his hands (Fig. 13*b*). Assistant priests held smoking copal censers and sprinkled *balche* as the high priest, with the long flint knife in his hand—"the hand of God," the Maya called it—advanced toward the victim, for in a ceremony of such importance only he could perform the sacrifice. Balam felt himself swept by a wave of emotion, in which impulses of elation, pity, and sadism were strangely mingled. The Olmec, his arms and legs curving down from the small of his back resting on the sacrificial stone, was between Balam and the sun, now low in the afternoon sky. His shadow on the stuccoed floor lay like the arc of a grotesque bow at Balam's feet.

The high priest, bending over the victim, struck a savage blow at the base of the left ribs. At the moment of impact the body gave a last convulsive jerk. The high priest wrenched out the heart and raised it above his head, facing toward the setting sun. His clothing was stained deep red and more blood had spattered his face. A second time the heart was raised to the west, the direction of the god Venus, who would soon be visible if the world were to be spared. A great shout arose from the congregation squatting in the court below as the priest walked to the edge of the platform, showing the heart to those assembled there.

The body was placed to one side as the second victim was brought forward and similarly dispatched, and then the third. The former slave of Balam's father was the fourth victim. Balam felt a certain shame that this simple, harmless youth should die. It was considered an honor to contribute a victim, but it would have been easier to bear had the man been sullen or had he shown bravado; this eager faith was upsetting. Balam averted his gaze, watching instead two flies that hovered around the gaping wound in the stomach of one dead man. He did not look to his front again until the shout of the crowd told him all was over.

The fifth man, who had revealed terror, struggled as he was brought forward, and had to be dragged to the block. Even after he had been thrown on it, and was tightly grasped in the requisite position, he continued to try to free himself. Balam frowned beneath his mask. Such conduct was unseemly, and by such ignominy the man was disregarding the welfare of the whole community, for such a spectacle must be offensive to the god Venus. The man had already jeopardized the well-being of all by his careless carving of an error on the stela. Now he was once again upsetting the rhythm of the ritual. His struggles soon ended, however, and his body was placed beside those already sacrificed. The whole ceremony had taken but a few minutes.

Balam and Tutz moved forward to take their place in the procession. At the head walked the high priest and his three assistants. Behind came five more priests wearing masks of the Venus god, each carrying a bowl in which reposed one of the hearts of the sacrificial victims. The four sky monsters swung in behind them and were, in turn, followed by other priests with smoking censers of copal; junior priests and attendants, carrying offerings to be dedicated to the new stela, brought up the rear.

The procession passed down the stairway of the pyramid, across the court of the Venus Temple, passed the end of the ball court, and so into the great ceremonial court. A halt was made in front of the newly erected stela, which stood on the east side of the court. Because of its width, the court was still lighted by the rays of the setting sun. The blues, reds, yellows, and greens of the freshly applied stucco glowed in the soft light. At the foot of the monument a large hole, reaching to level with the base of the butt, stood ready to receive the offerings, stout transversal poles against the butt holding the mass of carved stone in position.

Balam and Tutz had to mount several steps of the pyramid, against the base of which the stela was set, in order to occupy their position to the east of the ceremony and still be visible. Thus overlooking the stela, Balam again had a full view of the proceedings. He was relieved that Tutz and he had made the difficult trip down and up the steep steps without mishap; it had taken many rehearsals to co-ordinate their movements. As soon as all were in their assigned positions, the priests, junior priests, attendants, and all the spectators gathered in the great court and squatted on their haunches. From bags they drew sharp points of obsidian and bundles of sticks all cut to the same size. The drums set at each corner of the great court were thudding to a slow rhythm. Gradually the tempo increased until the beats cascaded in the same sequence with great rapidity. Balam's pulse quickened to the pounding measure; he wanted to shout and dance. It was almost unbearable to have to stand motionless. Now the trumpets and rattles and conch shells were sounding and antlers were beating on turtle carapaces.

The high priest raised his hand as a signal to the assembly, and then, lowering it, plunged an obsidian point in quick succession into his tongue, the lobes of his ears, and the fleshy parts of his arms and legs. Every man, for there were no women present, did the same save the eight novices inside the sky monsters. Then the sticks were passed through the gashes.

The high priest and his attendants advanced in turn to the pit in front of the stela, and cast in the blood-smeared sticks and pieces of bark cloth on which the blood had dripped; the ordinary people arranged their bloody sticks on the ground before them. The music had slowed and died. The lower part of the stela was now in shadow.

In turn, the five impersonators of the Venus god approached, holding the bowls with the hearts in them. The high priest took a heart from each in order. He smeared the first over the face of the god carved on the front of the stela and then dropped it in the center of the pit before the stela. The corners of the stela were rubbed in turn with the remaining four hearts, which were immediately dropped in the hole, one at each corner. As the high priest performed these acts, the assistants and junior priests squatted behind lines of braziers, from which rolls of smoke rose and, carried by the breath of evening wind, wreathed the stela. More attendants advanced carrying bundles of quetzal feathers, carved jades, finely worked flints, *balche*, food, and cacao beans. The high priest raised each offering in turn to the west and next to the stela, and then cast it into the pit.

When all the offerings had been deposited in the pit, attendants scooped earth into the cavity, and as soon as it had been tamped down, masons hurriedly laid a floor over it.

By then the sun was on the point of setting, and as it sank below the horizon, Balam could see the dim light of the god Venus growing brighter each minute; the world had been given respite from destruction for another twenty years. The day 5 Imix had started. He raised a hand and quietly jerked the pole resting on his right shoulder, the signal he had agreed to give Tutz if Venus was visible.

At a sign from the high priest, the drums began to beat a triumphant fast measure. The flutes joined in. Priests lighted a fire, and into it the men threw their blood-stained sticks and offerings of copal. Young men from the college hastily lighted pine torches in the blaze and ran with them to all the pyramids in the ceremonial center. Soon the court was ablaze with fires burning before every temple and stela. Other fires illumined the ball court and the market place; on the outskirts lights began to twinkle in the houses of the theocrats.

The assembly was beginning to disperse. The four sky monsters wended their way back to the storeroom of the masks. When the cumbrous masks and serpent bodies had been doffed, Balam's empty stomach reminded him of the feast that was to follow. Everyone was in a happy mood. The eighty days of tension were over, the ceremonies in which they had participated had been crowned with success, and the day 5 Imix had started without any untoward occurrence. Balam had completely forgotten his father's slave, whose heart now was buried at the base of the stela.

Tutz, who was barely seventeen, started some horseplay, catching the end of his partner's loincloth and twisting it round his leg in an effort to trip him. The keeper of the paraphernalia chided him half jokingly, to which Tutz replied that he was hard-hearted, "with a face like a tree trunk," as the Maya saying goes. All laughed, for the master of the paraphernalia was known to everyone as one of the kindliest of men.

When the two friends left the building, it was completely dark, and many of the fires had died down. They walked to the edge of the ceremonial center, entering the residential quarter of the nobility. Frogs were croaking their monotonous chorus; drooping leaves of cohune palms were silhouetted against a sky silvered by a moon ten days old. Passing one house, the boys' nostrils caught the odor of turkey stewing in chile sauce. They quickened their pace.

THE DAILY ROUND

For Ix Zubin the day began a little before 4:00 A.M. After hurriedly making her morning ablutions, she squatted to blow on the ashes of last night's fire so that its flames would supply illumination. Next, carrying a heavy jar outside the door, she strained its contents, maize, lime, and water, through a colander, a simple affair made by punching holes in a gourd. As the lime-impregnated water sank into the ground, she washed the maize several times. The hulls, softened by many hours' immersion in lime and water, came loose easily, and soon the corn was ready for grinding on the *metate*.

She was not the only one at work. All over the hamlet the lights of fires flickered through the polework of the walls of huts, and the indescribable but, once heard, unforgettable *cric, cric, cric* of muller on grinding stone witnessed that she had risen no earlier than her neighbors. With rhythmic stroke she drove the muller forward over the corn; gradually the pile of dough increased. The pot of black beans, left from last night, was put on the fire, together with more wood to insure a good supply of embers. Squatting by a smooth block of wood, she took some of the damp dough and began to flatten it with her fingers on a broad leaf.

The noise of patting and the soft rustle as the leaf was turned were the signal for her husband, Cuc, to rise. Dawn had not yet come, but as he stood in the doorway of the hut, his eye caught Venus blazing on the eastern horizon, reminding him that he planned to hunt that day. He re-entered the hut and sought his pottery incense burner and some copal incense, neatly wrapped in corn husk. Stopping by the fire, he raided some of the embers his wife had just placed beneath the pottery griddle and put them in the incense burner. Setting the censer on the ground outside the hut, he squatted on his haunches behind it so that he faced the east. He prayed to the sun, the morning star, and Ah Ceh, god of the chase, that his hunting would be successful, excusing his wish to destroy life by explaining his need and his poverty, and promising not to kill more than he needed. As he prayed, he dropped pieces of the waxy copal on the embers, telling the gods that this was his gift to them—a humble gift, but, as they knew, he was not rich.

Re-entering the hut, he found the first of the tortillas, the round and very thin cakes of corn dough which his wife had been patting into shape on the leaf, on the hot griddle. Deftly Ix Zubin tossed those that were ready into a deep calabash, and placed a cloth over the mouth to keep them hot. Cuc sat on a low stool fashioned from a log, and, with a piping hot tortilla rolled to serve as a spoon, scooped some beans from the pot. Sprinkling a little chile on top, he started his breakfast, as his wife continued to shape the tortillas expertly and to keep them rotating on to the pottery griddle and thence to the calabash.

So far not a word had been exchanged. Custom demanded that the man be the first to speak, but Ix Zubin could contain herself no longer. With head turned, as though she were addressing the fire, she said, "I dreamed of a snake last night." A smile lit Cuc's face, for, as everyone knows, to dream of a snake means that a baby is coming, and they had been married some time without any blessed event. Children were needed, for in a year or two Cuc would no longer be working with his father-in-law, but would have his own fields, and children were almost a necessity to help bring home corn and firewood and to aid their mother in the home. Furthermore, to be childless brought shame on a wife, and might bring about divorce. Cuc knew that already one or two catty women had whispered asides on the subject when Ix Zubin had stopped for a gossip while filling her water jars at the stream.

His breakfast finished, Cuc took his bow and arrow, quiver, tumpline, and netted bag, and crossed to his father-in-law's hut. A gray band across the eastern sky, which had not yet reached as high as the morning star, showed that dawn was at hand. The time for the best hunting was passing, as one had a better chance of finding game in the hour before dawn. On the other hand, the day was Manik, day of the god of hunting.

As Cuc and his father-in-law left the hamlet, they paused at the eastern outskirts where a small shrine and a large pile of stones stood beside the path. Similar shrines were at the north, south, and west exits of the little settlement. These were dedicated to the gods set at the four sides of the earth and the sky. Both hunters placed a stone on the rock pile, and prayed briefly but earnestly to the red rain god of the east to send the now much-needed rain.

Near the village chances of getting game were slim, but not far from their milpa there was a small stretch of savanna, an area of poor, sandy soil, where only grass, pine, and a few scrubby trees and bushes grew. Cuc had burned off the patches of grass some time ago so that the deer might be attracted by the tender grass that would spring up in its place. They circled this place so as to approach it from the direction in which there was least danger of the wind's carrying their scent to any game that might be there. Two deer were, in fact, feeding near the center of the patch of grassland. The two men carefully approached as close as they could, taking advantage of the cover afforded by clumps of pine and the low *nance* bush. Once within range, the older man took aim, and the arrow, flying straight, entered the deer near the heart. The wounded animal ran some distance and then collapsed. Cuc had not shot at the second deer, for he, like all Maya, knew that if one shot more than one needed, the gods of hunting would be annoyed and would not send game another time.

Cuc fished his fire-drill out of his netted bag, and started twirling one stick in a hole in the softer wood of the other. A few minutes later a thin wisp of smoke curled up from the dry punk, and hard blowing soon produced a flame. His father-in-law, meanwhile, had first propped up the dead deer and then collected some dry wood. A small fire was soon blazing, and as soon as some embers had formed, the older man placed them on a stone, and on top laid hunks of copal. As the black smoke, with its sweet scent strangely blended with a certain acridity, billowed up, he began to address the deer, and through it the god of hunting, begging the deer's pardon for having killed it, and explaining that, as the crops had not been too good that year, his family needed food.

When this little ceremony was concluded, the deer was cleaned and skinned, but that was not a difficult job. With an obsidian blade Cuc slit the skin on the underside from lip to tail and down the inside of the legs. Much of the skin could be loosened with the fist, but the head gave a little more trouble, and here more than one obsidian blade had to be used. The meat was cut up and suspended from the branches of a near-by tree so that it would be out of reach of animals.

These tasks had taken some time, and it was midday before the two men reached their milpa. They went to the temporary hut in the center of the clearing, where tools were kept, and where later on corn would be stored in husk. Leaving their bows and arrows, quivers, and bags there, they set to work to weed around the hills of young corn. The men were pleased with its condition, despite the lack of rain. "Our Grace," the holy maize, was putting out healthy leaves, their greenness more vivid against the background of ash, blackened stumps, and charred trunks of the burnt field.

Soon after one o'clock Ix Zubin arrived with a bag of parched maize dough, which, mixed with water, assuaged their thirst and hunger at the same time. They had planned to carry home firewood, but now, with the deer to be loaded, only Ix Zubin would be free to do that job. She collected a heavy load and, tying it with strips of bark, set out for home with head bent forward to sustain the weight, borne by a tumpline across her forehead. The men worked till the middle of the afternoon, and then returned to the savanna to pick up the deer.

Arrived back at the village, Cuc produced his horn, a conch shell with its top sliced off, and holding it to the side of his mouth, awoke the echoes of the hills with a series of long low blasts. People, hearing the call of a successful hunt, hurried to the hut, where each family received a little of the meat. A haunch was sent to the village priest or medicine man, an important man in the village, but not of high rank in comparison with the priests at the ceremonial center. The family's share of the meat was rather larger than usual, as a number of families had been summoned to work on pyramid building and were camped near the great ceremonial center, eight miles distant.

Cuc bathed in the stream, changed his breechclout and was ready for his evening meal by five o'clock. Ix Zubin had prepared deer-meat tamales, a great treat and, to top off the meal, chocolate mixed with ground maize and spiced with chile. This was also a rarity, for most of the cacao they harvested went to the priests and nobles, who drank it twice a day and exported the surplus to Yucatán, where it fetched a good price in embroidered mantles. Cuc ate alone, Ix Zubin waiting on him, as it is right and proper for any wife to do.

His dinner finished, Cuc got up from the low stool on which he sat and, leaving his wife to eat her meal, started for a stroll through

Fig. 22.—Animation in portraiture of gods. Movement contrasts with the static quality usual in portraits of the gods. All are of stone except *a*, from a molded pottery vessel, and all are late Classic period (A.D. 680 to A.D. 800). *a*, The maize god (San José, British Honduras). *b, d*, Long-nosed rain god holds container from which rain pours (Zoomorph O, Quiriguá). *c*, God in dancing posture in coils of snake (Altar O, Quiriguá). *e*, Long-nosed god incised on fine-grained stone (Palenque). *f*, God emerging from conch shell holds maize plant, out of which grows the head of the maize god. (*b, d, f after Maudslay*.)

the hamlet. He usually stopped at the hut of his friend Cantul for a few minutes' conversation, but hesitated to go there that night. Cantul's second son, a bright boy of eight and a general favorite with the hamlet, had been taken to the ceremonial center three days ago. Tomorrow, together with several other children, he was to be sacrificed to the Chacs, the rain gods. Cantul was trying to hide his grief, and it would be better not to go there for fear of making things worse. The thought of that cheerful youngster's being sacrificed next day saddened Cuc. He pictured the boy's frightened and bewildered face peering out of the litter in which he would be carried, his healthy brown skin almost hidden under the mass of jade he would wear, and the mask of the rain god pressing heavily on his brow. It was only a few days since Cuc had helped him make a bow. Yet someone must be the victim; the corn needed rain, and the Chacs needed blood. Man must keep his bargains; the gods were generous, but they, too, needed strength for their work, and they would not, if they could, send their gifts to a people who were ungrateful. For two years the hamlet had not been called on to supply a candidate for sacrifice, and last time it had not cost them anything, as they had been able to hand over that stranger from Chetumal.

With these thoughts in his mind, Cuc wandered to the communal hut, where the village elders were trying a case. Cuc, being one of the young men of the village and consequently without standing in the community, took an inconspicuous position at the back of the hut. The trial was about a minor matter. One man was complaining because his neighbor's dog had stolen some of his meat. Ah Buul, the chief elder, tried to put himself in turn in the place of complainant and defendant, sympathizing with each in his quiet voice and participating in their statements.

After the complainant had stated his case, Ah Buul commented: "Yes, that is so. Meat is hard to get. One hunts long for it. As you say, you have a large family, and the children had been looking forward to enjoying the meat and now the dog has eaten it. That is so. It is not just. A man should not be robbed in that way. You did right to complain."

Then the defendant stated his case, and again the chief elder sympathized with him: "Yes. That is so. A man has his work to do and cannot be watching his dog all the time. The dog was well fed, as you say. He had three tortillas this morning, and who would imagine that he would want to steal meat after such a good meal? There is much truth in what you say about the duty of a person who has meat putting it out of reach of any marauder, and our neighbor was at fault in not doing so. Still, perhaps it would have been wiser to have tied the dog before leaving the hut or taken him with you, as you say that your wife was busy making pottery. Both of you have some right and some carelessness on your sides, and so, if you agree that it is fair, I think our neighbor who is the owner of the dog should replace half the stolen meat next time he is successful in hunting. He is a good hunter, one of the best in the village, and his dog will be strong after eating that much meat. Do you both think that is a just arrangement?"

Cuc did not wait to hear whether the judgment would be accepted by complainant and defendant. He knew it would. Quiet compromise and the spirit of live and let live were too deeply ingrained in his and his neighbors' characters to let him doubt the result. Everyone, and all the trees, the crops, and the animals had their rights. One must not violate these rights or try to take more than was his due. All such matters should be looked at from the other point of view as well as one's own.

Wandering back to his hut, Cuc found Ix Zubin steeping tomorrow's corn in the jar of lime water. In a corner of the hut was the load of pottery jars to be sold at the great market which would be held tomorrow after the sacrifice. It was time for bed. They would have to rise early, long before dawn, for it was the day on which the ceremony to the Chacs was to be held, and everyone in the hamlet would be going to the ceremonial center to watch the sacrifice from the great court, and afterwards would visit the market. He wondered whether those traders from the highlands would be there. He hoped so, as he needed some more obsidian blades, but he was afraid he would not have much heart for bargaining for them with his cacao after seeing young Cantul sacrificed."

Cuc sighed. If Ix Zubin's dream came true, he hoped that their child would never be chosen for sacrifice, but, if it were, he hoped that he would receive the blow in the same quiet way Cantul had; it was unbecoming to show grief when the needs of the gods affected one personally.

The frogs were croaking. Perhaps rain was on the way. He must remember to get some rushes so Ix Zubin could mend the bed mat.

THE ARCHITECT AT CHICHÉN ITZÁ

Ah Haleb, master architect at Chichén Itzá, had a busy day ahead of him. Like many a successful man before and after him, he fully realized that if you want a thing well done, you must be on the spot to see that your instructions are properly followed. In his case this would mean being at half a dozen places at the same time.

As he left his hut, the sun was only a hand's breadth above the eastern horizon. Instead of following the path that led directly to the great ceremonial center, he took another trail that would take him to the north side of the city. Ten minutes' brisk walk brought him to a clearing in the wood where many men were at work. Here were the lime kilns.

On the far side of the clearing a new kiln had been started. In the center a pole, about nine feet high, had been set up, and, on the ground around it, large logs of hardwood had been laid at intervals like the spokes of a great wheel with a diameter of about twenty feet. Ah Haleb inspected this arrangement to assure himself that the spaces between the radiating logs had been filled adequately with smaller timbers, and the crevices packed with slender branches and chips, all of freshly cut hardwood. Close by, a stream of men brought wood to raise the levels of other kilns to the requisite height of six or seven feet by adding more layers with their tightly chinked radial spokes.

The foreman approached Ah Haleb with a suggestion that the completed kilns be fired, as the day was windless and looked as if it would remain so. There were several of these kilns awaiting firing. On top of the completed drums had been added a layer of limestone chunks, none bigger than a baseball. This layer was about two feet deep at the perimeter, but sloped up to a height of three feet at the center. The whole mass looked for all the world like a giant birthday cake with a generous conical layer of frosting on top, and with the summit of the central pole serving as a solitary candle.

Ah Haleb, aware that the foreman was a better judge of weather conditions than he, authorized the firing. Men ran forward to remove the central pole from each kiln and drop glowing embers in the resulting well. In a few minutes dense clouds of smoke began to billow upward, as the fire, fanned by air sucked through interstices in the layers, began to eat its way outward from the central well. Later the smoke would yield to sheets of flame, the drum of wood would collapse inward, shooting its roof of limestone chunks into the center of the inferno. Not until the following morning would the fire burn itself out.

The architect inspected kilns which had been fired a week or two before. The lime, slaked by dews and rains, had swollen to a powdery mass several times its original bulk. Satisfied with their condition, he directed his steps to the great court of Chichén Itzá. Passing between the tall pyramid of Kukulcan and the sacred cenote, he came to the Temple of the Warriors and its great colonnade, the building of which had engaged his attention for the past year (Plate 6c).

The strictly architectural work of erecting the pyramid and the temple above was completed. Outwardly the building was finished; there only remained the minor matter of applying a coat of stucco to the exterior surfaces. Inside the temple sculptors and painters were at their tasks. Both groups of artists worked independently and with considerable latitude within the broad limits fixed by Ah Haleb on the instructions of the high priest. The architect derived much satisfaction from watching the slow embellishment of his creation, but that was a pleasure which could await his leisure; the work on the colonnade needed his close attention.

There the task of erecting the corbelled vault was going forward. The four lines of columns, with their square drums not yet sculptured, and the solid end-walls of the colonnade had been completed several months previously (cf. Plate 8c). The great squared beams of sapodilla wood, some ten feet long and one foot thick, had been slung into position to span the intervals between the columns, and now formed four parallel lines the length of the colonnade, like the double tracks of a twentieth-century elevated railway. To counteract any lateral thrust during the erection of the vaults above them, which might cause buckling and collapse, Ah Haleb had had a line of logs placed on the floor on each side of each row of columns. Against them were wedged at short intervals transverse braces which extended diagonally to the beams of the parallel lines of columns. Looking down the long axis of the colonnade, these pairs of braces formed a series of huge X's one behind the other. As soon as the vaults of stone and cement were completed and had hardened into a monolithic mass, the braces would be removed, and the sculptors would be set to work carving the faces of the columns.

Above the beams the vaults had risen to a height of a couple of feet. This was the most ticklish work of all. In recent months Ah Haleb had more than once awakened from a nightmare in which the columns had buckled under a badly balanced weight, and the whole colonnade had come toppling to the ground. Had he known what playing cards are, he would have compared himself to a man building a house of cards, but with the comforting knowledge that, once the building was finished, its strength would grow day by day with the hardening of the mortar.

The erection of the vaulting was slow work to be entrusted only to his most skilled masons. The walls of the vaults were being built a course at a time, with long intervals between work to let the mortar harden. A new course was being added today, and the masons were busy laying the specially cut stones used in the vaulting. These were shaped like knee-boots, with the leg part tapering to a point and the sole, which was to form the surface of the vault, carefully dressed. Each vault stone was laid in a bed of the finest mortar and tilted to the requisite angle, so that its lower front edge nested on the top front edge of the stone below it. As soon as one stone was laid, the other wing of the *V*, which was to form the soffit of the parallel vault, was laid, and the space between the tails of the two stones filled with a mass of rock and mortar, and leveled flush with the tops of the newly laid stones.

Satisfied that the work was going forward evenly, Ah Haleb ducked through the lines of X's of the bracers and under the occasional ladders, up which the masons' assistants carried their pails of mortar, and so left the colonnade. His next stop was at the place where the mortar was being mixed. Two large piles marked the spot, one of lime, the other of *sascab*, a white marl, which was mixed with the lime as we use sand. Most of the mixers could be trusted, but Ah Haleb had to watch for carelessness. Too weak a mixture used in any one part of the vault might lead to the collapse of the whole structure. For this work a mixture of one part of lime to one and one-half parts of *sascab* was being used, double the strength of the mixture used in the fill of pyramids or other places where the stress would be much less. The architect stopped to watch one of the mixers stir the mass with a wooden paddle, sampled the resulting mixture by rubbing a little between his fingers, and, enjoining the mixer not to weaken the proportions, passed on.

Re-entering the colonnade, he made his way up the stairway of the pyramid. He glanced, as he had done every day for the past four months, at the friezes of sculptured warriors of the military orders of jaguars and eagles strung along each terrace of the pyramid (Fig. 13*c*). As always, his eyes were attracted by one carved stone set upside down, marring the whole appearance of the frieze. He frowned. He had been ill at the time that carelessness had occurred. As soon as he had got back on the job and had seen that stone sticking out like a sore thumb, he had wished to have it turned right-side up, but the high priest, who was with him at the time, had ordered it to be left as it was, saying that perfection was for the gods alone, and in any case the back wall of the colonnade vaulting would eventually hide it. That was true, but Ah Haleb felt this sloppiness almost as a personal affront. The mason who had blundered had been ordered to make a penitential offering of blood drawn from his own body, and had been demoted to the rank of a helper; at that, in Ah Haleb's opinion, the fellow had been lucky to have got off so cheaply.

Entering the temple, the architect paused to accustom his eyes to the dim light. The artists responsible for the murals were not at work, for the light was bad; they would work in the afternoon when the western sun streamed through the triple entrance to the temple. Considerable progress had been made with the painting of the great mural; the bold preliminary outlining in a tawny red had been completed several days before and had given Ah Haleb a good idea of how the scenes would appear. Now some of the second outlining in black was finished and filled with the requisite colors. In one place a scene representing an attack across water was taking form, and the light blue of the water and the greens of some of the trees had already been filled in (Plate 17*a*); at another place a large feathered serpent was coming to life, but looking strangely naked without his coat of plumes, as yet unpainted.

Near the entrance, where the light was best, sculptors were at work on the sides of several columns. Here the design to be carved in low relief had been outlined with charcoal on the dressed stone surface. The task of pecking away the background with coarse hammerstones was proceeding smoothly, and, in some instances, the incising of the main details had already begun. This was being done with sharp stone flakes which, with alternating strokes on each side of the shallow line, were producing V-shaped grooves. The chinked layers between the drums of the columns had been covered with stucco, over which the charcoal outlines swept to indicate the areas where the outline would have to be carved in the stucco.

One of the charcoal outlines represented a warrior dressed in the garb of the Mexican god Tezcatlipoca, a sight which did not please the architect, who was still a Maya rebel despite the fact that the Mexicanized Itzá had long been masters of the city. There was, however, nothing that he could do about it. At the far end of the temple some of the little Atlantean figures which would support the flat top of the altar were being assembled, and Ah Haleb noticed that they were not all of the same height. He wondered what to do about that, and then decided it would be best to sink the tallest in the floor. Their feet would not show, but at least the tops of their heads would be even, making a level support for the flat top. It was extremely dark at that end of the temple except just before sunset, and few people would ever know of this indignity to the figures of the gods. Ah Haleb can hardly be blamed for not foreseeing that some eight hundred years later archaeologists of Carnegie Institution of Washington would detect his little subterfuge.

Leaving the temple, the architect passed to a quarry not far off the edge of the great court. There some sculptors were at work on elements which would be assembled to form the decoration of the entablature of the front of the colonnade. Previously some of this work had been rather carelessly executed; intervals had not been properly measured, with the result that carved lines on adjacent stones sometimes did not meet. Ah Haleb was determined this should not happen again. It was customary to carve the designs on columns after they had been erected, but stones for friezes and the mosiac decoration of façades were sculptured at the quarry. There was no logical reason for this custom that he could see.

Lines of dressed stone were arranged by sizes. To one side was a row of veneer stone for the plain areas of the façade. Behind were enough boot-shaped stones to complete the vaulting of the colonnade, and beyond was a line of the specialized capstones which would be used to close the vaults. The architect wished that these were already in position. In the weeks to come he was going to have little peace of mind, for with each new course added to the vaulting the danger from side-thrusting would grow.

From the quarry he walked to the other end of the city where work had recently started on a small pyramid. The site had been roughly leveled, and the space to be occupied by the pyramid had been laid out. Inside this area a second rectangle had been marked on the ground, corresponding to the area of the pyramidal core. Not until it was erected would the outer skin of the pyramid be built. Lines of workers were bringing loads of stone to the scene of operations.

Masons and their assistants were busy erecting the core. This work was not done all at a time. Instead, the area had been divided into rectangles, each about six by four feet, and each was built to a height of about six feet before the next unit was started. Already the rectangular blocks at each corner were well advanced. The masons had laid the undressed stone and mortar to form the four walls of each block, a course at a time, and, after leveling them off, had filled the area enclosed within each rectangle with rocks and weak mortar. This was work that needed close watching, for masons, in a hurry to finish their tasks, often filled the centers of each block with large rocks placed so that there would be as much space between them as possible, and then used a minimum of mortar, blocking the cracks with stones so that the mortar would not fill them. Such sloppy work, if undetected, might cause serious settling after the pyramid had been completed and the temple erected on its summit. By that time it would be too late to remedy the defect. The architect had placed one of his keenest foremen in charge here, and therefore was confident that there would be no unsubstantial building this time.

The lime kilns for this construction and the *sascab* pits must be visited. After that Ah Haleb would be free to go home to work on the drawings for the temple that would eventually crown this new pyramid. He had promised to have them ready for inspection by the high priest within a few days.

244

On his way home the architect stopped at a small shrine to make his daily offering of copal to the creation gods. People generally paid little attention to those gods, who lived far away in the thirteenth heaven, but Ah Haleb felt that he was in a sense under their protection, for in his own way was not he, too, a creator?

MARRIAGE À LA MODE

Young Ah Pitz Nic was bored and restless, and, looking around at his fellow inmates in the men's house, he realized why. One by one, friends of his own age had left to get married, and now those in the men's club were mostly boys sixteen to nineteen years old, on whose juvenility he looked with that feeling of mature superiority attained after twenty birthdays. If all went well, he would not have to stay much longer in the men's house, for the preliminaries to his marriage had been negotiated, and "negotiated" was the right word in more senses than one.

Nic had first noticed Ix Bacal as he and his friends from the men's house went down to bathe one day in the cenote. Coming round a bend in the trail through the woods, they had caught her and her companions by surprise, and Nic had had a good look at her before the girls could turn their backs on him in the Maya way, for with a large pottery jar of water on your head you can't turn your head quickly. It was extraordinary how often in the next week or so Nic happened to be passing that bend at the time the water carriers were coming back from the cenote. Not long after that, Nic shot a deer, and on the way back detoured to pass by the hut in which the girl lived, for he knew her name and where she lived. Some of his friends chaffed him about that detour. In the stories of the sun's wooing of the moon, the young sun god had stuffed a deerskin with ashes and carried it past moon's hut day after day to impress her with his ability to keep the larder full, until one day he slipped before her house; the deerskin scattered its load of ash broadcast, to sun's considerable humiliation. Now the fellows wanted to know if Nic's deer was real or stuffed, and one of them solemnly presented him with a stuffed skunk skin as he was leaving on his next hunting trip.

Nic had talked the matter over with his father while his mother pretended to be busy with her weaving, although taking care not to miss one word of the conversation. Nic's father would be sorry to lose his son's help in weeding and harvesting his cornfield and for bringing home loads of wood, but since his eldest daughter's husband had recently come to work for him, young Nic's marriage would not really represent a loss of labor. The elder Nic promised to get a marriage broker to sound out the Bacal parents.

He had been as good as his word, for he had engaged the offices of the marriage broker and had arranged that he and his wife would accompany Nic to the Bacals' hut to make an offer of marriage in the near future. Unofficial word had been sent to Ix Bacal's parents of the proposed visit, which would be on the day 1 Caban, the day of the moon goddess, in whose charge were such matters as marriage and parenthood. Nic and Ix Bacal had not exchanged a word, but the boy had felt reassured that so far as she was concerned, there would be no trouble, for passing by Ix Bacal's hut a few days after word had been passed to the Bacal family of the proposed visit, he had found her brocading a design of corncobs and flowers on the cloth on her loom. As *nic* means little flower and *bacal* is corncob, Nic felt quite sure that this was a message of encouragement to him. The trouble was that her views on the choice of her future husband were not of much consequence; that was a matter the older generation decided in consultation with the priest.

The visit of the marriage broker and Nic's parents to the Bacal hut had gone well. As was usual on such occasions, nothing about a proposal of marriage was so much as mentioned in the course of the first hour of conversation. Much attention was paid to the condition of the corn crop, the chances of damp weather producing a lot of rust damage to the ears, the best ways of warding off locust invasions, and the failure of the series of sacrifices the previous year to end the drought naturally to be expected in a year which began with the malignant day Cauac.

The arrival of gourds of cocoa mixed with corn and sprinkled with chile pepper gave a new turn to the conversation, for in Yucatán little cacao was grown and the expensive drink was seldom served by families, such as that of Ix Bacal, which were not of the aristocracy. It was a sign that the suit was not unsatisfactory to the Bacal family; it could also be a sign that the Bacal family thought themselves a bit superior, and the bridal price would be high. The matchmaker had the answer ready for that line of reasoning.

Finally, when every other subject had been thoroughly discussed, the matchmaker brought forward the proposal that the two families should be united by the marriage of young Nic to the Bacals' daughter. The good nature and the skill of the young man as a farmer and hunter were set forth at length and with the exaggeration of a man selling a gem.

Ah Bacal (*Ah* is the masculine prefix, as *Ix* is the feminine) expressed his complete surprise at any suggestion of marriage for his daughter, although, of course, as he pointed out, he had realized that with her skill in weaving, which was almost beyond belief, and her amazing ability to cook, she must necessarily attract every young man in the neighborhood. In addition, he continued, one could see from her build that she would bear many children, and in looks she could stand comparison with even the young moon goddess herself. In the family, he concluded, she was affectionately known as Ix Kukum, "Lady Quetzal Feather," because she was so precious.

The matchmaker replied with a fuller catalog of Nic's virtues, and then, after some general discussion of the merits of both young people, he came to the point. Young Nic was so much above the average that his parents thought that there was no call to make the customary present, but in order to keep to custom, they would engage that the boy should serve his future father-in-law for three years after marriage, help him with all the agricultural work, hunt with him, look after his bees, and help to keep the household supplied with firewood. In addition, he would make a payment of a quarter of a load of cacao beans, eight red beads made of the valuable spondylus shell, thirteen corn-husk packets of copal, and two loads of unspun cotton.

Ah Bacal declared the payment ridiculous. His daughter was called in and asked if she was willing to marry Nic, provided the payment could be arranged; and to that question, with every attempt not to show her interest, she replied affirmatively. Ah Bacal then proposed five years' service and a doubling of the cacao and cotton payments. This proposal was promptly but politely turned down by the matchmaker, who pointed out that Ah Bacal had no sons to help him in his work and was not as strong as he had been, and therefore should be extremely glad to get such a hard-working son-in-law. That was really the matchmaker's trump card, for young Nic had a good name as a hard worker; he had wisely held it back to trump Ah Bacal's counter proposal. The bargaining continued for a long time, but finally it was agreed that service for four years and the payments as first proposed might be the basis for an agreement. On a subsequent visit presents of decorated gourds and pottery were exchanged to seal the bargain, which was celebrated with a meal brought by the visitors. Later, Nic's father walked over to the men's hut to give his son the news and to hand over a gaily brocaded loincloth, a gift from his future in-laws.

Even then the matter was not really settled, for the local priest had to be consulted. Next day, the matchmaker, with a load of corn as fee, interviewed the priest, who pronounced that there was no serious conflict between the gods on whose days the young people had been born. Indeed, the mating would be extremely favorable since Nic's natal day was 3 Kan, and Kan was the day of the maize god, and three the number of the rain and lightning god, who helps the crops to grow. What auguries could be better for marriage to a girl whose name was corncob? Her birthday, 7 Etz'nab, was ruled by the jaguar god and the god of sacrifice, both of whom might be regarded as neutral so far as this marriage was concerned. Finally the priest suggested several days favorable for the marriage.

Some time passed before there came a slack season, during which the parents could be sure of getting together a group of kinsmen and friends to build a new hut behind that of the Bacals for the couple, but the actual building of the hut took only two days. Early in the morning of the first day all the men went out to the woods, some to get four corner posts and the wood for the beams that rest on them, the ridge pole, and the *A* frames which support it; others to get the lighter rafters and the roof-rods. The four forked corner posts were first placed in position, and in their forks were laid the longitudinal beams. Meanwhile, two of the helpers had returned from the woods with coiled lengths of suitable liana, with outer covering removed, and strips of bark. With these the beams were lashed to the corner posts, the *A* frames to the beams, and the ridge pole to the *A* frames (Fig. 24*d*). As the work of lashing these together and then lashing, one by one, the rafters and the roof rods into position progressed in the capable hands of four of the most experienced men, the rest returned to the forest for more liana and for loads of the fan-shaped leaves of the *guano* palm.

By late afternoon when work stopped, the frame of the house was finished, and large piles of palm leaves with stems chopped short were ready for the men to start thatching next morning. The walls had not been started, for in a Maya house, unlike ours, the roof is not supported by the walls, but by the four corner posts and the two longitudinal beams (Fig. 24*a*).

Meanwhile in the Bacals' hut there had been much activity. Scores of venison and turkey tamales had been made, pots of beans were boiling, sweet potatoes were cooking slowly in a covered pit in the ground, and thick tortillas of maize and ground squash seed were being kept hot in large covered gourds. As soon as work stopped, the men and boys returned to their huts to wash and change their loin-cloths, and then returned to the Bacals' hut for the customary feast.

Next morning the thatching was started, and more poles were set up and lashed with liana to form the walls and the doorway. This was a simple task uncomplicated by such problems as windows, just as the thatchers had not needed to worry about a chimney. Early in the afternoon the hut was completed, long before the festival meal was ready for the workers. It was a cheap way of obtaining a home; every item in its construction had come from the woods around, and the labor had been obtained at the cost of two meals and an obligation to repay it by volunteering for similar projects undertaken by one's helpers, a not unpleasant way of working together for mutual advantage. The work had not been hard, and there had been some fun. Nic and a friend who, like all Maya, loved a practical joke, had untied some of the liana lashings, which held one of the roof rods where Uc was thatching, taking advantage of that fat youth's short absence to get a drink of *posol*. When Uc, returning to his job, stepped on that roof rod, it bent under his weight, throwing him off balance, so that he disappeared through the roof frame and hung there suspended between roof and floor. Everyone was laughing too hard to rescue him as he dangled there like a trussed-up tapir, calling for help. Then two of the men had placed a notched pole within Uc's reach, but it had slipped, landing Uc and all his excess pounds on top of his two would-be rescuers. That was something that Uc would not be allowed to forget for a long time.

Next evening the hut was consecrated by the local priest. Copal was burned in the four corners, and *balche,* turkey meat, and tortillas were offered in sacrifice. Nic with the help of his father-in-law had constructed a bed of poles with pole slats tied with liana across the top, as well as various odds and ends such as shelves and suspended trays of the same material. The fireplace—three stones forming a triangle—had been the easiest job, but the table for Ix Bacal's metate had to be made with more care of solid wood, for the backward and forward sweep of the muller on the metate would cause any table not strongly made to collapse in very quick order. Furniture, such as pottery storage jars and cooking vessels, gourds, pottery griddle, baskets, a bark cover and a reed mat for the bed, and a bark bucket, had been provided; all was ready for the couple to move in.

The evening before the wedding ceremony Nic was subject to a lot of chaff in the men's house. Several Kekchi traders from the Alta Verapaz, in the distant highlands of Guatemala, had arrived that day, bringing obsidian cores to trade for the famed textiles of Yucatán, and were lodged in the men's house. They joined in the conversation as they sat round the fire pressing blades one by one off the cores to have them ready for the next day's market—it looked so simple, but the Yucatec Maya could no more do it than the Kekchi could do the same with a flint core. One of them was teasing young Nic, telling him that he ought to go to the Guatemala highlands to seek a wife. "In my land," he said, "the girl has to go to the man's home before the marriage and give a demonstration of grinding maize and making tortillas. You ought to do that up here. Another thing, if the girl is found to have been free with her favors before marriage, you can send her home, and get back your payment. Down by Lake Atitlán a fellow shows he is interested in a girl by breaking the pottery jar she is balancing on her head as she goes down to the lake to fill it. If she likes him, she says nothing; if she protests, that means she isn't interested, and the fellow has to buy her a new jar. That is a delightful custom, and the pottery makers are all for it."

This last remark was not taken too seriously by the young fellows in the men's house, for travelers from far away have a habit of telling tall stories, but the trader assured them it was true. "The lad waits on the path, and you should hear the excited chatter when a jar is smashed, although the blow is a gentle one. You fellows," he continued, "who complain about the high cost of a bride ought to go to Campeche, for there a bride costs only a bow and two arrows, and you can leave her any time during the first year after marriage."

Next morning Nic's mother presented to Ix Bacal the wedding skirt and brocaded blouse she had woven for her, and laid out for her son a new loincloth with the ends decorated with parrot feathers and a shoulder mantle she had made for him. Nic's father had made him a pair of sandals and a necklace of beetle wings, and his uncle

brought him a surprise gift of a charming pair of ear ornaments of hardwood with a carved design of flowers inlaid with red and yellow pigment.

The ceremony itself was held that evening in the Bacal house following a feast and the ceremonial drinking of *balche*. Speeches were made by the fathers of the bride and groom, and the bride's uncle added an unscheduled address somewhat marred by the cumulative effects of the nips of *balche* to which he had been helping himself with unbecoming alacrity. At the conclusion of the ceremony the party adjourned to the newly built house in which the priest again burnt copal. The bridal pair, who still had never spoken to each other, were ceremoniously seated on a mat, where they were blessed by the priest after prayers to sundry gods for their well-being had been said.

An hour before sunrise next morning Ix Bacal was busy preparing tortillas. Nic arose and ate his breakfast, waited on by his wife. A few minutes later he was following his father-in-law along the trail which led to the latter's cornfield to work the first day of his four-year contract; honeymoons are not a part of the Maya way of life.

DEATH AND LIFE

In a thatched house in the northern highlands of what is now Guatemala an old man was dying. Outside, in distant fields, men were about their daily work with a feeling of urgency, for the sun was nearly two "months," that is, forty days, past the spring equinox, and life-giving rains would soon end the dry season and cause the corn seed to quicken. Outside the hut, but close by, women also were working with a feeling of urgency, but they were racing not life, but death. They were weaving the last rich mantles for the old man's burial, and they were weaving for the last time, for they, too, were about to die.

Inside the hut a middle-aged man watched his father, the head chief, and wondered when death would come. The sorcerers had made their divinations, pouring heaps of *pito* beans or corn on the ground and counting them into piles of four, and had followed them with ceremonies on neighboring mountaintops. A visiting sorcerer from the territory of the Mam in the western highlands had made his divination in the strange method of the Mam—rubbing his legs and watching for the twitching of the muscles. His left leg had twitched, a sign of bad news. All the divinations had pointed to a verdict of death within a few days; the only difference was the exact day. The old chief had heard the results and had made up his mind to die with that acceptance of the inevitable which is so alien to us, but so common in the Orient and among American Indians. The old chief's favorite diviner had said that day, 10 Camel, would see the end. It was the day of the death god, a fact which may have influenced the result of the divination; it certainly affected the old chief's will to live. He had decided that he would die that day, and when an old

Indian, be he Maya or Aztec or Iroquois, makes up his mind to die at a certain time, he usually does so.

The old chief lived through the night, but when the chill dawn came, he breathed his last. His waiting son placed a jade bead in the dying man's mouth to receive the departing spirit, and then rubbed it gently over his father's face. The event had been anticipated, and all was prepared: the embroidered mantles to cover the dead man's shoulders were woven; men to summon chiefs of neighboring groups were standing by, waiting for orders to run with their messages; the household goods to be placed in the burial shaft had been assembled; the food for the old chief's last journey to the underworld was ready; and the tomb itself was dug. A watchful eye was being kept on the slaves to see that none tried to run away.

All through the next day the neighboring chiefs, each in his litter carried by slaves and followed by a retinue of head-men arrived at intervals; their housing and entertainment presented problems which tested the organizing abilities of the new head chief.

Burial was on the third day. A procession of local chiefs and head-men and the chiefs who had come from near and far for the funeral, together with numerous attendants bearing gifts and household possessions climbed the hill to the burial shaft, accompanying the dead chief. A forlorn group of frightened slaves also marched on their last journey, for they were to die so that their souls could minister in the next world to their master's soul.

The dead chief had been decked with jewels—jades, shell necklaces, and a few ornaments of gold and gold-copper alloy (four or five centuries earlier these would have been unknown, for metal did not reach the Maya until the end of the Classic period). He wore on his breast a large mirror of iron pyrites, the polygonal plates of which were fitted mosaic fashion on a back of painted slate; in the lobes of his ears were earplugs of apple-green jade; leg-bands from which hung little copper bells, so that they had jingled at each step he had taken in life, were tied beneath each knee; and sandals with high heel-guards of worked leather were on his feet. A cotton loincloth with an elaborately embroidered design was wrapped around his waist, the ends, decorated with feathers, hanging down in front and behind. Over his shoulders had been laid mantle after mantle

a

Fig. 23. *a*: Tomb of an important chief beneath part of a pyramid at Kaminaljuyú. The pit, dated about A.D. 550, originally had a roof of perishable materials. The chief and his attendants (or family?) were seated cross-legged, but with decay the bodies slumped. The attendants, perhaps slaves sacrificed to accompany their master in the next world, were two adolescents of fifteen to seventeen years and a child of about eleven. In the tomb were many jade beads, jade earplugs, shell beads and ornaments, iron pyrite mirrors, obsidian points, an alabaster vase, many fine pottery vessels, the skeleton of a dog (to lead his master to the abode of the dead), jaws of a jaguar, the skull of a coyote, and (not shown in the illustration), a corn grinding stone and muller, and traces of a sort of wooden litter. Some four hundred shell tinklers which formed a rectangle around this litter had probably been attached to a textile over the litter. (*After A. V. Kidder.*)

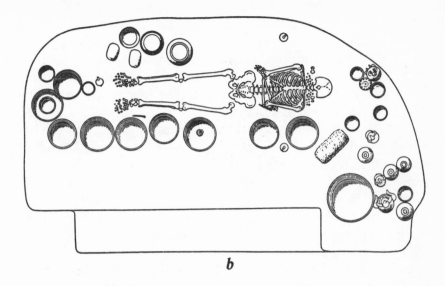

b

Fig. 23. *b*: Burial of a priest at Uaxactún, about A.D. 550. A man placed full length, with red ocher on his bones. There were no teeth or facial bones. Thirty-five pottery vessels of the early Classic period, earplugs and beads of both jade and shell, jaguar teeth, a sting-ray spine, traces of copal, charcoal, and a bone tube were with the burial. The sting-ray spine perhaps indicates that the dead man was a priest, since it was used by priests in blood-drawing ceremonies. (*After A. L. Smith.*)

of cotton brocaded with intricate designs and shoulder cloaks of gorgeous featherwork, the "trousseau" which his women slaves had been making for many months for this new life in the next world.

Thus adorned and squatting on his haunches, the dead chief had been placed in a large wooden box—coffin one could scarcely call it because it was almost cube-shaped. The box rested on a litter borne on the shoulders of four slaves.

At the top of the mountain the procession halted, and the box was lowered into the wide, deep pit already prepared. Attendants advanced in turn to deposit the rest of the dead man's possessions: more jades; iron pyrite mirrors; vessels of pottery, Mexican onyx, wood, and gourd; featherwork of quetzal, macaw, parrot, and ocellated turkey plumage; knives and points of obsidian; flint-pointed spears; shields; dishes of corn, meat, beans, and chile sauce; cups of *posol* and spiced cacao; sleeping mats and cotton cloaks; and presents brought by neighboring chiefs. Next, the dead chief's favorite dog was killed and placed in the pit, for his shade would guide his master's shade on the long journey to the other world (Fig. 23a).

Then it was the turn of the slaves, both those of the household and those who had been brought by visiting chiefs. One by one they were slain and laid in the pit, and with them were placed their tools. Corn-grinding stones, looms, spindles and spindle whorls, brooms, and potter's clay and temper were laid with the women slaves; stone axes, planting sticks, blowguns, spears, knives for dressing skin, and pack traps with the men. The pit was now almost full; earth was thrown in to fill the spaces between bodies and utensils, and tamped down. Shortly a masonry altar would be built over the pit, and on it incense would be burned to the gods and food deposited so that the departed spirits could feed on the spirit within it. How often and how widely in time and place have such funerary rites been performed so that the shades of departed kings and chiefs could live in the next world as they had lived in this!

That evening the new head chief entertained his father's mourners with a banquet. After polite speeches had extolled the virtues of the dead man, conversation became more general, although death and burial dominated it. One chief from the Chiapas side of the Cuchumatanes Mountains explained how similar were the burial rites near his home, save the corpse was placed in a huge pottery jar. An elderly man who had traveled from one end of the Maya area to another described a peculiar burial custom practiced by the Cocom family which ruled at Mayapán, in distant Yucatán.

"They cut off the head of the dead chief," he said, "boil it to remove the flesh, and then saw off the back part. On the front half they model the features of the dead man with a kind of bitumen, and what is more, they keep these permanent portraits of the dead ancestors in their household shrines, and offer food to them on all their festivals. There is another strange custom in parts of Yucatán. A son orders a wooden statue of his father with a hollow in the back of the head. He burns part of the corpse and fills the hollow with the ashes, and then covers the mouth of this hollow with the corresponding piece of skin from the back of the dead man's head, and buries the rest of the body. Families keep these wooden statues with the statues of their gods, and venerate them. It is certainly a strange custom."

The speaker could not see the skeptical expressions on the faces of some of his listeners who sat in shadow beyond the light from pine torches. Modeling features of the dead man on his skull did not strike them as unusual, for they knew a somewhat similar custom had once obtained in their own country, but the account of the sealing of the hole in the wooden statue with a piece of skin from the back of the dead person's head sounded like a traveler's tall story. They need not have been skeptical. A century or so later, Bishop Landa reported both customs; and a wooden statue with a hole in the back of its head, dredged from the well of sacrifice at Chichén Itzá, is now in the Peabody Museum, Harvard University.

Normally, the visiting chiefs would have started home the next morning, but the new head chief had asked them to stay to take part in the *hetz' mek* ceremony for his daughter who would be three (twenty-day) months old that day. The *hetz' mek* is carried out when a girl is three "months" old because three is woman's sacred number (the fireplace at which a woman will spend much of her life has three stones arranged as a triangle); it is performed when a boy is four "months" old because four is man's sacred number (to represent the four sides of the cornfield on which a man will labor all his days).

The girl was brought into the room in her mother's arms and handed to the wife of one of the chiefs. On a mat in the center of the room were placed nine objects which a woman would use in her daily work. They included a spindle and a hank of cotton, a miniature loom and batten, a bone needle, a tiny water jar, a cooking pot, a miniature grinding stone and muller for grinding corn, and a collander. The woman picked up the spindle and hank of cotton, and placing it in the child's hands, said, "Take it so that you will learn to spin cotton," and at the same time guided the child's hands in a rough imitation of twirling the spindle. Next, after carrying the child on her hip once around the mat, she picked up the miniature loom and helped the child to go through the motions of weaving, and so on until nine circuits of the mat had been made and the child had been instructed in the use of all the implements. The ceremony was then repeated with the husband of the "godmother" as instructor. At its conclusion everyone felt sure that the girl would later be an asset to the group, although, truth to tell, as the daughter of a head chief, she would not be called on to grind maize or sweep floors.

Next day, in a tropical downpour, the visitors left for their homes. A chief and half a score of slaves had ceased to belong to the group; a new member had been received into it. Except for the family of the departed head chief, the interlude was over; the heavens had opened, the precious jade, the life-giving rains, had come, and with them nature had been revivified; death no longer intruded on the community.

VI. Maya Religion

To feel the pulses of hearts that are now dead.—Thomas E. Brown

COSMOLOGY

Our sources for Maya religion are the writings of the Spaniards, largely friars, of the sixteenth century, religious references in the Maya books of Chilam Balam, the residue of paganism recovered by ethnologists working among present-day Maya after sifting out all European accretions and new ideas developed from that blending, and lastly, religious representations sculptured on ancient monuments or painted on murals or in the three surviving books of hieroglyphic writing.

The material is not too promising. For one thing, all sources except the last are subsequent to the big intrusion of Mexican ideas into the Maya area about A.D. 1000, and it is hard to tell how many of the religious beliefs and practices about which they speak are truly Maya. Although most of the religious ideas introduced from central Mexico appear to have been followed only by the new ruling caste which arose as a result of those invasions, it is possible that some of them may have been accepted by the Maya masses, perhaps in altered form. Furthermore, it is almost impossible to disentangle these Mexican threads from the Maya ones because of the strong similarity in the fundamental religious beliefs of all Middle American peoples.

In interpreting religious sculpture of the Classic period in the light of what we know of practices at the time of the Spanish Conquest, particularly in Yucatán, we have to make the somewhat dangerous assumption that Maya religion was static and that the same gods were worshiped and the same rituals followed in, say, eighth-

259

century Copán as in sixteenth-century Yucatán. So far as the general cosmological structure is concerned, I think that may well be the case; but there were differences, local and probably temporal as well. For instance, in the highlands of Guatemala, mountains were personified and identified with deities of the earth. This cult of mountain gods was of great importance in that rugged land, but it never took hold in the flat country of northern Yucatán.

The cosmological ideas of the Maya were involved. They appear to have believed that the sky was divided into thirteen compartments, in each of which certain gods resided. These may have been thought to be arranged as that number of horizontal layers one above the other, or as steps, six ascending on the east and six descending on the west, with the seventh at the top so that compartments one and thirteen, two and twelve, and so on were on the same level. The sky was sustained by four gods, the Bacabs (Fig. 13*a*). who stood on the four sides of the world. An association of supreme importance in Maya religion is that of colors with directions. Red is the color of the east, white of the north, black of the west, and yellow of the south; there may have been a fifth color, green, for the center. Almost every element in Maya religion and not a few parts of the Maya calendar are connected with one world direction and its corresponding color. Thus the red Bacab stood at the east, the white Bacab at the north, the black Bacab at the west, and the yellow Bacab at the south.

At each of the four sides of the world (or perhaps at each side of one of the heavens) stood a sacred ceiba (the wild cotton tree), known as the Imix ceiba, and these trees, too, were associated with the world colors. They appear to have been the trees of abundance, from which food for mankind first came; their counterparts in Aztec mythology helped to sustain the heavens. In a ritual of the four world directions in the Book of Chilam Balam of Chumayel, we read: "The red flint is the stone of the red Muzencab [the sky bearer who also functioned as a bee god]. The red ceiba of the dragon monster is his arbor which is set in the east. The red bullet tree is their tree. The red sapodilla, the red vine . . . . Reddish are their yellow turkeys. Red toasted corn is their maize."

The rotation of the directions follows this quotation, each with associated deities, flora, and fauna of the required color. On each tree perched a bird of the requisite color. There is reason to believe that a fifth green tree was set in the center. Highly conventionalized representations of world-direction trees with birds perched on them appear on reliefs at Palenque and Piedras Negras. Of the ceiba tree, still considered sacred, many legends and superstitions survive, although the old cosmological beliefs have largely disappeared under the impact of Christianity. It is almost certain that the Maya, like the Mexicans, believed that the world rested on the back of a huge alligator or crocodile, which, in turn, floated in a vast pond. I am inclined to think that there may have been four of these terrestrial monsters, each assigned to a world direction and each with its distinguishing features.

There seems no reason to doubt that the Maya, like the Aztec, believed that there were nine underworlds, one below the other or again stepped, with the fifth the bottom-most. At any rate, the nine lords of the night, who have an evil aspect, are as prominent in the Maya calendar as in the Aztec. In Aztec belief these lords ruled the nine underworlds; Mictlantecutli, one of the nine lords and chief god of the underworld, and his wife ruled the fifth. The numbers thirteen, nine, seven, and four have great ritualistic and divinatory importance in both Maya and Aztec cultures.

The Aztec believed that the world had been created five times and had been destroyed four times, the present age being the fifth. Each age had been brought to a violent end, the agents being respectively ferocious jaguars, a hurricane, volcanic eruptions, and a flood. The traditions that have survived among the Maya on the number of creations and destructions of the world are somewhat at variance. That we are now in the fourth age is the view expressed in two sources. Nevertheless, it is probable that Maya belief was in agreement with the Aztec in assigning the number five to the present age.

We have no information on the spans of time the Maya assigned to these ages. Actually, as the Maya priests reckoned hundreds of millions of years into the past, it is probable that they grasped the concept of time, and therefore perhaps a world, without beginning. This intellectual conception of a few priest-astronomers may have existed alongside a popular belief in various creations and destruction of the world.

THE GODS

Most Maya gods were in groups of four, each associated with its world direction and color. The gods in each group could be regarded either as individuals or collectively as a single deity, somewhat as in the Christian doctrine of the Trinity.

Gods could have both good and bad aspects. The Chacs sent the rain, but they also sent hail and long periods of damp which produced rust on the ears of corn. The Chac might therefore be shown as a beneficent deity or as a death-dealing power. In the latter case he could be represented with a skull replacing his head and with other insignia of death. Gods could change their localities and resultant associations. The sun god was, naturally, a sky god; but at sunset he passed to the underworld to become one of the lords of the nights, and emerged at dawn with the insignia of death. To depict him during his journey through the underworld, it was necessary to add attributes, such as those of the jaguar, or black, the color of the underworld, or maize foliage, which also connoted the surface of the world and the underworld. In a similar manner celestial dragons could become terrestrial monsters. These varying aspects of deities make the elucidation of Maya religion more difficult. Many, perhaps we can say most, Maya gods blend the features of animals or plants with a human aspect. The Maya may have made their gods in their own mental image, but hardly in their physical image.

Sky Gods. The sun and moon were the most important of the celestial deities (Fig. 25e–g). Around them was built a veritable cycle of legends. Sun and moon, prior to their translation to the skies, were the first inhabitants of the world. Sun was patron of music and poetry and was a famed hunter; moon was the goddess of weaving and childbirth. Sun and moon were the first to cohabit, but moon, who was unfaithful to her husband, earned an unenviable reputation for looseness, and her name became synonymous with sexual license. Since flowers of the *plumiera* tree (frangipani) were the symbol of sexual intercourse, they came to be associated with both sun and moon. The monkey had the same symbolic qualities. We find both these traditions reflected in hieroglyphic writing. From parallel beliefs in central Mexico we can add to the functions of the moon that of being goddess of maize and of the earth and probably all its crops. Sun and moon were finally translated to the sky. Moon's light is less bright than that of sun because one of her eyes was pulled out by sun. A widespread belief, still prevalent in Middle America, but clearly not shared by the Maya priest-astronomers, is that eclipses are due to fights between sun and moon. Honorific titles such as "lord" and "lady," "our father" and "our mother," or "our grandfather" and "our grandmother" were bestowed on sun and moon almost throughout the Maya area.

Itzamna was an outstanding deity in the hierarchic pantheon, but seems to have had few devotees among the rank and file. As with other Maya gods, there were actually four Itzamnas, one assigned to each world direction and color. There can be little doubt that the Itzamnas are the four celestial monsters (often represented as two-headed alligators or lizards; sometimes shown as serpents with one or two heads) which are so prevalent in Maya art of all periods (*itzam* actually means "lizard" in Yucatec). In the bottom third of the page depicting a New Year ceremony in Codez Dresden (Plate 31*a*), a priest, impersonating Itzamna, offers a decapitated turkey to the sacred column set up for the New Year. Among the Chorti Maya of the eastern fringes of the Central area, sky monsters, known as Chicchan, are thought to be half human, half snake and are associated with world directions and colors. There are also terrestrial manifestations of the Chicchan. These celestial monsters are deities of the rain and, by extension, of the crops and food. They are probably local variations of the Chacs.

Other dwellers in the skies were the deities who were the planets, and the Chacs. Of the former the Venus god was of supreme importance in the Maya hieroglyphic records; the Chacs, like the Itzamnas, are rain gods, and have ophidian attributes (Fig. 22*b, d, e*). It is possible that they merely represent a different manifestation of

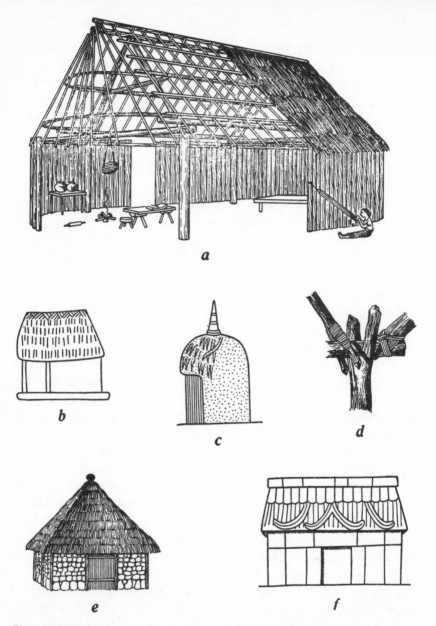

Fig. 24.—Maya Huts.

a: Typical Yucatec hut as still used. Interior shows bed (nowadays replaced with hammock), table with corn grinder, table with jars, tripod table for making tortillas, stool, hanging tray, three-stone fireplace, and woman weaving. Part of wall and most of thatching removed to show construction.

b, *c*: Huts depicted on murals at Chichén Itzá. This is the only record of round huts in the Maya lowland area.

d: Joins are secured with lashings of bark or native vines; no nails are used.

e: Zutuhil house in the highlands of Guatemala. Walls are of dry rubble lava masonry; thatch of grass capped with inverted bowl.

f: Stone model of Maya hut in the façade of the *Monjas* building at Uxmal (about A.D. 900).

(*After Wauchope with additions.*)

the Itzamnas, but it is, perhaps, a shade more probable that they are elements of the simpler and older religion which survived, particularly among the peasants, in rivalry with the more occult deities, such as the Itzamnas, favored by the hierarchy. At any rate, the worship of the Chacs is predominant among the present-day Yucatec Maya who have forgotten even the name of Itzamna.

The Chacs, as we have seen, were four in number and similarly set at the four sides of the world. They are popularly believed to send rain by sprinkling a little water from calabashes which they carry. Were they to empty these calabashes at one fell swoop, the world would be flooded. Because of these gourds, they are sometimes known as "the sprinklers." They cause lightning. They also carry stone axes, which they hurl to earth, and these are thunderbolts. Polished stone axes, dating principally from the Mexican period and later, are found in many parts of the Maya area, and are known as Chacs' axes. The association of stone axes with thunderbolts is world wide.

The Chacs are sometimes thought to be of gigantic stature, and the little frogs, called *uo*, whose croaking announces rain, are their attendants and musicians. An amusing legend recounts the experiences of a mischievous boy who was taken as an attendant to the abode of the Chacs in the sky. Ordered to sweep the Chacs' residence, he swept out the frogs despite their indignant protests, and then, purloining the water gourd of one of the Chacs, he almost flooded the world by sprinkling too much water from it.

Kukulcan, as Quetzalcoatl was called in Yucatán, was the tutelary of Mexican invaders and, as such, was but a flash in the Maya pan. Of supreme importance in the art of the Mexican period, he appears to have been regarded as alien by the great body of the Maya. His ephemeral character is well illustrated by the fact that his name is quite unknown among the present-day Maya.

Earth Gods. Of the gods of the soil, those who have charge of the crops are the most important. A deity of vegetation in general and of maize in particular, a youthful personage who incorporates features of the young corn, is frequently represented in Maya art (Plate 10*b*; Figs. 22*f*, 25*a*, *d*). His head is used as a symbol for the number eight. In the more rugged parts of the Maya area gods of the soil are associated with prominent mountains, springs, the confluences of rivers, and other outstanding manifestations of nature. There is a little evidence that there may have been a group of seven deities associated with the surface of the earth, just as there were thirteen sky gods and nine gods of the underworld.

Various crops, such as beans, had their indwelling god, but the maize god, always depicted as youthful and often with maize growing from his head, was a god of all vegetation.

The jaguar god (Fig. 20), corresponding to the Mexican Tepe-yollotl, god of the interior of the earth, is an important Maya deity of the surface of the earth or its interior, for the two regions overlap. Mam, a scarecrow figure, was reverenced during the five nameless unlucky days at year end. At their conclusion he was treated with contempt, undressed, thrown on the ground or shut up until the next year end. The earth deities share a number of attributes, of which the water lily, shells, and other aquatic symbols, the Imix sign, and attributes of death are the most prominent.

Gods of the Underworld. The Aztec believed that there were three abodes of the dead. Warriors who had died in battle or on the sacrificial stone and women who had succumbed in childbirth went to a celestial paradise. The former escorted the sun from the eastern horizon to the zenith; the latter from the zenith to the western horizon. Persons who had died of sundry diseases, such as dropsy and epilepsy, and those who were drowned or had been struck by lightning (the axes hurled by the rain gods) went to Tlalocan, the home of the Mexican rain gods, called Tlalocs. This was a paradise in which all edible plants grew in great profusion and, according to one source, formed the lowest celestial compartment. The third abode of the dead was Mictlan, apparently the lowest compartment of the underworld, whither departed those who had not qualified for either of the other two lands of the dead. The god and goddess of death ruled this realm.

How closely these concepts were paralleled in Maya belief is not certain. There is no evidence of a celestial abode for warriors, which may have been an outgrowth of Mexican warrior cults, but there was definitely a Maya equivalent of Tlalocan and, at least in later times, an underground abode of the dead, ruled perhaps by Cisin, whose name implies the stench of the charnel house, and who is probably the death god so frequently represented in Maya codices (Plate 31*a*, middle third of page; Fig. 17, No. 22).

The glyphs of the nine lords of the nights and of the underworlds have been identified, but their names are unknown, although the first of the series, the night sun or the sun god during his nightly passage from west to point of rising in the east, is easily recognized (p. 262; Fig. 17, No. 19, Glyph 8).

Deification of Periods of Time and Numbers. The twenty days which formed the Maya "month" were regarded as gods and were the recipients of prayers. The days were in a way embodiments of gods, such as the sun and moon, the maize deity, the death god, and the jaguar god, which were drawn from their various categories to be reassembled in this series. The numbers which accompany the days were also gods and perhaps correspond to the thirteen sky gods, although they are also in the same sequence as thirteen of the day gods. The fact that in this series of thirteen occur gods of the underworld or the surface of the earth does not seriously militate against their identification as the original thirteen gods of the heavens, for Maya deities pass elusively from one region to the other. Similarly, all periods of time appear to have been regarded as gods, and Maya divinities form and reform in bewildering aggroupments, thereby supplying the priest-astrologer with means to hedge on his prophecies, but sorely perplexing the modern student.

Sundry Gods. In addition to the deities assigned to sky, earth, and underworld, there were various gods not so easily placed, albeit temporarily, in those categories. At the time of the Conquest, the Maya had various gods who were the patrons of trades, such as the tutelaries of merchants, beekeepers, and tattooers. It is not improbable that several of these were merely manifestations of specialized aspects of gods whose main functions were of a more general nature. Various deified heroes reported for sixteenth-century Yucatán probably reflect Mexican influences, but deities of animal origin, such as the bat, the dog, and the Moan birds, owls which stand above the celestial dragons and also sent rain to mankind, were worshiped during the Classic period, as was the god of the flint or obsidian blade. On the other hand, we have no information on a Maya god of fire, although among the Mexicans that deity was of considerable importance. The Maya recognized a supreme being, the creator god, but, like the Mexicans, appear to have accorded him little worship, presumably because he was regarded as remote from human affairs.

Work among the present-day Tzotzil Maya of Chiapas reveals the importance in their communities of the worship of ancestors—that is, the supposed founders of the lineages. There is some evidence for similar cults in Yucatán at the time of the Spanish Conquest, and the names of two or three or those deified ancestors have been recorded. In that connection it is worth noting that the family oratories found in houses of persons of consequence at the late site of Mayapán seem to have been primarily for ancestor worship. Such lineage cults may derive from a time when a clan organization was far stronger among the Maya than at the time of the Spanish Conquest. They may have resulted from Mexican influences, for the best-known lineage god, Zacalpuc, was a Mexican invader.

The cult of the unpleasant god known to the Aztec as Xipe Totec, who wears a human skin cut off at wrists and ankles to show his own hands and feet and a mask of human skin over his face, was found all over Middle America, including the Maya area. He is a god of vegetation, and his flaying rites are widely shared with a goddess of the soil. His portrait is perhaps on the vase shown in Plate 30. The original home of this god is unknown; the Aztec discredited his cult to the Tlapanec, a small group on the Pacific Coast of the state of Guerrero.

Caves were used throughout the Maya area as ossuaries and for religious rites, particularly in honor of the god of the interior of the earth and of the rain gods. For their ceremonies the Maya used "virgin" (uncontaminated) water. Water dropping from the roofs of caves was a sovereign source of virgin water, the more inaccessible the cave, the better guarantee of purity. Consequently, the most hidden and dampest of "rooms" often contain huge numbers of complete or broken pottery and stone vessels often sheathed in lime from dripping stalactites.

Close by Chichén Itzá a warren of underground caves, called Balankanché, devoted to the worship of the Mexican rain gods, the Tlalocs, and also to Xipe Totec, has recently been discovered. The serried ranks of incense burners, miniature *metates* and mullers and pottery plates (miniature implements and humans [children] were features of the Tlaloc cult in central Mexico) frequently grouped around stalactites are as they were left when the caves were last used some nine centuries ago by the Mexicanized invaders of Chichén Itzá, who had probably used an ancient center of Chac worship for the cult of their Mexican cousins, the Tlalocs. The Maya in the neighborhood had a tradition of ancient use of these caves, and their name for them Balankanché, means "hidden seat," a case of folk memory going back nearly a millenium.

I believe the outstanding characteristics of Maya religion to be these: (1) Reptilian origin of deities of the rain and of the earth; features of snakes and crocodiles, merged and fantastically elaborated, alone or blended with human characteristics, distinguished those gods (Plate 14b; Fig. 13b, c). Deities with purely human form are not common in Maya art. (2) Quadruplicity of various gods together with association with world directions and colors, yet a mystic merging of the four in one, a process somewhat comparable to the Christian mystery of the Trinity. (3) Duality of aspect, for deities could be both benevolent and malevolent and in some cases, seemingly, could change sex. This duality also extends to age, for in the case of several deities, functions are shared between a youthful and an aged god. Malevolence is expressed in art by the addition of insignia of death. (4) Indiscriminate marshaling of gods in large categories so that a god might belong to two diametrically opposed bodies, becoming, for instance, a member of a sky group as well as of an underworld group. (5) Great importance of the groups of gods connected with time periods. (6) Inconsistencies and duplication of functions arising from the imposition of concepts originating among the hierarchy on the simpler structure of gods of nature worshiped by the early Maya.

It is interesting to reflect that the Maya, who had resisted the earlier impact of alien cults such as that of Kukulcan, accepted Christianity, but not as a substitute for their old gods. Instead, they quietly amalgamated the two religions to their liking. Maya gods and Christian saints were welded into a smoothly functioning pantheon with the Christian God at the head. In Yucatán the Chacs were mounted on the horses of the Spaniards and renamed after the archangels, and the moon goddess was merged in the Virgin Mary; in highland villages of Guatemala, saints of the Catholic church, mountains, and

Maya day names share the prayers said by shamans at crosses set at the world directions. The crosses themselves are the recipients of prayers.

In some parts there is a division between the functions of saints and of pagan gods; the former rule the towns and their activities, the latter guard the forest and milpas and those who work in them. Nevertheless, very few Maya could tell you which are the Christian and which the pagan elements in his religion. Indeed, all would be indignant at any suggestion that they were part pagans.

THE SOIL AND THE MAIZE

Looking back on what I have just written, I realize that it is a dull, lifeless catalog, in the same category as one of those cards, not written with the milk of human kindness, which social workers label Case History No. 1286391. Such treatment may suffice for the celestial gods, but I have dismissed the maize god in two lines, and that won't do.

Maize was a great deal more than the economic basis of Maya civilization; it was the focal point of worship, and to it every Maya who worked the soil built a shrine in his own heart. Without maize the Maya would have lacked the leisure and the prosperity to erect their pyramids and temples; without their mystical love for it, it is improbable that the peasants would have submitted to the unceasing and stupendous program of building directed by the hierarchy. The Maya laborer knew that he was building to conciliate the gods of sky and soil, on whose care and protection his maize field was dependent.

Love of the soil is found among peasants the world over, but I doubt that there is a more strongly mystical attitude toward its produce than in Middle America. To the Maya, corn is peculiarly sacred. Even today, after four centuries of Christian influence, it is still spoken of with reverence and addressed ritualistically as "Your Grace." It is the gods' supreme gift to man, to be treated with full respect and not a little humility. Before clearing the land or sowing, the Maya fasted, practiced continence, and made his offerings to the gods of the soil. Each stage in the farming round was a religious celebration.

More than two hundred years ago a friar summed up the highland Maya's attitude toward maize in these words: "Everything they did and said so concerned maize that they almost regarded it as a god. The enchantment and rapture with which they look upon their milpas is such that on their account they forget children, wife, and any other pleasure, as though the milpas were their final purpose in life and source of their felicity." This is very much to the point, but the writer made one mistake. The Indians did regard the maize as a god, although they took good care not to let the friars know it.

A somewhat similar attitude is revealed by the comment of a Mam Maya from western Guatemala on the white custom of burying in niches. The Indians, he said, consider it better to feed the earth with their dead bodies in payment for the products it gives them when they are alive—"The earth gives us food; we should feed it."

In our urban civilization the productivity of the land is something rather remote which is taken for granted. It is associated more with chain stores and can openers than with the soil, and, if our thoughts go a step back of that, we envision a man on a tractor or behind a team of horses, something picturesque, but unrelated to our efforts to earn our daily bread.

The Maya, who has to struggle against climate, tropical pests, and a too exuberant vegetation, sees things in a very different light. His livelihood depends literally on the sweat of his brow, not on the steaming flanks of a pair of horses. Even now, with the benefit of crops introduced from the Old World to vary his diet, 80 per cent of his food is maize. He eats it with every meal year in and year out, and so the failure of that one crop is a disaster to him. The maize seems to be fighting beside him in an unending defense against every kind of enemy, trying to survive in order that the man and his family may also live.

The conception of a crop as a live being, an ally striving at our side, is utterly alien to our way of thinking, but it was and is fundamental in the Maya pattern of thought. No wonder that the Maya personified the maize and regarded it with a reverential love which we could never feel for anything inanimate. Maize is the gift which the gods could bestow on man only after considerable effort. The story is given in Maya legend:

Maize was once stored beneath a great mountain of rock. It was first discovered there by the marching-army ants, which made a tunnel to its hiding place beneath the rock and began carrying the grains

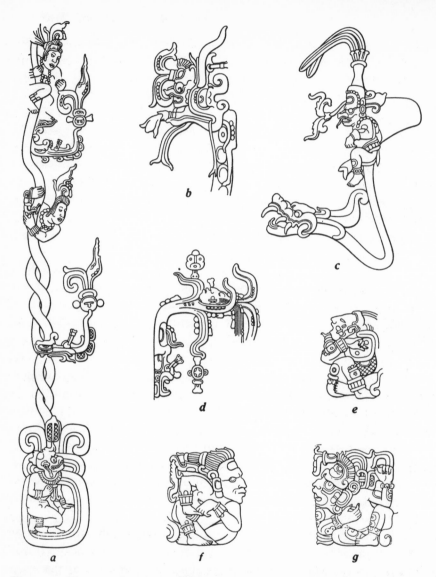

Fig. 25.—Maya gods of the Classic period. *a*, Representations of the youthful maize god with maize headdresses clinging to the body of a snake (Copán). *b*, The long-nosed god emerges from a serpent's jaws (Copán). *c*, The long-nosed god forming the head of a staff which terminates in an alligator's head (Quiriguá). *d*, The head of the maize god as an ear of corn on a maize plant (Palenque). *e*, The moon goddess grasping the moon sign (Quiriguá). *f*, *g*, The sun god (Quiriguá).

away on their backs. The fox, who is always curious about his neighbors' doings, saw the ants carrying this strange grain and tried some. Soon the other animals and then man learned of this new food, but only the ants could penetrate to the place where it was hidden.

Man asked the rain gods to help them get at the store. In turn, three of the rain gods tried, but failed, to blast the rock apart with their thunderbolts. Then the chief rain god, the oldest of them all, after many refusals, was prevailed upon to try his skill. He sent the woodpecker to tap the surface of the rock to find the weakest spot. When it had been discovered, he told the woodpecker to take cover under an overhanging ledge while he tried to split the rock. With all his strength he hurled his mightiest thunderbolt against the weak point, and the rock was riven asunder. Just as the thunderbolt struck, the woodpecker, disobeying orders, stuck out his head. A flying fragment of rock hit him on the poll, causing it to bleed freely, and ever since the woodpecker has had a red head. The fiery heat was so intense that part of the maize, which had been entirely white, was charred. Some ears were slightly burned, many were discolored with smoke, but some escaped all damage. There resulted four kinds of maize—black, red, yellow, and white.

This legend is repeated in the Book of Chilam Balam of Chumayel in allegorical language: "Three, seven, eight thousand was the creation of the world, when he who was hidden within the stone, hidden within the night was born," and "occurred the birth of the first precious stone of grace, the first infinite grace. . . . Not yet had he received his divine rank. Then he remained alone within the grace. Then it was pulverized. There were his long locks of hair . . . his divinity was assumed when he came forth."

The precious stone of grace is jade, which in Mexican allegorical writing is the ear of corn before it ripens. The passage states that the green corn, like precious jade, is hidden within the rock. Then the rock is smashed asunder, and the maize is born and becomes divine. The maize god always has long hair, perhaps derived from the beard of the maize in its husk. Hence the reference to the long locks. The full passage is of some length and is replete with allegory and mysticism (in one paragraph Christian ideas have led to the identification of Jesus, as the Bread of Life, with the maize god). Parts are beyond our comprehension, but the general presentation well illustrates the reverential approach to this great source of food. In fact, the attitude of the Maya toward the soil and the fruits he grows reveals more about his mentality and his customs than any other single facet of his culture, for the Maya culture is fundamentally one of farming, with a complex religious structure as an outgrowth.

Before each task the Maya makes his offering to the gods who guard his field. Ceremonies at sowing time among the Mopan Maya of southern British Honduras will illustrate the religious setting.

The night before sowing, the helpers gather at the hut of the owner of the field. At one end of the hut the sacks of seed are laid on a table before a cross, and lighted candles are placed in front and to each side of a gourd containing cacao and ground maize. The seed is then censed with copal, and afterwards the hut, inside and out, is completely censed. The men, who have brought their own hammocks, lounge in them, passing the night in conversation and music and the enjoyment of a meal served at midnight. Sometimes the group prays in the church for a good crop. The purpose of this vigil is to insure that the crop will not be endangered by the incontinence of any member of the group (the Mam, the Chorti, the Kekchi, and other Maya groups observe periods of continence of up to thirteen days at sowing time).

Looking back thirty years, I can see the group, most of them deep in shadow, for the guttering candles throw only a small circle of light. One or two are sitting in their hammocks; a third is lying back in his hammock with one foot dangling over the edge. Everyone is wrapped in a thin blanket, for the April night is cold and the chill air has no trouble in finding the spaces between the poles that form the walls of the hut. Conversation in soft, singsong Maya starts and dies like puffs of wind. Outside, the constellations of the tropics dawdle across the sky; they seem so close, one feels like raising his hand to push them on their course. Curiosity can hardly be delaying them; they have seen such vigils for many centuries. At daybreak the owner of the land goes to his field ahead of the rest of the party. There, in the center of the field, he burns copal and sows seven handfuls of maize in the form of a cross oriented to the four world directions, and recites this prayer:

O god, my grandfather, my grandmother, god of the hills, god of

274

the valleys, holy god. I make to you my offering with all my soul. Be patient with me in what I am doing, my true God and [blessed] Virgin. It is needful that you give me fine, beautiful, all I am going to sow here where I have my work, my cornfield. Watch it for me, guard it for me, let nothing happen to it from the time I sow until I harvest it.

Rites of the same general type precede clearing the land and burning off the scrub when it is dry. Typical of the religious context of the agricultural year are the ceremonies to the Chacs still held in villages of Yucatán when rain is needed. Not a man in the village fails to attend. The first task is to fetch the water needed in the preparation of the food offerings. This has to be virgin water from a sacred cenote where women never go. Once this has been brought, no one must return home, for if anyone had intercourse with a woman during the ceremony, the rains would not come. Accordingly, the men sling their hammocks within the cleared area, usually on the outskirts of the village.

Following two days of preliminary ceremonies, the shaman offers at dawn of the third day thirteen tall gourds and two shallow gourds of *balche* to the Chacs and guardians of the milpas. Following a chant by four assistants, the *balche* is distributed among the assembly, and everyone must take a little, for *balche* purifies one of evil. Birds are then brought forward. Four assistants called chacs hold each bird in turn by its wings and legs while the shaman pours *balche* nine times down its throat and dedicates it to the rain gods. After that the birds are killed.

Thirteen times *balche* is sprinkled on the altar, and after each sprinkling is offered to the members of the congregation. By noon the food is ready, and the main ceremony can commence.

A boy is tied by his right leg to each post of the altar. These four boys represent frogs, the attendants and musicians of the rain gods. As the ceremony proceeds, they croak in imitation of frogs announcing the approach of a storm. An older man, selected to impersonate the chief Chac, is reverently carried to a cleared space a few yards east of the altar. He is provided with a calabash and a wooden knife, for, as was related earlier, calabashes are carried by the Chacs and water sprinkled from them causes rain. The wooden knife represents the implement with which they produce the lightning.

275

From time to time this impersonator makes sounds like thunder and brandishes his wooden knife. Sometimes in place of a single impersonator of the chief Chac, four men, one at each corner of the altar, represent the four Chacs of the world directions. Each time the shaman recites a prayer or offers *balche*, they dance nine times around the altar.

The altar is piled with food and drink. Thirteen tall gourds and two dishes of *balche*, nine pails of broth from the sacrificial birds, four lots each of nine piles of tortillas made of maize and squash seeds, and nine piles of various other kinds of tortillas are placed on it.

After this provender has been offered to the gods (a time-consuming ceremony), all retire so that the gods can feast on the offerings without interruption. When it is judged that the gods have concluded their repast, the shaman returns and pours *balche* on the head of the impersonator of the chief Chac. The food, minus the spiritual essence already extracted from it, is divided among the men, and except for one or two minor ceremonies the rain petition is finished.

Great stress is laid on imitative magic. The croakings of the frogs, the noises like thunder, the impersonation of the rain god with the symbols of rain and lighting are basically magic. Important, too, is the use of the sacred numbers seven, nine, and thirteen. The purification pattern runs through the ceremony: virgin water must be used, theoretically the sacrificed birds are virgin, continence is essential, and *balche* is a purifier. In ancient times this ceremony would probably have been not a village, but a district, rite, and children might have been offered instead of turkeys.

Yet, these rites must not be regarded as so many ethnological data; they are the expressions of Maya preoccupation with the living maize and the gods who nourish him and give him drink. Much of the ancient pomp and ceremony is no more, but we can be sure that the Maya peasants, gathered in the courts of Tikal or Palenque for some ceremony, recognized with satisfaction the representations of the maize god, the Chacs, and the earth gods carved on the façades and roof combs of the temples, and were content to continue building to their glory and serving the priests who served them. They had given their hearts to the land and could have anticipated Kipling's lines: "And Memory, Use, and Love make live us and our fields alike."

CREATION MYTHS

The fullest creation myth is given in the Quiché-Maya book of legend and history called the *Popol Vuh*, but it recounts only three creations, whereas it is probable that the Maya believed the world had been created four or five times. According to the *Popol Vuh*, at the beginning there was only water. The creator gods cried, "Earth," and the land appeared. They covered it with trees, marked the courses for the rivers, and filled it with animals, assigning to each species its habitat. As the animals could not speak and so could not offer praise or supplication to their creators, the gods decided to make a superior species of mud. These beings could speak, but they had no intelligence and no strength, and, being of mud, they dissolved in water. The dissatisfied gods destroyed them.

The gods then made beings of wood. These spoke, ate, and reproduced themselves, but they had faces without expression, and, being of wood, they were dry, bloodless creatures with yellow flesh. Their intelligence was limited, and they showed no gratitude toward their creators. The discouraged gods sent rains to destroy them. These waters, like black resin, darkened the face of the earth. Then the animals turned against these Pinocchios. Jaguars and eagles devoured them; sticks and stones rose and hit them. Their dogs and even their water jars, cooking pots, grinding stones, and griddles joined the revolt, chasing them to the rooftops, up trees, and into caves. Their dogs said, "Why did you give us nothing to eat? You scarcely looked at us, but you chased us and threw us out. You always had a stick ready to strike us while you were eating." Their griddles and cooking pots said, "Pain and suffering you have caused us. Our mouths and our faces were blackened with soot; we were always put on the fire and you burned us as though we felt no pain. Now you shall feel it, we shall burn you."

From the few puppets which escaped are descended the monkeys. In the final creation the flesh of the ancestors of the Quiché was made of a gruel of yellow and white maize, which was taken from its hiding place beneath the mountain. These first men, four in number, were too gifted. They could see to the uttermost part of the earth. The gods, not wishing man to be almost their equal, dulled their eyes with a light mist, just as one obscures a mirror by breathing on it, and their vision was limited. Wives were created for these four men. Then the dawn came; the morning star arose; the sun rose. These men worshiped their makers. They were the ancestors of the Quiché, the Cakchiquel, and other Maya peoples of the highlands.

The incident of the revolt of the utensils appears also in Peruvian mythology. In all Middle American creation myths the culminating point is not the creation of man, but the dawn. It must be remembered that the Maya did not set the human race so far apart from the rest of created life as we do, but then the Maya had, and still has, a deeper sense of his relative unimportance in creation.

SACRIFICES

A point well illustrated in the above brief abstract is the demand the gods make for worship and sacrifice. In Maya eyes the gods were not benevolent dispensers of indiscriminate charity; they did not grant favors, but traded them for offerings of incense, food, and blood. It is a rather pleasant concept, revealing somewhat of a desire on the part of the Maya not to be over-beholden to anyone and disclosing also an absence of abasement. In the Kekchi prayer the traveler asks the earth god for game after gently reminding him that he has received an offering.

Human sacrifice was certainly practiced by the Maya in all periods of their history, but never on the same scale as by the Aztec, who wallowed in the blood of their sacrifices. It is probable that the practice was most developed in the Mexican and subsequent periods, when militarism had its basis in a system of strengthening the gods with human blood.

I have described in Chapter V a sacrificial scene. I shall now quote the most dramatic account we have of such a ceremony. It comes from testimony given in Yucatán in 1562 when charges of relapses into paganism by baptized Indians were being investigated. It was found with a mass of similar documents some years ago by France Scholes in the Archives of the Indies, Seville. The inquiry was held only twenty-one years after the final conquest of Yucatán, when the hold of Christianity on the natives was still weak. The number of Franciscan friars had been quite inadequate to instruct the masses of converts in the fundamentals of Christianity or to wean the natives, particularly the older generation of the former ruling class, from their pagan practices and beliefs.

The witness was Juan Couoh, appointed schoolmaster at Yaxcaba by the friars, a young Maya who had probably been educated by the Franciscans. He appears to have been torn between his loyalty to the old ruling caste and his loyalty to the new religion in which he had been educated. In the Maya spirit of compromise, he kept a foot in each camp, for although a catechist, he confessed to having kept hidden in a cave sixty idols which had belonged to his father and to making sacrifices to them. He also admitted to having been present at a ceremony in a near-by church, at which a deer and some turtles had been sacrificed. He then went on to relate this story:

I was in my house one Tuesday evening, when at midnight Diego Pech, the cacique of Yaxcaba, sent for me to read a letter for him. On my way there I passed by the church where I saw Pedro Euan, principal of Yaxcaba, who in ancient times had the office of sacrificing men and boys to the idols. He had a youngster from Tekax, in the Province of Mani, with his hands tied behind his back. This boy, Francisco Cauich, had gone on a holiday to Yaxcaba to visit some relatives, who lived there. He was seated next to the pedestal of the altar in the church, and, as I have said, with his hands tied behind his back. A large candle was burning. I asked them what they were doing there, and Pedro Euan replied, "Why do you want to know? Go and read the letter in the cacique's house, and then return here and you will find out what we are doing."

I continued on to the cacique's house, where I found assembled Diego Pech, the cacique, Juan Ku, cacique, Juan Tzek, principal, Francisco Pot, Gaspar Chim and Juan Cambal, all three former pagan priests, Lorenzo Ku, school bailiff, and Diego Ku, his father. These I recognized; I don't recall if others were present.

When I arrived, Diego Pech reproached me, saying that I was greatly indebted to him for support in the past, yet I was repaying him by getting the town mixed up with the friars, although I didn't really believe them when they said I was like a son to them. He went on to say that they were going to sacrifice a boy and I must agree to this and witness the ceremony.

I replied that it was a very serious matter, and it was not right that it should be done. Christians did not do such things. Diego Pech told me that I must do as he ordered, and he sent for Pedro Euan, who was guarding the boy in the church. When Pedro Euan came, he berated me for not wanting to do as I was told. I replied that I would refuse. They could do as they wished, but I should take no part in it. Then Pedro Euan caught me by the hair [the symbol of taking a prisoner who would be sacrificed], and said, "If you obstruct us and do not agree to take part, we will do to you what we are going to do this boy." I was so frightened that I gave way and agreed to what they said.

Then all rose and fetched ten idols, which they had brought from Diego Pech's maize field, and the other things necessary for the sacrifice, and took them to the church. When they entered they neither prayed nor bowed to the altar, but went and placed the ten idols in a line on some leaves of the *copo* [a *Ficus*, used in Maya ceremonies]. In front they laid a large mat, and on top of it they placed a large flint knife with its handle wrapped in a white cloth. Then Gaspar Chim and Pedro Pech, former pagan priests, took two large candles, and all sat down on small stools, and they ordered the Indian by the altar to be brought, and they seated him in their midst. His hands were tied, his eyes were covered with a cloth, and he wore no shirt, only short drawers. Gaspar Chim said that I would tell the friars about this, and under the threat of being myself sacrificed, I promised not to tell of what I saw. Then Diego Pech said to the youth whom they were going to sacrifice, and who was crying, "Be of good heart. Do not be upset. We are not going to harm you. We are not sending you to hell, but to glory in the sky, as our ancestors used to do."

"Do as you will," the boy replied. "God who is in heaven will aid me."

Then Gaspar Chim said "Untie him and do what must be done before it dawns and people are around."

Thus they untied the youngster and threw him on the mat. The priests handed over the candles they held, and four of them caught hold of the boy and placed him in a supine position, holding him by his hands and feet. Pedro Euan, taking the flint knife, made an opening on the left side of the youth's heart, grasped the heart and cut the arteries with his knife. He gave the severed heart to the priest, Gaspar Chim, who made two cuts like a cross in its extremity and then raised it on high. Next he took some part—I do not know what it was—and placed it in the mouth of the largest of the idols which was that of Itzamna. Then they took the boy's body and heart and his blood, which they had collected in a large gourd, as well as the idols, and all went with them to the cacique's house. I do not know what they did there. As they left they again warned me not to speak to the friars of what I had seen. "Even if they burn us alive, we must not say a word," they added.

I went to my house for what they had done seemed very evil.

In translating this passage, I have converted Couoh's testimony from indirect to direct speech and abbreviated a few sentences. Whether the schoolmaster was as unwilling a witness of the ceremony as he made out will never be known. If the local leaders feared that he might give them away, why did they summon him from his house at midnight? Perhaps they thought that they could thereby involve him so deeply in the proceedings that he would not dare to speak. In any case, it is a tense story of overwhelming drama, the horror of which is enhanced by the knowledge that it took place in a building dedicated to the worship of Him who said, "Whoso shall offend one of these little ones . . . ."

This belief that the deities who sent the rain desired offerings of children was widespread, for such sacrifices were customary not only in Mexico, but in various parts of South America. In testimony in another case in the investigations of relapses into paganism, it was brought out that the bodies of three children who had been sacrificed were thrown into a deep cave, the mouth of which was then covered with a large stone. A similar disposal of the bodies of children sacrificed to the rain gods was practiced in central Mexico. However, skeletal material recovered from the sacred cenote at Chichén Itzá includes remains of men and women as well as children.

Perhaps an adult was needed to bring back the message of the gods. Child victims of sacrifice were usually orphans, distant relatives adopted by the head of a household, or youngsters kidnaped or purchased from another town (Francisco Cauich was from another town). We learn that in one sale the price was five to ten red beads, that is, of *Spondylus* shell; in another the little victim was bought for a fathom of large beads. Children were frequently chosen as sacrificial victims because of the idea that sacrifices should be *zuhuy*, as the Maya say—that is, uncontaminated, virgin, whether speaking of beings or, just as we do, of virgin forests or lands. *Zuhuy* water came from depressions in rocks or was collected from plants; it had not been contaminated by contact with the soil. On the other hand, the sun and some other gods required the nourishment of adult victims; small children would hardly supply the needed strength.

Sacrifice by removal of the heart (Figs. 12*d*, 13*b*) was the usual method, but in some ceremonies the person to be sacrificed was tied to a stake or wooden frame (Fig. 2) and shot with arrows by the assembled men, who danced around him. At the beginning of the ceremony, the victim himself danced, but later, while the rest continued their steps, he was tied to the stake and a white mark placed over his heart to mark it as the target. Such active participation of the one who was to die in the preparatory ceremonies was usual in Mexican ritual, and, in fact, this form of arrow sacrifice almost certainly derives from Mexico, where it was particularly associated with the worship of Toci, the mother goddess of fertility.

On certain occasions the body of the victim was rolled down the steps of the pyramid to the bottom, where it was flayed. The priest then dressed in the skin for a dance. This custom of flaying the body and then donning the skin was quite common in Mexico, where it was practiced in honor of the god Xipe Totec in ceremonies sponsored by the warrior orders of Jaguars and Eagles, as well as in festivals of certain goddesses of the soil and crops, including the above-mentioned Toci.

Sometimes the victim was hurled from a height onto a pile of stones below, and then his heart was removed. This again was a form of sacrifice associated with the worship of Toci, but in Yucatán it was incorporated in ceremonies in honor of Itzamna.

Tying the victim to a stake and then removing the heart is reported from Yucatán, the Petén, and from the Usumacinta valley. This was the fate of two martyrs of the Christian faith, the Dominican friars Cristóbal de Prada and Jacinto de Vargas, who fell into the hands of the Itzá of Tayasal in March, 1696. Each was tied hand and foot to an X-shaped frame of crossed poles, and his heart removed. The head of a Franciscan friar, also a victim of the Itzá, was placed on a stake. Testimony at a post-Conquest trial for relapses into paganism brought to light a particularly cruel ritual, in which a young girl was tied to a stake and then beaten to death with a thorny pole. The pole was of ceiba, a wood peculiarly sacred to the Maya because, as we have seen, the trees set at the four corners of the world were ceibas.

Adult victims were confined in wooden cages. Among the Lacandón, we learn, it was customary to place the prisoner in these cages only at night, and guards slept on top to prevent their escape. By day the future victims were allowed to roam the town, but with attendants vigilant against any attempt to escape.

The bodies of persons who had been sacrificed were given to participants of rank in the ceremony; the hands, feet, and head were reserved for the priests and his assistants. To judge by Mexican beliefs, the victim represented the god in whose honor he died. Therefore, by eating his flesh, one endowed himself with certain of the qualities of the deity in question.

The marked similarity between these less usual forms of human sacrifice, as reported by Spanish observers of the sixteenth century, and practices in central Mexico suggest that most of them were adopted in the Maya area as a result of Mexican influences. One thinks immediately of the Toltec invasions, but it is possible that some were transmitted with the early influences from Teotihaucán apparent, particularly at Kaminaljuyú, in the early Classic period. Indeed, there are representations of the Mexican rain gods, the Tlalocs, on Maya stelae of the Central area, and the little scene of the arrow sacrifice (a spear is used, for at that time the bow was unknown) is scratched on the walls of a room at Tikal (Fig. 2).

Human sacrifice is shocking, but one can appreciate that it is logical if he accepts the premise that the gods need human blood to give them strength to perform their tasks, and its corollary that it is the duty of a devout people to provide it. There is, too, some mitigating evidence that on some occasions, at least, the victim was given a drug before the ceremony. This might have been to spare him suffering, but it is equally possible that it was an insurance against any unseemly struggle to resist. At least it can be said in defense of the Maya that everyone (including those to be sacrificed) believed that the victims died for the good of all. One doubts whether such unanimous approval supported the execution of Salem's witches, who were victims of mass hysteria, not chance sufferers for the common weal.

In addition to human beings, offerings to the gods included animals, agricultural products, cooked meat in sauces, copal incense, rubber, flowers, and such precious objects as jade, shell beads, and prized feathers. The range of sacrifices may be gauged from this comment by Bishop Landa: "They always smeared the faces of their demons with blood of everything there was, namely birds of the sky, animals of the land, or fish of the sea. And other things which they had they used to offer. They removed and offered the hearts of some animals; others they offered whole. Some were alive, some dead; some raw, some cooked. They also made great offerings of bread and wine, maize preparations and *balche* [fermented honey], and of every kind of food and drink which they used."

In many parts of the Maya area, particularly in the western highlands of Guatemala, offerings of turkeys, various preparations of maize, beans, and squash seeds, as well as flowers, are still made to pagan deities. As we have seen, offerings are still made in Yucatán to the Chacs, and in the remoter villages of the peninsula no Maya will start to clear his land or plant his crop without an oblation, usually of copal and *posole*, to the gods of the soil (the black smoke of the copal represents the rain clouds; *posole* is a popular maize gruel). The sacrifice of one's own blood was very common. Usually a cord set with thorns was passed through the tongue, a method represented in Maya sculpture and on the murals of Bonampak. The blood was allowed to drip on strips of bark-paper, which were them offered to the gods (Plate 12). Landa tells that the stings of sting rays were used by the priests in drawing blood, and, as already noted, these are frequently found in graves. He also says that blades of reedy grass were passed through the holes in tongue and ears. Another writer mentions that in the Alta Verapaz blood was drawn twice a day from arms, nose, tongue, ears, and all members of the body, sixty, eighty, or one hundred days (i.e., three, four, or five "months") before a big festival. The usual sources of blood were tongue, ears, elbows, and the penis. Sacrificial blood-letting was also prevalent throughout Mexico.

THE PRIESTHOOD

In Yucatán the head of the hierarchy was called Ah Kin Mai or Ahau Kan Mai. Possibly the priesthood in each of the chiefdoms of Yucatán was organized independently under its local Ah Kin Mai. The head priest had certain administrative duties, such as examining priests and assigning them to areas where they were needed. He also taught hieroglyphic writing, genealogies, ceremonies for the cure of sickness, calendrical computations, astronomy, divination, and the ritualistic round. In addition to instructing divinity students in these subjects, he advised the civil rulers on the prospects for any undertaking, such as war or marriage. This, of course, meant consultation of the astrological aspects, and divination by balancing the good and bad values of the days involved. It is probable that high priests had a considerable say in civil matters, for they were members of the council which elected a successor to a chief. They officiated only at the most important sacrifices involving the whole community.

According to Landa, the Ah Kin Mai was succeeded by his son, and the priesthood in general was recruited from the sons of priests and the younger sons of the nobility who showed an inclination for that vocation. His statement, if correct, indicates that the priesthood, even in those times of lay dominance, was sufficiently powerful to keep its chief office from passing to the family of the civil ruler. In any case, one can presume that the two families at the head of the civil and religious organizations were closely related by marriage and descent. That a high priest was succeeded by his son finds support in information from the Verapaz, where the high priest was elected from a certain lineage, a kind of Maya tribe of Levi. He ranked next in importance to the head chief, and was a member of his advisory council. Among the Tzotzil Maya of Chiapas, as in Yucatán, the priesthood was recruited from the sons of the nobility; among the Cakchiquel there were two high priests, apparently of equal rank, who were elected by the head chief and his council. One was in charge of sacrifices and the liturgical side of religion; the other was in charge of the religious and astrological books and was responsible for all divinatory matters. Actually, the civil high chief, the *halach uinic*, also performed certain priestly functions, for, as already noted, his title is translated as either "governor" or "bishop" in an early Maya-Spanish dictionary.

The regular priests were called *Ah Kin*, "he of the sun," in Yucatán. They performed the round of communal sacrifices and, after consulting their hieroglyphic books, made divinations. The *chilans* were prophets and soothsayers. They prophesied after consulting the divinatory almanacs and also received divine inspiration through visions. The *chilan* retired to his house, where, in a trance, he received his message from a god who placed himself on the ridge-pole of the house. The priests assembled to hear the prophecy or the message with faces bowed to the ground. It is probable that the *chilan's* visions were induced by narcotics, such as tobacco mixed with lime. More potent drugs such as peyote or *Datura* may have been used here as elsewhere in ancient America, although neither of these is native to the Maya area. Hallucination mushrooms were of great importance in the highlands. Before consulting their books, the *chilans* sprinkled the wooden covers with *zuhuy* water, brought from deep in the woods where no woman had penetrated.

Presumably the *chilan* was a priest who had specialized in this branch because of his gift of vision, for no one without training as a priest could have had sufficient knowledge of the divinatory side of the calendar. The functions of regular priests and *chilans* overlapped to a considerable extent.

Tearing out the heart of a sacrificial victim was the duty of a group of priests known as *nacons*. They passed it to the *Ah Kin*, who carried out the remaining ceremonies. Four elderly men, known as *chacs* (same title as that of the rain gods), served as lay assistants to the priests. Among their duties was that of holding the arms and legs of the victim when he was sacrificed; they also made new fire on ceremonial occasions by twirling a stick.

An important duty of all members of the priesthood was divination. In its most advanced form this consisted of consulting the 260-day almanac and other periods of time and calculating the effects of the different influences; but there were other and simpler forms of divination which survive to this day as part of the training of village shamans or calendar priests. These are used principally for ascertaining such matters as the causes of sickness or the names of those who have caused it by black magic, the location of lost articles, whether a sick person will recover, or whether a girl will make a good wife. Usually seeds of the *pita*, beans, grains of maize, or more rarely, pebbles are poured out of the shaman's bag and counted off in pairs or in fours. The answer depends on the number left over. Thus, in the Quiché town of Chichicastenango, if one or two is left over, a lost article will be found; if the remainder is three, the article will never be found. Sometimes the divination has to produce the same result four times running to be reliable. An early writer describes how a divination was made with maize to discover the direction in which a girl had fled.

Twitching of the muscles of the calf is another form of divination. The method varies in its details from village to village. In Mam territory a twitch of the left calf is bad; of the right, good; and no twitch at all is also good. In many areas the pulse is able to control the answer.

The Lacandón bring the hands together. If the nails of one hand slip under those of the other, the answer is negative; if they are in line, the answer is yes. The Kekchi make divination by watching the death struggles of a turkey.

There are, too, many omens and portents known to every Maya. Thomas Gage, an English Dominican friar in charge of Amatitlán, near Guatemala City, wrote that the Pokoman Maya "are given to much superstition, and to observe cross ways, and meeting of beasts in them, the flying of birds, their appearing and singing near their houses at such and such times."

The treatment of sickness was an important part of a priest's duties, the first task being to divine the cause of the sickness, often found to have been "sent" by an enemy or to have been caused by "evil winds" or failure to make the required sacrifice and prayers to the gods or to carry out some ritual correctly. The Maya were keenly interested in medicinal plants, and there is a considerable body of medical literature written in Yucatec with European characters. None of these treatises antedates the eighteenth century, but Ralph

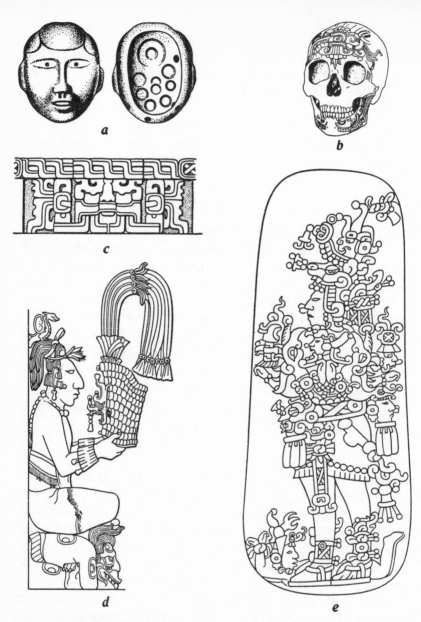

Fig. 26.—Sundry art forms.

a: Front and hollowed back of jade mask from Camp 6, British Honduras, showing marks of tubular drills used to remove cores, probably reused as beads.

b: Restoration of human skull with carved design. Found on the floor of a tomb at Kaminaljuyú and probably a trophy.

c: Large stucco mask on a façade at Benque Viejo, British Honduras.

d: Seated figure offering a "crown."

Note treatment of hair and the snail on the head, as well as the human stool. From a sculpture recently found by the Mexican archaeologist, Alberto Ruz, at Palenque.

e: Incised design on the Leyden plaque. This is the second earliest dated piece yet found in the Maya area (A.D. 320). It was found near the modern town of Puerto Barrios, Guatemala, but was carved at Tikal.

Roys believes that they were compiled from earlier sources. They contain some European recipes translated into Yucatec, but these do not appear to have affected the native lore to any marked extent. A surprisingly large number of the Maya medical texts deal with the treatment of symptoms and are based on objective observation of the effects of certain plants on the human system. Some of these plants appear in the United States Pharmacopoeia.

CEREMONIES

Ritualistic feasts and the preliminary periods of fasting and continence succeeded one another almost without a break. Fortunately, Landa describes those celebrated in Yucatán. Typical was the ceremony of the makers of wooden idols held in the month Mol, if divination showed the time to be favorable.

The carving of idols was regarded as dangerous work, which might bring illness or death to the maker or some member of his family, and so the carvers were persuaded with difficulty to undertake a commission of this nature. The idols were made of Spanish cedar, called the "god tree" in Yucatec.

As soon as the wood was ready, carvers, priests, and the old men called chacs—one might call them lay readers—shut themselves in a temporary hut enclosed with a fence until the work was concluded. Only the person who had ordered the idols and, therefore, was responsible for bringing food and water to the group was allowed to enter the enclosure. The food was not plentiful, for all participants fasted before and during the period of fabrication. The object of secluding the workers was probably to insure that they remained continent and to confine the danger of this work to those who, by fasting and continence, had purified themselves and thereby gained a certain immunity from peril. Incense was constantly burned to the gods of the four world directions, and workers frequently smeared blood drawn from their own bodies on the idols in process of manufacture. When the men were resting, the idols were kept in a large urn, in order, one supposes, to reduce the danger from them, since a belief that idols come to life and wander around harming people exists among the present-day Maya.

When completed, the idols were placed in an arbor erected for that purpose, and the soot with which the participants, as fasters, had smeared themselves, was removed. Following ceremonies of purification and consecration, the idols were wrapped in cloths, placed in a rush hamper, and handed over to the person who had ordered them. Payment was in local currency (cacao, shell beads, etc.) and in gifts of venison and birds. The priest then addressed the idol makers, praising them for their courage in view of the latent dangers had fast or continence been broken. A feast and carousal concluded the ceremony.

The foregoing outline illustrates the Maya conception that the effectiveness of rites depended on the physical purity of all participants. Ritualistic drinking, such as concluded this ceremony, was more than a release from tension; *balche*, the drink of fermented honey, was holy. By drinking it, one drove evil from the body, and the resulting exaltation, physical and spiritual, brought one in closer touch with the gods.

The ceremony of purification which followed immediately on the completion of the idols consisted of collecting various objects used in the rites and depositing them outside the village. Thereby evil was safely removed from the group and, presumably, from the new idols, and deposited where it could do no harm. This process was followed in most Maya ceremonies, and I myself have witnessed it at the dedication of a new hut in British Honduras. The slaying of a scapegoat, described below, for the sins of a Quiché town is merely a variation of the same theme.

Success of a ritual depended on the purity not only of the participants but also of all the elements used. The floor had first to be swept and the utensils purified. Water used must be "virgin" water from sources uncontaminated by human touch; children were most acceptable as sacrifices because of their purity; animals sacrificed were theoretically virgin; among the Aztec, and almost certainly among the Maya, too, some physical imperfection disqualified a person as a sacrificial victim. Moreover, the actual ritual had to be followed without deviation. For instance, a Lacandón drummer made a mistake in the beating of a drum at the sacrifice of a human. The ceremony was immediately stopped and the drummer himself came very near being sacrificed for his crime.

The deeply religious attitude of the Maya is well illustrated by the ceremonies still held at Momostenango, in Quiché territory, on the return every 260 days of the feast of 8 Batz (the day 8 Monkey). The Guatemalan ethnologist Antonio Goubaud wrote a magnificent description of this festival on which I have drawn.

All the Indians of Momostenango feel bound to observe this day, and those who are absent return for its celebration. They firmly believe that failure to do so will bring illness or even death.

On the afternoon preceding 8 Batz, the Indians begin to arrive at the church, and by 8:00 P.M. the interior is completely filled with them, kneeling in prayer in parallel rows, face to face. The murmur of the fervent prayer fills the church and hundreds of candles twinkle on the floor, their flames dimmed by the pale gray smoke of copal incense rising from scores of clay censers. There is an atmosphere of intense spiritual emotion.

At dawn the next morning the Indians go to the pagan altars on high ground about half a mile from the town, and by 9:00 A.M. a huge crowd has assembled—estimates of attendance vary from 15,000 to 20,000. The altars are mounds up to ten feet high, consisting largely of fragments of pottery which have been offered there. In front of each stands the calendar priest or shaman, and around is gathered the group for whom he is praying.

People approach the calendar priest, give their names, make a payment of a tiny sum of money, and explain for what they want the prayers. The subjects covered are usually forgiveness of sins, gratitude for past blessings, and desire for future well-being, physical, spiritual, moral, and economic. The calendar priest burns a packet of copal incense in the niche in the altar. These niches, about twenty inches wide by fifteen inches deep, are formed of potsherds, which for this occasion are decorated with pine boughs.

Each ceremony is very long. The calendar priest prays interminably, mentioning to the earth god the most intimate details in the life of the suppliant. Sometimes he offers a little *aguardiente* to the god, and afterwards drinks it himself, for he believes himself closest to the supreme deities when slightly intoxicated.

Near by, on secondary altars, the newly initiated shamans pray, but being inexperienced, they are less sought after. Women shamans also have their altars. The rites continue until dusk, when the shamans move to the top of a near-by hill, where they continue praying and burning copal throughout the night. On the two following days prayers continue, and almost all the Indians remain in the town to participate in these further ceremonies.

The two sites for these rituals are called respectively "Little Broom" and "Big Broom." As among the Aztec a broom symbolized forgiveness of sins (it sweeps out the dirt), it is quite likely that these places were thus named because 8 Batz ceremony is essentially an occasion for general confession. That the ceremony is very ancient is demonstrated by the name of the town, for Momostenango means the "place of the altars."

Throughout the Maya area confession, particularly by a sick person, was customary, for illness was commonly thought to be the result of past sin. Confession might be made to a priest, or failing him, a son could confess to his parents, or a husband to his wife, or a wife to her husband. Until a few years ago the Ixil Maya, on the northern boundary of the Southern area had intra-family confession on New Year's Day. In Yucatán, Landa tells us, quarrels often result from the confession of a spouse who told all in the expectation of dying, and then lived to face constant upbraiding from his or her matrimonial partner. In the Alta Verapaz a woman named by a confessor as having committed adultery with him was condemned without trial, for certainly no one would lie in the ceremony of confession.

An interesting example of a scapegoat is reported among the Quiché. A very old woman was taken out to a cross-roads outside the town, accompanied by all the local population. The people surrounded her and, all together, confessed their sins in loud voices. When they had finished, a priest drew near and hit the old woman over the head with a stone until she died. The people then covered her body with a pile of stones and returned home convinced that they and all their neighbors were thereby purified of their sins.

DANCES

Dances were intimately associated with religious ceremonies. The sacrificial victim himself might take part in the dance preliminary to his sacrifice; his relatives and friends also participated. The old dances, because of their pagan context, were prohibited by the friars who introduced in their place dances of Spanish origin which are still performed by the Indians. However, one of the old sacrificial dances survived among the Quiché and Zutuhil for a century after the Spanish Conquest. In a deposition dated 1624 the Spanish priest of the town of Mazatenango describes the dance:

It represents the sacrifice and offering to the devil of an Indian prisoner of war as was done in ancient times, and this the dancers themselves state. There are four men who attack and try to kill a fifth, who is tied to a stake. The four are disguised respectively as a jaguar, a puma, an eagle, and an animal I do not recollect. These animals they say were their familiars. They go through the dance to the accompaniment of yells and of sad and horrible sounds, frightening just to hear, which they make with some long, twisted trumpets, like sackbuts [cf. Plate 17*b*]. When it has been danced in other towns I have seen that when the trumpets are blown, the whole town is filled with excitement, and everyone, including even tiny children, comes rushing and panting to be present.

This dance almost certainly is that which the Aztec performed in honor of Xipe Totec. Four warriors were dressed to represent the military orders of Jaguars and Eagles, and in turn fought a prisoner, tied by a long cord to an altar, whose only defense was a sword in which plumage replaced the obsidian or flint blades. After he had been slain, the victim's skin was removed and worn by one of the participants.

A dance in Yucatán is thus briefly outlined:

The Indians prepared a float [or litter] and placed on top of it a sort of narrow turret about six feet high and somewhat like a pulpit. This was covered from top to bottom with painted cotton cloths, and two flags were at the top, one on each side. A handsomely dressed Indian, visible from the waist up, was in this tower. He had a rattle of the kind they use in this land in one hand, and a feather fan in the other. All the time he kept shaking his body and whistling to the beating of an upright drum which another Indian, alongside the float, was playing. With him were many other Indians who sang to the same drum, making a great row and giving many piercing whistles. Six Indians carried the float on their shoulders, and even they moved forward singing, dancing, and wiggling their bodies to the sound of the drum. That turret was very handsome, and swayed a great deal, and one could see it from far off because of its height and its bright colors. That dance was called Zonó, and is one of those they used in ancient times.

Ceremonial dances are painted on the Bonampak murals, and persons on several stelae are shown in similar attitudes (Plate 15a). There is full evidence that in many of the celebrations masked dancers impersonated the gods. Dances to insure success in hunting and to obtain good crops were also performed.

The essentially religious nature of these dances is demonstrated by the fact that the performers first observed a period of continence and fasting, as well as by the fact that dances came to be associated after the Spanish Conquest with church festivals.

Of a very different nature is the erotic snake dance which still survives in several Quiché-Maya towns of the Guatemalan highlands. The Quiché name of the dance, the doubling of the maize, refers to the bending of the ears when they are ripe to protect them from rain and birds. There are variations from place to place, but usually about twenty men take part. All are in their usual clothes but have their faces masked, except for one man, who is dressed as a woman. All carry rattles. The day before the dance men go out to collect snakes, the hiding places of which are announced by local prayer-makers. The jaws of poisonous snakes are sewed together with a thread, and all the snakes are taken in a jar or a cloth-covered gourd to the house of the woman impersonator.

After preliminary dancing each man grasps the woman impersonator and goes through the motions of coition with her, or she is held by two other dancers for that purpose. The other dancers shout, make obscene gestures, wave their rattles, and call out indecent remarks. Next, each dancer in turn takes one of the snakes collected the previous day and inserts it in the neck of his shirt. The snake disappears, to emerge at the end of one of the man's sleeves or trouser legs. The snakes are collected, replaced in the gourd or jar, and at the end of the dance are taken to surrounding woods and released,

Fig. 27.—Incised decoration on bone, perhaps human. One of nearly ninety from the splendid Tomb 116 in pyramid of Temple 1, Tikal. Delicate design brought out by rubbing incised lines with cinnabar. Long-nosed god as fisherman. Creel on back similar to one on Formative sculpture from Pacific Coast. Shells as symbol of water as in water scenes from central Mexico. Note surprise on paddler's face (about A.D. 700). (*Specially drawn for this book by Andy Seuffert with permission of University Museum, Philadelphia.*)

a close parallel to the end of the Hopi snake dance. The dancers constantly whip one another mercilessly.

Throughout Middle America snakes are associated with rain and the rattle is an attribute of gods of the soil, and sporadically over the area the sexual act is enacted as a magical rite to insure a large maize crop. This is the exact opposite of the usual Maya practice of continence before each stage in the farmer's year. There is a possibility that the dance was brought to Guatemala by Mexicans, who had a snake-swallowing fertility dance something like this but without the erotic features. However, I am inclined to see this as a very primitive magical dance which probably had its roots in the Formative period and survived as a sort of *sub rosa* alternative to the official imposition of continency.

Speaking of dances of Spanish origin, Thomas Gage writes: "When I lived amongst them, it was an ordinary thing for him who in the dance was to act St. Peter or John the Baptist, to come first to confession, saying that they must be holy and pure like that saint whom they represent, and must prepare themselves to die. So likewise he that acted Herod or Herodias, and some of the soldiers that in the dance were to speak and accuse the Saints, would afterwards come to confess of that sin, and desire absolution as from blood-guiltiness."

This quotation illustrates how completely the dancer identified himself with the part he took. That was a natural attitude in a society which had always held dancing to be essentially a religious ritual.

RELIGION AND THE INDIVIDUAL

Every feature of Maya life had its religious aspect, and no important move, whether by the community or by the individual, could be made without consulting the portents. The priests weighed the favorable and unfavorable factors, and announced what days were favorable for such matters as making war, starting to build a temple for the community or a hut for the individual, holding puberty ceremonies, having a communal hunt, starting to clear land, sowing, and harvesting. Public fasts were followed by organized celebrations, and a perpetual round of sacrifices of food, drink, and copal incense kept the gods nourished and satisfied. The individual maintained the same cycle of private worship and sacrifice on a small scale—

continence, fasting, prayer, and offerings of food and incense before and during each crisis of his private life, whether it affected his family life or the agricultural round.

One example of a modern Maya prayer has already been given. I shall close this chapter with two others. The first is a Lacandón chant collected by A. M. Tozzer; the second, a Kekchi prayer recorded by Carl Sapper. It will be seen that all three follow the same pattern. I have been told that such prayers resemble quite closely mediaeval Christian prayers, but the similarity must be fortuitous, since the Lacandón have had almost no contact with Christianity.

The Lacandón prayer is offered by a father for his son:

Guard my son, my father. Cause any evil to cease, cause the fever to cease. Do not allow evil to trample him under foot. Do not allow a snake to bite my son. Do not permit my son's death when he is at play. When he is grown up, he will give you an offering of posol. When he is grown, he will give you an offering of tortillas. When he is grown, he will give you an offering of bark bands. When he is grown up he will remember you.

The Kekchi prayer, together with copal incense, is offered when on a journey to the Tzultacah, the gods of the earth, of the hills and valleys:

Thou, O God, Thou lord of the mountains and valleys. I have given thee a morsel for thee to eat, for thee to drink. Now I pass beneath thy feet, thy hands, I a traveler. It grieves thee not, it troubles thee not to give me all kinds of great and small animals, thou my father. Thou hast many animals—the trogon bird, the pheasant, the wild boar. Show them, therefore, to me. Take them and set them on my path. Then I shall see them, behold them.

I am beneath thy feet, beneath thy hands. I am fortunate, thou lord of the mountains, thou lord of the valleys. Everything in abundance is possible to thy power, to thy name, to thy being. Of all I may partake. Today, it may be, I was forced to eat my tortillas, yet I am in good hunting lands. It may be that God does not see that there is any living beings here. Perhaps I may bring hither, I may carry back, a small trogon bird.

Now I see, and behold thee my god, thee my mother, thee my father. It is only that of which I speak which I intend. What I have brought you is in truth not much and of little good for thy eating and for thy drinking. Whether it be so or not, what I say and what I think, O God, is that thou art my mother, thou art my father. Now I shall thus sleep beneath thy feet, beneath thy hands, thou lord of the mountains and valley, thou lord of the trees, thou lord of the liana vines. Tomorrow is again day, tomorrow is again light of the sun. I do not know where I shall then be. Who is my mother? Who is my father? Only thou, O God. Thou seest me, thou protectest me on every path, in every time of darkness, from every obstacle which thou mayest hide, which thou mayest remove, thou, O God, thou my lord, thou lord of the mountains and valleys.

It is only that which I say, which I think. Whether it should be more, whether it should be less than I have said. Thou dost tolerate, thou dost forgive my sins.

This prayer seems to summarize the whole attitude of the Maya to the divine powers. The supplicant starts off by calling attention to the offering he has made to them, and then asks, in return, that they should send him game to hunt as he has nothing to eat but his tortillas. As a good Maya he does not ask for more than he needs, for he will be content with one trogon bird (about the size of a grouse). He acknowledges that he is in the hands of the divine powers who are to him as a father and mother, and who protect him wherever he may be. He makes his act of adoration in the beautiful expression, "I am beneath thy hands, beneath thy feet," and in conclusion, renders thanks that his sins have been forgiven him.

VII. Maya Civilization in Retrospect

There is a spirit in man: and the inspiration
of the Almighty giveth them understanding.
—Job 32:8

DEVELOPMENT

Why cultures follow certain paths is a highly specu-
lative subject about which very little is known. Opinions differ on
the motivations of well-studied civilizations of the past, even when
the written observations of their contemporaries are at hand to guide
modern judgment. How much more must they be at variance when
the little-known Maya civilization is the subject of discussion. In
these final pages I give an opinion on what caused Maya culture to
develop in the unique way it did and what caused it to decline. It is
an attempt to guess the acrostic with more than half the lines unsolved, and so I may easily find myself holding a very different view
a few years hence, for each year new discoveries fill gaps in our
knowledge of the past.

I knew well Jacinto Cunil, a Maya of Socotz, in western British
Honduras, for thirty-six years, and our friendship was cemented by
godparenthood, which to the Maya is a peculiarly intimate relationship. I came to respect him and love him, for he was kindly and
upright, loyal, and the old-fashioned kind who believed in doing an
honest day's work for his wages. Jacinto's life and character seem an
epitome of the whole Maya philosophy of life.

Socotz, like most villages on the edge of the Petén forest, is a
recruiting ground for *chicleros*. The chicle contractors pay big wages,

and those they sign up to spend the rainy season bleeding gum in the forest get large advance payments. For a week or so after these advances have been made, money flows freely in the little towns and villages. Most of it is spent on drink and shoddy store goods—silk scarfs of gaudy colors that will run the first time they are exposed to a shower, boots that are more cardboard than leather, and so on. When the splurge is over, the *chicleros* start for the forest camps to work off their indebtedness.

Jacinto would have none of that; for him a man's life should revolve around his milpa. For most of the year he worked on the road for considerably less than a *chiclero* earns in a good season. He quit when the dry season came in order to clear his land, as his ancestors had done for several thousand years; a full crib of corn meant more to him than all the trash in the stores of near-by Benque Viejo. Most evenings he visited round the village, where he was liked and respected (several times he was asked to serve as "mayor"). The orderly routine of the village clearly appealed more to him than the squalor and shiftlessness of get-rich-quick chicle camps. At the hour of the Angelus his children came to him for his benediction. That, of course, is not an old pagan custom, but it is in the Maya traditions of religion in everyday life and respect for parents. Most lowland Maya are light-hearted and seem to enjoy life—well adjusted, as the current expression puts it. Jacinto, perhaps, took life a little more seriously, but essentially, he, too, was a happy man.

On archaeological trips Jacinto kept an eye open for the hives of wild bees. Honey is a treat for any Maya, but, more important, the hives yield wax. Jacinto strained the black wax and took it home at the end of the season to use in his private intercessions, for candles of black beeswax are more efficacious than store candles in religious rites. Jacinto was a keen hunter. If game was plentiful, he smoke-dried the surplus. As soon as he had as much as he could carry home, he stopped hunting, for he did not kill for sport, and more than once I heard him condemn *chicleros* who killed more game than they could use.

I know the names of only a few trees and plants and manage to get those few mixed; I walk close to a beehive and cannot see it; I frighten game away as I blunder noisily through the forest behind my guide; I lose a trail marked so clearly that any fool except a gringo can see it; and I cannot even put a good edge on a machete blade. Jacinto was very patient with me; as an individualist, he accepted the idea that it takes all kinds to make a world.

Jacinto died in 1964. His death was in keeping with his life, epitomizing the age-old Maya love of the soil. He had gone to his corn-field to burn the dry vegetation, earlier felled, prior to sowing. It seems that there was a change of wind, and he was overcome with the smoke. A heart attack may have been a contributing factor, for he had had a lifetime of practice in avoiding the fire peril. His death came from the soil, around which his whole life had revolved. His body lies in Socotz, almost in the shadow of the archaeological site of Benque Viejo, first settled by his ancestors in early Formative times, some 2,500 years ago, and slowly converted into the religious center for the upper Belize valley. From there he can hear the Angelus ring in Socotz church and perhaps the conch trumpet of some ghostly pagan priest sounding from the highest pyramid of Benque Viejo.

Jacinto had those sterling qualities which, I believe, made his forebears what they were; and, incidentally, he lacked that failing—drunkenness (controlled in pre-Columbian times)—which charac-terizes the present-day Maya. Pondering whether my attitude toward the Maya, past and present, might be too sentimental and idealistic, I turned to the writings of Karl Sapper, German geographer and ethnologist, who lived for several years on very intimate terms with the Kekchi-Maya of the Alta Verapaz, and to the judgment of Alfred Tozzer, who has lived among the Lacandón.

Sapper says of the Kekchi that by family training and racial custom they seek to instill control of every kind of mental excite-ment, to teach moderation in all actions, and to inculcate subordina-tion to superiors. He comments that the quick gestures and loud speech of most Europeans and North Americans are evidence to the Indian of deficiencies in our training and of the low status of our civilization. As a testimony to Kekchi honesty he notes that in his twelve years of residence among them nothing of his was stolen (my experience has been the same). Endurance, he believes, is the form of energy most esteemed by the Indian.

Tozzer writes of the Lacandón that their morals are good and their family life happy, seldom disturbed by discord or strife. He notes that they view with disgust the loose morals and infidelity of the whites and *ladinos* with whom they come in contact, and that generally they are truthful, honest, generous, hospitable, and mild.

Tozzer, unlike Sapper, does not specifically mention the two characteristics which I believe to have had most influence on Maya culture—moderation in all things and the attitude of live and let live—but their presence can be deduced from the whole tenor of his report. Each writer emphasizes the deeply religious character of the Maya group he studied. These judgments on Maya character re-assure me that my assessment is not unduly idealistic or influenced by sentimentality.

The general character and religious devotion of the Maya in pre-Columbian times were surely the same as today, and, I believe, they largely decided the path Maya culture followed. Devoutness, discipline, and respect for authority would have facilitated the emer-gence of a theocracy, and as long as the priestly caste met the spiritual needs of the rank and file, there would, I believe, have been little opposition, overt or covert, to it. The hierarchic group had a vital function in Maya society, that of intermediary between the gods and man. The priests were able to relieve, season by season, the loving anxiety with which the Maya peasant brooded over his soil and his crops, and, remote in the mysterious, dark rooms of their lofty tem-ples, they gave expression to the deep mysticism with which that relationship was impregnated. The priests alone comprehended the orderliness of the universe, for they alone understood the influences emanating from the regnant gods of the innumerable cycles of time. They only, with their assessments of malignant and benevolent aspects, could help the crops by choosing favorable days for every stage in the farmer's year.

This doctrine of orderly predestination had a profound effect on Maya life; it could hardly have arisen had not the Maya been an orderly people, for the Maya made their gods in their own image and conceived a universe suitably regulated to their existence.

Yet, the Maya, with his deeply religious spirit, surely was not satisfied with cut-and-dried formulae for insuring good crops. His emotionalism called for more than the passive role of following in-structions as to days favorable or unfavorable to his sundry under-takings; it demanded the spiritual comfort of sacrifice. Here, again, the priest group could comply, and at the same time strengthen its hold on the people. Endurance and honest labor are virtues of which the Maya now, and presumably then, are proud. The perpetual building of religious structures and the endless enlargement of existing nuclei in the ceremonial centers gave the people the opportunity to offer to the gods the oblation of their labor and endurance, and—perhaps more important—gave them the feeling of participation, without which no religion can endure. To the devout such labors were acts of devotion to the loved gods of the soil; to the less mystical they were insurance for full corn bins. The priestly group seems to have been well aware of the value of meeting psychological needs by combining mystery and detachment with group participation. The rites inside the narrow, dark temples were for the few; the figures of the rain gods, with their ophidian or reptilian guises, and the portraits of the youthful maize god, visible from afar on the façades of the buildings, were for the common people. Maya art of the Classic period surely reflects spiritual adjustment in its serenity and beauty.

I once saw stelae texts as purely calendric and astronomical. It is now clear that there was no such abnegation of glory; rulers did leave memorials of their accessions. Yet these were joined to ritualistic and astronomical data, and it may well be that rulers were deified (Spanish sources tell us of such), and as deities in their own title or as personifying long-established gods they had divine right to such glory. The prince-archbishops of Renaissance Salzburg may present a parallel—hard to tell the spiritual and mundane percentages in their make-up.

I have tried to show the Maya as one of several coeval cultures in Middle America, each of which reacted on the other. I would suppose that the three great characteristics of Maya temperament—devoutness, moderation, and discipline—were shared by the makers of the other great cultures—Teotihuacán, La Venta, Monte Albán, and Tajín—and for that reason their similarities far outweigh their differences. However, in none of these centers did architecture or science approach the Maya level, and in at least two (Teotihuacán and Monte Albán) artistic achievement was far behind the Maya.

Archaeology perhaps yields the explanation for this disparity. At Teotihuacán and Monte Albán (and later at Tula) there are many rooms built around small patios, and they are almost certainly residential. At Teotihuacán these residential buildings far outnumber religious structures. Nothing comparable has been found in Maya cities of the Classic period. In the present state of our knowledge it would be dangerous to assert that no buildings in Maya ceremonial centers are residential, yet we can be reasonably certain that no early Maya city of the lowlands had such a high proportion of residential buildings as Teotihuacán (I have supposed that there were no permanent residents within the actual limits of a ceremonial center). It is, perhaps, a fair deduction that at Teotihuacán, and probably at Monte Albán, too, secular influences (not necessarily militaristic, for the worship of rain gods is depicted constantly at both sites) challenged religious domination in relatively early times and undermined the singular devoutness which carried the Maya to their intellectual and artistic peaks. A contributing factor may have been Teotihuacán's geographical position, for on the frontier of civilization there can have been little tranquility under the constant threat of attack by uncivilized tribes.

DECLINE

The attacks of uncivilized tribes in the remote north were, I believe, the indirect cause of the eclipse of Maya civilization, its gradual decline, and final collapse. Central Mexico, like the northern frontier of the Roman Empire, was exposed to the incursions of barbarians from the north (the Aztec was one of the later groups to arrive), and its peoples in self-defense had to accept a militaristic orientation of their culture. The transformation of the sun god into a war god was perhaps the first step. With the growth of a warrior class comes the theory that the sun needs human flesh to give him strength each morning, and with it develops the heresy that war is not solely a matter of defense, but is primarily to obtain food for the sun and, concomitantly, for the glorification of the warrior caste. Teotihuacán, more interested in rain gods than deified warriors, was an early victim. Tula, which rose after the fall of Tetihuacán but surely before the end of the Maya Classic period, was aggressively militaristic despite the pacific teachings of its patron, Quetzalcoatl. The new cult of war, we must suppose, spread southward like a blight, destroying or transforming the older and gentler cultural growths in its path.

Pressure of these new ideas or even of invaders affected the high-lands of Guatemala, Campeche, and Yucatán before they reached the heart of the Maya lowlands. Indeed, actual contacts between the outside world and that nucleus of Maya culture may have been almost nil, but indirect influences from outside may have had a decisive effect on the Maya theocratic society. The ruling group appears to have adopted some of the new religious cults and practices which had developed in the north, and it is possible that the masses were alienated by these innovations and the consequent relegation of their loved gods of the soil to secondary places. It is reasonable to suppose that they would not have labored willingly to build to the glory of gods in whom they were not interested, especially if they associated those religious innovations with a developing interest by their leaders in war. Perhaps the priests, increasingly absorbed in their theories of the philosophy of time, began to lose the allegiance of the masses before foreign influences widened the gap. In either case the prole-tariat would have questioned whether the hierarchy any longer acted wholeheartedly for the common welfare. Once that doubt had gained a hold, the old order was doomed.

In the Central area the collapse came slowly, first to one city, then to another. If the above outline of what happened is correct—one must realize that it is a theory deduced from a minimum of fact—the overthrow of the old order may have been achieved by passive resistance or by the slaughter of the ruling caste (the Maya is slow to anger, but once aroused is implacable). Certainly it was final, for the Maya peasant, bereft of the hierarchy, never developed another civilization or rebuilt the old. Culture remained on a low level until the coming of the Spaniards, perhaps because revitalizing influences from outside failed to make themselves felt in those isolated regions.

In Yucatán and the Guatemalan highlands the situation was different, for in those areas foreigners from Mexico established them-selves as new ruling castes and, by their introduction of militarism and the sacrificial sun cult, forced the native Maya reluctantly to follow suit. Rival factions fought for control, and central govern-ment was finally imposed by the most powerful group in each area—Mayapán in Yucatán, the Quiché in the Guatemalan highlands. Those new rulers claimed to be of Toltec descent.

Such Mexican features as the worship of Quetzalcoatl and Tezcatlipoca and the sun cult, as well as the warriors' orders that maintained them, lost ground in the final centuries before the Spaniards arrived; the ruling class was no longer Mexican in speech when the end came.

In the fifteenth century the two incipient empires of Mayapán and Utatlán, seat of the Quiché, were overthrown. The two dominions disintegrated into numerous petty states constantly at one another's throat, effectively destroying any hope for a Maya renaissance.

The lack of stability and the submergence of old values in the centuries after the close of the Classic period are reflected in the decadence of the arts. Sculpture, architecture, and ceramics degenerated, sinking with each change for the worse in political and religious life to the pitiable level which the Spaniards encountered.

The course Maya culture took in the centuries of the Classic period has few, if any, close parallels in history. Perhaps the nearest to it is the Jesuit mission state in sixteenth- and seventeenth-century Paraguay. Both were hierarchic and pacific, and each fell because of warfare from without (direct impact in Paraguay; probably indirect in the Maya area), but there is one vital difference. In Paraguay, European religion and culture were imposed by a European hierarchy on the Guarani natives; in the Maya area the growth was largely or (in the eyes of orthodox anthropologists) entirely native.

The later stages of Maya history—warfare, the universal state, tyranny, and fission—form a sequence which appears over and over again in history, as Arnold Toynbee has demonstrated.

In the Classic period, Maya character, free to work out its own salvation, produced a unique and fascinating culture; in the later periods it was weakened by the impact of alien attitudes in conflict with its ideals. Immoderation swamped moderation to produce a stereotype culture not differing markedly in its dull history from a dozen others. Yet one sees in the writings in the books of Chilam Balam and in the character of the present-day Maya that below the surface the old attitudes survived. Captive Greece conquered Rome. Through the anguish of the last century of pre-Columbian history one can detect signs of a re-emergence of Maya attitudes, and had the discovery of the New World been postponed a century or two, Maya culture might have bloomed again, perhaps in another soil. Without much doubt the Aztec would have conquered the Maya, but then history might have repeated itself, for the Maya were to the Aztec as Greece was to Rome.

Maya civilization, I believe, was the product of Maya character, but there was another essential ingredient—a creative minority with the imagination and mental energy to start Maya lowland civilization on its course and keep it on that course for several hundred years.

That ruling group might have been indigenous or it might have come from anywhere in the highlands between central Mexico and El Salvador, for, as we have seen, all that vast region was at the same cultural level during the Formative period. The important point is that the lowland Maya in their harsh setting of tropical rain forest outstripped their neighbors dwelling in highland and plateau country where conditions were so much more favorable.

The great civilizations of the world—of Egypt, Mesopotamia, the Indies, and China—developed in hot climates, but in lands that were fairly open, for the most part in the valleys of great rivers. Civilizations, such as those of Cambodia and Java, which have existed in tropical forest, were introduced already fully developed and did not long endure. Maya lowland civilization (surely La Venta, too) is, so far as I know, alone in having developed and reached maturity in thickly forested tropics.

Arnold Toynbee has pointed out that civilization responds to challenge, but if that challenge is too great, the civilization is abor-

tive. I cannot imagine a more formidable antagonist than those endless miles of jungle and forest, a Goliath which the Maya David
faced with torch and stone axe. Worse still, this was a Goliath who
could not be slain outright. Driven back, he recaptured lost ground
as soon as David's back was turned.

Perpetual warfare to keep the forest at bay with inadequate
tools should by all the laws of the Medes and Persians have been too
great a price to pay for civilization. Undoubtedly it would have been
to the Medes and Persians; for some reason it was not to the Maya.
Perhaps the reason was that blood brothers of Jacinto Cunil, not
Medes and Persians, formed the backbone of Maya civilization.

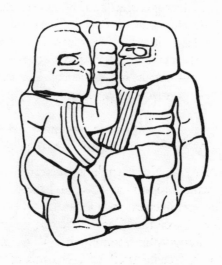

Synopsis of Maya History

circa 1500 B.C.—*circa* A.D. 200

Rise of agricultural civilizations on approximately the same cultural level and with essentially the same religion throughout Middle America. Period divisible into several phases. Pyramids built and hierarchy probably starting to emerge. Good plain pottery and figurine cult. Elementary hieroglyphic writing and simpler components of calendar. Strong development on Pacific Coast and in Guatemalan highlands. Maya lowland situation less clear, but at end of period the lowland Maya of the Petén and Yucatán were erecting pyramids. Their sculpture was still largely influenced by the early styles they had shared with their non-Maya neighbors.

CLASSIC PERIOD:
circa A.D. 200—A.D. 925

Early (A.D. 200–A.D. 625). No sharp division from Formative period. Corbeled vaulting which appears at close of Formative fully developed. Expansion of architecture and stela cult. By A.D. 500 many Maya centers (Tikal, Uaxactún, Copán, Piedras Negras, Yaxchilán, etc.) are erecting hieroglyphic monuments. Maya art develops its characteristic features, freeing itself of archaisms of the Formative period. Cultural peak at Kaminaljuyú and other highland Maya cities (at Teotihuacán also). Toward close of phase a period of quiescence in lowlands.

Florescence (A.D. 625–A.D. 800). Greatest era of sculpture, hieroglyphic writing, and building for the lowland Maya. Finest painted pottery, superb mold-made figurines, and best lapidary work. Great progress in astronomy and advanced arithmetic. Great expansion in number of ceremonial centers and of stelae (nineteen cities are known to have dedicated hieroglyphic monuments in A.D. 790). Marked decline in Guatemalan highlands.

Collapse (A.D. 800–A.D. 925). One by one ceremonial centers of Central area abandoned, possibly because of revolt against hierarchy, perhaps an indirect result of chain reaction to barbarian pressure north of Mexico City. Mexican influences infiltrate west side of peninsula of Yucatán, and affect some Puuc cities, many of which are abandoned at end of period or shortly afterwards. In Central area a return to cultural level approximating that of the Formative period, probably with the village or group of villages as the political unit. Occasional visits to abandoned ceremonial centers for simple rites and burials of petty chiefs. Waxing Mexican influence in Yucatán.

MEXICAN PERIOD:
A.D. 925–A.D. 1200

Mexicanized groups conquer Chichén Itzá, introducing art and some architectural features of Tula, the worship of Quetzalcoatl and other Mexican gods, and warfare to obtain flesh and blood to sustain the sun. Itzá said to have conquered other cities, but archaeological picture for rest of Yucatán not clear. Rise of secular power at cost of priesthood. Showy architecture and art much inferior to that of Classic period. Metal, plumbate, and turquoise important features. Fall of Chichén Itzá at end of period.

PERIOD OF MEXICAN ABSORPTION:
A.D. 1200–A.D. 1540

Mayapán establishes "empire" in Yucatán, and the Quiché do the same in Guatemalan highlands. Central rule and tyranny. Ruling groups gradually shed their Mexican culture (except warfare), becoming Maya in speech and religion. Worship of Quetzalcoatl and other Mexican gods declines. Secularization of culture continues. Ceremonial centers become real cities. Architecture and the arts sink to new lows. Following revolts against Mayapán and the Quiché in the fifteenth century, small independent chieftainships established with perpetual warring among themselves. Cultural decline continues until Maya civilization ended by Spanish conquest of Guatemala in 1525, and of Yucatán in 1541. Itzá in remote Tayasal remain independent until 1697.

Selected Reading

Published material on the Maya is very extensive, but much of it is technical. Many of the titles listed below are not readily obtainable, but can be consulted in good public libraries. Those dealing with specific ruins have been chosen partly because they well illustrate architecture, sculpture, and the minor arts. All the titles under the heading "General and History" contain extensive bibliographies.

The following abbreviations are used:

C. I. W. Pub.: Carnegie Institution of Washington *Publication*
P. M. M.: Peabody Museum of Archaeology and Ethnology, Harvard University, *Memoirs*
P. M. P.: Peabody Museum of Archaeology and Ethnology, Harvard University, *Papers*

ARCHAEOLOGICAL REPORTS
(All are well illustrated.)

Altar de Sacrificios. A. L. Smith and G. R. Willey. "New Discoveries at Altar de Sacrificios, Guatemala," *Archaeology*, Vol. XVI (1963), 83-89.

Bonampak. K. Ruppert, J. E. S. Thompson, and T. Proskouriakoff. *Bonampak, Chiapas, Mexico*. C. I. W. Pub. 602. 1955.

A. Villagra. *Bonampak, la ciudad de los muros pintados*. Mexico, 1949.

Calakmul. K. Ruppert and J. H. Denison. *Archaeological Reconnaissance in Campeche, Quintana Roo, and Petén*. C. I. W. Pub. 543. Washington, 1943.

Chichén Itzá. K. Ruppert. *The Caracol at Chichén Itzá, Yucatán, Mexico*. C. I. W. Pub. 454. Washington, 1935.

K. Ruppert, *The Mercado, Chichén Itzá, Yucatán, Mexico*. C. I. W. Pub. 546, Contribution 43. Washington, 1943.

E. H. Morris, J. Charlot, and A. A. Morris. *The Temple of the Warriors at Chichén Itzá, Yucatán*. C. I. W. Pub. 406. Washington,

1931. 2 vols. (One vol. of text, one vol. of illustrations of sculpture, murals, and architecture.)

A. M. Tozzer. Chichén Itzá and Its Cenote of Sacrifice, P. M. M. Vols. XI and XII. Cambridge, 1957.

Copán. G. B. Gordon. *Prehistoric Ruins of Copán, Honduras.* P. M. M., Vol. I, No. 1. Cambridge, 1896.

J. M. Longyear. *Copán Ceramics. A Study of Southeastern Maya Pottery.* C. I. W. Pub. 597. Washington, 1952. (More than pottery; a history of the site.)

General. A. P. Maudslay. *Archaeology. Biologia Centrali Americana.* London, 1889–1902. 5 vols. (Four vols. of magnificent plates covering Chichén Itzá, Copán, Palenque, Quiriguá, Tikal, Yaxchilán, and smaller sites. One vol. of text.)

Guatemala highlands. A. L. Smith. *Archaeological Reconnaissance in Central Guatemala.* C. I. W. Pub. 608. Washington, 1955.

Kaminaljuyú. A. V. Kidder, J. D. Jennings, and E. M. Shook. *Excavations at Kaminaljuyú, Guatemala.* C. I. W. Pub. 561. Washington, 1946.

Mayapán. H. E. D. Pollock, R. L. Roys, *et al. Mayapán, Yucatán, Mexico.* C. I. W. Pub. 619. Washington, 1962.

Naranjo. T. Maler. *Explorations in the Department of Petén, Guatemala, and Adjacent Region.* P. M. M., Vol. IV, No. 2. Cambridge, 1908.

Palenque. A. Ruz. Various articles in *Anales del Instituto Nacional de Antropologia e Historia.* Mexico, 1954ff.

Piedras Negras. T. Maler. *Researches in the Central Portions of the Usumasintla Valley.* P. M. M., Vol. II, No. 1. Cambridge, 1901.

W. R. Coe. *Piedras Negras Archaeology: Artifacts, Caches, and Burials.* Museum Monographs. Philadelphia, 1959.

Quiriguá. E. L. Hewett. "Two Seasons' Work in Guatemala," *Archaeological Institute of America Bulletin,* Vol. II (1911), pp. 117–34.

San José. J. E. S. Thompson. *Excavations at San José, British Honduras.* C. I. W. Pub. 506. Washington, 1939.

Seibal. T. Maler. *Exploration of the Upper Usumatsintla and Adjacent Region,* P. M. M., Vol. IV, No. I. Cambridge, 1908.

Tikal. T. Maler. *Explorations in the Department of Petén, Guatemala.* P. M. M., Vol. V, No. 1. Cambridge, 1911.

A. M. Tozzer. *Prehistoric Ruins of Tikal, Guatemala.* P. M. M., Vol. V, No. 2. Cambridge, 1911.

Tikal Reports. Museum Monographs. Philadelphia, 1958 onward.

W. R. Coe. "A Summary of Excavation and Research at Tikal, Guatemala: 1956–61," *American Antiquity*, Vol. XXVII (1962), 479–507.

Tulum. S. K. Lothrop. *Tulúm, an Archaeological Study of the East Coast of Yucatán.* C. I. W. Pub. 335. Washington, 1924.

Uaxactún. A. V. Kidder. *The Artifacts of Uaxactún, Guatemala.* C. I. W. Pub. 576. Washington, 1947.

    A. L. Smith. *Uaxactún, Guatemala: Excavations of 1931–37.* C. I. W. Pub. 588. Washington, 1950.

Uxmal. See "Architecture" (Marquina and Proskouriakoff).

Yaxchilán. T. Maler. *Researches in the Central Portion of the Usumacintla Valley.* P. M. M., Vol. II, No. 2. Cambridge, 1903.

ARCHITECTURE

W. R. Bullard, "Maya Settlement Pattern in Northeastern Petén, Guatemala," *American Antiquity*, Vol. XXV (1960), 355–72.

G. Kubler. *The Art and Architecture of Ancient America: The Mexican, Maya, and Andean Peoples.* The Pelican History of Art. London and Baltimore, 1962.

I. Marquina. *Arquitectura prehispánica.* Instituto Nacional de Antropología e Historia. Mexico, 1951. (Profusely illustrated.)

T. Proskouriakoff. *An Album of Maya Architecture.* C. I. W. Pub. 558. Washington, 1946, Norman, 1963. (Drawings of Maya buildings and sites restored to their original appearance. A very few are reproduced above.)

ART

T. A. Joyce. *Maya and Mexican Art.* London, 1927. (Outstanding pieces in the British Museum are illustrated.)

P. Kelemen. *Medieval American Art.* New York, 1943. 2 vols. (One vol. of text and one vol. of plates. Magnificent illustrations. Maya very well represented in this book, which covers the whole New World.)

G. Kubler, *See* "Architecture."

T. Proskouriakoff. *A Study of Classic Maya Sculpture.* C. I. W. Pub. 593. Washington, 1950.

H. J. Spinden. *A Study of Maya Art.* P. M. M., Vol. VI. Cambridge, 1913. (By no means out of date.)

S. Toscano. *Arte precolombino de México y de la América Central.* Universidad Nacional Autónoma de México. Mexico, 1944.

GENERAL AND HISTORY

S. G. Morley. *The Ancient Maya*. Stanford, 1946.

T. Proskouriakoff. "Historical Implications of a Pattern of Dates at Piedras Negras," *American Antiquity*, Vol. XXV (1960), 454–75. (Very important as first evidence of records of Maya dynasties.)

R. L. Roys. *The Indian Background of Colonial Yucatán*. C. I. W. Pub. 548. Washington, 1943. (Excellent account of Maya life in Yucatán just before the final collapse.)

J. E. S. Thompson. "A Trial Survey of the Southern Maya Area," *American Antiquity*, Vol. IX (1943), 106–34.

———. "A Survey of the Northern Maya Area," *American Antiquity*, Vol. XI (1945), 2–24.

A. M. Tozzer. *Landa's Relación de las cosas de Yucatán*. P. M. P., Vol. XVIII. Cambridge, 1941. (The very full notes make this volume a mine of information.)

HIEROGLYPHIC WRITING

S. G. Morley. *An Introduction to the Study of the Maya Hieroglyphs*. Bureau of American Ethnology *Bulletin* 57. Washington, 1915.

J. E. S. Thompson. *Maya Hieroglyphic Writing: An Introduction*. Norman, 1960.

———. *A Catalog of Maya Hieroglyphs*. Norman, 1962.

PRESENT-DAY MAYA

A. Goubaud. *The Guajxquip Bats, an Indian Ceremony of Guatemala*. Guatemala, 1937.

O. La Farge. *Santa Eulalia. The Religion of a Cuchumatan Indian Town*. Chicago, 1947.

M. Oakes. *The Two Crosses of Todos Santos*. New York, 1951. (This book makes the Mam Indians live. Superlative plates.)

R. Redfield and A. Villa R. *Chan Kom, a Maya Village*. C. I. W. Pub. 448. Washington, 1934.

J. E. S. Thompson. *Ethnology of the Mayas of Southern and Central British Honduras*. Field Museum of Natural History Anthropological Series, Vol. XVII, No. 2. Chicago, 1930.

A. M. Tozzer. *A Comparative Study of the Mayas and the Lacandones*. New York, 1907.

C. Wisdom. *The Chorti Indians of Guatemala*. Chicago, 1940.

TRAVEL

Gage, Thomas. *Thomas Gage's Travels in the New World*. Edited and with an introduction by J. Eric S. Thompson. (First published in 1648,) Norman, 1958.

T. W. F. Gann. *Maya Cities*. London and New York, 1927. (One of six books of travel and Maya archaeology by this author.)

A. C. and A. P. Maudslay. *A Glimpse at Guatemala*. London, 1899. (Written with great charm and published in a beautiful edition.)

J. L. Stephens, *Incidents of Travel in Central America, Chiapas, and Yucatán*. New York, 1841. 2 vols.

——. *Incidents of Travel in Yucatán*. New York, 1843. 2 vols. (Both sets of volumes are classics. Fine engravings of drawings by F. Catherwood.)

J. E. S. Thompson. *Maya Archaeologist*. Norman, 1963; London, 1963.

WRITTEN MAYA SOURCES

Recinos, Adrián (trans. and ed.). *Popol Vuh: The Sacred Book of the Ancient Quiché Maya*. English version by Delia Goetz and Sylvanus G. Morley. Norman, 1950.

——, and Delia Goetz (trans. and eds.). *The Annals of the Cakchiquels*, with *Title of the Lords of Totonicapán*. Norman, 1953.

R. L. Roys (trans. and ed.). *The Book of Chilam Balam of Chumayel*. C. I. W. Pub. 438. Washington, 1933.

—— (trans. and ed.). *Ritual of the Bacabs*. Norman, 1965.

List of Special Decorations

Moan bird. From wooden lintel, Tikal.   *title page*
Attendant with folded arms. From painted vessel, Nebaj, El Quiché.   3
Spider monkey scratching head. From painted vessel, Pusilhá.   30
Armadillo beating drum. From painted vessel, Chama, Alta Verapaz.   33
Chief carried in litter with dog beneath. From painted vase, Ratin-
    lixal, Alta Verapaz.   41
Seated man in formalized design. From painted vessel, Copán.   42
Bat god (vampire). From painted vase, Chama, Alta Verapaz.   49
Hummingbird. From painted vase, Pusilhá.   57
Twined plant motif, probably water lily, from painted vessel. Pusilhá. 66
Three glyphs of the "full-figure" type.   108
Jaguar holding offering within two vessels placed lip to lip.
    From painted vase, Uaxactún.   109
Jaguar diving into underworld. From floor of plate, Uaxactún.
    (Other leg hidden behind element of design.)   110
Skulls impaled on poles. Part of design in stone around the
    Platform of the Skulls, Chichén Itzá.   140
Man in formalized design typical of painted pottery of Honduras.
    Copán.   156
Two elaborate glyphs of the day Ahau flanking Initial Series
    introductory glyph of the month Ch'en with moon goddess
    as patroness.   202
Hunter slaying deer. Pottery figurine whistle, Lubaantún,
    British Honduras.   222
Masked chief painted black and wearing jaguar pelt. Painted vase,
    Chama, Alta Verapaz.   223
Chief in litter. Pottery figurine whistle, Lubaantún, British
    Honduras.   251
Woman grinding maize with child on her back. Pottery figurine
    whistle, Lubaantún, British Honduras.   259

One of the Bacabs emerging from a conch shell. Painted vase,
  Chama, Alta Verapaz.   262
Bust of a woman. Pottery figurine whistle, Lubaantún, British
  Honduras.   278
Textiles designs. From sculptured figures on lintels and stela.   292
Throne, Piedras Negras. From a stone lintel, Piedras Negras.   298
Death god diving earthward. Dresden Codex.   299
God of hunting. Madrid Codex.   307
Ball-game players. Note visors, gloves, and belts. Pottery figurine
  whistle, Lubaantún, British Honduras.   308

*All except the skull rack and the two figures
from codices are of the Classic period.*

Index

Adobe: 51, 86

Adultery: 292

Agriculture: 23; beginnings, 45–46; and abandonment of cities, 102–104; *see also* cornfields, maize, *and* plants (cultivated)

Ah Canul: 148, 161

Aké (Yucatán): 75

Albite mask: 54

Alcoholism: 31, 301; religious, 291

Alta Vera Paz (Guatemala): 21, 33 (illus.), 41 (illus.), 49 (illus.), 212, 223 (illus.), 262 (illus.), 284, 292

Altar de Sacrificios (Petén): 37, 63, 86, 107–108, 218; *Plate* 30

Altars: 9, 59, 65, 81, 94, 121, 138, 144, 152, 162; modern, 275–76, 291

Amaranth: 45–46

Ambergris: 222

Ancestor worship: 144, 147, 268, 285

Aqualung archaeology: 134

Archaeology: objectives, 64; checks with modern sources, 39, 120, 138, 198; *see also* research and exploration

Architecture: 58, 72, 83, 84, 96, 187–89, 239–44; pyramids, 7, 10, 21, 51, 53, 54, 71, 75, 83, 85; courts, 7, 71–81; temples, 8, 67ff., 81, 117ff., 141–42, 149; palaces, 9, 83, 85, 87; highland, 21, 51, 151–52; vaulting, 21, 22, 56, 74ff., 128–30, 141, 187–88, 240–44; perishable materials, 21, 51, 55, 65, 73, 85, 88–90, 142, 150, 155, 187, 264; inner pyramids, 51, 54; acropolis, 55, 72, 73, 151; roof combs, 58, 77; special assemblages, 65–84; beam and mortar roofs, 73, 75, 142–44, 187; aqueducts, 74; drains, 74; underground pas-

sages, 74; trap door, 74, 77; tower, 75; round buildings, 75, 117, 141; gateways, 75; localisms, 77; crossties, 78, 82; shafts, 79; columns, 83, 121, 128–29, 142, 144; façade decoration, 83–85, 132, 264, 288; Puuc, 83, 111, 136; upper stories, 83, 84, 87; Río Bec and Chenes, 85, 111; pilasters, 102; capstones, 116, 188, 244; Mexican period, 117ff.; influence of rites, 128–30; colonnades, 129–30, 142, 152, 240–41; beams, 129–30, 240; Mayapán, 141–42, 149; engineering factors, 118; emotional outlet, 188–89; wood ceilings, 190; construction, 244; *Plates* 2–8, 17, 24, 26; *see also* bridge, houses, lintels, masonry and mortar, *and* stairways

Area, Mayan: 17–19; southern 19–22; central, 22–26; northern 26–27

Arithmetic: 168, 178–82; zero concept, 178–79, 182

Art: 202–19; Formative, 21; modern, 31; Classic period, 61, 77ff.; idealized beauty, 61(*f*), 66; decadence, 102, 141, 154, 219, 306; foreign influences, 102, 107, 111, 127; Mexican period, 121ff.; Mayapán period, 141ff.; humor, 204, 208

Astrology: 165–66, 174, 177, 189, 285

Astronomy: 62, 80, 94, 163, 169–78, 197; *see also* eclipse tables *and* Venus

Atlantean figures: 243; *see also* Bacabs

Axes: 214; emblem of Chacs, 226, 265; *Plate* 22e; *see also* celts

Bacabs: 131, 260, 262 (illus.); *Plate* 31a

Balche: 225–26, 275–76, 284

318

Ball courts: 7, 73, 81, 85, 87, 89, 152, 153, 183, 190; abandoned, 149; players, 308 (illus.)

Banners: 124, 293

Bark: cloth, 212; paper, 197, 284; bedcover, 250; bucket, 250; bands, 297

Baskets: 134, 218; *Plates 12a, 18c*

Bats: 49 (illus.), 96, 190, 267; metaphorgram, 191

Bearded figures: 223 (illus.); *Plate 31b*

Becan (Campeche): 126

Beds: 144, 250

Bee god: 157, 260, 267

Belize Valley: 93, 301

Bells: 79, 134, 146

Benches: 82, 87, 144; *see also* daises

Benque Viejo (British Honduras): 288c, 301

Berlin, Henry: 97, 197

Birth goddess: 260

Blood drawing: 69, 160, 224, 230, 284, 289; from fingers, 101; *Plate 12*

Blowguns: 147

Bonampak (Chiapas): 68, 83, 95, 97, 101, 102, 207; *Plates 10, 17*

Bonework: 8, 217–18, 255, 295; *Plate 31b*

Books, hieroglyphic: 34, 35, 163, 173, 193, 195, 197, 299 (illus.), 307 (illus.); *Plate 31a*

Books of Chilam Balam: 38, 112, 117, 119, 197, 273; quoted, 127–28, 136, 158, 159, 260

Bows and arrows: 106, 126, 147; copper head, 215; bride payment, 251; sacrifice, 282

Bracelet, shell: 153

Brainerd, George W.: 89

Bricks: 86, 195

Bridge: 74

British Honduras: 17, 22, 26, 127, 157, 219, 288

Broadheadedness: *see* head

Bullard, William R.: 88–91

Burials: 8, 68, 79, 87, 106, 144, 217, 218; rites, 56, 252–58; urn, 56, 256; ossuary, 144, 147; Mayapán impoverished, 146; *see also* tombs

Butterfly pectoral: 123

Cacao: 20, 25, 93, 151, 184, 222, 235, 246; as currency, 219–21

Cages, prisoner: 283

Cakchiquel Maya: 28, 133, 150–51, 285

Calakmul (Campeche): 63, 64, 177; *Plate 10c*

Calendar: 9, 13, 162–69, 174–83, 225; deification, 14, 163, 175, 246, 252, 267; correlated with European 40, 59; Initial Series, 59, 60, 180, 200; computations, 94–95; 260-day almanac, 163, 174–76, 246, 291; journey, 163–64; survivals, 163; localisms, 164; start, 172, 177–78; *see also* divination, heiroglyphs, katun, time, uinal, *and* Venus

Campeche (Mexico): 17, 26, 96, 105, 111, 115, 251

Cancuén (Petén): 86

Cannibalism, ritualistic: 283

Canoes: 218, 220–21, 295; *Plate 17a*

Caracol (British Honduras): 86

Carbon–14 dating: 40, 46, 50, 51, 53, 56

Carnegie Institution of Washington: *vii*, 37, 126, 243

Causeways: *see* roads

Caves: early cultures in, 45; rites, 161, 268, 279, 281

Ceiba tree: 23, 260–61, 283

Celts: stone, 145; copper, 215

Cenotes: 27, 138, 146, 275; sacrifices at, 133–34, 136; dredging, 134–35, 210

Ceremonial centers: 7–9, 60, 66–88; description, 7–9, 99; building, 8, 89–90; unsuited to residence, 66–67, 99; not urban, 69; modern, 70; relations between, 93–97, 98; unfortified, 94; and the peasant, 97, 105, 127; abandoned, 100–108, 112, 115, 126; reused, 106–108, 138, 146; shife to fortified sites, 125–26, 151–52; *Plates 2, 3*

Ceremonies: 224–32; nullification, 229, 290; purification, 290; *see also* blood drawing, cannibalism, caves, cenotes, Chacs, continence, cornfields, fire, idols, New Year, sacrifice, *and* water

Cerro de las Mesas (Veracruz): 60, 63

Chacs: rain gods, 123, 132, 134, 136, 193, 225–26, 237, 262–65, 269, 273; rites for, 275–76, 281; assistants, 275, 286, 289;

Plate 31a (top right and bottom left); see also rain gods

Chalchitán (El Quiché): 152; *Plate 26b*

Chaneabal Maya: 28

Character and attitudes: 13, 14, 30, 98, 112, 156–62, 178, 226, 237–38, 270–71, 274, 276, 283, 296, 298, 300–308; bearing on civilization, 9, 10, 26, 301–302, 306–308

Chenes (Campeche): 115; see also architecture

Chiapas (Mexico): 17, 19, 22, 25, 28–29, 47, 70, 75, 91, 105, 208, 212; early stelae, 53

Chiapanec tribe: 17, 94

Chichén Itzá (Yucatán): 37, 67, 75, 79, 100, 112–38, 140 (illus.), 149, 208; old name, 133; destruction, 137–38; partial reoccupation, 138, 146; *Plates 5a, 6c, 7a, 8c, 14c*; see also cenote, Itzá, and Tula

Chicle and chicleros: 4, 5, 23, 24, 38, 157, 299–300

Chiefs: see ruling class

Children: upbringing, 160, 257–58, 259 (illus.); economic value, 104, 233, 246; see also sacrifice

Chile: 25, 45

Chol Maya: 27, 99; *Plate 1c*

Chontal Maya: 24, 27, 99, 107, 119, 128, 220–21

Chorti Maya: 27, 263, 274

Christianity, Maya fusion with: 70, 167, 269, 273, 279–80, 291

Chuh Maya: 28

Chutixtiox (El Quiché): 151; *Plate 26a*

Cities, residential: 140; see also ceremonial centers

City states: 97–99, 139; see also ceremonial centers and political organization

Civilization: possible laws of, 14, 15, 26, 306; climate and, 307–308

Civilization, Maya: unique character, 13, 308–309; area, 17; secularism and, 112, 113, 140, 147, 304; decline, 112, 145, 147–48, 304–306; absorptive nature, 132–33, 154, 305, 306; Maya character and, 161, 302, 307; creative minority 307

Clans: 89, 92–93

Climate: 20, 24–26; and man, 307

Clothing: 184, 212, 235, 253; sleeveless tunics, 95, 101, 116, 124; *Plates 9–14*, 17, 18, 20, 30

Cobá (Quintana Roo): 24, 75, 185–86

Cocoms: 56, 148–49, 153, 257

Codices: see books, hieroglyphic

Comalcalco (Tabasco): 86, 107

Communal labor: see co-operation

Concrete: 56, 187

Confession: 292

Continence, ritualistic: 68, 160–61, 174, 274–75, 294

Co-operation: 248–49, 274, 296; intellectual, 171; bearing on character, 161, 171

Copal: 9, 25, 60, 134, 172, 233, 274

Copán (Honduras): 22, 25, 27, 63, 65, 71, 80–81, 94, 99, 193, 203; artifacts, 42 (illus.), 156 (illus.), 217, 218; sculpture, 61, 80–81, 122, 123, 204, 272; *Plates 2, 6, 11, 16, 29, 31*

Copper: 20, 79, 88, 134, 146, 152, 215–17, 221

Coral: 88

Cornfields: 26, 193, 235, 301; clearing, 23; rites, 160, 274–76, 284

Corn grinders: 20, 27, 232, 254, 259, (illus.); miniature, 268

Cosmology: 260–61; see also creation and world

Cotton: 27, 52; armor, 125; see also clothing and textiles

Cozumel (Quintana Roo): 119, 135

Creation: 152, 261; legends, 201–202, 261, 277–78

Cremation: 257

Crocodile, mythical: 261, 263, 272

Crown: 288; feather, 39; gold, 152

Crystal, rock: 146

Cunil, Jacinto: 299–301, 308

Currency: 215, 219, 282; see also cacao

Daily life: 232–39

Daises: 68, 80, 88, 108, 130, 298 (illus.); *Plates 8c, 10a, 18c*

Dances: 69–70, 215, 236, 268, 293–96; *Plates 15a, 18a*

Dates, Maya, correlated with European calendar: 40, 59

Death: god, 175, 252, 266, 299 (illus.); insignia, 262

Decapitation: 153

Defended sites: 125–26, 139, 151–52; Classic period absence, 96; buildings, 148; *Plate 26a; see also* island sites, maguey, moat, palisades, tower, *and* wall

Discoveries of ruins: *viii*, 32–38, 59, 126

Disease and illness: 287, 292; introduced from Old World, 24, 104; and abandonment of cities, 104; glyphs 181, 193; divination, 285

Divination and omens: 163–65, 193, 194, 198, 225, 233, 246, 252, 285–87

Divorce: 233

Dogs: 41 (illus.), 175, 190, 193, 213, 277; guides to next world, 254; *Plate 20c*

Dragons, celestial: *see* sky monsters

Drains: stone, 74; pottery, 210

Dreams: 233

Dress: *see* clothing

Drills: tubular, 212, 288; copper-lined, 217

Drums: 33 (illus.), 72, 82, 198, 199, 294; pottery, 210

Duality: religious, 262, 267, 285; political, 97, 286

Dye: logwood, 25; *see also* paint

Dzibilchaltún (Yucatán): 53

Eagles and Jaguars, orders of: 115, 124, 130, 131, 142, 293

Earplugs: pottery, 210; gold, 217; jade, 254, 255

Earth revered: 157, 271

Earth gods and monsters: 123, 157, 175, 261, 263, 265, 291; attributes, 262

Eclipses: tables, 62, 80, 173–74; cause, 263

Education: 160, 301

El Baúl (Escuintla): 60

El Cayo (Chiapas): 97

El Salvador: 17, 19, 210, 219; *Plate 18b*

El Tajín (Veracruz): 19, 71, 182

Engineering knowledge: 185

Environment: 17–27, 99, 116, 140, 307

Eroticism: Maya reaction to, 127, 158; in dance, 294; *see also* phallicism

Etzná (Campeche): 100

Fans: 41 (illus.), 201, 223 (illus.); feather, 293

Fasting: 68, 160–61, 174, 224, 270, 290, 294

Fauna: 7, 9, 23, 27

Feathered serpents: *see* serpents

Featherwork: 10, 39, 205, 210, 293; export, 25

Fire: glyph, 181; making, 234, 286; walking 225–26

Fireplace: 250, 257, 264

Fish: 218, 295; net sinkers, 210; metal hooks, 215; creel 218; god, 191; sacrificed, 284; *Plate 17a*

Flint: 25, 145, 149, 213, 280; god, 267; *Plate 22*

Floors: stucco, 9; paved, 74, 152

Flora: 5, 7, 23–25

Flowers: loved, 100; sex symbol, 263; sacrificed, 284

Flutes: 210

Folk tales: 157, 262–63, 265, 271–73

Folk memory: 269

Food: 233, 235, 260; preparation, 232–33, 249, 300; with dead, 256; sacrifice, 274, 284

Forest: 5, 7, 22–23, 38; effect on Maya, 26; encroachment, 38, 103, 138, 308

Förstemann, Ernst: 37, 173

Fortifications: *see* defended sites

Frescoes: *see* mural paintings

Frogs: religious import, 265, 275; glyph, 108 (illus.)

Furniture: *see* house-hold utensils

Games: *see* ball courts

Glottochronology: 28

Gods and goddesses: 262–70; impersonators, 216 (illus.), 275, 276, 283, 296; attitude to, 237, 278, 298; *Plates 12, 17b, 19c; see also* Bacabs, Chacs, creation, death, earth, Itzamna, Ixchel, jaguar, Kukulcán, long-nosed, maise, Mam, merchants, moon, mountain gods, serpents, sky, sun, *and* underworlds

Gods, Mexican: Tezcatlipoca, 118, 123;

Chicomecoatl, 123; sun, 123; Tlalchi-tonatiuh, 123, 124, 131, Chacmol, 130; Xipe Totec, 147, 268, 293; Toci, 282; Tlalocs, 203, 217; *Plates 8c* (extreme right), 30

Gold: 20, 27, 132, 134, 146, 152, 215, 217

Goubaud, Antonio: 291

Gourds and calabashes: 210, 226, 233, 265, 275, 294

Government: *see* political organization

Graffiti: 10, 11

Granite: 25

Grijalva River estuaries: 107

Guatemala: highlands 19–22, 92; highland post-Classic, 150–51; *Plates* 25, 26; *see also* Pacific Coast *and* Petén

Hammocks: 183, 274; *Plate 8b*

Head: index, 29, 57; deformation, 30, 43, 53, 61, 106, 107, 132

Headdress as crown: 39

Hematite: 20

Henequen: 212

Hierarchy: *see* priests *and* ruling class

Hieroglyphic writing: 79, 80, 108 (illus.), 172, 176, 180–81, 189–97, 202 (illus.), 217, 218; expanded to speech, 16, 200; origins, 21, 53, 190; distribution, 21, 22, 65; in highlands, 66, 85; subjects, 62–63, 197; name, 62, 97; known by few, 92; uniformity and localisms, 96, 97, 99; emblem, 97, 98, 193; non-Maya, 107; decline, 141; rebus, 189–91, 193, 196; research, 194–95; *Plate 31*

History, periods of: hunters, 44–45; Formative, 46–57, 86, 87, 134, 183, 309; Classic, 57–109, 126, 128, 135, 186, 309–10; Mexican, 87, 110–39, 310; Mexican absorption (Mayapán), 139–50, 153; synopsis, 309–10; *see also* civilization, Maya

History: on stelae, 62–63, 197; repetition, 118, 165, 198; in prophecies, 120, 198

Holmul (Petén): 86

Honduras: 17, 49, 88, 149, 215, 219, 221

Household utensils and furniture: 48, 229, 232–33, 264; revolt of, 277; *see also* beds, benches, shrines, *and* stone

Houses, residential: 55, 142–45; building, 248–49; consecration, 250, 290; stone models, 264; round, 264; *Plates, 17a, 24a; see also* architecture, kitchens, *and* settlement patterns

Houses, specialized: men's, 73, 142, 245; community, 237; *see also* architecture

Huaxtec Maya: 19, 28, 214

Hummingbird: 57 (illus.)

Humor: in art, 204, 208; *see also* jokes (practical)

Hunac Ceel: 136–38

Hunting: 147, 156–57, 222 (illus.), 234; mammoth, 44–45; god, 232, 307 (illus.); dance, 294; prayer, 295

Ichpaahtún (Quintana Roo): 63, 125

Idols: 279–80; making, 93, 289; copal, 134; rubber, 134; wood, 134; stone, 145; pottery, 147, 210

Incense burners: 9, 138, 147–48, 172, 208, 268, 291; *Plates 19c,* 27; *see also* copal

Intellectual achievement: 169–83; impractical nature, 13, 187, 189

Intelligence: 30

Inventions: 183

Invasions of Yucatán: 119, 120

Iron pyrites: 20, 52, 214

Island sites: 127, 139; *see also* Tayasal

Itzá: at Chichén Itzá, 114, 117–21, 132–39; identified as Chontal, 119; at Tayasal: 153–54, 161, 166–67, 283

Itzamna: 135, 263, 281, 282; *Plate 31a* (bottom)

Ixchel: 135, 193; *see also* gods (moon goddess)

Ixil Maya: 292

Iximché (Sololá): 151, 152

Izamal (Yucatán): 75, 120, 135–37, 139

Jade: 21, 79, 106, 134, 217, 219, 254, 255; source, 20, 26; in mouth, 21, 106, 253; working, 26, 50, 212; masks, 56, 79, 213, 288; dated, 133; symbolic values, 191, 258, 273; teeth inlay, 214; *Plates 21, 28a*

Jaguars: 23, 27, 109 (illus.), 110 (illus.), 254; pelts, 27, 101, 223 (illus.), 298 (illus.); tunic, 95, 101; stone, 152, 204; gold, 152; ridiculed, 204; god, 206, 266;

kilt, 216; teeth, 255; *see also* Eagles and Jaguars
Jimbal (Petén): 100
Jokes: 231; practical, 30, 241, 249
Justice: 93, 157–58, 237–38

Kabah (Yucatán): 115, 116
Kaminaljuyú (Guatemala): 21, 37, 56, 66, 86, 112, 113; burials, 51–53, 85, 254; artifacts, 203, 208, 210, 218; *Plates* 19, 25
Katun: 62, 120, 166, 168, 181, 198–200; commemoration, 65, 162; prophecies, 120, 166–67; sequence, 120
Kekchí Maya: 28, 160, 211, 274, 287, 297, 301
Kitchens: 144
Knives and points: *see* flint *and* obsidian
Kukulcán: 75, 117–21, 265; *see also* serpents (feathered)

Labná (Yucatán): 115, 116; *Plate* 24
Lacandón Maya: 24, 37, 70, 92, 155, 212, 283, 287, 290, 297, 301–302; *Plate* 1*b*
Lacanhá (Chiapas): 63
Lacquer work: 210
Ladders: 10; *see also* poles (notched)
Lake Amatitlán: offerings recovered from, 134
Lake Atitlán: 20, 221, 250
Lake Petén: offerings recovered from: 134, 153
Land ownership: 93
Landa, Diego de: 34–35, 118, 135, 257; quoted, 117–18, 284
Languages: Maya, *xv*, 27–29, 94, 99, 192; glottochronology, 28; Mexican loan words, 124
La Muñeca (Campeche): 100
La Venta (Veracruz): 19, 50ff., 66, 183, 212, 303, 307
La Victoria (Quezaltenango): 47
Legends: *see* creation *and* folk tales
Leyden plaque: 288
Lime: 48, 86, 187, 232, 286; sizing, 197; kilns, 239–40
Limestone: 9, 22, 25–27, 85, 86, 187; crystalline, 83
Lineage: 268; god, 268; *see also* ancestor worship

Lintels: stone, 65, 80; wood, 80, 129; *Plates* 12, 13
Literature: 200; *see also* Books of Chilam Balam *and* Popol Vuh
Litters: 10, 41 (illus.), 253, 293; in burial, 52, 254
Loltún (Yucatán): 53
Long-nosed god: 216, 225–26, 236, 272, 295; *Plate* 14*b*
Looting, ancient: 52, 137–38, 144, 149
Lowland Maya: early inferiority to highlands, 21, 53; later superiority, 21, 22, 28, 56; trade with, 25, 26
Lubaantún (British Honduras): 83, 86; figurines (illus.), 222, 251, 259, 278, 308

Macaws: 23, 27
MacNeish, Richard S.: 45–46
Magic: 296; imitative, 276
Maize: 20, 260–76, 294; origin, 45–46, 273; wild, 46; god, 164, 175, 181, 236, 265, 271–73; glyph, 180, 183; divination, 252, 287; foliage as earth symbol, 262; goddess, 263; reverence for, 270–71; rites, 274–76; man of, 277; *Plate* 10*b*; *see also* cornfields *and* food
Maler, Teobert: 36
Mam: Maya, 28, 150–51, 271, 274, 287; god, 266
Marble vessels: 52, 88, 213
Markets: 69, 73, 222
Marriage: 220, 233, 245–52; cross-cousin, 92
Masks: jade, etc., 52, 56, 79, 215; on buildings, 54, 55, 83, 132, 288; gold, 152; worn, 216, 223 (illus.); headdress, 225; *Plates* 5*c*, 7, 24*b*, 28*a*
Masonry and mortar: 64, 72, 86, 88, 100, 187–88; mortar, 21, 87, 241–42; tile veneer, 83, 142; lime-encrusted mussels, 86; degenerate, 106; Mayapán, 142; *see also* concrete
Mats and matting: 52, 239, 250, 280, 290
Maudslay, Alfred P.: 7, 35–36
Maya, modern, confirm archaeology: 39, 70, 90, 108
Mayapán (Yucatán): 37, 75, 90, 120, 125, 135–37; domination, 138–49; destruction, 144–45, 149; *Plate* 26*c*

Medical lore: *see* disease and illness
Mercenaries, Mexican: 147, 161
Merchants: 220–22; gods, 198–99, 215; *see also* trade
Metal: 127, 146, 183, 215–17; absent from Classic period, 146; *see also* copper *and* gold
Metates: *see* corn grinders
Metaphors: 111, 231; glyphic, 191–92
"Mexican": definition, 19
Mexican influences: 21, 60, 85, 102, 105, 112ff., 202, 259, 283, 305; Maya reaction to, 127, 158; *see also* Teotihuacán *and* Tula
Mexican barracks: 148
Mexican period: *see* history
Militarism: in Classic period, 94, 95, 98, 101; rise, 112–15, 123–24, 140–41, 150–51, 304; and sun worship, 113–14, 266; religious effect, 127, 129, 147; *see also* Eagles and Jaguars *and* mercenaries
Milpas: *see* cornfields
Mirrors: 20, 52, 214, 253, 254
Moan bird: title page (illus.), 267
Moat: 125–26
Monkeys: 7, 23, 27, 30 (illus.), 277
Monte Albán (Oaxaca): 19, 53, 66, 112, 182, 210, 303
Moon: age recorded, 62; goddess, 135, 181, 193, 211, 246, 260, 262–63, 272; glyph, 180, 193; merged with Virgin Mary, 269; *see also* eclipse
Mopan Maya: 27, 157, 274
Morality: *see* character and outlook
Morley, Sylvanus G.: viii, 29, 59, 103, 200
Morris, Earl H.: 188
Mosaic work: 39, 213, 288 (d, crown); *Plate 28a*
Motul (Yucatán): 135
Mountain gods: 157, 260, 265
Mural painting: 56, 82, 83, 95, 101, 108, 113, 122, 127, 184, 198–99, 207, 208, 242, 264, 294; *Plate 17*
Music: 210, 260, 265, 293; *Plate 17*

Naachtún (Petén): 67
Nahuatl language: 17
Nakúm (Petén): 67, 98
Names: 62, 92, 216; *see also* hieroglyphic writing (emblems)
Naranjo (Petén): 102
Narcotics: 52, 286
Negative painting and batik: 183
Nets: 212; sinkers, 210; carrying bags, *Plate 17a*
New Year: 164, 263, 292; eve, 174; *Plate 31a*
New World: populating, 43–44, 47; culture compared to that of Old, 15–16
Next world: 53, 56, 77, 256, 266–67, 280
Nohpat (Campeche): 75
Nose ornaments: 152; *Plates 9b, 16*
Numbers: ritualistic, 65, 213, 257, 258, 261, 266, 275–76; divine, 108 (illus.), 163, 248, 267; *see also* arithmetic

Oaxaca (Mexico): 19, 213; *see also* Monte Albán
Obsidian: 20, 52, 88, 213–14; no lowland source, 25; working, 213–14; axe, 214; pyramid decoration, 214; *Plate 22e*
Offertory caches: 138, 149, 213f., 229–31
Old World: comparisons with New, 16–17; origins in, 43–44; contacts, 47
Olmec: *see* La Venta
Onyx (Mexican): 213, 254
Opossum actors (Bacabs): *Plate 31a*
Oxkintok (Yucatán): 63, 75, 100, 116; *Plate 15a*

Pacific Coast, Guatemala: 17, 20, 21, 47, 88, 151, 219; early stelae, 53, 59, 60
Paint: 20, 184, 208, 212, 295; body, 52, 255; *see also* mural painting *and* pottery
Palenque (Chiapas): 32, 58, 65, 67, 74–75, 79, 96, 99, 102, 133, 193, 208; sculpture, 39, 61, 236, 261, 288; architecture, 58, 67, 76; *Plates 5, 13, 15, 16, 23, 27, 28*
Palisades: 125, 126
Paper: *see* bark paper
Parasols: 82
Parrots, stone: 81
Pasión Valley: viii, 97, 98, 193
Pearl, mother of: 217
Pearls: 79
Peasants: *see* political organization, religion, *and* ruling class
Petén (Guatemala): 22, 103, 125, 153;

roads, 75, 186; post-Classic, 160–108, 127, 139, 140
Petén, Lake: *see* Lake Petén
Phallicism: 112, 116; *see also* eroticism
Philosophy: 13–14, 158–60, 202; of time, 162–69; *see also* character and attitude *and* time
Physical appearance: 29–30, 43; ideal, 61, 107; *Plates* 1, 9–14, 15, 16
Piedras Negras (Petén): 62, 65, 92, 96ff., 108, 133, 193, 298 (illus.); sculpture, 68, 80, 261; *Plates* 3, 9, 10, 14
Pilgrimages: 133, 135, 138
Pine: torches, 79; boughs, 291
Pipil Indians: 17, 150
Plants, cultivated: 9, 20, 45, 46, 183–84; *see also* cotton, cacao, *and* maize
Plaster: *see* stucco
Pokoman Maya: 28, 51, 134, 287
Polé (Quintana Roo): 119
Poles: notched, 48; vault ties, 82
Political organization: 88–100, 285; centralized, 139ff.; *see also* ruling class *and* social organization
Pollen counts: 25
Popol Vuh: 39, 277
Population: 24, 27, 29, 140; movements, 28; estimates, 29; density, 53; post-Classic, 104, 127; *see also* settlement patterns
Pottery: 52, 53, 56, 208–10; polychrome, 21, 88, 208, 209; stucco-decorated, 21, 203; hieroglyphs on, 22; earliest, 46–47; figurines, 49, 57, 107, 208; changes, 64; thin orange, 85, 210; spindlewhorls, 88, 106; slate ware, 88; archaeological values, 90, 138, 209–10; post-Classic, 106–107; fine gray, 107; fine orange, 107, 210; plumbate, 108, 116, 138–39, 209–10, 213; Mayapán red, 138, 146; decline, 147; modeled, 208; stamps, 210; utensils and ornaments, 210, 250; *Plates* 18–20, 27, 28, 30; illustrations of, *see* pp. 316–17
Prayers: 157, 211, 232, 274–75, 291, 297–98
Predestination: 14, 164, 167, 302
Priesthood: 9, 68–69, 97–98, 122, 132, 135, 255, 279, 285–86, 296, 302–303; novitiate, 11, 224–32, 291; seclusion, 69; village, 235, 250, 275, 291; *see also* rulers
Prisoners: 95, 101, 283
Prophecies: 118, 120, 136, 166, 198, 200, 286
Proskouriakoff, Tatiana: 59, 92, 111, 197, 216; *Plates* 2, 3, 6–8, 24, 26
Pumas: 124, 130, 293
Purificatory rites: 276, 289, 292
Pusilhá (British Honduras): 29 (illus.), 57 (illus.), 63, 66 (illus.), 74, 86
Puuc (Yucatán): 83, 99, 115, 147; *see also* architecture

Quarrying: 243–44
Quetzal bird: 20, 23, 167; feathers, 39, 41 (illus.), 131(*b*), 205
Quetzalcoatl: 151, 304; *see also* Kukulcán *and* serpents (feathered)
Quiché Maya: 28, 133, 150–51, 287, 291–94
Quintana Roo (Mexico): 13, 17, 26, 111
Quiriguá (Izabal): 13, 62, 81–82, 86, 100, 102, 172, 178, 180, 236, 272; *Plates* 11*b*, 32

Rainfall: 20, 24, 26
Rattles: 198, 199, 293, 296
Religion: 233, 259–98; Asiatic influences, 47; Formative, 56–57; shifts, 105, 304; hierarchic *versus* peasant, 105, 132, 207, 270, 302, 305; Mexican period, 121–24, 305; effect on buildings, 123, 128–30; decline, 140–41, 147, 149; bearing on art, 141, 145, 203, 204; ancestor worship, 144, 147; family cults, 144, 147; outstanding features, 269; mixed with Christianity, 269–70, 273; intoxication and, 291; *see also* calendar (deification), ceremonies, Christianity, continence, cosmology, duality, fasting, gods, idols, incense burners, next world, pilgrimages, prayers, predestination, sacrifice, shrines, *and* world directions and colors
Research and exploration: *vii–viii*, 32–39, 172
Reservoirs: 11, 74, 87
Rings: jade, 79; copper, 146, 152; ball-court, 152

Río Bec (Campeche): 99, 115, 126; *see also* architecture
Ritual: *see* ceremonies
Rivers: 23, 24; absent in Yucatán, 26
Roads: 7, 24, 75, 134, 150, 185–87, 189
Roys, Ralph L.: 128, 136, 152, 158, 201, 289
Rubber: 7, 23, 27, 134, 183–84, 284
Ruling class and hierarchy: 9, 56, 62, 68, 90–93, 97–101, 133, 136–37, 206, 211, 216, 218, 285, 305; glyphs of, 96; and peasant, 105–106, 126–27, 135, 207, 302, 305; possible revolt against, 105–106; foreign, 107–108; Mexican period, 124, 136, 137; last stronghold, 126; at Mayapán, 139, 148; residences, 143–44; deified, 267, 303; *see also* crown *and* political organization

Sacrifice: human, 11, 68, 72, 88, 98, 101, 121, 122, 131 ff., 216, 227–29, 282–84, 293; arrow or spear, 10, 282; children, 35, 88, 106, 134, 237, 279–81; *pechni*, 39; attendants, 52, 77, 79, 152, 253, 254, 256; hearts, 124, 130; decapitation, 101, 153; flaying, 268, 282; non-human, 275–76, 279, 284, 291, 297; *Plate 31a; see also* cenotes
Salt: abstention, 69; turtleshell containers, 218; trade, 221–22
Sandals: 134, 184; of jaguar skin, 101
Sandstone: 81, 86
San Isidro Piedra Parada (Quezaltenango): 53
San José (British Honduras): 67, 87–89, 106, 107, 236
San Lorenzo (Campeche): 102
Santa Rita (British Honduras): 108, 127, 139, 198–99, 215
Sapodilla wood: 11, 23, 129–30, 210, 260
Sapper, Karl: 29, 160, 297, 301
Savanna: pollen, 25, 103–104; and deserted cities, 102–103; for hunting, 234
Sayil (Yucatán): 83, 115, 129; *Plate 3a*
Sculpture: 203–207, 242–43; Formative, 53; Classic period, 64, 80–81, 96, 100; foreign influences in Petén, 102; degenerate, 102, 111, 142, 145; Yucatec Classic, 111, 117, 142, 145; phallic, 112;

reused, 117, 147; Mexican period, 123–24, 131–32, 205; Mayapán period, 142, 145; animated, 236; techniques, 242–43; *Plates 9–16, 25, 29, 32*
Sea routes: 48
Seibal (Petén): 37, 100, 102; foreign rule at, 107–108; *Plate 9b*
Serpents: 10, 122, 131, 236, 263, 272; feathered, 118, 121–23, 130–31; gods, 137, 192, 263; rattles, 226; dance, 294; *Plates 9b, 12b, 14b,c, 16c,d, 17a, 30*
Settlement patterns: 70, 88–90, 99, 100; *see also* ceremonial centers *and* cities
Sex: Maya attitude toward, 30, 262–63, 271; licence, 295; and maize, 296; *see also* eroticism
Shells and shellwork: 52, 88, 153, 179, 217, 236, 254, 255, 295; inlay, 56, 213; for building, 86; Bacab symbol, 131, 262 (illus.), trumpet, 217, 235; currency, 219, 282
Shields: 95, 114, 124, 130, 206, 307 (illus.); *Plates 11b, 18c*
Shrines, family: 144, 147
Sin: confession of, 292; scapegoat, 292
Skull: 134; rack, 124, 140 (illus.); on building, 152; incised, 218, 288; modeled, 257; *see also* decapitation *and* head deformation
Sky: monsters, 47, 81, 224–27, 260, 263; gods, 267; *Plate 32*
Slate: stelae, 86; mirror backs, 214, 222
Slaves: 93, 149; slain, 52, 77, 79, 152, 253–54, 256
Smith, A. Ledyard: 152, 255
Snakes: *see* serpents
Social organization: 47, 56, 93; Mexican effects, 119, 124; *see also* political organization, ruling class, slaves, *and* houses (specialized)
Songs: 200–202, 262
Soot: 210; fasting sign, 290
South American influences: 17, 146, 183, 278, 281
Spanish Conquest: 153; impact on Maya, 91, 167; reaction to, 159; *see also* Christianity
Spears: 10, 95, 101, 102, 114, 115, 206, 222 (illus.), 307 (illus.); *Plates 10c, 18c*

Spear-thrower: 10, 102, 114–16, 123, 134, 210

Spindlewhorls: 88, 106

Stairways: 8, 51, 54, 83, 121, 130; interior, 75, 87; within pyramid, 76–77; ceremonial, 80

Standards: 10

Stelae: 9, 59, 72, 80, 81, 86, 87, 136, 162, 204, 294; materials, 9, 81, 86; Formative, 53; Pacific Coast, 53, 59; earliest dated, 53, 59–60; broken up, 53, 59; cult, 61–66; subject matter, 62–63; absent in some lowland sites, 63, 83; highland, 66, 85; latest, 100–101, 105; degenerate, 102; reset, 106; *Plates* 9–11, 13, 15, 25

Stephens, John L.: 34, 84

Sting ray: 56, 148, 255, 284; glyphs on, 218

Stone: volcanic, 20, 86, 264; building, 20, 25, 81, 83, 85, 86, 147; tools and utensils, 20, 23, 212; thrown, 126; reused building, 136, 138, 147; *see also* flint, granite, limestone, marble, onyx, sandstone, *and* slate

Stucco: 214; floors, 9, 81; on buildings, 11, 54, 72, 83, 86–88, 142, 152, 288; on pottery, 21, 203; modeled, 54, 55, 79, 102; painted, 136; *Plates* 16a, 23

Sun: disk, 102, 123, 199; and militarism, 113–15, 266, 304; god, 123, 131(*b*), 135, 175, 262–63, 272; legends, 245

Superstitions: 108, 289

Sweat houses: 73

Symbolism: 192, 263, 273, 275, 284, 292, 295; gestures, 39, 95, 276; in sculpture, 203; *see also* time

Tabasco (Mexico): 17, 19, 118, 119, 140, 219, 221

Tattooing and scarification: 216 (illus.); god, 267; *Plate* 16c

Tayasal (Petén): 140, 153, 161–62, 166, 198, 200, 283

Teapa (Tabasco): *Plate* 27c

Teeple, John E.: 96, 173

Teeth: decoration, 214; jaguar, 255; *Plate* 28b

Tehuacán (Puebla): 45–46

Temperament: *see* character and attitudes

Temples: *see* architecture

Tenochtitlán (Mexico): 89

Teotihuacán (Mexico): 17, 19, 59, 66, 112, 113, 181, 210, 303–304; influences, 21, 85, 203

Textiles: 31, 52, 56, 134, 211, 221, 292 (illus.); painted, 293; *Plate* 12; *see also* clothing *and* weaving

Tikal (Guatemala): 3–11, 37, 40, 55–56, 67, 71–73, 75, 90, 97–100, 129, 193, 203; stelae, 9, 60, 65, 106; post-Classic, 127, 140; artifacts, 214, 217–18, 222, 288, 295; *Plate* 4

Tila (Chiapas): 100

Time: concept, 9, 13, 63, 94, 162–69; future confounded with past, 14, 167; *see also* calendar

Tlalocs: 123, 266

Tlatilco (Mexico): 50

Tobacco: 286

Toltec: *see* Itzá, Mexican influences, *and* Tula

Tombs: 51–53, 56, 77–79, 85, 152, 254, 256

Topoxté (Petén): 127, 139

Tortoiseshell: 218

Totemism: *see* clans

Totonac Indians: 55

Tower: 75; defensive, 126

Toynbee, Arnold: 15, 26, 306, 307

Tozzer, Alfred M.: 37, 297, 301

Trade: 25–27, 52, 56, 85, 88, 209, 215, 217, 220–22

Travel: *see* litters *and* time

Trees: 184; breadnut, 9, 23; glyphs, 180, 181; world directional, 260; *plumiera* (plumeria), 263; *Plate* 17a; *see also* bark, cacao, ceiba, copal, cultivated plants, forest, pine, rubber, *and* sapodilla

Tribute: 141

Trumpets: wooden, 293; shell, 217, 235; *Plate* 17b

Tula (Hidalgo): 19, 114ff., 128, 132, 146, 209, 217, 303; influences at Chichén Itzá, 115–24, 129–32; ancestors, 133, 150

Tulúm (Quintana Roo): 63, 125, 139, 208

Turkey: 23, 260

Turquoise: 146, 152, 212
Tutul Xiu: 133, 149, 153
Turtle: sacrifice, 279; *Plate 17a*
Turtle carapaces: music, 218; salt storage, 218; *Plate 17b*; *see also* tortoiseshell
Tweezers, copper: 146, 215
Tzeltal Maya: 28
Tzibanché (Quintana Roo): 210
Tzotzil Maya: 28, 96, 285; *Plate 1a*

Uaxactún (Petén): 37, 54ff., 67, 75, 98–100, 106, 107, 109 (illus.), 110 (illus.), 186, 208, 214, 255; *Plates 2a, 5c*
Ucanal (Petén): 102
Uinal (20-day month): 175, 181–82; birth, 201–202
Underworlds: 115, 261, 262; gods, 79, 266–67
Usumacinta Valley: 105, 283; estuaries, 107
Utatlán (El Quiché): 151
Uxmal (Yucatán): 75, 83–85, 112, 116, 120–21, 133, 135, 136, 264; *Plates 6, 8, 16*

Vanilla: 23, 25
Venus, planet: 105, 118, 169–73, 225, 278
Veracruz (Mexico): 19, 49, 55, 88, 111, 112, 118, 119, 213
Vigils: 224
Villages: Spanish creation, 90; organization, 91
Virgin: vestal, 73, 84; concept, 282

Wall panels: 80
Warfare: *see* militarism
Water, virgin: 192, 268, 275

Wax: 300
Weapons: 185; *see also* bow and arrow, flint, obsidian, spears, spearthrowers, *and* stone
Weaving: 31, 151, 211–12, 262, 264a; moon, goddess of, 260
Wells: 27
Whistle and whistling: 31, 208, 293–94
Women: 232–33, 235, 259 (illus.), 278 (illus.), shortage, 104; weaving house, 212; taboo, 275; shamans, 291; impersonator, 294; *Plates 1d, 17a, 20a,c,d*
Wood: utensils, 134, 275; carved, 210; statues, 257; beings, 275; idols, 289; *see also* lintels *and* trees
World: directions and colors, 47, 131, 225–26, 233, 260, 262, 265, 274, 276, 289; glyphs, 181; end of, 165–66, 225–27; *see also* creation

Xelhá (Quintana Roo): 125
Xinca Indians: 185
Xpuhil (Quintana Roo): *Plate 7b*
Xultún (Petén): 71, 100
Xupá (Chiapas): *Plate 20c*

Yaxchilán (Chiapas): 62, 71, 96–99, 102, 193; sculpture, 61, 65, 80, 96, 122, 216; *Plates 12, 13, 14*
Yaxhá (Petén): 98
Yaxhuná (Yucatán): 49, 75, 185
Yucatán (Mexico): 17, 26, 27, 96, 115; language, 27, 28, 38, 99; Maya, 29; *Plate 1d*

Zaculeu (Huehuetenango): 151, 213, 217
Zoque Indians: 17, 94
Zutuhil Maya: 150–51, 221, 264, 293